Leo Strauss and the Theopolitics of Culture

SUNY series in the Thought and Legacy of Leo Strauss
———————
Kenneth Hart Green, editor

Leo Strauss and the Theopolitics of Culture

Philipp von Wussow

Cover image of Leo Strauss courtesy of Jenny Strauss Clay.

Published by State University of New York Press, Albany

© 2020 State University of New York

All rights reserved

No part of this book may be used or reproduced in any manner whatsoever without written permission. No part of this book may be stored in a retrieval system or transmitted in any form or by any means including electronic, electrostatic, magnetic tape, mechanical, photocopying, recording, or otherwise without the prior permission in writing of the publisher.

For information, contact State University of New York Press, Albany, NY
www.sunypress.edu

Library of Congress Cataloging-in-Publication Data

Names: Wussow, Philipp von, author.
Title: Leo Strauss and the theopolitics of culture / Philipp von Wussow.
Description: Albany : State University of New York, 2020. | Series: SUNY series in the thought and legacy of Leo Strauss | Includes bibliographical references and index.
Identifiers: LCCN 2019019665 | ISBN 9781438478395 (hardcover : alk. paper) | ISBN 9781438478401 (pbk. : alk. paper) | ISBN 9781438478418 (ebook)
Subjects: LCSH: Strauss, Leo.
Classification: LCC B945.S84 W87 2020 | DDC 181/.06—dc23
LC record available at https://lccn.loc.gov/2019019665

10 9 8 7 6 5 4 3 2 1

Contents

Preface — vii

Introduction: Leo Strauss and the Theopolitics of Culture — ix

Part I
The Return of Religion, the Remnants of Neo-Kantianism, and the Systematic Place of "the Political"

1. Hermann Cohen on the Systematic Place of Religion — 5

2. Post-Cohenian Quarrels: Rosenzweig, Natorp, Strauss — 11

3. Strauss on Paul Natorp and Ernst Cassirer — 19

4. Returning to Cohen: "Cohen and Maimonides" on Ethics and Politics — 31

5. Strauss and Carl Schmitt: Vanquishing the "Systematics of Liberal Thought" — 41

Part II
The Argument and the Action of *Philosophy and Law*

6. A Hidden Masterpiece of Twentieth-Century Philosophy — 57

7. Strauss's Introduction — 65

8. Leo Strauss and Julius Guttmann on the History of Jewish Philosophy ... 91

9. A Complex Afterlife: Julius Guttmann, the "Jewish Thomism" Affair, and the Turn to Exotericism ... 135

Part III
"German Nihilism" and the Intellectual Origins of National Socialism

10. Genealogies of National Socialism ... 163

11. Strauss's Argument ... 193

Part IV
Strauss on Modern Relativism

12. From "Culture" to "Cultures": Émigré Scholars, the Rise of Cultural Anthropology, and the Americanization of Leo Strauss ... 219

13. Cannibalism: Leo Strauss and Cultural Anthropology ... 227

14. Irrationalism and the Remnants of the Social Question ... 239

15. Two Types of Relativism ... 247

Part V
Jerusalem and Athens

16. Jerusalem and Athens or Jerusalem versus Athens? ... 255

Conclusion: Leo Strauss and "the Natural Way" of Reading ... 285

Notes ... 299

Bibliography ... 351

Index ... 367

Preface

I first read Leo Strauss as a recent post-doc at the Hebrew University of Jerusalem. At that time I sought to veer away from my home ground of twentieth-century continental philosophy and simultaneously began to study political philosophy and Jewish philosophy. Needless to say, I learned soon enough that reading Leo Strauss requires proper training in all three fields. But most of all, it requires the close and continuous encounter with his writings—the type of "listening" that is at odds with the derivate discourses of Straussians and anti-Straussians alike.

It's been a long way from this initial study work to the completion of this book. It involved three different university affiliations, the loss of numerous handwritten materials in a car burglary in Rome, and some surprising changes in the outline of this book. Among other things, it was clear from the beginning that *Philosophy and Law* (1935) would be an important text for my argument, but the plan to write a long commentary on the book materialized only at a late stage. The initial idea to trace Strauss's inconspicuous critique of "culture" through five or six different contexts of his work, however, remained unchanged. The hesitation over the exact number is due to a peculiarity in the first part of this study, which traces the emergence of Strauss's philosophical project from the templates of Hermann Cohen and his disciples and defectors. The encounter with Carl Schmitt appears as an appendix to the Cohenian problem here, although one may be tempted to treat it as a context of its own (or even as the founding moment of his political philosophizing). Tracing the late ramifications of neo-Kantian thought through even the most unexpected places of his writings has been a guiding motif of this work.

Although this study is unmistakably the product of many long hours in university libraries and archives, it would not have been possible without the help of others. Paul Mendes-Flohr, who first introduced me to the study of German-Jewish thought, has been a steady supporter of my work from time immemorial, and the most vivid example of a great human being. Christian Wiese has been a most wonderful employer and colleague, and he went out of his way to support my *Habilitation* at Goethe University on the basis of this study. Jeffrey A. Bernstein introduced me to a number of people in the United States, and the vivid exchange of ideas on even the most intricate details of Strauss's writings had a great impact on the formation of this study.

The completion was made possible with the help of a grant from the Deutsche Forschungsgemeinschaft (German Research Council).

I truly appreciated the conversations with many great colleagues, among them Leora Batnitzky, Cedric Cohen Skalli, Peter Gostmann, David Janssens, George Y. Kohler, Menachem Lorberbaum, Thomas Meyer, Peter Minowitz, David Myers, Dietrich Schotte, Eugene Sheppard, David Weinstein, Christoph von Wolzogen, and Michael Zank.

I am grateful to Nathan Tarcov for allowing me to quote from Strauss's unpublished writings and correspondences, Kenneth Hart Green for his generous offer to publish the book in the SUNY Press series "The Thought and Legacy of Leo Strauss," and Michael Rinella of SUNY Press for his indispensable help with the preparation of the text. I also wish to thank the unknown reviewers who pushed me to clarify a number of points in earlier versions of the text.

Lina Bosbach read every draft and supported the completion of this study in many other ways.

Introduction

Leo Strauss and the Theopolitics of Culture

For the time being, Leo Strauss remains the unlikely case of a first-rate philosopher who has yet to be discovered, despite the enormous amount of scholarship invested in his legacy. Strauss has been studied widely in the fields of political science, intellectual history, and modern Jewish thought, but his philosophical project remains difficult to grasp. This is in part due to the fact that his works do not seem to have a central idea or thesis. Instead, they are exceedingly multilayered, stretching across a variety of fields, epochs, and thematic concerns. Strauss is not only a major reference for the renewal of political philosophy in the twentieth century, he has also had a major impact on the historiography of medieval Jewish philosophy and he has made a partly unexplored contribution to the logic of modern social science. Furthermore, he advocated a largely atypical notion of philosophy, according to which the problem of belief and unbelief is the central issue of philosophical investigation. Last but not least, he sought a way out of the impasse of modernity by consciously "returning" to Platonic philosophizing.

It is difficult to find a single master thesis or a common thematic thread behind these heterogeneous aspects of Strauss's work. But perhaps there is a recurring conceptual pattern or a critical purpose—or at least a "direction" of philosophical investigation—despite the great variety of concerns? To understand the philosophical project of Leo Strauss, I suggest reading his works with regard to a specific constellation of culture, religion, and the political. In particular, this study carves out Strauss's largely unknown critique of "culture," his occupation with a latent culturalism that allegedly holds its grip on modern philosophical thought.

This focus may not be self-evident. His objections to the notion of "culture" initially appear to be rather vague. Moreover, "culture" is not the central theme of Leo Strauss's writings. It is, however, a theme that leads to and accompanies the central themes. As this study argues, Strauss's conception of political philosophy was formed in the polemics against the notion of "culture." The problem had an extraordinary importance for the inner workings of his philosophical endeavor. As he understood the notion, "culture" signified a void in the discourse of twentieth-century philosophy, which has come to be seen in the problematic conjunction of "culture" with religion and the political.

The place where the new philosophical concern came to be most visible is Strauss's unrecognized masterwork *Philosophy and Law* (1935), where he introduced the topic into the historiography of Jewish philosophy. In the first chapter—masked as a review essay of Julius Guttmann's seminal book *Philosophies of Judaism* (1933)—Strauss sought to demonstrate that Guttmann could not understand the original problem of religion because he was trapped in the assumptions of the philosophy of culture; but as he argued, "religion cannot be rightly understood in the framework of the concept of 'culture.'"[1] First, culture is to be understood as the spontaneous product of the human spirit, while religion is *given* to man. Second, culture is to be understood as a set of "domains of validity," each constituting "partial domains of truth," whereas religion makes a claim to universality. In a next step Strauss rephrased these two incompatibilities as a contradiction between two oppositional claims to universality: "The claim to universality on the part of 'culture,' which in its own view rests in spontaneous production, seems to be opposed by the claim to universality on the part of religion, which in its own view is not produced by man but *given* to him." With their respective claim to be universal, culture and religion do not coexist peacefully side by side. Instead, they clash with each another and seek to submit each another to their respective semantic structure. In Guttmann's *Philosophies of Judaism*, religion wins the fight against culture. As Strauss described the outcome of the quarrel, Guttmann "finds himself driven to a remarkable distancing from philosophy of culture by the fact of religion as such, which thereby proves to be one crux of philosophy of culture."[2]

Now that Strauss had described the conflict between religion and culture, he added an inconspicuous third element. In his footnote to the passage quoted above on religion as the "crux" of philosophy of culture, he continued: "The other crux of philosophy of culture is the fact of the political,"[3] referring to his review of Carl Schmitt's *The Concept of the Political*. With this addition, the conceptual framework of culture, religion, and the political was completed.

This study follows the conceptual triad of culture, religion, and the political through different aspects of Strauss's work stretching across a variety of spatial and temporal contexts. Each of the five parts can be read on its own to a large extent, but the triad also provides a recurrent theme or *leitmotif* throughout the book. Such an interpretation of Strauss's philosophy inevitably finds itself in an uneasy position between "systematic" and "historical" philosophizing. The present study, with its emphasis on close reading of Strauss texts, seeks to situate them in their proper context of discussion while exploring a thoroughgoing systematic concern. It is therefore compelled to combine the "systematic" and the "historical" pursuit of philosophical scholarship in a way that is open to attack from all sides.

Most notably, perhaps, the argument of the book cannot be properly laid out in terms of "contextualism" as it is widely understood. Only to a small extent does it situate a text or teaching in the immediate historical context of its creation. Rather, it traces how a major theme was imported from a prior discourse that belonged to an entirely different temporal and spatial context, and how it was adapted to a new situation. In each case, the connection is still visible in the voids and ruptures of arguments and conceptual strategies. I show in each chapter of my study how a prior discourse—often from a remote context—provides the conceptual template for the new discourse. The larger consideration is that philosophical discourses are not essentially a direct response to an immediate context. The recourse to earlier conceptual patterns is philosophically far more relevant than the immediate responses. However, the inevitable modifications of these patterns are being made in accordance with the historical situation.

Strauss may have been up to something when he emphasized—and maybe overemphasized—the essential difference between philosophers and intellectuals, who respond to their political and cultural situation. One need not evoke the dreadful image of timeless and spaceless philosophizing to see the difference: philosophers respond to their immediate contexts, too, but they do so in a different way. When they reflect upon "their time," they resort to conceptual patterns and genealogical lines that reach much farther down both in history and in the structure of their argument. Such patterns and lines are also to be found throughout the writings of Leo Strauss. He had a knack for running the same conceptual patterns through the most divergent texts and contexts, and he even ran them through the same texts again and again without ever coming to the same conclusion twice. There must be some systematic thread that keeps his philosophizing together.

My attempt to introduce a "systematic" concern into Strauss scholarship may seem odd, for Strauss is not known as a systematic thinker, and he did not present his ideas in a systematic fashion. Phrased in terms from the philosophical discourse of his time, he appears to be a *Problemdenker*, not a *Systemdenker*.[4] He clearly belonged to the postidealist world in which philosophers no longer wrote the huge and comprehensive philosophical systems of previous generations but expressed their philosophical ideas in a series of commentaries to previous philosophical works. Some of the main ideas are scattered across all of his work, and the only way to get hold of these ideas is to analyze them in a variety of concrete situations.

Strauss himself described the prevalence of systematic thinking without a system, and even without the slightest attempt to explicate one's ideas in a systematic fashion, in his dissertation *Das Erkenntnisproblem in der philosophischen Lehre Fr. H. Jacobis* (1921). A major methodological question of this study was whether a "systematic difference" can also be claimed for an "anti-systematic thinker" such as Jacobi. As Strauss maintained, Jacobi was unwilling to bring his ideas into a systematic form, but the "objective systematic content" (*sachliche Systembestand*) of his philosophy could be discerned "without being systematically explicated."[5]

Strauss wrote the study in a moment when the old philosophical systems were no longer viable, whereas the anti-systematic fervor of the day seemed to lead straight into relativism. The crucial issue was "that there are several types of reason," and it was far from clear how the "multiplicity of standpoints" would allow for a unified philosophical perspective. In this situation Strauss proposed "that a philosophy which understands itself, and which does not wish to be exposed to a degrading relativism, must think of the truth as an independent, coherent existence [*Bestand*], which it does not create but seek, find, and recognize."[6] Subverting the distinction between *Problemdenker* and *Systemdenker,* Strauss pointed to a connection between systematic thinking and "a strictly definable complex of problems in its own lawfulness."[7] This early outline reverberated in his introductions to Moses Mendelssohn, where he pointed to Mendelssohn's distinction between systematic (philosophical) and poetic form, as well as to the problem posed by the plurality of systems.[8] How did these ideas morph into the foundational writings of Strauss's political philosophy from the early 1930s onward?

The place in Strauss scholarship that is located most closely to the matter is the question of whether there are "technical" discussions in his work. Most prominently, Stanley Rosen ventured that there are no such technical discussions in Strauss's writings.[9] Whether he had a very specific kind of technical discussions in mind (after all, the claim is based on a comparison between Strauss and Aristotle) or whether he looked only in some of the writings (those "middle works" upon which Strauss's fame and notoriety is based) we do not know. But the rhetorical question "whether or not [Strauss] was capable of this sort of technical work"[10] must be reposed with regard to his writings of the 1930s. These works are replete with many technical discussions, and from there we also find some technical work in his later writings. Strauss himself contributed to the fact that this layer was disregarded by his readership, for he often spoke out against "technical terms" in philosophy[11] and held that political philosophy was to be written in nontechnical language that stems "from the marketplace."[12] He also alluded to "technical terms" as an indicator of exoteric writing.[13]

The technical layer in Strauss's works, however, is to be found not in the terminology but in the discussions of the systematic division of philosophy. These discussions may not arouse the suspicion of most Strauss readers. But they indicate the place where we should look if we seek to understand the inner workings of his philosophy. Furthermore, these technical discussions are replete with historical references that situate Strauss within the overall discourse of early-twentieth-century German and Jewish philosophy. I argue in Part I that this occupation with the division of philosophy stems from his early intimate acquaintance with Marburg neo-Kantianism, especially with the works of Hermann Cohen. He discussed the problem of political philosophy within the framework of the prior discussion on the place of religion in the system of philosophy. Paradoxically, Strauss preserved this systematic preoccupation of neo-Kantianism in his lifelong polemics against neo-Kantian philosophy of culture.

Strauss's controversial interpretation of Carl Schmitt's *The Concept of the Political* is a follow-up to the Cohenian question, as we can trace from the discussion on the systematic place of the political in his "Notes on Carl Schmitt, *The Concept of the Political*" (1932).[14] The argument with Schmitt extends his occupation with neo-Kantianism up to the point at which Schmitt himself appears as a covert neo-Kantian. As I shall argue, the "horizon beyond liberalism" opened up at the beginning of the "Notes on Carl Schmitt" was in the first place a horizon beyond the polemical antagonism between liberalism and illiberalism. According to Strauss, Schmitt remained within the horizon of liberalism when he sought to understand the political as an equivalent to the moral, aesthetic, and economic domains. This version of the problem—locating the political among the forms of culture—is largely characteristic of the first version of "Der Begriff des Politischen" (1927). Schmitt openly turned to illiberalism when he gave up on this disposition in the second and third editions. Opting for a conception of the political as "intensity" instead—a violent suspension of all other domains—he provided the "systematic" theoretical foundation of the total state. Strauss did not follow Schmitt in this regard. As he pointed out, Schmitt's illiberalism was just another variation of the liberalism he despised.

Schmitt's failure to regain "a horizon beyond liberalism" also reflected the larger systematic predicament of contemporary political thought. Not coincidentally, the "Notes on Carl Schmitt" led to the point at which only the conscious return to premodern political philosophizing would lead out of the Schmittian impasse. A larger point of this demonstration concerns the relationship between philosophy and politics. Throughout, Strauss argued for a preponderance of the philosophical perspective over the political one, or for the notion that "philosophy is of higher ranks than politics."[15] As he explained:

> [The philosopher] is ultimately compelled to transcend not merely the dimension of common opinion, of political opinion, but also the dimension of political life as such; for he is led to realize that the ultimate aim of political life cannot be reached by political life, but only by a life devoted to contemplation, to philosophy. This finding is of crucial importance for political philosophy, since it determines the limits set to political life, to all political action and all political planning.[16]
>
> Man is more than the citizen of the city. Man transcends the city only by pursuing true happiness, not by pursuing happiness however understood.[17]

Statements such as these should be taken literally. Even the most "political" of Strauss's texts offer a critical philosophical perspective that surpasses their political contexts. It is this perspective that explains Strauss's actual position in the political debates that surround his legacy, to wit, his stance on National Socialism and on various illiberal movements and intellectual formations. From early on, he searched for an understanding of politics that would no longer be "merely political."[18] He may have sympathized with Mussolini for a short period of time, and he may have leaned toward the Revisionist branch of Zionism associated with the name of Ze'ev (Vladimir) Jabotinsky. He also engaged with Carl Schmitt before Schmitt turned to National Socialism and no longer replied to Strauss's letters. But most of all, he was concerned with philosophy, its meaning and purpose and its legitimacy vis-à-vis politics and society.

In the 1930s, Strauss largely shifted the technical work to the context of medieval philosophy and, in particular, to the transformations of medieval thought into modernity. Major philosophical insights are often described with regard to a seemingly insignificant shift in the systematic disposition of a concept or doctrine. Strauss's discovery that became a key quote for *Philosophy and Law* pertains to the "classification of the sciences," namely, to the question of the place of prophetology in the whole of the sciences.[19] At one point in the book Strauss sought to clarify his obsession with the division of philosophy more generally. Against Julius Guttmann—who described medieval philosophy within the framework of neo-Kantian philosophy of religion—he wrote:

> If one starts from the division of philosophy into theory of knowledge, logic, ethics, aesthetics, and philosophy of religion, thus assuming, for example, that the problems of natural theology and rational psychology are to be treated under philosophy of religion . . . then one is in fact compelled to look for the originality of medieval philosophy exclusively or primarily in philosophy of religion. That one would arrive at a different conclusion if one started from the ancient division of philosophy—much more obvious, after all, in a study of the older philosophy—into logic, physics, metaphysics, ethics, and politics; and furthermore, that it is not merely a technical question whether to label a problem "metaphysical" or "religio-philosophic" needs no further elucidation.[20]

Strauss bothered with a "technical question" here to show "that it is not merely a technical question." As he warned, "a 'method' is never an indifferent, impartial technique, but always pre-determines the possible content."[21] These and other methodological considerations provide an excellent guide through the inner workings of *Philosophy and Law*. Part II of the present study provides a detailed commentary on *Philosophy and Law* and its afterlife.

The principal task is to outline how the book works as a book, despite its heterogeneous parts and its multiple philosophical contexts. Needless to say, this commentary is not meant to provide a comprehensive interpretation; it merely serves to outline a path through the extremely difficult text in order to prepare for such an interpretation. If this meticulous work is helpful, it is a first step toward the future recognition of *Philosophy and Law* as one of the greatest philosophical works of the twentieth century, along with the *Tractatus*, *Being and Time*, and *Dialectic of Enlightenment*.

The systematic question also serves as a guide through Strauss's work on medieval philosophy, most notably through his evolving views on Maimonides after *Philosophy and Law*. A typical proposition in the article "Some Remarks on the Political Science of Maimonides and Farabi" (1936) goes as follows: "It is difficult to understand the exact meaning of Maimonides' prophetology if one does not know first the philosophical place of this doctrine."[22] Strauss first recited the Maimonidean division of philosophy into speculative philosophy and practical philosophy—the latter being divided into ethics, economics, and politics—and argued that this disposition is well founded in the Aristotelian tradition. Second, he examined some seemingly minor deviations from that division: Maimonides mentions happiness when speaking of politics, not of ethics; he divides practical philosophy into four parts but later drops one of them; and he attributes to politics the treatment of "divine matters." Third, Strauss suggested that the difficulties pertaining to these deviations can be solved only by acknowledging that Maimonides is strongly influenced by Farabi—namely, a philosopher who fought for philosophy against religious dogma. The systematic disposition was so important for Strauss here because it seemed to decide about the philosophical character of medieval Jewish thought: it would provide the only reliable clue to the question whether a work of Maimonides was actually a *philosophical* or a *Jewish* book. This, in turn, would also give access to the precise way in which political things are intertwined with divine things.[23]

Strauss discussed the same division in "The Literary Character of the *Guide of the Perplexed*" (1941) and stretched the matter much further. The preeminent characteristic was the exclusion of any philosophic subject from the *Guide*, and Strauss concluded that it was not a philosophical book.[24] The discovery of "exotericism" in Maimonides and his predecessors led to a turnaround in the hermeneutics of medieval thought. As the 1963 introductory essay on Maimonides shows, Strauss was still occupied with the structure of the *Guide for the Perplexed*, but the way he described this structure had changed. To give a typical example:

> The *Guide* consists then of seven sections or of thirty-eight subsections. Wherever feasible, each section is divided into seven subsections; the only section that does not permit of being divided into subsections is divided into seven chapters. The simple statement of the plan of the *Guide* suffices to show that the book is sealed with many seals.[25]

At this point the systematic question had moved into the background. Instead of the underlying division of philosophy, Strauss paid greater attention to the outer division of a text, or to its surface. As in the quote above, there was a new word that indicated this new approach: the *plan*. In "How to Begin to Study *The Guide of the Perplexed*," Strauss simply started from a description of the sections, subsections, parts, and chapters as the indicators of its "plan." Such meticulous descriptions of textual surfaces became the epitome of Straussian hermeneutics in the wider public perception.[26]

Despite the dramatic shift in his philosophic and hermeneutic approach from 1937 onward, there is also a fundamental continuity. The original hermeneutic innovation of Straussian political philosophy preceded the discovery of exotericism and the shift of attention from the systematic division to the literary character of a text. It is to be found in his attention toward what he later called "the argument and the action" of a text.[27] Strauss paid great attention to the tension between argument and action, and in particular to the argument *of* the action. As Seth Benardete explained the title of Strauss's late work *The Argument and the Action of Plato's Laws*: "The 'and' in the title is misleading; it does not mean that some sort of action is represented while the argument is being developed; it means that the action has an argument, and that that argument is the true argument of the *Laws*."[28]

To better understand the notion of the argument of the action—and its continuity in Strauss's thought—we must seek to trace how it applies to the composition of his own writings. For lack of a better term, I suggest that a major aspect of the Straussian art of writing is the predominance of *directional* arguments. These arguments indicate a movement from one understanding to another, and they contain instructions on how to get from one to another. Strauss's directional arguments suggest that the propositional content of a text must be discerned from its dramatic movement. This feature also explains why Strauss was immensely occupied with the questions of *how to begin*, and *how to proceed* from there.

Strauss must not be read in the same manner he read, but his advice that the philosophical argument is contained in the dramatic action is certainly useful for reading Strauss. As he explained in a landmark article on Plato: "For presenting his teaching Plato uses not merely the 'content' of his works (the speeches of his various characters) but also their 'form' (the dialogic form in general, the particular form of each dialogue and of each section of it, the action, characters, names, places, times, situations and the like); an adequate understanding of the dialogues understands the 'content' in the light of the 'form.'"[29] Strauss imitated these features of Platonic dialogues in his philosophical prose. His own texts, to be sure, do not have the type of dramatic elements—characters, places, or situations—mentioned in the quote. But he often seemed to transpose the philosophical concepts and their systematic interrelationships into a dramatic situation, in which they all of a sudden and unexpectedly gain a new life of their own. To quote Benardete on Strauss's Plato again: "Strauss was not the first to . . . suggest that the drama altered the apparent meaning of the argument; but what is peculiar his discovery was that once argument and action are properly put together an entirely new argument emerges that could never have been expected from the argument on the written page. Something happens in a Platonic dialogue that in its revolutionary unexpectedness is the equivalent to the *periagōgē,* as Socrates calls it, of philosophy itself."[30] It is not difficult to trace these features in Strauss's own writing, for his texts often appear to have a peculiar spatial dimension. Strauss was a master of translating a philosophical subject into a dramatic situation, in which a new argument emerges from the interplay between the concepts—the "characters" in philosophical prose—over the course of a text.

These peculiarities notwithstanding, we shall be cautious not to imitate Straussian hermeneutics for reading Strauss. In particular, we shall not presuppose that Strauss himself *practiced* exoteric writing, or that he wrote "between the lines."[31] In most cases, it is more precise to understand the respective text "as it stands."[32] Reading Leo Strauss, one must make a shift toward the argument: To see the dramatic action of a Strauss text, one must read it closely and follow the argument. This can be a difficult task. As a rule of thumb, readers invoke exotericism where the plain argument is either too simple or too difficult to understand. One common challenge to reading comprehension is to identify whether the position stated in the text is Strauss's own. As Steven B. Smith explained: "One of the great challenges in reading Strauss is the question of voice. When is Strauss speaking in his own voice and when is he reconstructing, often in his own distinctive idiom, the words of someone else? He no doubt deliberately and provocatively ran these together. Strauss often restated the views of dangerous writers like Nietzsche and Heidegger with a power and clarity greater than those writers had expressed themselves."[33] Beyond "dangerous writers," Strauss applied this ability also to thinkers who were not easily accessible to readers. As he explained with regard to Cohen's *Religion of Reason*, his remarks were an attempt at "reproducing or imitating difficulties" that the author had not resolved.[34]

This mimetic reproduction of philosophical positions and their internal difficulties adds to the directional character of Strauss's texts, or to the fact that their propositional content must be discerned from the dramatic action. "Exoteric" readings often occur where the reader has lost track of the argument and action. But these directional arguments are not in any meaningful sense written "between the lines." In principle they are accessible to careful readers. Their rhetorical elements—and the continuous interplay between philosophy and rhetoric—pertain to the educational function of philosophy as Strauss came to see it.

Part III of the present study will follow up on this theme in an interpretation of Strauss's "German Nihilism" (1941), which is an extraordinarily "rhetorical" text. The rhetorical elements, however, serve a clear philosophical purpose. I argue that the text is a parable on liberal education toward philosophy, placed within the context of the debates around 1940–41 on the intellectual origins of National Socialism. As I seek to show, the text responds to a forgotten genre at the border of philosophy and politics, in which scholars sought to locate the origins of National Socialism in the history of German philosophy, particularly in German Idealism, Romanticism, or Nietzsche. The genre had been established during World War I and was resurrected for a brief and intense period during World War II. It also retained a strange afterlife in postwar debates on the alleged political complicity of philosophy. The principal fallacy of the genealogies of National Socialism was due to a confusion in the relationship between politics and culture. As they sought to trace the peculiarities of German politics in German *Kultur,* they paradoxically repeated what—so they thought—was the fallacy of German philosophy: a characteristic overemphasis on culture, to the detriment of politics with its corresponding notion of civilization. A major key to Strauss's counterinterpretation of National Socialism in his "German Nihilism" text is the critical reversal of the distinction between culture and civilization. Located particularly within the heated debates of 1940–41, the text served to clarify the relationship between philosophy and politics.

As to the inner development of Strauss's thought, it has often been argued that "German Nihilism" marks the transition of a German-Jewish scholar of the Weimar era to the American research context. I propose to move this debate to another playing field, namely, Strauss's discourse on American social science and his scathing critique of modern relativism. Part IV of the present study argues that Strauss's transition to American social science is to be located in a shift from "culture" to "cultures." There is a quote in *Liberalism Ancient and Modern* that captures this shift better than any other:

> It is not easy to say what culture susceptible of being used in the plural means. As a consequence of this obscurity people have suggested, explicitly or implicitly, that culture is any pattern of conduct common to any human group. Hence we do not hesitate to speak of the culture of suburbia or of the cultures of juvenile gangs, both nondelinquent and delinquent. In other words, every human being outside of lunatic asylums is a cultured human being, for he participates in a culture. At the frontiers of research there arises the question as to whether there are not cultures also of inmates of lunatic asylums. If we contrast the present-day usage of "culture" with the original meaning, it is as if someone would say that the cultivation of a garden may consist of the garden's being littered with empty tin cans and whisky bottles and used papers of various descriptions thrown around in the garden at random. Having arrived at this point, we realize that we have lost our way somehow.[35]

Quotes such as this are likely to be noticed for their irony and wit, but there has been little effort to understand them in their theoretical and historical context. As I show from numerous traces—often to be found in remote articles and unpublished lecture manuscripts—the actual target of this critique of "cultures" was the new science of cultural anthropology, with Ruth Benedict as its principal spokesperson in the wider public discourse. According to this viewpoint, all values are relative to a social or cultural group. The absurd notion that juvenile gangs or inmates of lunatic asylums constitute "cultures" provided the extreme case for the thesis that all values are "relative" to any group.[36] The ostensibly more open-minded and flexible notion of "cultures"—or of *a* culture as opposed to culture—thereby came to be regarded as a problem. In the words of Geoffrey Hartman, "[I]t is 'a culture' that tends toward hegemony, while 'culture,' understood as the development of a public sphere, a 'republic of letters' in which ideas are freely exchanged, is what is fragile."[37]

Strauss occupies a special place in the wider discourse on relativism, although he is practically nonexistent in the more technical philosophical debate. For some, he is a bulwark against the tide of Western relativism, while for others, he is the high definition of an "absolutist" invoking the threat of relativism for demagogic purposes. To the extent that the so-called Strauss wars have any specific philosophical and moral content (beyond the more obvious political content), they revolve for the most part around the relativity or permanence of ideas, values, and philosophical problems. But Strauss was by no means the staunch antirelativist he has come to be regarded as in the wider public perception. To revaluate his contribution to the understanding of modern relativism, it seems useful to keep a certain distance from both sides. In other words, we shall neither presuppose nor merely debunk Strauss's antirelativism. His critique of modern social science can neither be taken to be true nor understood as untrue in its entirety, as if social science were still the same as it was for him in the 1950s. The debates on "relativism" in the 1950s and '60s are for the most part a matter of recollection at best. Hence, one must first recontextualize the Straussian discourse on relativism to revaluate his understanding of social science. This procedure will help to see the strengths and weaknesses of the actual arguments against "modern relativism."

For the thesis of a fundamental plurality of cultures, the theoretical project of cultural anthropology provided some extreme cases such as cannibalism, the killing of parents, and female genital mutilation. Initially Strauss's sometimes enigmatic contributions to this discourse seem to be rather unspecific. He generalized the matter to the point at which he concluded that modern social and political science as such has become relativistic and that it is therefore methodologically incapable of addressing the fact of the political. But his arguments are often highly idiosyncratic interventions into specific theoretical situations. In the first place, one must rehearse the arguments and rhetorical strategies pertaining to the theoretical matrix of "relativism" and "absolutism." One must analyze them in their respective textual situation. Second, Strauss's discourse is not a unified theory but a loose set of strategies and arguments in a complex matrix of relativism and absolutism. Third, Strauss was occupied with relativism only in a comparably short span of his philosophical career. And fourth, he did not reframe his arguments as a contribution to an ongoing debate. Their precise function is to disrupt a debate. As he sought to demonstrate, the debate had lost track of its subject matter and purpose. He therefore designed his arguments as a disruption that would prepare for a change of perspective.[38]

For the most part, then, Strauss's arguments do work, even as their function is limited. There are basically three types of arguments: commonsense arguments, historical arguments, and arguments that combine a commonsense understanding with a historical perspective. Commonsense arguments often come in colloquial phrases—"forgetting the wood for the trees" is the most common phrase. The purpose is to remind the reader of a triviality, "if a necessary triviality."[39] Historical arguments usually seek to put a modern problem into a larger historical perspective. Their main purpose is critical, and for the most part they come in brief and fairly dry statements that seek to strip a contemporary teaching of its normative claim: "this conclusion . . . is known to every reader of Plato's *Republic* or of Aristotle's *Politics*."[40]

Both these types of argument are not yet very spectacular. Strauss's specialty was to combine a commonsense argument with a historical argument. Even these combinations seem trivial at first, but they are well thought out and surprisingly strong. When Strauss sought to remind his contemporaries of "a necessary triviality" he typically followed a concept or debate to its ultimate relativistic consequences to state that "we have lost our way somehow."[41] The inconspicuous claim functions as a brief allusion to a larger change of perspective: The debate had been on the right way, but at some point it strayed off course. It is therefore necessary to make a fresh start.

Another characteristic element of this change of perspective is the understanding that this new start must involve some kind of return to an earlier position, which had been refuted in the debate that eventually strayed off course. Each time, Strauss proposed an untimely "return" to Platonic political philosophy (supplemented by Aristotle's *Politics*). He did not merely speak as a Plato scholar here, but as the principal spokesman for a full-fledged return to Platonic philosophizing. But how is it possible for a twentieth-century philosopher and/or Jewish philosopher—a modern—to return to premodernity, and why did he insist?[42] As we shall see in various textual situations, Strauss often evoked the return to Plato to facilitate a change of perspective on modernity. The contrast between modernity and premodernity creates a tension within the modern world, and this contrast is primarily a *critical* difference introduced by Strauss into twentieth-century philosophy. Whereas some of his contemporaries sought to judge modernity by its socioeconomic flipside, for Strauss it was to be tried in a "pre-modern court."[43]

But Strauss was also radically modern. As he explained in 1935, "[T]he return to pre-modern thought . . . led . . . to a much more radical form of modernity."[44] There is no better context to study this paradox in action than his life-long occupation with the theme of Jerusalem and Athens. Strauss was a major proponent of a view that understood philosophy from its opposition to revealed religion, and one of his principal contributions was to renew the conflict between reason and revelation in the middle of the twentieth century. He took reason and revelation as representatives of two types of wisdom, and he associated these types of wisdom with the names of two cities, Jerusalem and Athens.

Part V provides a fresh commentary on the seminal article "Jerusalem and Athens" (1967) in its basis and its genesis. As to the basis, Strauss outlined an understanding of religion *after* the critique of religion: he described a notion of religion that is no longer exposed to the critique of religion proposed by Karl Marx, Friedrich Nietzsche, and Sigmund Freud. Marx, Nietzsche, and Freud offered three—maybe *the* three—comprehensive post-traditional interpretations of Judaism in modernity. They represent the three options for a radical critique of religion to argue where religion stems from: class struggle, the will to power, or neurosis. Religion, then, is a sign either of injustice, mediocrity, or immaturity. Despite their internal differences, their respective views on religion have a lot in common. Marx called it "the opium of the masses," Nietzsche spoke of "alcohol and Christianity" as "the two great European narcotics," and Freud compared religion to "intoxicating substances."[45] They all expected a future without the drug of religion to be blissful and bright. But Marx, Nietzsche, and Freud did not account for the possibility that one could be thoroughly religious without falling back behind their critique. They presupposed that the religious interpretation of reality had been discredited, and that the common man only held on to it for narcotic purposes. A new interpretation would successfully replace the religious interpretation. The one thing necessary for humanity was a new purpose—the classless society, the overman, or the man of unprejudiced science. These purposes were the core elements of a new, secular "belief," which was based on the idea of the perfectibility of man.

Strauss was not the first to detect the fundamental weakness of this critique of religion, but he took the matter to another level. Following his reevaluation of the critique of religion and its premises, we may describe the epistemic situation of religious belief as follows: it is possible to refute religion, of course, but it is just as possible to refute the refutation, and both refutations take place on the very same grounds. Religious and non-religious or antireligious beliefs and attitudes are a matter of choice, an act of the will. Religious and antireligious discourses are a matter of rhetorical persuasion. A philosophical critique of the critique of religion is therefore not needed to rehabilitate or reestablish religion, it is justified by the purpose of philosophy itself. The veracity of philosophy depends upon its relationship to religion and theology, for this relationship illuminates the epistemic precondition of philosophy.[46]

Strauss was also somewhat ahead of the discourse on belief and unbelief when it came to the proper conceptual strategies. With a strong sense for the structural asymmetries in the conflict, he was careful not to prematurely resolve the case in favor of one side. As Pierre Manent put it, Strauss's account was "so impartial that it seems impossible to say where he stands."[47] The relatively high symmetry of Jerusalem and Athens developed over a long span of time, evolving out of his passionate—perhaps even preposterous—resistance to mediation through "culture." Strauss had started from a highly asymmetrical understanding of the conflict between Jerusalem and Athens and only successively came to an understanding of the conflict as one that cannot be resolved in either direction. And while he became less and less convinced that the mere decision for the philosophical life could settle the matter, he came to emphasize that the possibility and necessity of philosophizing depended upon its clear delineation from the life of obedience to God.

I start from an outline of the emergence of the topic and the conceptual strategies in Strauss's work. "Jerusalem and Athens" in particular, with its unique outline of a philosophical interpretation of the Bible and a theological interpretation of Greek philosophy, is an extremely well-crafted text, displaying certain hypermodern arguments and rhetorical means that deserve close attention. Another aspect of "Jerusalem and Athens" is how it brings together Strauss's two critiques of culture—the critique of German philosophy of culture (represented in text by Hermann Cohen and *his* understanding of Jerusalem and Athens) and the critique of cultural anthropology (represented by some unnamed scientific observers of Jerusalem and Athens).

Strauss did not fully develop the intricate connection, but in the void between the two concepts of culture the text announces a third type of culturalism, which had come up in the 1950s and '60s. This new type of culturalism was closely linked to the emergence of postcolonialism—a multiplicity of "cultures" becoming nations and eventually founding nation-states. Both the political events and their repercussions in the academic discourse brought about a *first* wave of reaffirming the roots of "Western civilization," for which Strauss became a spokesman. As Judith Shklar contended in 1964:

> The conspicuous concentration on "the West" today is clearly a response to the Cold War and to the political organization

of ex-colonial, non-European societies which now challenge the European world. These events have made us all culturally self-conscious. . . . The question is whether it is valid to extract a quintessence of "the West" by subtracting from its history all that it shares in various degrees with the rest of mankind. The result inevitably gives Europeans an unwarranted appearance of consistency and uniformity. The aim of this exercise, moreover, is not difficult to guess: as always it is a matter of defending the "essential" West against other ideological forces, revolutionary, national, and violent. The difficulty is that these too are Western.[48]

Shklar summed up the argument against the resurgence of "the West" well. It is based on the plurality of what constitutes the West, generalizing the claim that the idealizing view of the West excludes some of its many aspects while highlighting others. We must not diminish the scope of this criticism to see that at least the more intelligent proponents of "the West," such as Strauss, have little to fear from it. They had known about this plurality all along. When Strauss recast Jerusalem and Athens as the "two roots of Western civilization," he was well aware that he had not described all its branches and fruits. It was the ongoing conflict between the two roots or "pillars" of the West that safeguarded its vitality, with all its heterogeneous elements.

A *second* wave of reaffirming the roots of "the West" began as a response to the conflicts at the border of culture, religion, and the political in the twenty-first century. This wave has ignored many of the lessons of the first wave, including those of Strauss. The current return to "the West" also witnesses the renewal of an older quarrel between two highly politicized notions of culture: the largely conservative notion of culture as a reaffirmation of the roots of Western civilization has again entered into a principal argument with the liberal notion of culture as an agent of social change. This principal argument can now be seen again after a time when the argument in favor of "the West" was virtually absent from the discourse on culture. As Susan Hegeman noted about the conservative appropriation of the term *culture*: "A classic rhetorical tool of liberal discourse is now being appropriated by the Right." Her response reflects the shock caused by the loss of a monopoly:

> What does it mean that "culture," undeniably a central term of a left-leaning academic discourse in previous decades, has now become accessible to this kind of manipulation? . . . I believe we

are in danger of ceding the domain of culture to those who we already know have a deliberately limited understanding of it.[49]

We shall be glad that the debate is open once again. But we shall also welcome any serious contribution that would lead the way out of this highly politicized situation. And we shall remind ourselves that neither the reaffirmation of the West nor the hope for social change exhausts the meaning of culture.

There are three ways in which the relationships between culture, religion, and the political are being played out here: as a conflict between the religious and the philosophical life, as the conflict between philosophy and politics, and as the resistance to mediation by way of "culture." It is important to notice these different concerns. But it is also crucial to see that they are all part of an inconspicuous larger concern, namely, to secure the possibility of philosophy. The possibility of philosophy had to be negotiated in the force-field of culture, religion, and the political. We may seek to pose the pertinent conflicts differently than Strauss did, but it seems useful to further acquaint oneself with the contexts, problems, and strategies of his philosophical project to see the scope and magnitude of the issues at hand.

Part I

The Return of Religion,
the Remnants of Neo-Kantianism,
and the Systematic Place of "the Political"

Introduction

Leo Strauss did little to draw his readers' attention to a systematic layer in his thought. His writings typically combine the loose form of the essay with some unfathomable principle of organization and densification. One can best describe them as theologico-political treatises that are traditionally situated on the border of commentary, wisdom literature, and political treatise. Strauss often seems to rely on loose observations and on tiny details he found on the textual surface, but he also had a knack for the long (and sometimes exhausting) mimetic reproductions of an author's view.

Reading experiences with this kind of writing vary. But no matter whether readers see the contours of some hidden teaching or the absence of any genuine teaching in Strauss's writings, they all find it difficult to come to terms with his concept of political philosophy. Often his own statements are not particularly helpful here. An obvious starting point is the terminological attempt to distinguish political philosophy from political thought, political theory, political theology, social philosophy, or political science.[1] Another option is to start from Strauss's historical and historiographical considerations and hence to arrive at a concept of political philosophy that is based on the traditions—both ancient and modern—on which he wrote. Both approaches have produced valuable insights, but they have not led to a systematic understanding of Strauss's concept of political philosophy.

As I wish to suggest, a more systematic understanding must start from the relationship between political philosophy and philosophy proper: Is political philosophy one philosophical discipline among others or a key to the whole of philosophy? Partial answers in Strauss's writings point in both directions. He argued for political philosophy as "a branch" of philosophy and emphasized the need to distinguish political things from things that are not political.[2] But he also argued that the phenomenon of "the political" could only be understood if it was no longer represented as one of several cultural fields or "provinces."[3] And contrary to the understanding of political philosophy as a "branch" of philosophy, he argued that the term *political* indicated "a manner of treatment" of all philosophy, as in, "the political, or popular, treatment of philosophy."[4] He seriously considered political philosophy to be "the rightful queen of the social sciences,"[5] and ultimately the queen of the philosophical disciplines.

Overall, then, Strauss understood political philosophy both as "a branch" of philosophy and as a comprehensive view on philosophy. It was both the quest for knowledge of political things and a guide to the political treatment of philosophy. Strauss qualified these two different notions with many historical considerations, but there is a principal conflict at work here that runs through many of his writings: He could either opt for a precise systematic location or for a systematic omnipresence of the political—or he could avoid a decision altogether and leave the problem unresolved.

Strauss had a knack for leaving problems unresolved. He loved to point out the intricacies of philosophical problems, but he was suspicious of all solutions. All too often his discussions of a problem disembogue into a cascade of paradoxes that leave the reader perplexed. The problem of the systematic status of political philosophy is no exception here. But it is also more severe than any other. It is perhaps the best example of problems that cannot be solved, only understood. Speaking in terms of theory construction, both options had their advantages and disadvantages. In particular, both were replete with political ramifications. The first option by and large amounted to a containment of the political and rendered its full articulation impossible. This was the situation from which Carl Schmitt had started, and Strauss understood well Schmitt's rejection of situating the political "next to, and equivalent to, the other 'provinces of culture.'"[6] But he also had good reason to treat political philosophy as a branch of philosophy. For the other option was to politicize philosophy altogether, and that left little space for sound political judgment. It was Carl Schmitt who embodied the pitfalls of this option even before his eventual turn to National Socialism.

Strauss henceforth moved between the two options, demonstrating why the scope of political philosophizing must be both restricted and widened. It must be widened to see the whole of philosophy with regard to its political dimension and restricted to prevent an all-out politicization of philosophy.

The question of whether political philosophy is "a branch" of philosophy or a key to the whole of philosophy did not come out of nowhere. It was built upon the template of a nearly forgotten problem in the Marburg School of neo-Kantianism: *the place of religion in the system of philosophy*. In a nutshell, the question can be stated as follows: If philosophy is divided into the Kantian triad of epistemology, ethics, and aesthetics, what is the place of religion? Does religion belong to ethics? Should the Kantian triadic structure be changed by adding religion as a fourth pillar of the system? Or does it actually destroy the system altogether? The place of religion in the system of philosophy has been a major issue in the late thought of Hermann Cohen, and it became a bone of contention in the canonization of Cohen's philosophy through Franz Rosenzweig and others during the 1920s. It was the subject if a variety of dissertations written by young Jewish thinkers in the late 1920s and early 1930s. The problem still resonated in the quarrels over the neo-Kantian legacy during the Weimar Republic, which Strauss knew as a firsthand witness and critical commentator. Religion became recognizable through this discussion as the paradigmatic noncultural, which did not fit into the system of philosophy as it was devised by neo-Kantian philosophy of culture.

It was Strauss who transferred the problem to the new context of political philosophy. He discussed "the political" within the conceptual framework that was built and prepared in the prior discussion on the place of religion within the neo-Kantian system of philosophy. When he argued in his "Notes on Carl Schmitt" that the political cannot be located within the systematic structure of the philosophy of culture, he understood Schmitt's *The Concept of the Political* in terms he had acquired from the prior debates on the systematic place of religion. He formed these terms into a structural analogy between religion and the political. This analogy caused a string of secondary problems, but the general idea is indeed sustainable: neither religion nor the political can be located in the systematics of "culture."

The historical and theoretical context of neo-Kantian philosophy of religion is hardly known today, even by historians of twentieth-century philosophy, but it was an integral part of the world from which Strauss had emerged. The guiding questions vanished in the overall turn against the philosophical systems. They were pushed aside and eventually forgotten through the predominance of phenomenology and the resurgence of theology in the 1920s. Strauss later claimed these two related developments as the double origin of his own philosophical endeavor.[7] Together with a number of diatribes against the remaining neo-Kantians, his accounts of the intellectual climate in German thought of the interwar period—often to be found in his late semiautobiographical recollections—have given the impression of a profound hostility toward the Marburg School. Strauss was a master of the polemical discourse against neo-Kantianism. But like no other of his generation, he also shows how the philosophical systems exerted a subterranean influence long after their purported demise.

To see the systematic problem of Strauss's political philosophy in its historical genesis, then, we must seek to understand the prior problem of religion in neo-Kantian philosophy. We must seek to understand what initially seemed to speak against the inclusion of religion, why the matter turned out to be a serious challenge to the overall system and how it became a bone of contention over the neo-Kantian legacy in the 1920s and thereafter. In the first place, we must acquaint ourselves with Hermann Cohen, the post-Cohenian debates in Jewish philosophy, and Strauss's complex position on Cohen throughout his work.

1

Hermann Cohen on the Systematic Place of Religion

Strauss himself pointed to the template of Hermann Cohen's question of how "religion 'enters into the system of philosophy'"[8] in a number of writings, from his early review essays to the late introductory essay to Hermann Cohen's *Religion of Reason out of the Sources of Judaism*. Cohen, the mastermind of the Marburg School, who was widely regarded as the last great systematic philosopher and a preeminent figure of German-Jewish thought, built his system upon the Kantian division of philosophy (epistemology, ethics, and aesthetics), to which he added a slight Hegelian touch. There are two versions of the system. The first was devised as a tripartite commentary on Kant (*Kants Theorie der Erfahrung*, 1871; *Kants Begründung der Ethik*, 1877; *Kants Begründung der Ästhetik*, 1889) that was meant to elevate Kantian idealism back to its former glory. The second version, a more independent outline of the system along the same lines, comprised *Logik der reinen Erkenntnis* (1902), *Ethik des reinen Willens* (1904), and *Ästhetik des reinen Gefühls* (1912). The common denominator of these three parts, which also designate three independent "directions of consciousness" or "directions of culture,"[9] lies in the word *rein* (pure). It means that all content of the system is constituted purely by the human mind, so that it is free from all empirical determination; but it also invokes the purity of the heart by which the individual would stand before God.[10] The purity of knowledge, will, and feeling assures that the system is independent and free from reality, for Cohen thought that only such independence would guarantee that reality could be changed. Hence, the emphasis on philosophical idealism was connected from the beginning to his social idealism. Idealism designated that reality, with its characteristic features of poverty and social suffering, could be profoundly transformed.

The problem with religion was that it is not pure in this sense: it is historical; it is replete with mystical elements; and most notably, there are many religions, so that religion is not universal. It needed to undergo what Cohen called the "transcendental inquisition," just as did all basic facts of culture: "We start from their facticity and then ask for their right."[11] Yet the system itself seemed to demand the inclusion of religion to be comprehensive. And, pushing back against the predominant historical and psychological accounts of religion, Cohen reiterated that religion needed to be properly integrated into the system of philosophy: "There is only one kind of philosophy: systematic philosophy."[12] Cohen was aware of the common "contempt for systematic philosophizing" in his time, but he saw it as a matter of "incompetence" on the part of his colleagues.[13]

Most likely, he would in turn be criticized for the misrecognition of religious reality. The standard argument was provided by Alfred Jospe, who wrote in his 1932 dissertation that "the methodology of neo-Kantianism eliminates the tangible reality by putting the spontaneity of thinking at the beginning. Deforming the concept of reality into the idea of truth, and identifying truth with science, it strips man of his tangible existence and God of his sense of reality." As Jospe argued, Cohen's social idealism excluded "man's necessary, natural reality"[14]—and this common sentiment against neo-Kantianism was prevalent in German philosophy as well as in Jewish thought.

Some careful readers cautioned that Cohenian idealism does not truly exclude any claims of reality. As Heinz Graupe noted in his dissertation on the place of religion in the Marburg system of philosophy, the "characteristic elasticity" of the system makes it possible to include the claims of religion in the methodological process.[15] Another option was to argue that the religious teaching transcended Cohen's idealistic position.[16]

Adding to the general problem of system and reality, Cohen was also bound by the tripartite structure he had adopted from Kant. After all, the three parts were meant to represent the three pillars of human culture. Each of them was determined by a particular "direction" of consciousness, and there was nothing left to be added as an independent fourth part. To name only the most severe restrictions: Religion could not be a part of aesthetics, because the feeling could not stand for two parts of the system at once.[17] Ethics was conceived as *the* part of the system that dealt with all human affairs; therefore the integration of religion *alongside* ethics would strip the latter of its unique status within the system. And despite many points of contact, a fusion of epistemology and religion would have stripped the former of its purity. Finally, there was the "danger of a false, not methodologically-systematically founded independence of religion."[18] Faced with these problems, Cohen initially drew the conclusion that religion was to be dissolved into ethics.[19] In the course of this examination, he was led to profound changes in the theoretical design, but he nevertheless kept the basic structure of the system intact. Three phases are to be distinguished: first, the attempt to fit religion to the system; second, a modification of the system; third, the resolute non-location of religion in the system.[20]

Cohen's *Ethik des reinen Willens* (1904) is the major reference point for the first phase, although the projected "dissolution of religion into ethics" (*Auflösung der Religion in Ethik*) can be identified in his work as early as 1896.[21] "Ethics," wrote Cohen in 1904, "absolutely cannot acknowledge the independence of religion. . . . It can . . . acknowledge religion only as a state of nature, whose cultural maturity falls into ethics. . . . Religion must merge [*übergehen*] into ethics."[22] This solution was untenable, and Cohen hastened to add that it described a future endgame for religion, not an actual task. As should be noted, it was not only the desire to keep the Kantian system intact that led him to this solution. A formative impulse was to emphasize the universal aspect of mankind as opposed to the particularistic nature of religions and confessions.[23] Only an ethicized religion would overcome the shortcomings of each particular religion. Without being founded and integrated in philosophy proper, religion would inevitably fall back into mysticism. This perceived danger reflected Cohen's stance on Judaism and German culture. Cohen had maintained a principal distinction between systematic philosophy and Judaism for most of his life, and this distinction was in itself a statement on Judaism. His theoretical work was designed as a contribution to the European project of science and morals. This work would force the non-Jewish world to recognize the cultural value (*Kulturwert*) of Judaism.[24] The preemptive erasure of all markers of Jewish particularism was seen as a prerequisite to the admission of Jewry into German culture.

As Strauss emphasized, Cohen was the principal spokesman of German Jewry in the early twentieth century. His theoretical considerations were not merely a reflection of historical events. He created the model by which German Jews of the early twentieth century understood themselves as being Jews *and* Germans. Outside of this context, his theoretical solutions often seem to lack the plausibility of each of the two positions they are meant to combine. One must see them rather as *political* solutions within the German-Jewish context in order to be able to understand their necessity—Cohen could not simply decide in favor of the independence of religion or dissolve religion altogether. Strauss's late words on Cohen point in this direction: He sought to explain the obscurity of Cohen's solutions by way of his impossible position as a German Jew *before* the collapse of the German-Jewish "symbiosis":

> While Cohen had a rare devotion to Judaism, he was hardly less devoted to what he understood by culture (science and secular scholarship, autonomous morality leading to socialist and democratic politics, and art). . . . Cohen's goal was the same as that of the other Western spokesmen for Judaism who came after Mendelssohn: to establish a harmony between Judaism and culture, between *Torah* and *derekh eretz* [the way of the land].[25]

It was fully in line with this double task that Cohen defended the dissolution of religion into ethics to be a *praise* of religion. In his *Der Begriff der Religion im System der Philosophie* (1915), he stipulated that the truth content of religion is measured by the grade to which it is capable of such dissolution.[26] By the time Cohen drew this line of argument, however, it had by and large become defensive, cited primarily to justify his older position. He had come to doubt whether "ethics is indeed capable of dealing with all problems that traditionally arise in religion." The doubt culminated in the question whether God can be properly understood as an "accessory [*Zubehör*] of man."[27] Thus, the problem arises anew whether religion can be said to have a "share in the system of philosophy."[28]

Cohen now sought to articulate the reality of religion that still lived in him, but he needed to accommodate it to the system of philosophy. The provisional solution in *Der Begriff der Religion*—the second phase—is that religion possesses some kind of "share in the system of philosophy," but it does not form an independent element in the systematic structure. The God of religion is now understood as an enrichment to ethics, for ethics would remain a torso without an infusion of "being" (*Dasein*) granted by religion.[29] Religion is not the foundation at the beginning but the conclusion at the end. It is not the safe ground upon which ethics is built but the keystone by which ethics will eventually be completed.

Cohen meant to secure this harmony through a conceptual double strategy toward religion that would limit its scope and secure its unique status. His solution is that religion possess not independence (i.e., systematic autonomy) but uniqueness or peculiarity (*Eigenart*). Thus, it acquires a precarious position in the system of philosophy, to which it nevertheless does not belong: there is no religious consciousness beyond the scientific, moral, and aesthetic consciousness. Cohen was not entirely satisfied with this solution, either. Once again he had avoided adding religion as a fourth realm of culture beside the three cultural realms of science, morals, and art, but he nevertheless deemed it necessary to eventually assume a fourth element: He planned to add "psychology" as a fourth part of the system that would encompass the other three parts. In the closing pages of *Ästhetik des reinen Gefühls* (1912) Cohen projected this fourth part as the "hodegetic [i.e., path-guiding] encyclopedia of the system of philosophy."[30] This move would conclude the transformation of the Kantian system into a philosophy of culture. As Rosenzweig understood it, this fourth part was meant to unite the system as a whole and overcome the unreality of each of the disciplines; for each of these disciplines was separated from the others despite their common relationship to culture, whereas the man of culture is homogenous.[31] Apart from minor references in Cohen's writings, the plan never materialized. Instead, Cohen wrote *Religion of Reason out of the Sources of Judaism*, the unfinished master work on religion published after his death. It marks the third stage in Cohen's revaluation of religion.

The systematic solution in the *Religion of Reason* is not entirely different from the solution in *Der Begriff der Philosophie*, but Cohen posed the problem in a different way here, so that the solution reaches a step farther beyond the systematic premises. The short but dense discussion in the second part of the introduction, stretching over less than two pages in the original text, deserves a careful reading. Cohen's starting point was that ethics, as a branch of the system, "claims to govern all human affairs," so that it must deny a share in the knowledge of human affairs to any other kind of knowledge, "including religion." This leads to an alternative "in which either of two choices seems to be equally fatal for the problem of the religion of reason." According to the first choice, religion falls under the domain of ethics, which covers the whole range of reason; but then the autonomy of religion (qua religion of reason) is in question. In this case the project of a religion of reason would have no basis. According to the second choice, ethics "is not sufficiently able to master the entire content of the concept of man," so that religion must "fill this gap." Cohen clearly favored the second option over the first, but he named two possible difficulties with it. First, he cited his own systematic objection against the admission of religion. But, surprisingly, "the fact that religion would have to enter the system of philosophy" was no longer a principal danger for Cohen, who for a brief moment seemed to conceive the possibility of such an admission of religion into the system. As he declared, "[T]he considerations against it, even historically, would have little weight." At this point, the systematic question had moved into the background. Cohen saw a far more severe problem "in the fact that the methodological concept of ethics would become ambiguous," for ethics as the comprehensive doctrine of man would then be no more than a part of the doctrine of man: "Should ethics have to share its labor with religion?" Cohen's main objection to the admission of religion was that ethics, then, could "do only half of the job."[32]

In his last work, then, Cohen no longer argued against the admission of religion in the name of systematic coherence. His deeper concern was the claim to universality of one element of the system, namely, ethics. This danger was a steady companion of the philosophy of culture. The problem of one element in the system attempting to impose itself on the other elements, denying their right to exist as independent parts, became much more significant in the philosophy of Ernst Cassirer, as we shall see below. But Cohen, too, in his last discussion of the philosophical problem of religion, detected a fundamental conflict within the idea of culture and its various "directions" or forms.

Furthermore, Cohen also sensed a danger for religion itself if it were to become entirely independent: the possibility that religion might "install" itself as the religion of reason (*dass sie . . . sich einrichten könnte*).[33] Apparently Cohen feared that religion would glide into a cushy comfort zone and lose its idealist sting if it were to form an independent domain. Therefore, it should retain its precarious status rather than come to rest in the system. Cohen thought that this methodological issue would explain all dangers pertaining to the history of religion in its relationship to theoretical and practical culture. As he emphasized in his conclusion of the paragraph: "There cannot be two kinds of reason with regard to the doctrine of man."[34] Paradoxically, then, the uniqueness of religion is guaranteed precisely by the fact that it is *not* properly located within the system of philosophy. This systematic non-location could be interpreted in various ways. The most far-reaching claims, however, were made by Franz Rosenzweig in his seminal introductory essay to Cohen's *Jüdische Schriften* (1924).

2

Post-Cohenian Quarrels

Rosenzweig, Natorp, Strauss

Rosenzweig's account of Cohen combines firsthand knowledge of Cohenian thought with great rhetorical boldness. It was devised from the beginning to disregard the "school."[1] Therefore, Rosenzweig sought to avoid all methodological issues and base his characterization to a large extent on anecdotes or personal experiences. But even within this setting he came to a principal statement on the systematic question, and this statement took a unique turn:

> All intellectual sharpness is being summoned to furnish proof that religion possesses uniqueness, but not independence. No peculiar systematic element of consciousness pertains to it, in the way that recognition pertains to logic, the will to ethics, the emotion to aesthetics; neither may religion presume to assemble these powers of the consciousness within itself, for such is irrefutably the task of the homogeneous cultural consciousness, as will be elaborated in the psychology. And yet, or rather precisely because he clearly and strictly maintains the concept of culture and its parts, Cohen prevents this philosophy of religion from becoming—philosophy of religion, i.e., he does not integrate religion into the compartments of culture as a subject among others, nor does he stage an argument between religion and culture on the whole; this being the Scylla, that the Charybdis of this century's efforts for the concept of religion. It is precisely the fact that

religion is being denied systematic independence that saturates it . . . with systematic—one is compelled to say—omnipresence.[2]

The watchword here is "omnipresence." It suggests that religion spreads over all other "compartments of culture" (epistemology, ethics and aesthetics), either by affecting each compartment *or* by invalidating the systematics of culture altogether. Rosenzweig had a proclivity toward the second option. The first was rather characteristic for Paul Natorp, another main figure of neo-Kantian philosophy, who belonged much more than Rosenzweig to the enterprise of the philosophy of religion. As Rosenzweig understood the problem, Cohen kept the system of philosophy intact to prevent religion from its degeneration into a philosophy of religion. This derogative use of the term *Religionsphilosophie* was widely known in the German discourse on religion and culture in the 1920s, and Strauss employed it at length in *Philosophy and Law* in his polemical discussion of the Protestant tradition inaugurated by Friedrich Schleiermacher's *Über die Religion* (1799). For proponents and opponents of the new theology in the early 1920s alike, "philosophy of religion" stood for a purely subjective attitude toward religion based on the affection of the self by a vague religious feeling.

A fine example of the assumed dangers of the religio-philosophical approach can be found in Paul Natorp's earlier work, *Religion innerhalb der Grenzen der Humanität* (Religion within the Boundaries of Humanity, 1894). Natorp attempted to locate a religious a priori in the human consciousness long before Cohen. He sought to combine the Schleiermacherian notion of religious feeling, but that did not sit well with Cohen's systematic approach, to which he sought to adhere. This was seen most clearly by Hans Leisegang, who wrote a devastating critique of Natorp's approach:

> This feeling has no object, since every possible object is being dealt with by the other powers of cognition, of the will and of the artistic imagination, so that no specific realm remains for religion beside the true, good and beautiful. Thus, unlike in Schleiermacher, the feeling cannot have the infinite as its object. Therefore Natorp replaces the feeling of the infinite with the infinity of the feeling. Religion is not to aim directly for the infinite, for transcendence; it is not to cross the barrier of the human, but to make an impact solely in science, ethics and art, in culture and humanity by completely relinquishing the claim to transcendence. . . . Thus, religion . . . has no value of its

own; it is wholly absorbed by the ideas of the good, true and beautiful, through which all culture is created. With this result, the link to Schleiermacher has become entirely pointless, whom one need not evoke to achieve this result.[3]

Faced with the irreconcilable tasks of articulating an overflowing religious "feeling" and locating it within the Kantian system of philosophy, Natorp saw no other way than to neutralize religion. His solution was not particularly attractive for his contemporaries. Cohen himself proved to be much more difficult to dismiss, precisely because he resisted the desire to incorporate religion into the realm of culture altogether. His systematic precaution is not merely a failed attempt to acknowledge the independence of religion, for there were very good reasons to limit the scope of religious experience. As Natorp himself noted, the best Cohen could have achieved by emphasizing the independence of religion was to provide a transcendental foundation of religion, which would have won him "a logically good conscience vis-à-vis culture."[4]

Furthermore, Cohen also had a clear political motivation in limiting the scope of religion. One need not go as far as Helmut Holzhey, who read Cohen's self-limitation thesis as an attempt to curb religious fundamentalism.[5] The topical question concerning the politics of religion, which is common to Cohen's own problem *and* the question of religion today, may be stated as follows: If religion is a part of ethics, it serves the human community; it is a part of culture; it wholly belongs to the human world. God is then a mere "accessory (*Zubehör*) of man,"[6] as Cohen quipped—and this what he sought to avoid. Only if religion remains at least in part independent from ethics is it capable of reaching beyond the realm of human traffic. Therefore, religion has little to gain from its integration into the system as an independent part, and hence as a cultural "direction" or form among others. The experience of God revealing himself to man is fundamentally different from the experience provided by cultural forms and activities; it is the disruption of these activities. To follow Cohen's lead: as a part of ethics, religion would appeal to common values of humanity, and these values could be deliberated upon, but it would not provide an outside perspective on human deliberations and purposes. Only if religion is located beyond the systematics of culture proper, then, can it resist its own neutralization.

Strauss professed intimate knowledge of the matter in his early writings. It appears that he frequently changed his position in accordance with each specific situation, and each position is somewhat disputable. Just like his general double role as a devoted adherent and a fierce critic of Cohen,[7] his seemingly enigmatic statements on the relationship between the philosophical system and religion often leave commentators perplexed. But there is a common denominator: in each case Strauss defended the systematic coherence of Cohen's philosophy of religion against its critics and argued for a continuity between the system of philosophy and the articulation of Judaism in Cohen. The lines of argument changed in accordance with their targets—they could be directed against a postsystematic understanding of Judaism, a strictly Kantian interpretation of religion, or a protestant emphasis on the individual religious feeling. But in all cases they pointed to the intricate connection between the system and the demands of Judaism.

The earliest example is to be found in the article "On the Argument with European Science" ("Zur Auseinandersetzung mit der europäischen Wissenschaft," 1924). Strauss addressed the Protestant theologian Georg Wobbermin here, who had criticized Cohen's philosophic-systematic approach toward religion in the name of religious experience (*Erlebnis*). Wobbermin's general criticism against the systematic-philosophical approach was that the system had not taken religion into account from the beginning. Cohen's task to locate religion within the system of philosophy, then, was the ultimate attempt to "determine the concept of religion itself from the context of the system that had been devised without regard to [religion]." For Wobbermin, this endeavor amounted to a deformation of religious experience, and ultimately the "rape of religion," by the philosophical system.[8] Strauss concluded that Wobbermin had read only the title of Cohen's 1915 work, whereas "a reading of the entire work" would have led him to a different conclusion: "the entire context of Cohen's philosophic system rests on religious presuppositions . . . system and science are decisively *prepared* by religion."[9] Later in the same text Strauss characterized "the inner connection between Cohen's entire philosophical system and Judaism" in such a way that the system "in every respect *fulfills* itself in his theology."[10]

This position on the relationship between the philosophical system and religion in Cohen's work is indeed "unique to Strauss,"[11] but it also resembles the position of Natorp's late lectures on practical philosophy (*Vorlesungen über praktische Philosophie*, 1925). Cassirer suggested in his obituary for Natorp that "the whole construction of Natorp's thought rests on ultimate religious convictions," and that a strong individual-religious basic feeling runs through the entire book,[12] including those parts not dealing with religion. Furthermore, Strauss's claim was decisively anticipated by Rosenzweig's argument regarding the omnipresence of religion in Cohen's system. Strauss simply stretched Rosenzweig's point a little farther.

A year later, Strauss had come to a different understanding of the subject matter. Most notably, he had come to doubt Rosenzweig's interpretation. In his review article for the *Jüdische Wochenzeitung für Cassel, Hessen und Waldeck* on Cohen's *Jüdische Schriften* he argued as follows:

> Cohen arrived at the necessity of the concept of God [on the ground of the Kantian system]. If one considers that, according to Cohen, the system of philosophy is to accomplish the foundation [*Begründung*] of "culture," i.e., of European culture . . . this path of Cohen's already constitutes a "return" from Europe to Judaism. When Cohen asks, what necessity of the system leads to the idea of God, he implicitly asks: What European necessity demands the preservation and development of Judaism? It follows from the aforesaid that Cohen's doctrine of religion, of Judaism, of God cannot be understood without knowledge of his system.[13]

On this basis, Strauss criticized Walter Kinkel, a staunch neo-Kantian who in his popular introduction to Cohen's work had advocated for a return to the "self-dissolution" of religion: "The great merit of Cohen in religion . . . is in our view the ethicization of religion."[14] As Strauss ironically commented:

> The only point in Cohen's system of thought Kinkel dislikes is the constitution of a philosophy of religion *next to* the ethics that, while not independent, is still particular [*eigenartig*]. This ceases to be surprising as soon as one notices the massive cluelessness of the author in regard to Jewish things. . . . Without a more specific perception of the context from which Cohen hailed and to which he "returned" it is impossible to understand his system as one culminating in Jewish theology.[15]

The claim that Cohen's system *culminates* in a "Jewish theology" is the centerpiece of Strauss's 1925 review essay. It was reiterated in the late introductory essay to Cohen's *Religion of Reason* (1972). The essay emphasizes the ambiguities and paradoxes in Cohen's stance on the relationship between philosophy and religion. One can rephrase the argument in the most simple form as follows: Cohen had initially transplanted key doctrines of Judaism into his ethics, so that they became a central part of the system itself. At the same time, he sought to show that ethics must be transcended by religion. The *Religion of Reason* would hence have to be understood as the crowning part of the system of philosophy. But qua being developed *out of the sources of Judaism*, the *Religion of Reason* transcends the system. Hence, there is an "obscurity" in the relationship between the system and Judaism, and this is due to the fact that Cohen was devoted both to Judaism and to "what he understood by culture." Religion therefore could not be reduced to ethics but needed to remain dependent on ethics.[16] This double devotion, and the speculative power invested by Cohen to mediate between the two, led to the paradoxical situation of his late philosophy. Strauss's concluding remarks on the matter come as a precaution with regard to passages in which "Cohen's heart speaks" or where he articulated the Jewish teachings against the backdrop of his system:

> This does not mean that he abandons the teaching of his *Ethics*; he keeps it intact as the ethical teaching; he merely supplements it by the religious teaching; but in so doing he profoundly transforms it.[17]

This framework of interpretation, situated at the border between Judaism and the system, is entirely different from the one employed by Rosenzweig, who had based his entire presentation of Cohen's teaching as a great *teshuva*, an act of repentance and return.[18] This solution created a principal disjunction between philosophy and Judaism, suggesting that Cohen had left the context of the philosophical system to facilitate the return to Judaism. Strauss believed as well as Rosenzweig that Cohen had "returned" to Judaism, but unlike Rosenzweig he held that this return followed from the very premises of Cohen's philosophy. As he maintained in 1925, the return to Judaism was a "European necessity," not a principal turn against Europe.[19] The point of departure was "the foundation of the system." By ignoring the part of logic (and hence the mathematical sciences), Rosenzweig had misconstrued the relationship between the system and Judaism:

> The inwardly justified extension of the system toward Judaism indeed motivates a retreat of logic in regard to the proportions [of the system], but not in regard to its constructive meaning for the structure, which turned out differently than initially planned.[20]

At this point, Strauss had dissolved the separation between systematic philosophy and Jewish thought, and that was not a casual byproduct of the article. Overall, then, the reason for a "return" to Judaism was to be found in the antinomies of the philosophical system, and Judaism had become an integral part of European thought. This road was different from the one taken by Rosenzweig, and it also differed from the project of *Philosophy of Law*, where Strauss presented the Islamic and Jewish notion of law as the "other" of philosophical reason. In this context his view on Cohen was different, too. At first sight it was closer to Rosenzweig's: both Rosenzweig and Strauss understood Cohen's concept of religion in terms of the "reality" of God and His revelation to man. They viewed Cohen in light of the opposition between the purported formal, ethicized "idea of God" and the unmediated, full experience of God as a reality.[21] But Strauss did not subscribe to Rosenzweig's interpretation of this opposition. He followed Rosenzweig to some extent, but he eventually argued that Rosenzweig was part of the same problem: The omnipresence of religion in and beyond the systematic structure of philosophy did not help much to articulate its "reality." The progress to the "new thinking" led to an ever greater distance from the reality of God. Upon the premises of existentialism, religion merely retreated farther into the subject, but that did not make God any more real.[22]

3

Strauss on Paul Natorp and Ernst Cassirer

Strauss's acquaintance with the intricacies of the systematic problem of religion stemmed from his early encounter with Cohen's writings, but he also viewed the matter through a variety of post-Cohenian criticisms and appropriations. The principal figures to discuss here were Paul Natorp and Ernst Cassirer, the two living monuments of the school's "disintegration."[1] Although his remarks on the subject initially give the impression of mere contempt and mockery, Strauss saw the transformation of the Cohenian system by the remaining neo-Kantians very clearly. As he noted about Ernst Cassirer—his doctoral advisor at the University of Hamburg, who was widely regarded as Cohen's heir[2]—the neo-Kantians *after* Cohen lacked the "sensitivity to the problems" that had been the hallmark of Cohen's systematic philosophizing.[3]

His take on Paul Natorp is entirely focused on the notion of *Kulturprovinzen* (cultural provinces), and this leads right into the heart of the systematic question and its afterlife in the 1920s. Today the term is almost solely known through Strauss and his "Notes on Carl Schmitt," where Schmitt poses against his will as a covert neo-Kantian.[4] It had floated around in neo-Kantian circles up to the late 1920s and was eventually forgotten with the demise of philosophical systematics. Karl Vorländer had already in 1894 written about the three cultural provinces of science, ethics (*Sittlichkeit*), and art; and Theodor Litt spoke in 1926 of the "great cultural provinces."[5] Natorp's writings do not give a direct match for the term *Kulturprovinzen*, but he interchangeably spoke of the three "provinces of the spirit," "scientific domains," or "great main directions of human culture."[6] There is a section in his *Die Weltalter des Geistes* (1918) that well captures his philosophy of the cultural provinces. From here one can easily see Strauss's discontent with the systematic concept of culture in its basis and genesis.

> These three dimensions of the spirit split off from the common angular point of the soul's inner life; this [inner life], an undivided whole, a concrete unity, continues to assert itself in religion. It does not disappear even once that the split has occurred, but now it seems . . . to gain a life of its own and thus—against the whole meaning of religion—to constitute a distinct province in the realm of the spirit.[7]

As Natorp argued, every "cultural province" strove to conquer and dominate the whole life of the spirit; and hence it became "not only expulsive," but outright "tyrannical" against the other provinces. But religion was the greatest tyrant of culture: Since it could not join the forces of cultural differentiation, it saw itself pushed into a purely defensive position. Here, it could only assert itself as a last, unanswerable but irrefutable question. In this perspective, the claim of religion has degenerated into a desperate reaction against the forces of modernization. The problem of Natorp's account was that it was based on a strict notion of "development" *without* a corresponding idea of progress. As he maintained, religion would become ever more "backward, unfree, fleeing the full gravity of development into which mankind has entered after all now, and which cannot be reversed, whatever may come out of it [*werde daraus was will*]."[8] Just as Strauss noted in a remark on Friedrich Engels, the idea of progress has been abandoned here, but the sole response is a reassuring "never mind."[9]

Natorp substituted progress by "development," a notion that maintains the duty to move along without a corresponding purpose. *Whatever may come out of it*: Natorp was nevertheless certain that "the differentiation must go on and on." As he added, the unity of world-knowledge would remain unabated "as a presupposition." But the goal of unity in that knowledge would "more and more become a far prospect, a prospect soon without any prospect. By and by one loses it out of sight; the progress of specialized research and the advancement of work on the particular, finite problem appear to be incomparably more urgent than the concern for keeping in tune with the . . . [other] domains of science."[10] The "development" toward ever-greater differentiation has become the holy duty of mankind, whereas the formal "presupposition" of unity has degenerated into an empty ritual without any corresponding cognitive effort.

Natorp left intact the basic tripartite structure of the Kantian system as he inherited it from Cohen, but he interpreted this structure in a different way. His attempt to reconcile the system with the claims of religion, in particular, shows that his progress beyond Cohen was ambivalent. Natorp sought to broaden the method to include human expressions hitherto unknown to the neo-Kantian enterprise, but paradoxically the system became more rigid and formalistic than it was in Cohen. The term *Kulturprovinzen* functions like a dialectical image of this paradox. It evokes the fate of the Cohenian system *after* Cohen, its formalism despite its turn toward reality, and the provincialism of the Marburg School at the time Strauss came to study with Natorp.[11]

But no matter how problematic this account of the *Kulturprovinzen* turned out to be, Natorp expressed the systematic problem of religion well. He sensed that religion did not fit into the "main provinces of the spirit" because it was different from the others, but he nevertheless counted it among these provinces. As he declared, the provinces of culture comprised "theory [= epistemology], praxis [= ethics], then art, religion, and what may have been omitted in this enumeration."[12] Despite his intention to provide the cultural provinces with a new idealistic foundation, the last remark shows that he was not entirely sure what even counted as a province of its own. This question was a steady companion in the discussions on the systematic of culture in the 1920s, and the place where it became most visible is the philosophy of Ernst Cassirer.

Cassirer changed the systematic disposition of philosophy dramatically by expanding the tripartite Kantian system (which had by and large remained intact in the Marburg School despite the internal differences regarding its precise interpretation) into an indefinite number of "symbolic forms." These "various fundamental forms of man's 'understanding' of the world," each of which "is subject to a particular law," would in sum encompass "the life of the human spirit as a whole."[13] In other words, symbolic forms were not mere parts of a system of philosophy; they were living proof of the awesomeness of human culture and its products. His stance on what is to be counted among the symbolic forms varied from text to text, and sometimes even within the same text. This variety points to the severe systematic problems he faced.

Cassirer began with language, myth, and art. These remained the three core forms throughout his philosophy of culture (with linguistics, art science, and religious studies as the corresponding positive sciences). Religion may *almost* be counted as a core form in its own right. Cassirer named it together with the other three in his earliest exposition of the symbolic forms, as well as in the first volume of *The Philosophy of Symbolic Forms* and in the final version in *An Essay on Man*. But sometimes he dropped the matter or, alternatively, treated religion together with myth. He thereby suggested that the difference between the two is only gradual. This issue became a lasting problem of his entire project, as we shall see below. In his *Language and Myth* ("Sprache und Mythos," 1925) Cassirer added scientific knowledge or cognition for the first time.[14] The succession of the three-volume *Philosophy of Symbolic Forms* suggests that the core of the system consists of language, myth, and cognition (with the three corresponding functions of expression, representation, and meaning).[15]

Cassirer successively faced new prospective symbolic forms, with some of them making only a brief appearance in his writings. Technology was described as a symbolic form in its own right in a 1930 article (whereas Natorp had subsumed the "technological dominion of nature" among cognition, thereby maintaining its close link with scientific knowledge of nature),[16] but he noted that it could not easily be located in the universe of symbolic forms, and the matter was dropped in later systematic considerations.[17] History deserved a chapter of its own, but it remains open whether it really can be counted as a symbolic form.[18] The same goes for law.[19] Politics is a contentious issue in this respect: as Cassirer's philosophy became more and more political, he still treated politics as a historian of political ideas, and he did not elaborate on politics as a symbolic form. Nevertheless, he increasingly sought to acknowledge the fundamental political conflicts between the various symbolic forms. He thereby came to see a deep conflict in his own approach.

The two conditional issues that determined the inclusion or exclusion of each prospective form into the framework of culture were, first, that it could be understood as a sole creation of the human mind and, second, that it could in principle be understood as one form among others. Substituting politics and the political through the history of political ideas was a prerequisite for the integration of politics into the framework of culture. But was politics a matter of "*ideal* oppositions"—i.e., ideas and concepts—or was it about "real powers"? Cassirer faced the possibility that he was dealing with "intellectual abstractions" rather than real politics, but in the end he assured himself that "both sides are inseparable from each other."[20]

Another possible element is conspicuously missing from Cassirer's systematic disposition, and it was Strauss who paid much attention to it. As he noted, Cassirer "had transformed Cohen's system into a new system of philosophy." The most striking difference was that "ethics had completely disappeared," whereas it had been the "center" of Cohen's system. "It had been *silently* dropped: he had not *faced* the problem."[21] Indeed, Cassirer did not lay out an interpretation of ethics as a symbolic form, and he did not explain why he chose not to do so. Even in *An Essay on Man*, with his most comprehensive enumeration of symbolic forms, he did not mention ethics. The reason why Cassirer could not develop a theory of ethics as a symbolic form is that his entire doctrine of symbolic forms was an implicit ethical teaching. He could not bring ethics into recognition in any other way than as a symbolic form, for a comprehensive and positive notion of ethics would have threatened the autonomy of symbolic forms. The only possible solution was the silent, implicit ethicization of his entire philosophical project.

The ethics of culture is that each claim to truth must be transformed into an expression of culture, and each expression is merely one cultural form among others. Cassirer gave the clearest outline of this ethical desire in the Davos debate with Martin Heidegger, where he argued that man "must transpose everything in him which is lived experience into some objective shape in which he is objectified," thereby denying legitimacy to each claim of unquestioned truth.[22] The second advice is that none of these shapes is entitled to rise above the others. These two imperatives are at the heart of Cassirer's implicit doctrine of ethics, which also contains many political implications. Most notably, it states that human culture is multifaceted, and it seeks to demonstrate how the multiple forms of culture could peacefully coexist side by side. But Cassirer knew well that such peaceful coexistence could not be presupposed. In his programmatic introduction to the first volume of *The Philosophy of Symbolic Forms* he explained:

> Every basic cultural form tends to represent itself not as a part but as the whole, laying claim to an absolute and not merely relative validity, not contending itself with its special sphere, but seeking to imprint its own characteristic stamp on the whole realm of being and the whole life of the spirit. From this striving toward the absolute inherent in each special sphere arise the conflicts and the antinomies within the concept of culture.[23]
>
> The particular cultural trends [*geistige Richtungen*] do not move peacefully side by side, seeking to complement one another; each becomes what it is only by demonstrating its own peculiar power against the others and in battle with the others.[24]

We find here—as well as in the article "Form and Technology"—a strong emphasis on *struggle* and *conflict* as the basic facts of modern societies. Cassirer was apparently influenced by Georg Simmel here. But unlike Simmel, who took much delight in watching his own conceptual distinctions shift or collapse, Cassirer strove to find a position from which he could not only describe but also settle these conflicts. Philosophy, being the "supreme authority and repository of unity," would be qualified to resolve the "struggles and conflicts" of the spirit. But there was a problem: The "dogmatic systems of metaphysics"—clearly the opponents of scientific and cultural pluralism in Cassirer's view—"usually stand in the midst of the battle, and not above it: despite the conceptual universality toward which they strive, they stand only for one side of the conflict, instead of encompassing and mediating the conflict itself in all its breadth and depth." By hypostatizing one logical, aesthetic, or religious principle, the old systems shut themselves off from the plurality of cultural spheres and forms. "Philosophical thought might avoid this danger . . . only if it could find a standpoint situated above all these forms and yet not merely outside them: a standpoint which would make it possible to encompass the whole of them in one view."[25] With such a standpoint, philosophy of culture would rise above the conflicts of culture.

As Cassirer outlined, the possibility of such a standpoint depended upon the proper systematic disposition of philosophy. The one thing needed was a "a systematic philosophy of human culture in which each particular form would take its meaning solely from the *place* in which it stands, a system in which the content and significance of each form would be characterized by the richness and specific quality of the relations and concatenations in which it stands with other spiritual energies and ultimately with totality."[26] It is the idea of *relation* and *inner connection* that Cassirer considered to be the groundbreaking novelty of his philosophy. Accordingly, the philosophical system consists of purely functional relations encompassing a variety of elements while leaving each of them in their own right. The punch line of this idea—that all forms and spheres have an equal share in reason—also carries a sociopolitical dimension.

The questionable part of this solution is its status vis-à-vis reality, namely, vis-à-vis real political conflicts. And here it seems that Cassirer grossly overestimated the significance of his metalingual solution to these conflicts. A closer look at the transitions between some of the symbolic forms—especially from myth to religion and from religion to art—shows why. Transitions from one symbolic form to another pose a great challenge to Cassirer's theory in general. Basically nonhierarchical, these forms are nevertheless structured by a teleological order. The teleology becomes visible through the historical dimension inherent in the formation of culture. Each form evolves dialectically out of another, so that religion emerges out of myth, before it is superseded by art, before modern science emerges at the top of the pyramid. Each time, the dialectical movement is instigated by the act in which man recognizes the symbols and forms more and more as his own, so that they lose their power over him. In myth, symbol and reality are inseparably intertwined, while all later forms successively abandon any pretension to be real. As Strauss summarized Cassirer's position, myth "creates a realm of 'meanings,'" but thereby "the moments of thing and meaning indiscriminately flow in one another."[27] Hence, myth has a share in the formation of culture and society, but only as an early stage in the history of mankind (and similarly as an early stage in the development of individual consciousness). Myth is superseded by religion, in which thing and meaning are in a constant tension. This tension is calmed by art, which succeeds religion. Art is the medium that liberates religion from the assumption that an image deals with reality; instead, the spirit recognizes it as an "expression of its own productive power."[28]

The implications of this teleology were not lost on Cassirer's colleagues. Heidegger wrote after reading the second volume of Cassirer's *Philosophy of Symbolic Forms*: "He sees everything he sees . . . from the highpoint of the Kantian concepts. Inevitably volume III [on] art will follow."[29] Strauss, too, sensed that the idea of aesthetic autonomy was the vanishing point of Cassirer's philosophy. With its strong emphasis on the creative powers of the human mind, it seemed to exclude any forces beyond human creation and control. Hence, a smooth transition from myth and religion to art is crucial for the philosophy of symbolic forms. The problem with this notion became openly visible when Cassirer discussed the political myths of the twentieth century and their intricate connection to aestheticism. As Strauss quipped in his 1947 review of *The Myth of the State*: "Cassirer seems to trace the romantic revolt against the enlightenment to aestheticism. But is not aestheticism the soul of his own doctrine?"[30]

Strauss had drawn a similar conclusion in an early review article, which traced the relation of religion and myth in Cohen and Cassirer. Arguing with regard to the Jewish stance on myth, he dismissed the link between Cohen and Cassirer: "Cassirer's theory of mythology is not a congruent expansion [*sinngemäße Erweiterung*] of the Cohenian system but its dismantling [*Abbau*]."[31] The crucial issue here between Cohen and Cassirer is what causes the suspension of myth. As Strauss saw correctly, the suspension is described by Cassirer in such a way that the human spirit regards the world of myth as its own product: man recognizes himself in the world of myth, so that myth loses its coercive character for him.

Now, Strauss claimed that this theory does "naturally" not apply to biblical history, and he rephrased the departure from myth in Cohenian terms on the emergence of monotheism. This move turned Cassirer's notion of the human origin of myth against Cassirer himself: when the formations of myth are revealed to be the "work of man," they lose their compulsory character; but myth, the work of man that compels man, is thereby "replaced not by the autonomous human spirit, but rather by a different, stronger compulsion, the 'one and only' compulsion," namely, by God. The products of myth, being of human origin, cannot compel man; but religion, being provided by God's revelation to man, does compel man.[32] This interpretive move is brilliant, but it did not come out of nowhere. Strauss simply confronted Cassirer with Cohen's notion of monotheism. In particular, he reminded Cassirer of the central role of Jewish monotheism for the transition from myth to religion: "It seems to me that it is no accident that Cassirer, in his attempt to sketch the relations between the mythic and the religious formation of concepts, refers to Vedic religion, to Parsiism, to Calvinism, and to Jansenism, but *not* to Judaism."[33] The purpose of this reminder is to show that the Jewish religion relates to myth not in the way of a dialectical development, a sublation (*Aufhebung*). Religion thus understood does not "develop" out of myth: it requires a decisive break with myth—"a passionate rejection" and "elimination" rather than a "sublation."[34]

After completing the three-volume *Philosophy of Symbolic Forms*, Cassirer scarcely touched upon the issue of myth. It reemerged in the 1940s in an entirely different mode. Most notably, he saw myth from a political viewpoint now. As he noted in 1944: "What we have learned in the hard school of our modern political life is the fact that human culture is by no means the firmly established thing that we once supposed it to be."[35] This remarkable statement is not without precedent in the thought of Cassirer, who privately announced in 1933 that he would never again write a word after Hitler had come to power.[36] But it was another matter to acknowledge the shift in his theoretical work. For hitherto the understanding that "culture" had not prevented the relapse into barbarism had paradoxically confirmed, rather than cast into doubt, his belief in culture as a means to create and protect the social order. He never abandoned this view entirely, but he severely questioned it in the conclusion of his last book, *The Myth of the State*.

The book contains a turnaround in the notion of myth—or more precisely, it is an attempt to reconcile a new notion of myth with his older notion, although the two notions are visibly at odds. Cassirer recounted the Babylonian myth of the creation of the world to illustrate "the relation between myth and the other great cultural powers." This notion is based upon the idea that myth is one of many "cultural powers." Myth contributes to culture and simultaneously is held in check by culture. The other notion of myth presupposes a qualitative difference between myth and all the other cultural forms: "Our science, our poetry, our art, and our religion are only the upper layer of a much older stratum that reaches down to a great depth. We must always be prepared for violent concussions that may shake our cultural world and our social order by its very foundations."[37]

In this notion, myth is not merely a cultural form among science, poetry, art, and religion: whereas the latter are literally superficial, myth stems from depth; and whereas they protect the social order, myth violently shakes the social order. In order to analyze the specifics of political myth, Cassirer abandoned his earlier idea that myth is not merely an enemy but also a formative element of culture. The decisive factor for this abandonment was his discovery of modern political myth. Although he understood it as a "fake" myth, it deeply affected his overall understanding of myth. The shift became fully visible in his concluding discussion of the Babylonian myth of creation, in which the god Marduk had to fight a mortal battle before he could begin to create the world:

> He had to vanquish and subjugate the serpent Tiamat and the other dragons of darkness. He slew Tiamat and bound the dragons. Out of the limbs of the monster Tiamat he formed the world and gave to it its shape and its order. He made heaven and earth, the constellations and planets, and fixed their movements. His final work was the creation of man.[38]

Cassirer's retelling of the Babylonian myth must be read as the central theoretical advice of his book.[39] It is remarkable how little Cassirer appears to notice that the image turns against his intentions. That image can hardly serve as a proof of the superiority of culture. First of all, it confirms the suspicion that the creation of man rests on a violent act. Culture is then not the free creation of autonomous man but is entangled in a mythical dialectic in which each higher form reproduces the original violent act by subjugating another form. Cassirer took no heed of these aspects and their implication of a dialectic of culture and barbarism. He stated:

> The world of human culture may be described in the words of this Babylonian legend. It could not arise until the darkness of myth was fought and overcome. But the mythical monsters were not entirely destroyed. They were used for the creation of a new universe, and they still survive in this universe. The powers of myth were checked and subdued by superior forces. As long as these forces, intellectual, ethical, and artistic, are in full strength, myth is tamed and subdued. But once they begin to lose their strength chaos is come again. Mythical thought then starts to rise anew and to pervade the whole of man's cultural and social life.[40]

Cassirer described the battle between culture and myth in terms of "darkness" and light, "forces" and counterforces, "strength" and "chaos," subduing and arising. These concepts closely resemble political distinctions—they all can be read as variations of mythical enmity and friendship. In a way, he reframed the political and military war between National Socialism and the Free World as a mythical battle between darkness and light. In this battle, the various cultural forms no longer stand idly by each other. Rather, Cassirer revaluated them from a political point of view, and this posed the question of right or wrong of each cultural form. Thus, Cassirer's concluding statement perfectly illustrates a process often found in the transition from "culture" to "the political": the suspension of the peaceful coexistence of a multiplicity facing the case of emergency. By dismantling his philosophy of culture—and hence to some extent his own lifework—Cassirer proved Leo Strauss's point that the political, as well as religion, is *the "crux" of philosophy of culture*.[41]

Strauss's review of *The Myth of the State* in *Social Research* is remarkably restrained, although the eventual collapse of the philosophy of symbolic forms was not lost on him. And yet one cannot help but notice a subtle call for repentance, *teshuva*, when Strauss urged Cassirer to "return" to Hermann Cohen and transform the philosophy of symbolic forms "into a teaching whose center is moral philosophy."[42] We shall follow this lead and return from Natorp and Cassirer to Cohen, and in particular to the multilayered question of Strauss's stance on Cohen. As we shall see, the claim on the centrality of moral philosophy is a core issue here. Technically speaking, this claim is concerned not with the division of philosophy but with the precise interpretation of that division: the issue is the predominance of one branch within the system of philosophy—despite its being located within the system—and not the inclusion or exclusion of one branch in the system. This is how Cohen's ethics became a role model for Strauss's political philosophy; and this is why Strauss was so concerned in his 1931 lecture "Cohen and Maimonides" with the relationship between ethics and politics. These considerations serve as a gateway from the systematic problem of religion to the location of "the political" in political philosophy.

4

Returning to Cohen

"Cohen and Maimonides" on Ethics and Politics

Strauss himself returned from Natorp and Cassirer to Cohen. This movement was possible on the assumption of a principal difference—despite their common allegiance to neo-Kantianism—between Cohen on the one hand, Natorp and Cassirer on the other. As Strauss maintained, that principal difference between Cohen and the Marburg School existed "from the beginning."[1] It was in the respective philosophical projects and not a matter of the school's decay in the 1920s. But it also had something to do with Cohen's precarious position as a systematic philosopher and Jewish thinker. Strauss did not join the ubiquitous diatribes against the system—or when he did, he hastened to add that its opponents fared even worse. By turning from the system to existence, as Rosenzweig did, reality retreated farther into the subject, and that did not make it more real.[2] More than any other commentator Strauss pointed out how the philosophical system and the claims of religion in Cohen were inseparably intertwined. Following up on his writings on Cohen, the connection is to be found in the word *and*. Cohen as understood by Strauss was "a passionate philosopher and a Jew passionately devoted to Judaism."[3] The *and* does not indicate a synthesis, it rather creates a precarious balance between the two equally important human pursuits. It also leaves open the precise relationship between the two pursuits—and hence Strauss could defend Cohen and yet maintain a completely different stance on Judaism, politics, and interpretation.

Cohen was the principal modern figure when it came to the the task of returning. He had created the model for the balance between philosophizing *and* being a Jew. Returning to Cohen was necessary because his model was no longer being understood, and he no longer seemed to speak to the time. In a 1925 article on the *Jüdische Schriften*, Strauss argued that the "process" that manifests itself in Cohen's writings was "completed," but "only as it were and on the whole. It is completed for German Judaism as a historical totality, though not for the particular Jew of the present generation. Each individual German Jew must undergo the process for which Cohen is and remains paradigmatic." Hence, the appropriation of Cohen's writings was "of the utmost urgency" even as it may have been outdated on the whole.[4] Returning to Cohen and carefully reading his writings, then, meant to go through a "process." Needless to say, going through that process was far from agreeing with Cohen. It meant coming to a principled stand on the issues that had occupied Cohen, but that stand was necessarily different from Cohen's own stand. In any case, a principled stand needed to evolve from an explicit argument with Cohen.

There is an early Strauss text that demonstrates this task extraordinarily well, although it is by no means a finalized article. The lecture manuscript "Cohen and Maimonides" ("Cohen und Maimuni," 1931), with its fragmentary arguments and sudden ruptures, is the document of a transition. It is replete with references to the emerging scholarly project of *Philosophy and Law*, but the ideas on Maimonides are reframed as a continuous argument with Cohen. Cohen had written on Maimonides in his seminal *Ethics of Maimonides* ("Charakteristik der Ethik Maimunis," 1908). Strauss's manuscript shows the extent to which the project of *Philosophy and Law* was initially devised as a counterinterpretation to Cohen, in which he developed some of his lasting ideas on Judaism, ethics, and politics.

Strauss's copious explanation of the "and" in the title demonstrates the reorientation in the most literal sense: It entailed a change of perspective. As he explained, the "and" between Cohen and Maimonides "gives the impression that we, as if sovereign spectators or even judges, wanted to allow both these outstanding men to *pass before* us."[5] This procedure would be appropriate for all "theory"-led approaches that are certain of their own epistemic superiority. Strauss started from the premise that Maimonides was inaccessible for current readers. He wanted "*to gain access to* Rambam by starting with Cohen: Cohen is to open for us the access to Rambam."[6] But what was the obstacle to the understanding of Maimonides? Why was it in need of guidance? "Because *initially* he is *not* accessible to us. He is not accessible to us because we live in a *totally different world*: in the world of 'modern culture,' as Cohen likes to say. We want to avoid this expression, because it makes a highly vulnerable and contentious issue appear all too self-evident."[7] Strauss's task therefore was to lead from a cultural understanding to "an original understanding of Rambam."[8]

The paradox here is that Cohen exemplified both the cultural understanding and the "original understanding" of Maimonides; Strauss wanted to arrive at a more "original" understanding, and yet he sensed that Cohen "is in an *original* manner what we are in a derivative manner."[9] These conflicting statements testify to the perception that any original interpretation of Spinoza, Maimonides, or even Plato needed to pass through the previous interpretations by Cohen. Cohen was an original thinker despite his belief in "culture." But an "original" understanding of Maimonides could only be achieved if Maimonides would no longer be understood in terms of "culture." As Strauss added, in following Cohen he would thereby "have to criticize Cohen." Rather than "blindly following" him, "it is a matter of following the right track of Cohen's and not allowing ourselves to be put off course by his aberrations."[10]

Statements such as these can be cited ad infinitum. They ultimately lead to the conclusion that Strauss *rewrote* Cohen. A number of theological-political treatises point this out openly—from his early articles on Spinoza and Maimonides to the late "Jerusalem and Athens," in which Strauss identified the turning points one by one. Notwithstanding the formal and stylistic differences, they all communicate with Cohen's own theological-political treatises in the way of a *contrafact*—a principal text written as the remaking of another text, with a new outlook being developed in close proximity to the prototype but with the opposite intention. This was also the manner in which Strauss developed his notion of political philosophy, and ultimately of politics. He returned to Cohen to *repeat* and *redirect* the Cohenian enterprise.

Strauss often started from observations on Cohen's modes of interpretation. In particular, he noted the fallacies of Cohen's "idealizing" interpretation, which grossly violated the principle of seeking to understand a thinker *as he understood himself*.[11] The notion of "idealizing" interpretation has a wide specter,[12] but Strauss put great emphasis on how Cohen pitted one philosopher against another to maintain a principal opposition between Plato and Aristotle or Hegel and Kant:

> [For Cohen] Plato and Aristotle represent an *eternal opposition*, the eternal opposition not only between *correct* and *false* philosophizing, but between philosophizing in a state of *fidelity* to the

most important concern of man and philosophizing in the state of *betrayal* of this concern.[13]

As Cohen understands Plato from the point of view of Kant, so he understands Aristotle from the point of view of Hegel. What especially concerns his understanding of Aristotle is that by its orientation to Hegel it is very often misguided.[14]

Strauss found this mode of interpretation deeply flawed,[15] but he also understood well that Cohen's strong antitheses had a "political side." He hastened to add that the term *political* does not refer to the "paltry dealings of party politics" here.[16] Clearly, a concept of the political was in the making *before* Carl Schmitt's 1932 book. And from the beginning Strauss was concerned with the methodological problem of how to bring the political into systematic recognition.[17] But Cohen provided him also with a different notion of the political. Most obviously, the political does not *create* the conceptual binaries but reveals what is important in them:

Politics is the field in which political, moral, (and) inner oppositions come to *decisive expression*, where with respect to these oppositions things go *all out* [*wo es . . . aufs Ganze geht*], where it *becomes manifest* what is important about these oppositions. And this becoming manifest is nothing external or supplementary, but the internal, the philosophic as it presses outward from within toward expression, toward deed, toward realization. This is a fundamental idea precisely of Cohenian ethics.[18]

Strauss read Cohen *politically* in more than one sense. First, he understood the stark oppositions in Cohen's thought as political oppositions. He sensed that they stemmed from an ethical impulse that pervaded Cohen's entire teaching. This ethical impulse made it necessary for Cohen to see the whole of philosophy from a political viewpoint. Thus, Strauss could understand even the most wrongheaded premises and conceptual oppositions in Cohen as being grounded in a political program. Second, he understood the difference between Cohen's position and his own with regard to the political teaching: he sketched his own understanding of politics in expressly disagreeing with Cohen's understanding; but even more importantly, he thereby outlined a different conception of the relationship between philosophy and politics. There was an obvious disagreement with Cohen's messianic social progressivism, which served as the basis of his socialist politics. This disagreement marks the point where Strauss himself was led by a *political* impulse to redirect the Cohenian enterprise, and here the political content of his political philosophy became visible. But there is also a crucial philosophical argument here—the demonstration that the ethical qua political teaching of Cohen needed to be transformed into political philosophy. As Strauss suggested, genuine political philosophy emerged when ethical impulse of progressivism was no longer presupposed. (He knew well that the same goes for antiprogressivism.) The point of departure, then, was the difficult transition from the ethical qua political teaching to genuine political philosophy. Hence, the relationship between ethics and politics is a transitional question both for the systematic location and the political limitation of political philosophy.

Strauss noted that Cohen's *Ethics of Maimonides* ("Charakteristik der Ethik Maimunis," 1908) did not treat ethics as one part of Maimonides's doctrine: "Ethics, as the doctrine of man, is the *center* of philosophy," he echoed Cohen's declaration in the opening paragraph of *Ethik des reinen Willens*. "It needs logic as its preparation and aesthetics as its completion—it is therefore not the *whole* of philosophy, but it is the *central* philosophical discipline."[19] From here, Strauss saw clearly that Cohen aimed at the center of Maimonides's doctrine: at its "human meaning" in its integrity as opposed to its purely theoretical meaning. Ethics is *the* center of philosophy, understood as the doctrine of man. All philosophizing is directed toward the practical life.

Strauss emphasized this ethical interest and insinuated that it was "more exactly" to be understood as the "political interest."[20] This *silent* substitution of ethics through politics serves as the starting point for a renewal of the quarrel between Plato and Aristotle. Following Cohen's "idealizing" opposition between Plato and Aristotle, the quarrel is between two different understandings of ethics *or* politics in its relationship to philosophy proper—between ethics or politics as a discipline or as a view on the whole of philosophy.

As we saw, Strauss found a middle position in Cohen: ethics is not the *whole* of philosophy but is its *central* discipline. Such a middle position was certainly useful for Strauss to avoid the two extremes in the systematic location of the political. But it also has a proclivity toward the diffusion of the central discipline beyond its systematic place. In Cohen it could only be contained by an act of the will—the will to keep the system of philosophy intact. In the quarrel between Plato and Aristotle, however, Cohen took sides for a wider notion of ethics. In particular, he was drawn to Plato's Socrates: "Socrates considered ethics not only as a science, but as the science par excellence. He proclaimed ethics as the core and focus of human cognition."[21] Cohen added that Socrates hereby "announced an agenda—the agenda of universal culture."[22] In other words, Cohen saw not only his own task but also that of an enlightened Judaism in the figure of Socrates.[23]

At this point the intricate textual situation—with its multiple references to Socrates, Plato, Aristotle, Maimonides, and Cohen—becomes increasingly confusing unless we consider what Strauss saw as a matter of course: even the most wrongheaded premises in Cohen's interpretation cannot be understood on the basis of his ethical and political interest alone. They were structured by the Jewish interest or, to be more precise, by the interest in the proper way in which Judaism contributes to the ethical and political fate of mankind. As Strauss highlighted, ultimately Cohen's Jewish interest is also the source of his enmity toward Aristotle, as perfectly captured in the sentence: "All honor to the God of Aristotle; but truly he is not the God of Israel."[24] Cohen even credited Aristotle with "enmity against the idea of the Good."[25] Strauss noted with much reservation that the "passion" in Cohen's criticism of Aristotle stemmed from "biblical depth."[26] But most importantly, Cohen was a Platonist—and an enemy of Aristotle—because he was a progressive Jew.

Cohen's interest in Jewish politics intensifies the inner-philosophical opposition between Plato and Aristotle up to the point where the glaring disproportion between philosophy and politics threatens the soundness of his philosophical judgment. The difference between the life of philosophy as being directed toward the political life (Plato/Socrates) and the life of contemplation, of *theoria* (Aristotle), functions as a cipher to negotiate the fate of humanity. As Strauss paraphrased Cohen: Whereas Socrates is concerned with the future of mankind, for Aristotle "the future is only a rebirth of the past and its unsurpassable wisdom."[27]

Strauss sharply noted the political ambiguity in what is commonly called Jewish political thought. The crucial point was the transition to political philosophy. But the problem also pointed to the ambiguity of the political itself:

> The word "political" is necessarily ambiguous. . . . This ambiguity is so fundamental that it cannot be gotten rid of by, for instance, the fact that one distinguishes between spiritual politics and special-interest politics. . . . The ambiguity is not at all to be avoided. It has its basis in (the fact) that human life is as such life together and this political life. That is why every human action and motivation and thought is in itself political. But it is not always *expressly* so.[28]

Strauss distinguished between the orientation toward political life "in an *express* manner," as in statesmen, when politics is "what they are occupied with," and some alternative orientation toward political life that is initially difficult to decipher. It is modeled upon Plato. Plato teaches that morality is the purpose of the world, whereas for Aristotle nature accomplished its good on the basis of its own principles.[29] As Strauss pointed out, Maimonides restates the Aristotelian viewpoint and qualifies it in the sense that the existence of the world has its purpose in the free will, or the wisdom, of God. He is also in agreement with Aristotle that man is *small* in comparison with the cosmos.

> If therefore man is *not* the purpose of the world, if there is something greater than he in the world, then he cannot be what (ultimately) matters; then politics cannot be the highest and most important science; then the highest thing is: contemplation of existing (things) and understanding of Being.[30]

Strauss qualified the view stated here in many ways. In particular he sought to demonstrate anew—both with and against Cohen—"that Rambam is in deeper harmony with Plato than with Aristotle."[31] The hidden Platonic tradition in Maimonides and his Islamic predecessors is *the* historical theme of *Philosophy and Law*. In the 1931 manuscript, Strauss employed this theme to point to the difference between Cohen's understanding of God as the God of morality and the notion of God as law. As he argued, the "idealized" difference between Plato and Aristotle does not lead anywhere if God is being understood in terms of morality. "Instead of morality, one must say: Law."[32] In other words, the structural equivalence between ethics and politics must be supplemented by the categorical difference between an ethical and a political understanding of Plato, and ultimately between ethics and politics.

Nevertheless, the Aristotelian thesis on the limitation of politics retained a vivid afterlife in this conception. The scope of politics needed to be both expanded and limited. Strauss was overall a Platonist, but there is also an Aristotelian strand in his thought. The return to Plato needed to be supplemented by a return to the Aristotelian *Politics*. In a way, then, the "idealized" interpretation was preserved in Strauss. He understood the conflict between Plato and Aristotle in a different way than Cohen. The main point of departure was that the quarrel between the two should not be understood within the *modern* horizon, that is to say, from the standpoint of the opposition between Kant and Hegel.[33] From here, Strauss traced the distortion in Cohen's view of Aristotle: "Cohen has not done justice to Aristotle." That injustice first came to sight as a "historical injustice,"[34] but it also led to the systematic misrecognition of politics. Finally, then, Cohen understood Maimonides as a Platonist, but he went only half the way by "replacing the idea of *law* with that of *morality*." Strauss traced the consequences of this substitution, which led Cohen "to his *defining* political position, to his passionate support for the politics of 'the great *Left* of humanity,' to the politics of progress."[35] Ultimately, the idea of progress set a limit to Cohen's understanding of Plato and Maimonides.

> We will not be able to understand Plato, and thereby also not Rambam, until we have acquired a horizon beyond the opposition progress/conservatism, Left/Right, Enlightenment/Romanticism, or however one wants to designate this opposition; not until we again understand the idea of the *eternal* good, the *eternal* order, free from all regard for progress or regress.[36]

From early on, Strauss had argued that the prevalent political oppositions were merely "ideological."[37] As he demonstrated at the end of his 1931 lecture, genuine political philosophy emerges only if the "horizon" of contemporary oppositions is being transcended. The programmatic statement outlines for the first time the paradox of Strauss's political philosophy. He understood political philosophy as the quest to recognize the fundamental political conflicts and oppositions, but he also sought for a perspective toward their depoliticization. Political philosophy was essentially the quest for a nonpolemical understanding of political things.

Strauss's principal strategy was to return to premodern philosophy. We will recognize this double task in his analysis of Carl Schmitt's "The Concept of the Political," in which many of the themes from "Cohen and Maimonides" recur. The catch-phrase in Strauss's "Notes on Carl Schmitt" is the notion of a "pure and whole knowledge" (*ein integres Wissen*). As Strauss wrote, such a knowledge "is never, unless by accident, polemical."[38] The first step for Strauss in his quest for a pure and whole knowledge was to refute the premises of cultural philosophy, which divided human knowledge into a number of independent "domains." But Schmitt also exemplified the grave dangers of this endeavor—the option to do away with the systematic confines of cultural philosophy and to politicize philosophy altogether. Strauss chose wisely not to follow Schmitt's path here. He followed Schmitt's lead to a "horizon beyond liberalism,"[39] but this horizon looked different from what

Schmitt might have imagined. Most notably, he understood this "horizon" as a systematic problem: Schmitt, too, faced the question of whether the political was a field among others or a comprehensive point of view. And as Strauss showed, Schmitt's "The Concept of the Political" was the point where the inconspicuous systematic question showed its exceedingly *political* face.

5

Strauss and Carl Schmitt

Vanquishing the "Systematics of Liberal Thought"

Strauss's review article "Notes on Carl Schmitt, *The Concept of the Political*" (1932) and the short-lived intellectual relationship with Schmitt have been subjected to a vast body of scholarly work. This work often displays an unusual amount of passionate response and fascination, far exceeding the confines of a mere historical interest. Two reasons stand out for this: For some scholars Strauss seems to provide a fresh access to an intellectual tradition that was discredited by Schmitt's eventual affiliation with National Socialism. At the same time, Strauss's engagement with Schmitt promises a clue to the actual political content of his political philosophy.

It seems useful to opt for a more modest approach and address, first and foremost, the systematic question that runs through Strauss's "Notes." This strand of thought also concerns our understanding of the genesis of his political philosophy, his political stance on Schmitt, and hence his own political position. They challenge the idea of a significant "dialogue" between the two as the foundational event of his political philosophizing,[1] the Strauss-as-a-secret-Nazi narrative,[2] and his alleged youthful flirtation with the Right.[3] Most of all, they cast doubt on the notion that Strauss ever was a Schmittian. Strauss was distinguished from Schmitt by way of a philosophical program that made him immune to the charms of Schmittian politics.

Strauss contended that "[Schmitt's] critique of liberalism occurs in the horizon of liberalism; his unliberal tendency is restrained by the still unvanquished 'systematics of liberal thought.'"[4] This claim has sometimes been read as a political statement—just as if Strauss might be *even less* liberal than the antiliberal proto-Nazi Carl Schmitt. But the contention is part of a larger systematic argument. Strauss's encounter with Carl Schmitt, then, is as a follow-up to his ongoing argument with neo-Kantianism. Strauss approached "the political" by tracing its systematic location within the whole of philosophy. Just like religion in the prior Cohenian debate, the political could either be ordered "next to, and equivalent to, the other 'provinces of culture,'" or it could be located beyond the cultural order. Both possible solutions had their obvious downsides, and Strauss did not propose one solution over the other. The principal strategy was to situate Schmitt in the conflict between the two possible solutions. Strauss's "Notes," then, must be understood as an appendix to the Cohenian problem.

Schmitt had apparently sought to avoid the systematic location of the political. According to Strauss, he asked for the essence of the political rather than for its genus (its origin and its belonging into this or that category) due to "his deep suspicion of what is today the most obvious answer":

> He pioneers a path to an original answer to the genus question by using the phenomenon of the political to push the most obvious answer ad absurdum. What is still today, despite all challenges, the most obvious, genuinely liberal answer to the question of the genus within which the peculiarity of the political and, therewith, of the state is to be defined is that [this] genus is the "*culture,*" that is, the totality of "human thought and action," which is divided into "various, relatively independent domains," into "provinces of culture" (Natorp). Schmitt would remain within the horizon of this answer if, as it first appears, he were to say: just as "in the domain of the moral the ultimate distinctions are good and evil, in the aesthetic domain beautiful and ugly, in the economic domain useful and harmful," so the "specifically political distinction . . . is the distinction between friend and enemy." However, this ordering of the political next to, and equivalent to, the other "provinces of culture" is expressly rejected: the distinction between friend and enemy is "*not equivalent and analogous* . . . to those other distinctions"; the political does *not* describe "a new *domain* of its own." What is hereby said is that the understanding of the political implies a fundamental critique of at least the prevailing concept of culture.[5]

Following this quote, Schmitt is moving between two possible answers to the question of the political. As Strauss phrased it, Schmitt pushed aside the most obvious answer to outline the contours of an "original answer." But the further course of the argument suggests the opposite direction: Schmitt searched for an "original answer" and remained caught within the horizon of the "most obvious," the "genuinely liberal" answer. In any case, there is an unresolved conflict between the two possible answers in the very heart of Schmitt's enterprise, and this conflict is due to a characteristic confusion between culture and politics. Therefore, the end of the quote suggests that the concept of the political could only be clarified through a critique of the concept of culture.

The reference to Natorp and the "provinces of culture" clearly situated Schmitt in the neo-Kantian framework. At the same time, Strauss expanded his systematic claim in his review essay. Not only is the political (as well as religion) structurally different from the "provinces of culture." The misrecognition of the structural difference, the unabated symmetric coordination, is "genuinely liberal." Hence, the two interrelated claims elaborate on how systematic presuppositions can be read as political principles.

Carl Schmitt was an eminently systematic thinker in his own right, albeit in a different sense than Strauss. Both sought to lay bare the systematic foundations of liberalism, but Schmitt had another conceptual framework at hand. In the doctrine of *The Concept of the Political*, the "systematic" aspect of liberalism pertained to the way it dissolves political questions into moral and economic questions: "In a very systematic fashion liberal thought evades or ignores state and politics and moves instead in a typical always recurring polarity between two heterogeneous spheres, namely ethics and economics, intellect and trade, education and property." The dissolution of state and politics into the domains of morals and economics creates "an entire system of demilitarized and depoliticized concepts." "These liberal concepts typically move between ethics (intellectuality) and economics (trade)."[6]

This outline has become a key element of the Schmittian Left. As Chantal Mouffe explained her stance on Schmitt, his critique "is more relevant now than ever. If we examine the evolution of liberal thought since then, we ascertain that it has indeed moved between economics and ethics."[7] Schmitt's text has the status of a profane revelation here. It proclaims a teaching beyond its time and context, anticipating the further course of liberalism rather than reflecting the fault lines of Weimar-era liberalism. Therefore, its content can be appropriated and retrofitted for the radical Left.

The predominance of economics is given with the "neo-liberal" application of "the idea of the market . . . to the idea of politics."[8] It is supplemented by the deliberative model of rational consensus (Habermas), which creates a link between ethics and economics. Mouffe argues with Schmitt that ethics and economics do not make the political disappear but merely obfuscate it. As she shows, the two spheres *recreate* the political distinction within their own realm: "nowadays the political is played out in the moral register." The we/they discrimination is retained, but "instead of being defined with political categories, [it] is now established in moral terms. In place of a struggle between 'right and left' we are faced with a struggle between 'right and wrong.'"[9]

Seen from the perspective of Strauss, Mouffe's appropriation of Schmitt against the "hegemony of neo-liberalism"[10] appears to fall back behind Schmitt. This is in part due to the static understanding of ethics and economics as the two pillars of liberalism. Technically speaking, Mouffe's argument boils down to the claim that two out of a number of cultural domains predominate the others. But Schmitt had something different in mind. He also wanted to uncover the conceptual "axes" of European thought and, in the last resort, the ultimate conceptual order of the "age." Ethics and economics are only a part of a larger historical scheme here.

Schmitt understood modernity as the "age of neutralizations and depoliticizations," which is divided into four stages: the theological, metaphysical, moral, and economic stages. Each stage has formed the central sphere for one century, from the sixteenth through the nineteenth century. Schmitt described this conceptual history as a continuous loss of substance and theopolitical edge. The driving force was the "striving for a neutral domain,"[11] arising whenever a prevalent domain had become too contested. This process has come to an end in the age of "technology" (i.e., the twentieth century). The thesis of the political is first and foremost a polemical counteridea to reverse the process of neutralization. Its purpose is to bring back this substance and theopolitical edge by repoliticizing culture.

Schmitt was aware that *The Concept of the Political* was transitional, and he rewrote the text several times.[12] From the beginning, scholars have paid much attention to the differences between the three editions. With the renewed interest in Strauss's review essay, much of this attention has been diverted to detecting Strauss's footprints in the text. As scholars suspect, Strauss's review article changed the way in which Schmitt understood his own project, up to the point where he altered the its disposition in response to Strauss.[13] But the scope of this premise is limited: it can be maintained only with regard to the changes from the second edition (1932) to the third (1933), whereas the more severe changes are in the transition from the first edition (1927) to the second (1932)—but these changes cannot possibly result from Strauss's review (after all, the 1932 edition is the one he reviewed). They certainly sparked his attention, though, and he let the reader know that he was aware of the differences between the two versions.[14] If we follow his lead to the differences in argumentation and presentation, the main focus shifts from the asymmetric "dialogue" with Schmitt to the way he addressed the systematic tension in Schmitt's construction.[15]

Strauss used roughly the same strategy he employed in his scathing critique of Julius Guttmann in the first chapter of *Philosophy and Law* (1935), as well as in his early critique of Martin Buber.[16] It was his uncanny ability to locate the strategic point of "culture" in its problematic relation to religion and/or the political that enabled him to "see through [Schmitt] like an X-Ray," as Schmitt had reportedly quipped in a private conversation.[17]

Schmitt did not make many important changes in the parts that he used for the second edition. But all significant changes he did make concern the systematic status of the political as compared to the other domains: the question was how the political would relate to morals, aesthetics, and economics (or, speaking in Schmitt's favored diction of nominalization: the moral, the aesthetic, and the economic). According to the 1932 text, the political compares to these relatively independent domains (*entspricht . . . den relativ selbständigen Sachgebieten*), but it does so "not in the sense of a distinct new domain."[18] At this point, Schmitt claimed that the political differed in its structure from the other domains: "It does not describe a domain of its own [*kein eigenes Sachgebiet*], but only the intensity of an association or dissociation of human beings."[19] This rather technical claim contains a remarkable shift from the first version of the text, in which the political was exactly the opposite, namely, one domain among others. Whereas the second edition was very outspoken about the political *not* being a domain among others (the moral, the aesthetic, the economic, etc.), the original argument was precisely that it is a domain (an *eigenes Gebiet*) among others. As Schmitt had maintained in 1927: "The political stands independently as a domain of its own next to other, relatively independent domains of human thought and action, next to the moral, the aesthetic, the economic, et cetera." The political was expressly a "domain" just "as any other domain of human life."[20] This earlier claim is replaced in 1932 by the transitional formula: The political comes into effect "in a characteristic way" but does not constitute "a distinct new domain."[21]

We can hardly overestimate the importance of this shift in the systematic location of the political. And yet Schmitt's clarification hardly solved the problem. A major stumbling block was his desire to secure the conceptual "autonomy" of the political.[22] It brought him into close proximity with neo-Kantianism, no matter how much he attempted to break away. In a way, Schmitt had tacitly accepted the neo-Kantian systematic premise, even as he attempted to secure a special status for the political: the political was neither fully integrated, nor did it facilitate a complete break with the systematics of culture. Formally, then, the political is the exception that temporarily *suspends* the systematic order but cannot altogether replace it. In principle this solution is not entirely different from the solution suggested by Hermann Cohen when he faced the "uniqueness" (but not systematic independence) of religion. Strauss was certainly up to something when he noted that Schmitt was compelled to make use of elements of liberal thought in his critique of liberalism.

As to the chapter "The Age of Neutralizations and Depoliticizations" ("Das Zeitalter der Neutralisierungen und Entpolitisierungen"), the changes from the original 1929 article to the book version seem purely cosmetic at first glance. But here even the slightest change provides a clue to the breaking point of culture and the political. In most cases, Schmitt simply replaced the terms *culture* and *cultural*. Most visibly, he departed from the original title "Die europäische Kultur in Zwischenstadien der Neutralisierung" ("European Culture in Intermediary Stages of Neutralization"), thereby replacing the problematic notion of "European culture" by the seemingly more neutral term "the age." Often he substituted *kulturell* by the apparently more neutral term *geistig* (spiritual); and in two cases he simply substituted *Kultur* by *Politik*.[23] These substitutions were so superficial that they sometimes killed Schmitt's narrative or even his sentence structure.[24]

Schmitt clearly made these changes to avoid the notion of culture, but he did not change the argument based on that notion. The changes are literally cosmetic: their purpose is to disguise the fact that concept of the political rests on a scheme of cultural history—or in his words of 1927, of "cultural development."[25] Schmitt sought to modify this scheme by way of politicization, and yet it bore all the signs of the systematic disposition he opposed.

But not all of Schmitt's revisions were superficial. A major change was announced by his new idea of the political as "intensity."[26] This notion brings about a little shift, albeit not a total change, in the semantic structure of the political. Systematically speaking, "intensity" suspends the coordination of cultural spheres without invalidating it altogether. At least, this interpretation suggests itself if we follow up on Schmitt's discussion of Harold Laski in the second edition.

Laski, a preeminent advocate for pluralism before his turn to Marxism, had argued that individual lives are conducted according to numerous associations and loyalties (religious institution, nation, labor union, family, sports club), so that "the State is only one of the associations to which [the individual] happens to belong."[27] Amartya Sen rephrased the same argument in terms of twenty-first-century identity politics:

> In our normal lives, we see ourselves as members of a variety of groups—we belong to all of them. The same person can be, without any contradiction an American citizen, of Caribbean origin, with African ancestry, a Christian, a liberal, a woman, a vegetarian, a long-distance runner, a historian, a schoolteacher, a novelist, a feminist, a heterosexual, a believer in gay and lesbian rights, a theater lover, an environmental activist, a tennis fan, a jazz musician, and someone who is deeply committed to the view that there are intelligent beings in outer space with whom it is extremely urgent to talk (preferably in English). Each of these collectivities, to all of which this person simultaneously belongs, gives her a particular identity. None of them can be taken to be the person's only identity or singular membership category. Given our inescapably plural identities, we have to decide in the relative importance of our different associations and affiliations in any particular context.[28]

The underlying sentiment is that the political is divisive, bringing those "inescapably plural identities" into binary oppositions. It suggests that those binaries *create* hatred and violence, whereas pluralistic semantic structures are peaceful and inevitable.

This basic presupposition of pluralism was a serious challenge for Schmitt. One cannot help but notice a certain helplessness when he retorted in *The Concept of the Political* that the political association is nevertheless the "decisive" one, because it is the only association on the basis of which the extreme case can be decided.[29] As he commented in a 1930 article, the "ethical consequence and result" of the pluralism thesis is "that the individual lives in unorganized simultaneity of numerous social duties and loyalties: in a religious community, economic associations such as unions, combines or other organizations, a political party, a club, cultural or social societies, the family and various other social groups. Everywhere he has a duty of loyalty and fidelity; everywhere ethics emerge: church ethics, professional ethics, union ethics, family ethics, association ethics, office and business ethics, etc. For all these complexes of duties—for the 'plurality of loyalties'—there is no 'hierarchy of duties,' no unconditionally decisive principle of superiority and inferiority."[30] The quote may be valid as a description of the situation, but it is purely defensive as to the proper response. As Schmitt acknowledged, "[T]he pluralist view corresponds to the actual empirical situation as it can be observed today in most industrialized countries. To this degree, pluralist theory is very modern and current."[31]

In other words, the case against pluralism had become indefensibly weak, and the pluralists were winning the argument. The problem was simply that individual lives are usually not determined by the extreme case, and Laski was right in most circumstances: in a liberal state, people *do* live according to numerous associations, and Schmitt could not deny this for any good reason.

Another option would be to understand the quarrel as a *temporal alternation* between the two modes, as suggested by Strauss in *The City and Man*: "Yet most of the time the city is at peace. Most of the time the city is not immediately exposed to that violent teacher War, and to unsought compulsions, and hence the city's inhabitants are of kindlier thoughts than they are when at war."[32] Schmitt could not refute Laski's argument, but perhaps he would find a way to secure the temporary *suspension* of the peaceful order. Accordingly, Laski's argument is valid "in our normal lives," or in Strauss's words, "most of the time." Such a contrast between the city as it is "most of the time" and the city "when at war" is not what Schmitt had in mind. The state of exception rather blurred the lines between war and peace: the exception referred to the *possibility* of war, not to the actual state of war. The political, then, is either located at the point of transition from peace to war, or it designates the ongoing presence of war within peace. In both cases, the bellicose effect of the political comes into its own already in times of peace.

This extension of war into peace contains an epistemic peculiarity, which accounts for the promise of the political and the widespread excitement over its periodic recovery. The promise of the political is a type of being-in-the-world that is organized through binary concepts, most notably through the binary of friendship and enmity. It involves as a change of experience, a process of awakening and entering into reality. Speaking in terms of

Walter Benjamin, thinking politically is "the art of experiencing the present as waking world,"[33] with the binary concepts causing the awakening from a postpolitical slumber. Hence, the political designates a sudden epistemic shift. The state of exception removes the plurality of associations and affiliations. The political association turns out to be of far greater importance than other affiliations, which play such a great role under normal circumstances (such as favorite sports teams, fashion brands, and ice cream flavors).

Schmitt suggested that this political turn would facilitate a shift from a meaningless type of being into an existentially significant one. But it is doubtful whether this promise of the political can be kept, at least on Schmittian premises. The liberal individual according to Schmitt has lost its relationship to politics and hence to reality. Its individuality is empty. But as Helmut Kuhn suggested early on, the "existential" individual of Schmitt's political is rather similar to the liberal individual, inasmuch as its content is nothingness, too.[34] Can the thesis of "the political" really provide a feasible epistemic alternative to the pluralism thesis of liberalism?

Adding to this doubt, the whole "epistemic" strand of thought is obstructed by another (and far more problematic) strand in Schmitt's concept of the political. Here, Schmitt is primarily concerned with state sovereignty—not with the epistemic presuppositions of the discrimination between friend and enemy, but with the *right* to such unconditional, unquestionable, and sovereign political judgment and decision. Speaking in terms of state sovereignty, the ultimate question of the political is: Who holds the right to declare the state of exception? Schmitt took over this strand of thought from his earlier book *Political Theology* (1922), in which he declared: "Sovereign is he who decides on the exception."[35] He transposed this notion into the framework of *The Concept of the Political* to argue that the viability of the state depended on its authority to decide over the status of friend and enemy. The suspension can be *imposed* by the sovereign, and his judgment and decision are not subject to justification or control by any standards of reason.

The claim to such sovereign judgment, however, does not sit well with the conception of "intensity." It can serve to justify the unrestricted and perhaps arbitrary decision about who is friend and who is enemy, but this decision alone does not yet intensify the sovereign's being-in-the-world. Unlimited sovereignty is rather at odds with intensity: in the moment of decision the sovereign is not "in the world." The world is merely the object of his arbitrary decision. But intensity presupposes that the subject is being "affected" or "governed" by its object, rather than imposing his own will on it. It seems that Schmitt's theory contains another promise that cannot be kept, at least not on the basis of its own premises.

As we saw above, Schmitt faced a systematic problem that resembled the problem faced by Hermann Cohen. Neither religion (Cohen) nor the political (Schmitt) could be located in the systematic framework of culture, and neither could thrive without the framework altogether. But there is also a difference between Cohen's notion of religion and Schmitt's notion of the political. In Cohen's late writings, religion did not spill over the other domains. Its non-location did not cast into doubt the validity of science. Schmitt's solution led to an expansion of the political onto other fields. Every other domain could all of a sudden be "politicized." Following Karl Löwith, this non-location of the political, which no longer occupied any specific domain but only a totality beyond all domains, provided the conceptual foundation for an all-out politicization in the "total" state.[36]

Strauss's point, however, was not that Schmitt was a fascist: he was a liberal with the opposite polarity. The problem was not that he was dangerous, but rather that he was not radical enough. Strauss expanded this line in a chain of arguments on the political problem in *The Concept of the Political*. A major strategy to bring home the systematic point was to dissociate Schmitt's critique of liberalism from its historical context. As he quipped in a letter to Hasso Hofmann in 1965, Schmitt's critique of liberalism was fundamentally sound as a critique of the liberalism of the Weimar Republic, but it was defective as a critique of modern liberalism as such.[37] This anticontextual remark points to the failure of Schmitt's endeavor: "[H]e remains trapped in the view he is attacking."[38] Following Strauss's 1932 analysis, Weimar-era liberalism had a peculiar double characteristic: it had visibly disintegrated, but it had not been replaced by another, more coherent political system or doctrine. Hence, it was insufficient to argue against the inconsistency of liberal politics, for the failure of liberal politics had not invalidated the almost inescapable consistency of the liberal doctrine. "What is needed rather is to replace the 'astonishingly consistent systematics of liberal *thought*,' which is manifest within the inconsistency of liberal *politics*, by 'another system,' namely, a system that does not negate the political but brings it into recognition."[39]

Strauss channeled Schmitt's task here, but he put far greater emphasis on the uncanny afterlife of liberalism in the systematic presuppositions. Hence, Schmitt was only a transitional phenomenon. Strauss emphasized the great "significance" of Schmitt's work but also pointed to the "basic difficulty" that it entails: since that "other system" does not yet exist, Schmitt finds himself compelled to make use of elements of liberal thought. Schmitt cannot gain a "horizon beyond liberalism" because he is himself caught in the liberal systematics he tries to overcome.

According to Strauss, the systematic preconception was in the notion of culture. The concept of culture prevailed over human thought and action by dividing the "totality" of human thought and action into "provinces of culture" (Natorp), "symbolic forms" (Cassirer), or "relatively independent domains" (Schmitt). As Strauss understood it, this division is the very systematic foundation of liberalism. Now, according to Strauss, the "prevailing" concept of culture is to be "replaced by another concept of culture," which is based on the "insight into what is specific to the political."[40] This different concept of culture is defined as the cultivation of nature:

> Following the prevailing concept of culture, however, not only are the individual "provinces of culture" "autonomous" in relation to one another, but, prior to them, culture as a whole is already "autonomous," the sovereign creation, the "pure product" [*reine Erzeugung*] of the human spirit. This viewpoint makes us forget that "culture" always presupposes something that is cultivated: culture is always the *culture of nature*. . . . "Culture" is to such an extent the culture of nature that culture can be understood as a sovereign creation of the spirit only if the nature being cultivated has been presupposed to be the *opposite* of spirit, and been *forgotten*.[41]

Strauss's "discovery" of nature around 1930 has a wide specter,[42] but there are two specific reference points in his Schmitt essay. First, the interest in the concept of nature is situated in the critique of "culture." And second, the concept of nature refers to the natural state of human life before culture, the *status naturalis*. The *status naturalis* is the foundation of culture, but this foundation was increasingly forgotten in the course of modernity. Strauss did not propose to *return* to nature, but instead he "naturalized" culture. Accordingly, culture is no longer its own self-referential starting point. It starts from natural man in his "dangerousness" and "endangeredness."[43] Understood as the cultivation of nature, culture refers to something beyond itself, which is not reducible to being another partial domain of culture. Therefore, the concept of nature provides Strauss with a solution to the problem that has bothered all serious critique of "culture" in modernity: the problem of how to see culture from outside. Hence, the notion of nature is at the core of the quest for a "horizon beyond liberalism" qua culturalism.

The principal figure to address here was Thomas Hobbes, for Schmitt's notion of the political was partly built upon the template of the Hobbesean state of nature. Strauss therefore returned to Hobbes to juxtapose Schmitt's understanding of nature with the Hobbesean state of nature. This juxtaposition of the two concepts of nature prepares for the final blow to the Schmittian enterprise. Strauss saw the difference as follows: Hobbes is the precursor of the liberal negation of the political. The state of nature is defined in order "to motivate the abandonment of the state of nature,"[44] for it is the state of all against all. The state of all against all must be abandoned in the name of civilization. Hobbes is "the author of the ideal of civilization" and, by this very fact, "the founder of liberalism."[45] Hobbes starts from the natural evil of man and lays the foundation of liberalism against the illiberal natural state of man.[46] In his quest for the "recognition of the reality of the political," Schmitt negates the liberal negation of the political. He therefore returns to Hobbes "to strike at the root of liberalism."[47] For Schmitt, the political is a basic characteristic of human life. It is *real* and hence inevitable, and it is *necessary* because it is given in human nature.

The opposition between the negation and the position of the political, Strauss wrote, must then "be traced back to a quarrel over human nature," namely, to the forgotten controversy over whether man is by nature good or evil.[48] Strauss agreed with Schmitt that man is in principle evil, but he disagreed as to what constitutes man's evilness. Schmitt held that good and evil are not to be taken in a moral sense but rather as "undangerous" and "dangerous," and he understood man's dangerousness as *the* presupposition of the political. Therefore, he preferred a notion of *natural* evil, and he believed that the political is *real* and *inevitable*. But as Strauss noted, this doctrine is irreconcilable with Schmitt's contention that the political is threatened and must be recovered: if the political is inevitable, it cannot be threatened, and vice versa. Strauss therefore concluded that the first option was not Schmitt's genuine answer: the genuine answer was to *affirm* the political and to provide man's dangerousness with a normative, moral meaning. Schmitt's affirmation of the political is legitimized by "warlike morals."[49] Furthermore, this "affirmation of the political is ultimately nothing other than the affirmation of the moral."[50] But the affirmation of the moral was obviously in conflict with Schmitt's polemics against the primacy of morals over politics. Schmitt actually opposed not the primacy of morals but the primacy of "specific morals,"[51] namely, of pacifist morals. But as Strauss pointed out, pacifist morals could not be decisively refuted by the antithesis of warlike morals. And here Strauss's analysis comes full circle:

> He who affirms the political as such respects all who want to fight; he is just as *tolerant* as the liberals—but with the opposite intention: whereas the liberal respects and tolerates all "*honest*" convictions so long as they merely acknowledge the legal order, *peace,* as sacrosanct, he who affirms the political as such respects and tolerates all "*serious*" convictions, that is, all decisions oriented to the real possibility of *war.* Thus the affirmation of the political as such proves to be a liberalism with the opposite polarity. And therewith Schmitt's statement that "the astonishingly consistent . . . systematics of liberal thought" has "still not been replaced in Europe by any other system" proves to be true.[52]

It was this "liberalism with the opposite polarity" that led Strauss to relinquish the notion of "the political" altogether in his subsequent works. The obvious exceptions confirm the rule, for they play out "the political" exclusively in the field of premodern philosophy.[53] Strauss did not follow Schmitt's affirmation of the political. He refuted Schmitt's thesis that "all political concepts . . . [have] a polemical meaning,"[54] arguing that this principle "is entirely bound to liberal presuppositions."[55] In his view, the very thesis of the political "is entirely dependent upon the polemic against liberalism."[56] Hence, "[Schmitt's] critique of liberalism occurs in the horizon of liberalism; his unliberal tendency is restrained by the still unvanquished 'systematics of liberal thought.'"[57]

With this barrage of paradoxes, Strauss's critique of Carl Schmitt has indeed come full circle. Accordingly, Schmitt's affirmation of the political was the last, most radical outcome of the systematics of liberal culturalism. It demonstrated the extent to which the "prevailing concept of culture" in fact prevailed, despite the common discontent with culture toward the end of the Weimar Republic.

Part II

The Argument and the Action
of *Philosophy and Law*

6

A Hidden Masterpiece of Twentieth-Century Philosophy

For most of the time since its publication in 1935, Leo Strauss's second book *Philosophy and Law* was known only to a small number of scholars, most of whom knew Strauss personally. This readership was by and large recruited from among a network of people he knew from Marburg or Berlin, who in the meantime had moved to various places all over the world. Via the teachings of these early readers the book maintained a presence in Jewish thought.[1] Judging from the responses in private letters and published reviews, virtually everyone had reservations about the book but nevertheless praised the magnitude and boldness of Strauss's effort. Objections were most frequently raised against the thesis of the introduction, and non-medievalists often could not follow the scholarly argument in the rest of the book. Like many books by German-Jewish authors published in Germany after the beginning of Nazi persecution, *Philosophy and Law* could not find any meaningful reception due to the lack of a wider audience. But it was also the rare and sometimes uneasy combination of a bold and idiosyncratic philosophical project and an obscure scholarly work on the inner workings of medieval Islamic and Jewish philosophy that prevented the book from gaining a wider traction: it was too philosophical for the scholars and too medieval for the philosophers.

As should be added, the text is also extremely difficult to understand. Most early readers sensed that Strauss had something important to say, but it was not clear what it was. The book had something of an "oracular light" to many of those readers, "as if it were a revelation without content, open to the most wide-ranging and incompatible of readings. *What* Strauss had in mind was simply not apparent, or at least not readily so."[2]

This situation has certainly changed with the renewed interest in Leo Strauss's early works. But despite a tremendous amount of recent scholarly work on particular aspects of *Philosophy and Law*, the larger philosophical project and the operating mode of the book have remained largely unclear. For the time being, the text is a stumbling block in current Strauss scholarship, an icon of the enigmatic interim period between the Nazi rise to power and the beginning of World War II. Within Strauss's overall work, it is situated between his early works and his writings on exotericism. Caught between "no longer" and "not yet," it cannot be easily located within any historical continuum of his work. It is no coincidence that a comprehensive interpretation of the book as a book has not yet been written.

If it were possible to interpret the book in its entirety, one might arrive at the understanding that the inconspicuous study is actually one of the "great books" of twentieth-century philosophy, along with Heidegger's *Being and Time*, Wittgenstein's *Tractatus*, and Horkheimer and Adorno's *Dialectic of Enlightenment*. These examples are not chosen at random, for they testify to a peculiar feature of great works in the twentieth century. *Being and Time* explored the relationship between philosophical thought and being, the *Tractatus* between philosophy and language, and the *Dialectic of Enlightenment* situated philosophical thought in the tension of myth, enlightenment, and modern capitalism. In short: the great masterworks of the twentieth century explicated the Other of philosophy: being (Heidegger), language (Wittgenstein), myth (Horkheimer/Adorno), or the law (Strauss). Turning to medieval Islamic and Jewish philosophy, Strauss traced the Other of philosophical thought in the remnants of a theologico-political order that would precede all philosophizing and, if recovered, provide it with a frame of orientation. Philosophy was to be understood from its opposition to the concept of the law, with its idiosyncratic blend of Platonic *nomos* and Jewish *halakhah*.

Philosophy and Law was not just a trailblazing study on medieval Islamic and Jewish political philosophy, it was also groundbreaking in its insistence that the conflict between reason and revelation is at the center of twentieth-century philosophy. Furthermore, the book forces its readers to rethink the relationship between culture, religion, and the political—a constellation that has become visible only around the turn of the twenty-first century. It seems that the latter is the main reason why it took so long until the significance of the book became recognizable to a broader philosophical readership: just as the *Dialectic of Enlightenment* appealed to audiences in the 1960s and '70s, *Philosophy and Law* has many features that are more likely to become readable today than at any other time since its publication. For as with Benjamin's dialectical images,[3] the constellation of culture, religion, and the political comes to readability only at a certain time. The following analyses are meant to foster that readability. They follow Strauss a long way through the course of his arguments, for the accessibility of his philosophical project depends upon a proper understanding of the text as a text.

The first question posed by the text is whether it is actually a proper book—a "work" in the sense of the classical "great books"—or a collection of separate studies. Fritz Heinemann contended in his review that *Philosophy and Law* was but "a series of loosely connected articles under a common title."[4] Current Strauss scholars have largely followed this lead. As Michael Zank wrote, the study consisted of "a few lectures and essays from the early 1930s . . . bundled together."[5] Often such claims are based on the complicated genesis of *Philosophy and Law*. But does this genesis really serve to debunk the book? Or is it indispensible to understanding its inner structure and argument? As it happens, the genesis of *Philosophy and Law* shows how the book *became* a book despite its heterogeneous parts.

Strauss had initially written the three chapters independently of each other and for a variety of purposes. The first chapter, completed in September 1933, was conceived as an extensive review essay of Guttmann's *Philosophie des Judentums*,[6] which Strauss apparently did not plan to publish anywhere.[7] In the context of the book it serves as a "methodological" introduction to the modern study of medieval philosophy. The third chapter is a slightly edited version of his article "Maimunis Lehre von der Prophetie und ihre Quellen," which had been completed by 1931 and was scheduled for publication first in the *Korrespondenzblatt der Akademie für die Wissenschaft des Judentums*, then in *Le monde orientale*.[8]

In November 1934 Strauss still believed that these two texts varied too much in form to be published together.[9] By mid-December, when the Schocken publishing house offered to publish them as a book, this perception had changed,[10] and Strauss began to revise and edit the texts and submit them to Schocken. Henceforth, he composed the short second chapter, "The Legal Foundation of Philosophy," to elaborate on a theme from the first chapter and create a link between the first and the third. This part contains the initial core of the scholarly project, a study of prophetology in Gersonides's (Levi ben Gershon) *Milkhamot Ha-Shem* that had become increasingly insignificant for Strauss in the meantime; but it also has a precise, albeit limited, function in *Philosophy and Law* that solely stems from its place in the book. At last, over the time of a few days, Strauss wrote the introduction in order to "motivate the publication" of these diverse articles.[11] This statement in a letter to Guttmann must be read literally. The introduction does not provide an all-encompassing summary or a universal key to the following chapters, but it does indeed "motivate" their publication in a setting that was entirely different from the context in which they had been created. The book came out at the end of March 1935, as Strauss reported to several of his correspondents.

With the history of the four parts in mind, it is certainly justified to consider the book as a patchwork, just as *Being and Time*, the *Tractatus*, and the *Dialectic of Enlightenment* are patchwork books. The differences notwithstanding, all these masterworks of the twentieth century testify to the fragmentary character of philosophy *after* the philosophical system. The "great books" of the twentieth century must be studied as carefully as the classic great books, but they must be read differently than the classics in their premodern integrity. We may be in doubt over the extent to which Strauss's notion of the "great books" is even relevant for his own great book. To name but a few differences: the assumption of a perfect author does not apply to the "great books" of the twentieth century. It is of little use to assume that structural incoherencies are part of a larger plan. The striving for systematic coherence has become the adversary of a great book. In the words of Walter Benjamin, another creator of great patchwork books: "Strength lies in improvisation. All decisive blows are struck left-handed."[12] Strauss's casual masterwork is certainly unsystematic in its structure, but it is also repetitive at times, with some interferences between the first and second and between the first and third chapters. As I shall argue below, it was not even written for any specific readership.

Another aspect of the fragmentary character of *Philosophy and Law* is that it does not have a clear core, a center from which the whole could be accessed and deciphered. It is impossible to discern *the* meaning of the text from a particular footnote or from the closing pages of the introduction. To a certain degree, each of the four parts stands on its own feet. Each chapter must to a certain extent be understood both on its own premises *and* with regard to its specific purpose in the overall book. To use one of Strauss's later expressions, each chapter follows a unique "argument and action," and in each case one must follow the argument and its dramatic character—its "action"—in order to discern the meaning of a claim in the context of the overall book. Julius Guttmann violated this principle in his reply to Strauss, and this violation was the inconspicuous starting point for his nearly malicious misrepresentation—despite his best intentions—of Strauss's position. The analytic separation and functional coordination of the various parts is indispensible for a more precise understanding of *Philosophy and Law*. It also sheds a new light on some rather obvious aspects of the book, namely, the relationship between belief and knowledge, or revelation and reason. Strauss rephrased these binaries several times in *Philosophy and Law*, as if he could not state his preferred version at once. He started in the introduction from the antithesis of orthodoxy versus the Enlightenment, then rephrasing it as orthodoxy versus atheism. Moving away from the modern antitheses, an important footnote in the first chapter substituted "belief and knowledge" with philosophy and law.[13]

For Ernst Simon, one of his early careful readers, this substitution seemed to contain an esoteric message. After all, the point was hidden in a footnote exactly in the middle of the book, and Simon believed that the most important things are to be found in the middle. Simon further assumed that Strauss had used Talmudic techniques of interpretation.[14] But Strauss was being neither "Talmudic" nor merely playful in his footnote. It serves a clear purpose in the plan of the book: he sought to replace the terms *belief* and *knowledge* in order to regain the political horizon of the problem—namely, the medieval tradition of Platonic political philosophizing outlined in the third chapter.

The binaries of "belief and knowledge" and "revelation and reason" had become equally problematic for Strauss. Belief or faith indicated a purely subjective and emotive attitude toward religion that is commonly represented by the name of Friedrich Schleiermacher, and in particular by his early addresses *Über die Religion* (1799) that based religion on the believer's intuition and feeling.[15] Strauss discussed the impact of Schleiermacher in the aforementioned middle of the book,[16] noticing a touch of Schleiermacherian romantic antirationalism in Guttmann's rational philosophy of religion. As to revelation, Strauss contended that philosophy of religion had long abandoned the reality of revelation. At last, philosophy did no longer represent reason or rationality, for modern philosophy had largely become irrational.[17] It was this alleged irrationality of present-day rationalism that motivated the turn to Maimonides as "the standard" of rationalism in the first place.[18] The term *knowledge* did not fit, either, for modern philosophy, with its unqualified dismissal of religion, did not seem to know what it was doing.

In a way, this conceptual readjustment merely prepared the way for a critical revision of the modern critique of religion. As Strauss had claimed in the introduction, the Enlightenment attack on orthodoxy had been insufficient and left the core of orthodoxy untouched. While the topic was not entirely new for Strauss, he now moved it to a diffferent field. The basic contention is a two-way argument: the refutation of religion had not been done in a thorough and cogent way; and hence it was possible to actually believe in revelation, the creation of the world, or miracles. This argument is notoriously difficult to contextualize. Most of all, its purpose is not apparent from the beginning: Strauss clearly did not speak as a believer. Occasionally he rather seemed to despise the arguments in favor of miracles, that is, the extreme case of an unfathomable God interfering with, or suspending, the natural order.[19] Strauss spoke against the refutation of the possibility, though, for philosophical reasons. As he argued, modern rationalism stands and falls with the impossibility. The mere possibility that the biblical account of the world could be true seemed to invalidate the modern notion of reason: if modern rationalism cannot decisively refute the biblical account of creation and all that comes with it, it is not rational in the full sense. Rationalism was sucked into the problem of the unclear relationship between philosophy and religion.

Philosophy and Law embedded the discourse on philosophy and law in a critique of reason, and this critique is the vantage point of his interest in the prophetology of Maimonides. The search for a "rational critique of reason"[20] is the ultimate philosophical justification of *Philosophy and Law*. Outside of the small circle of readers who knew his overall philosophical leanings, Strauss's turn to Maimonides has sometimes been understood as an odd choice of subject matter. Fred Wieck from The University of Michigan Press expressed this understanding most clearly in a letter to Strauss from 1956 on *Philosophy and Law*:

> The analysis of the contest between orthodoxy and enlightenment as the contest between orthodoxy and atheism is, patently, of the highest importance. A small book by you on this subject could save us years of confused talk, oceans of ink, and mountains of mistakes. What troubles me, however, is that your wisdom is concealed, disguised as a discussion of Maimonides addressed to a predominantly Jewish readership. This seems to be an inverted Trojan Horse technique, with the blessings inside, and I have my doubts on its effectiveness.[21]

The statement implies that Strauss's discussion of Maimonides is a mere disguise, that is, that it is not important for the argument of the book, so that this argument might as well be given in a plain and simple manner. Wieck suggested that Strauss rewrite the book for the American readership, for the "small book" he imagined was apparently not a mere translation of *Philosophie und Gesetz* but a popular elaboration of its introduction. Wieck was a precursor of those Strauss readers today who seek the core of *Philosophy and Law* in the introduction, and who regard the rest of it as too medieval or too Jewish to warrant a serious philosophical discussion.

In stark contrast, Fritz Heinemann criticized the book for its philosophical boldness, accusing Strauss of "a kind of postulatory dictatorship, a decision of the will, which does not derive from sharp, close interpretation and careful analysis, but rips into the whole in a bold sweep without proving the respective, often highly disputable assumptions."[22] Heinemann's polemic remarks were written from the perspective of a scholar, for whom the work was too philosophic. Strauss had apparently violated a scholarly consensus when he turned medieval Islamic and Jewish thought into a topic of political philosophy. Heinemann took this political turn for an all-out politicization of medieval Jewish scholarship, as if Strauss had drawn the subject matter into the abyss of contemporary politics. That was, of course, a mischaracterization of Strauss's notion of political philosophy. But this notion can be difficult to grasp, given how Strauss presented the historical thesis of *Philosophy and Law*. The text is full of layers and unexpected turns, changing freely between different epochs and thematic contexts. We must seek to describe this movement of *Philosophy and Law* as closely as possible.

7

Strauss's Introduction

Strauss anticipated readers who would take interest in his work on reason and revelation, but not in his scholarly work on medieval Jewish philosophy. He advised Alexandre Kojève—a decidedly "modern" reader—not to bother too much with the medieval stuff: "Just read the Introduction, and the first essay. The Introduction is very daring and will interest you if only because of that. And then write me your reaction."[1] Isolated from the rest of the book, the introduction will likely be seen as a document of Strauss's Nietzscheanism.[2] But its purpose is the opposite: it demonstrates why philosophy must return from Nietzsche to the medievals, and from there to Plato. In particular, it outlines the methodological premises that reflect the tension between contemporary and medieval thought.

We see this tension at work in the argument and action of the first two paragraphs. Strauss confronted modern rationalism with medieval rationalism by enacting the argument between the two as a contest among equals: he juxtaposed two rationalisms and asked "which of the two opposed rationalisms is the true rationalism." The surprising answer is that modern rationalism is a "sham rationalism"[3] leading to the self-destruction of reason,[4] whereas Maimonidean rationalism is the "natural model," the "standard" of rationalism. The present is to be confronted with medieval thought in such a way that its solutions turn out to be sham solutions, and its syntheses to be false compromises.

One can hardly overemphasize the unique, nay exceptional, character of this starting point, in which his five-year-long "change of orientation"[5] came to a simple and elegant formulation. Citing "the freedom of the question," Strauss made clear that he was no longer bound by the basic assumption of historicism—namely, that medieval rationalism was superseded or "overcome" by the early modern rationalism of Descartes and Hobbes, and this rationalism was in turn overcome by another rationalism, et cetera. Following this view, Maimonidean rationalism cannot be true for the fact that it was superseded by another doctrine.[6] By 1935, Strauss had concluded that this objection was a prejudice. He simply confronted and compared two historically distant doctrines of rationalism with each other as if they were coeval or simultaneous, and, even more important, as if medieval rationalism could be as true as modern rationalism.

Overall, the text moves freely between various epochs and contexts in an infinite interplay of quotes, which often appears to resemble the postmodern notions of simultaneity from the 1970s and onward. But despite its many layers and unexpected turns, there is also a recurring pattern, especially in the frequent methodological reflections. First, these reflections run along the modern/premodern divide, explicating the interplay between the present situation and a premodern standard of judgment. Second, they are organized so as to describe a *progression* from the present situation to a transtemporal standard. And third, this progression or inner movement gradually alters the status of his subject matter: "[M]edieval rationalism . . . changes in the course of our investigation from a mere means of discerning more sharply the specific character of modern rationalism into the standard measure against which the latter proves to be only a sham rationalism."[7]

This methodological progression well describes the course of the book. The introduction invokes Maimonides with regard to the modern quarrel between orthodox Judaism and the Enlightenment, asking how medieval philosophy might help break the impasse facing contemporary Jewry. The first chapter, treating the modern understanding of medieval Jewish philosophy (as exemplified by Julius Guttmann's *Philosophie des Judentums*), functions like a gateway: it starts from the modern prejudice, but in its course it shifts the balance toward premodern thought. The second and third chapters are entirely devoted to medieval rationalism, without further explicating its modern understanding.

The introduction casts the quarrel between orthodox Judaism and the Enlightenment as a preparatory "renewal" of the eighteenth-century *querelle des anciens et des modernes*.[8] Following Strauss, the present situation of Judaism is determined by the process in which the Enlightenment has undermined the foundation of the Jewish tradition. The popular sentiment was that the Enlightenment has been "overcome" in the meantime, that it is "shallow" or "trivial," and hence that the present stands in opposition to the Enlightenment. But Strauss argued that actually, "the present is at one with the Age of Enlightenment," because the debates are played out upon the Enlightenment premises; therefore, the original front lines of the quarrel are no longer visible: "How remote from our age is the quarrel about the verbal inspiration vs. the merely human origin of Scripture; about the reality vs. the impossibility of the Biblical miracles; about the eternity and thus the immutability vs. the historical variability of the Law; about the creation of the world vs. the eternity of the world: all discussions are now conducted on a level on which the great controversial questions debated by the Enlightenment and orthodoxy no longer even need to be posed, and must ultimately even be rejected as 'falsely posed.'"[9]

Clearly, the debate had reached a dead end. To renew the forgotten quarrel over the ancients and the moderns, Strauss first needed to address how it had become inaccessible in the first place. As he argued, the Enlightenment premises have become so self-evident that "at the outset . . . we find ourselves fully in the power of the mode of thought produced by the Enlightenment and consolidated by its proponents or opponents."[10] Similar lines of argument can be found in the lecture manuscript "Cohen und Maimuni" (1931).[11] Each time the old teaching is forgotten, the new teaching becomes self-evident, and the new teaching consolidates itself against the old one. And each time the opponents of the new teaching remain entangled in the polemical situation it created, consolidating the new teaching by way of their polemics.

Strauss's introduction names two examples of how the opposition in the name of the Jewish tradition remained entangled in the Enlightenment premises it opposed. One major attempt to save the Jewish tradition was to accept all these premises and create a "synthesis" of Enlightenment and orthodoxy, thus seeking to reestablish the traditional foundation of orthodoxy on a higher level. This is characteristic of mid-nineteenth-century Jewish Hegelians such as Salomon Ludwig Steinheim, Salomon Formstecher, and Samuel Hirsch. Strauss noted how the recreation of traditional contents could only succeed for the prize of their internalization—a gradual transformation into concepts of human consciousness in which creation, miracles, and revelation (the touchstones of Jewish theology) seemed to lose their meaning. As he concluded, internalizations "are in truth disavowals":[12] futile attempts to recreate the tradition in the mode of inner experience. Proponents and opponents alike are fully in the grip of the Enlightenment.

A second major attempt to save the Jewish tradition was made by Hermann Cohen, Franz Rosenzweig, and Martin Buber, the main figures of German-Jewish philosophy in the early twentieth century, whom Strauss referred to as the return movement (*Rückkehrbewegung*).[13] As he explained, they saw the limits of the nineteenth-century internalization of religion clearly, but their return to the Jewish tradition was carried out indecisively: neither Cohen nor Rosenzweig—Strauss had already dropped Buber from the discussion here—could accept the Jewish law, with its characteristic limitation to man's autonomy, without reservation. Their recovery of traditional Judaism against the Enlightenment critique was replete with elements of the Enlightenment and hence remained incomplete.

From here we are in a better position to understand Strauss's broad claim that all compromises and syntheses are untenable. It is based on the limits of the two earlier "return movements," and hence it is well founded in the modern history of German Jewry. German-Jewish philosophy in the nineteenth and twentieth centuries had indeed understood Judaism to a large extent within the framework of Kant, Hegel, and Schleiermacher. It was a good example of how a new movement remains entangled in the premises of what it opposes. Hence, Strauss's bold conclusion that the actual alternative between the Enlightenment and orthodoxy had to be recovered. The programmatic lines run as follows: "One must first of all, and at the very least, climb back down to the level of the classical quarrel between the Enlightenment and orthodoxy . . . the quarrel between the Enlightenment and orthodoxy, already longstanding and still ever-continuing, must be understood again."[14] In other versions, the quarrel must be "repeated"[15] or "resumed and re-understood."[16] In any version, Strauss assumed that the quarrel is "longstanding and still ever-continuing": the Enlightenment, as well as orthodoxy, "still lives today."[17]

Strauss's account of the quarrel oscillates between a seventeenth- and eighteenth-century debate on the one hand, and an ongoing battle between two transhistorical principles on the other. Neither "orthodoxy" nor "Enlightenment" is a historically clearly delineated concept in the introduction, but this is part of a larger strategy. Strauss sought to circumvent the derivative debates of the nineteenth and early twentieth centuries and their "foregrounds and pretenses." Going back to the seventeenth and eighteenth centuries was only a first step from here: Strauss built his narrative on orthodoxy and the Enlightenment already with regard to the other, much more serious quarrel between modern and Maimonidean rationalism. But it was also an inevitable step: had the Enlightenment been successful in its refutation of orthodoxy, there would be no need and no justification for the return to Maimonidean rationalism—but Strauss was convinced that the Enlightenment refutation had failed. Hence, the programmatic conclusion that "one must . . . drag out the dusty books that are to be considered the classical documents of the quarrel between the Enlightenment and orthodoxy." As Strauss described the task, one must "hear the arguments of both parties. Only by doing this, or more precisely, only by having the full course of that quarrel before one's eyes, may one hope to be able to attain a view of the hidden premises of both parties that is not corrupted by prejudices, and thus a principled judgment of right and wrong in their quarrel."[18]

Careful readers have concluded from these lines that the introduction is set up as a trial.[19] This observation on the spatial disposition of the text is apt, but it deserves to be further explicated. To the extent that the introduction does have the character of a trial, it is situated in an appeals court, in which a long-decided case—the case against orthodoxy—is retried. But the scope of the court metaphors is rather limited. The Straussian court may overturn the verdict of history, or the historicist assumption that "world history . . . is the final judgment,"[20] but it cannot arrive at a "principled judgment of right and wrong." The crucial problem is the position of the author as a judge. To the extent that Strauss reflected upon his own position in the trial, he did not claim the role of a judge. At the most, he is the lawyer of the orthodox side: being nonorthodox and hypermodern himself, he nevertheless tries to win his orthodox client a new verdict.

But even as he did not claim the role of a judge, Strauss sometimes seems to describe the quarrel from above, such as in the demand to "attain a view of the hidden premises of both parties." One must then imagine the author as an observer, who merely watches the renewed quarrel he initiated being played out.[21] In another version, Strauss identifies as a party to the trial between Maimonidean and modern rationalism. Acting as a lawyer to the Maimonidean side, Strauss sought "to awaken a prejudice" in favor of his client and "to arouse a suspicion against the powerful opposing prejudice."[22] The observer or judge is contemporary Jewry, and the whole purpose of the trial is to replace one prejudice with another. A third version of the setup shows how the case can at least partially be settled. According to the court metaphors in the first chapter, modernity is to be tried in a premodern court. Now following the Maimonides model, the court that settles the conflict is reason. Reason is both a party to the trial and the authority that settles the case. It does so, however, by declaring its own incompetence vis-à-vis the claims of revelation and, therefore, its compulsion to accept the suprarational claims.[23] As we shall see below, this self-critique of reason facing the fact of revelation is in the center of the philosophical project of *Philosophy and Law*. Overall, however, Strauss's precise role in the trial, and his own position in the text, remains ill defined, and his account of orthodoxy and the Enlightenment retained a high asymmetry.

In his occupation with the "hidden premises" of orthodoxy and the Enlightenment, Strauss was mostly concerned with the premises of the orthodox side. As he claimed, the Enlightenment has never addressed the ultimate premise of orthodoxy, namely, "the irrefutable premise that God is omnipotent and His will unfathomable. If God is omnipotent, then miracles and revelations in general, and in particular the Biblical miracles and revelations, are possible."[24] In other words: the Enlightenment refutation of orthodoxy has never even been carried out. Orthodoxy has not been proven guilty, and could not have been proven guilty, because the entire system of orthodox belief is irrefutable. Orthodoxy rests on the belief that God is omnipotent and unfathomable; this premise cannot be refuted; hence "all individual assertions resting on this premise are unshakable."[25]

This is a major argument in Strauss's introduction, and it has both its strengths and its weaknesses. It is built upon the demonstration that the thesis of God's omnipotence cannot be refuted; but the price of this demonstration is that the thesis cannot be proven to be true. Even if the Enlightenment was wrong in its pretension that it had refuted orthodoxy, that did not make orthodoxy right. In other words, the argument refutes a refutation, but it cannot found a position. Any principled judgment of right and wrong is impossible under the premise of a double negation. The renewal of the quarrel between reason and revelation qua Enlightenment and orthodoxy therefore comes at the price of a principal limitation. It is nevertheless surprisingly strong in the force field of culture, religion, and the political, where fundamental conflicts are not being settled in the orderly manner of a principled decision about right or wrong, but rather in the infinite clash of interpretations and rhetorical persuasions.

Strauss's argument is situated in a peculiar historical moment when the critique of religion employed by Marx, Nietzsche, and Freud had lost its traction, while the arguments in favor of a new type of religious faith had not yet been thoroughly articulated. This peculiar moment had been decisively prepared by Cohen, Buber, and Rosenzweig. But Strauss also reflects a certain disappointment with, and readjustment of, their respective arguments. The outstanding feature of the new understanding of religion is that it is immune to the critique of religion by Marx, Nietzsche, and Freud. It had become possible to be thoroughly religious *without* falling back behind the critique of religion. He later referred to this possibility as "post-critical Judaism."[26] To rephrase the critical insight in non-Straussian terms: one can believe in miracles, in God's creation of the world, and His revealing Himself to man; and there is no decisive counterargument as long as one believes in a thorough and sincere manner. It is, of course, possible to refute religion, but one can as well refute the refutation, and both are possible on the very same grounds. Religious or nonreligious beliefs and attitudes are a matter of choice, an act of the will. Religious and antireligious discourses are a matter of rhetorical persuasion.

This postcritical understanding of religion is not without dangers. Strauss criticized the Enlightenment on behalf of orthodox Judaism, but he did so by using the highest principles of the Enlightenment. But was this utilization of the Enlightenment against the Enlightenment possible without leaping into relativism? It seems as though, in order to invalidate the Enlightenment interpretation, Strauss needed to reap the benefits of relativism for a nonrelativistic purpose. This enterprise is built upon the principle of radical interpretation, which had been the hallmark of Marx, Nietzsche, and Freud. Strauss had learned it from Nietzsche in particular. Radical or infinite interpretation is also the point of comparison between Strauss and the French Nietzscheans of the 1960s.

Speaking in terms *not* employed by Strauss but familiar to him by way of Nietzsche: orthodoxy came to be regarded as a comprehensive interpretation of the world. It could not be refuted, only violently seized by another interpretation. As Michel Foucault argued in 1964, far from merely being an elucidation of meaning, interpretation also establishes "a relationship of violence." The reason why interpretation is infinite is that there is nothing to interpret. And there is nothing to interpret because everything is already interpreted; or there is nothing that is *not* already interpreted. Foucault wrote: "Indeed, interpretation does not clarify a matter to be interpreted, which offers itself passively; it can only violently seize an already-present interpretation, which it must overthrow, upset, shatter with the blows of a hammer."[27] Marx, Nietzsche, and Freud all created new interpretations in order to violently seize another interpretation.

From the outset, Strauss may seem to have had little to do with those theories of interpretation, which became an integral part of the postmodern cosmos. But he was familiar with "world-constructions" and interpretive violence.[28] Furthermore, he shared an epistemic starting point with Foucault and others, even as he proceeded in a different direction from there. The point of contact, of course, is Nietzsche and the idea of interpretation as an act of will. Just like the interpretation of Judeo-Christian morals (Nietzsche), the means of production (Marx), or dreams (Freud), the Enlightenment interpretation stood "in a relationship of violence" (Foucault) to the orthodox interpretation: it was a radical new interpretation put forward in order to violently seize another interpretation. It thereby could not demonstrate its superiority over the previous interpretation. It could only shatter that interpretation with the blows of a hammer.

Foucault was concerned with certain semiotic semblances between Marx, Nietzsche, and Freud to elucidate the structural principles of interpretive violence. This occupation with the structure of the sign has become largely irrelevant today, and we are likely to pay closer attention to some *thematic* features of radical interpretation. After all, the founders of radical interpretation did not seek to discredit just *any* other interpretation. The main driving force behind their violent acts of interpretation was the will to refute the religious interpretation.[29] This diagnosis effects a profound change in our understanding of interpretation. And here, Strauss—with his critique of the Enlightenment critique of religion—adds a unique voice to the debate. In return, the framework of radical interpretation helps to better understand the violent strategies and techniques of the Enlightenment as described by Strauss—the "weapons," as he called them.[30]

In Strauss's analysis, interpretive violence is not a foundational act that instigates something radically new. It is primarily a response to a principal "failure."[31] A major weapon employed by the Enlightenment was laughter and ridicule. Once Enlightenment thinkers realized they could not disprove the religious interpretation, they resorted to mockery. The principal strategy was to "laugh" orthodoxy out of its position, because it could not be dislodged by scriptural arguments or by reason.[32] Strauss emphasized that the violent seizure of the teachings of orthodoxy did not reach the heart of the matter. At best it was a retroactive legitimation of a liberty already acquired by other means. But inasmuch as it did not stem from a principal refutation of these teachings, it ultimately remained unsuccessful: "Thus the importance of mockery for the Enlightenment's critique of religion is an indirect proof of the irrefutability of orthodoxy."[33] Unlike the theorists of radical interpretation, Strauss had found a principal criterion here to determine whether the cause was just,[34] and he unhesitatingly concluded that the Enlightenment interpretation was unjust. The Enlightenment failed despite winning over orthodoxy—this is the critical difference that was lost to the great theories of radical interpretation.

A possible weakness in Strauss's appeals case is the notion of orthodoxy. As he continued: "As a result, orthodoxy was able to survive the attack of the Enlightenment, and all later attacks and retreats, unchanged in its essence."[35] This characterization seems odd, for which orthodoxy remained unchanged over the course of the nineteenth century? A recurring theme of Straussian historiography is how a teaching was forced to adjust and rebuild itself to counter an attack. The place in *Philosophy and Law* for the adjustment of orthodoxy is the discourse on the "internalization"[36] of Judaism in the nineteenth century. Strauss's rehabilitation of orthodoxy seems to have little in common with German-Jewish orthodoxy, which was by and large a *reaction* of nineteenth-century Jewry to the process of Jewish modernization.[37] In the same line of criticism, one may question Strauss's claim regarding the "victory of orthodoxy through the self-destruction of rational philosophy,"[38] for the orthodox world had little share in the development of philosophical rationalism. Orthodoxy may have been acquitted at this point, but that did not yet amount to a victory over the Enlightenment. At the most, the "victory" of orthodoxy is the epistemic possibility of an orthodox standpoint.

Superficially speaking, then, the notion of orthodoxy is a "construct," insofar as it does not match with German-Jewish orthodoxy and its inner dialectic. Strauss turned orthodoxy into a transhistorical principle instead, or, more precisely, he collapsed it into a much wider historical framework. In order to state the enmity between orthodoxy and the Enlightenment as strongly as possible, he evoked the position of ancient rabbinical Judaism in its quarrel with Greek philosophy. In other words, behind the fight between orthodoxy and the Enlightenment lurked the old enmity between Jerusalem and Athens—or, as he wrote elsewhere, "the issue" was "traditional Judaism versus philosophy."[39]

These ever-changing and overlapping binaries are so difficult to decipher because they combine a transhistorical principle with a variety of epochs and historical references. The quarrel of rabbinical Judaism against the influence of Hellenism adds a new element here. As it stands, it is the only possible reference to explain how Strauss came to present the quarrel as an ongoing life-and-death struggle. The famous Talmudic phrase "Cursed be a man who rears pigs and cursed be a man who teaches his son Greek wisdom" (b Sotah 49b) is only the most striking example of the *serious* fight between the two cities with their impregnable fortresses.[40] This imagery of the fight between reason, with its arsenal of criticism, and belief, with its fortress of revelation and miracles—with "Greek wisdom" (*ḥokhmat yavanit*) being a cunning of reason to bring Jerusalem to a fall, etc.—was preserved in *Philosophy and Law*.

From here we better understand the epistemic dimension of Strauss's criticism, namely, his radical counterinterpretation of modern science. As he argued, the Enlightenment may not have successfully refuted orthodoxy, but by attacking orthodoxy it defended itself against the attack of orthodoxy: "Even if . . . it could not prove the impossibility or the unreality of miracles, it could demonstrate the unknowability of miracles as such, and thus protect itself against the claims of orthodoxy."[41] Furthermore, this unknowability was valid only upon the premises of modern natural science, and the argument collapsed once it was discovered that modern science is but a "world-view." Now Strauss's claim is that modern science was actually *built* as a defense against miracles:

> The facts certifying this view allow for the opposite interpretation: Is not the very concept of science that guides modern natural science, ultimately, based on the intention to defend oneself radically against miracles? Was not the "unique" "world-construction" of modern natural science, according to which miracles are indeed unknowable, devised expressly for the very purpose that miracles *be* unknowable, in order to protect man against the grip of the omnipotent God?[42]

At this point, Strauss had entirely turned the Enlightenment critique against itself, using the highest principles of the Enlightenment against the Enlightenment. Follwing his counterinterpretation, modern science was invented as a protection against the possibility of miracles. The invention was a response to the Enlightenment "failure" to refute orthodoxy: the Enlightenment "was forced into constructing a world by this very failure."[43] To compensate for the fact that it could not refute the worldview of creation, miracles, and revelation, the Enlightenment invented the modern idea of culture and science:

> If one wished to refute orthodoxy, there remained no other way but to attempt to prove that the world and life are perfectly intelligible without the assumption of an unfathomable God. That is, the refutation of orthodoxy required the success of a system. Man had to establish himself theoretically and practically as master of the world and master of his life; the world created by him had to erase the world merely "given" to him; then orthodoxy would be more than refuted—it would be "outlived." Animated

by the hope of being able to "overcome" orthodoxy through the perfection of a system, and hence hardly noticing the failure of its actual attack on orthodoxy, the Enlightenment . . . devoted itself to its own proper work, the civilization of the world and of man.[44]

Strauss leaves open here whether the invention a comprehensive "system" of science and culture was due to an intentional coverup or an act of forgetting, or how the first paved the way for the second. But in either case, at this point he introduced a critique of culture that is remarkably different from the type of critique laid out in the first chapter of *Philosophy and Law* and elsewhere. Most notably, its principal purpose is not "methodological," and it is not meant to facilitate a change of perspective from "culture" to "politics." The critique of culture in the introduction is *genealogical*. Its purpose is to trace the roots of the Enlightenment from the modern notion of culture. Culture thus understood is a comprehensive system, which would overcome orthodoxy by way of its being complete. The Enlightenment, then, was not merely an interpretive construct.[45] The construction of a scientific and cultural world was meant to safeguard that there would no longer be a place for the orthodox world. Orthodoxy would simply be ousted from the "world" as created by the Enlightenment. The Enlightenment victory over orthodoxy was taken for granted as long as modern civilization seemed to succeed. With the crisis of culture, however, the viability of the project became doubtful.[46]

One cannot help but notice the short circuit between the roots of the Enlightenment and its most recent fruit, or between the ideal of "civilization" and the idea of "culture." The genealogical narrative is based on the notion that the latest idealistic interpretation was latent in the Enlightenment from the beginning, while the Enlightenment roots came to be seen in the latest idealistic philosophies of culture.[47] This strategy has posed a great challenge to identifying the actual targets of his attack:

> Modern "idealism"—perfected on the one hand in the discovery of the "aesthetic" as the purest insight into the creativity of man and, on the other hand, in the discovery of the radical "historicity" of man and his world as the definitive overcoming of the idea of an eternal nature, an eternal truth—finally understands modern natural science as one historically contingent form of "world-construction" among others."[48]

At this point, even the most careful readers may find it difficult to follow the text. The key problem is to identify the positions evoked in the quote. Laurence Lampert identified the discovery of the aesthetic with Kant and the discovery of historicity with Heidegger. Since the attack admittedly does not make much sense on this basis, he took it for yet another example of Strauss's "sophistic reasoning."[49] But the actual target in the quote, and the role model of modern idealism in its latest form, was Ernst Cassirer's *Philosophy of the Enlightenment* (1932). This magnificent study, a philosophical justification of the Enlightenment and a vigorous defense of liberalism completed during the final months of the Weimar Republic, was indeed the latest self-interpretation of idealistic scientism as described by Strauss in the quote above. Most notably, the "ideal of freedom as the autonomy of man and his culture" and the idea of symbolic forms as "world-constructions" are centerpieces of Cassirer's book. Cassirer also emphasized both the discovery of the aesthetic and "the conquest of the historical world."[50]

With the similarities and differences between the two revaluations of the Enlightenment in mind, some of the most impenetrable philosophical and rhetorical details in Strauss's introduction add up. Cassirer started from the same popular sentiment that the Enlightenment is "shallow." And just like Strauss he staged the philosophical revaluation of the Enlightenment as an appeals court, albeit with different personnel and intent: He sought to achieve "a revision of the verdict of the Romantic Movement on the Enlightenment,"[51] and he claimed that the Romantic judgment was still being accepted without criticism. Some historiographical differences should be noted as well: while Strauss constructed a comprehensive account of the Enlightenment qua the philosophical system, Cassirer sharply distinguished the Enlightenment of the eighteenth century from the deductive philosophical system of the seventeenth century. And while in Strauss's genealogy the erection of a comprehensive system is an essential characteristic of the Enlightenment, Cassirer further distinguished the deductive system of Descartes from the analytic method of Newton.

These constrictions of the historiographical perspective on Strauss's side are clearly within the limits of the genealogical perspective, with its characteristic interplay of blindness and insight: Strauss's genealogy may involve a decrease in historiographical differentiation if compared with Cassirer, but it came together with a highly condensed account of the Enlightenment and its hidden theologico-political problem. At the same time, Strauss offered a significant increase in differentiation with regard to the present meaning of the Enlightenment. While Cassirer's reverence for the Enlightenment ideal was unbowed, Strauss historicized this ideal: whereas Cassirer had turned it into a transhistorical principle and a stable guide to the faults and disavowals of the present, Strauss declared that the Enlightenment ideal was valid only for a brief epoch:

> This ideal was viable, rather, only during a peaceful interlude: in the interlude when the battle against orthodoxy seemed to have been fought out, while the revolt of the forces unchained by the Enlightenment had not yet broken out against her liberator; when, living in a comfortable house, one could no longer see the foundation on which the house had been erected, —in this epoch, after the decisive entry into the state of civilization, one could forget the state of nature, which alone was capable of legitimating civilization, and hence, in place of the primary ideal of civilization as the self-assertion of man against overpowering nature, one could set up the "higher" ideal of culture as the sovereign creation of the spirit.[52]

This historicization of the Enlightenment is an early example of how Strauss turned historicism against itself. The move against Cassirer leads to dramatic consequences: If modern natural science is but "one historically contingent form of 'world-construction' among others," the scientific interpretation of the world is not in principle superior to other interpretations. As we saw above, Cassirer evaded this consequence with the help of a Hegelian stepladder of knowledge, but this did little to evade the radical consequence implied in his philosophy of symbolic forms. Strauss saw this consequence sharply, and he used the insight to argue in favor of the Biblical interpretation. His bold conclusion was that the idealistic understanding of modern science "makes possible the rehabilitation of the 'natural world-view' on which the Bible depends." Modern science comes to be seen as but one of several possible "world-views," interpretations, or symbolic forms. The scientific "world-view" is not in principle superior to the Biblical worldview. The victory of scientism paradoxically marks the end of scientism, for it inadvertently rehabilitates the Biblical worldview.

This rehabilitation of the Biblical worldview should not be understood as an endorsement of this view. The point is epistemological: Strauss suggested that, upon the premises of radical interpretation, the biblical worldview is as legitimate as the scientific worldview. This equivalence comes with a peculiar epistemological twist. If the consequence of radical interpretation is relativism—and this is strongly suggested by Strauss—the introduction of the Biblical worldview uses the relativistic starting point for its own purpose, but this purpose is antirelativistic in its intention. For Biblical religion, with its center in the act of God revealing Himself to man, is not just another series of heterogeneous and indeterminate signs; it disrupts the infinite play of signs. And the quarrel between culture, religion, and the political is actually a bloody struggle.

Strauss's genealogy of the Enlightenment repeats the principle of radical interpretation, which violently seizes another interpretation. He both detected the Enlightenment violence against orthodoxy and repeated the violent act, shattering the Enlightenment with the blows of a hammer. The genealogical effort as such, being irreconcilable with the principle of understanding a doctrine as it understood itself, rests on an act of hermeneutic violence that must be committed to detect and describe a previous act of violence. As Strauss maintained, the Enlightenment was "forced" to create the world of modern culture to cover up its own failure.[53] According to this narrative, modern culture is not a spontaneous and free creation of man: it rests on an act of violence committed by the Enlightenment against orthodoxy. The subsequent development of the Enlightenment, then, is an attempt to cover up, and ultimately to forget, this act of violence.

Both the initial coverup strategy and the eventual act of forgetting correspond to Strauss's claim that the Enlightenment rests on "a new belief."[54] The proposition is likely to be understood as a typical refutation of the refutation of religion, with the obvious point that the attack on religious belief is grounded in another belief. Along this line of interpretation, it seems that Strauss borrowed a false conclusion from his opponents to reduce the status of modern science, reintroduce the "natural" understanding of the world, and elevate orthodoxy to a status equal to that of the Enlightenment. Stunned by the boldness of his rhetorical strategy, Laurence Lampert commented: "This is lawyerly sophistry of an entertainingly high order."[55] To be sure, Strauss's interpretation is both radical and playful, but it is hardly sophistic. And while it is indeed quite entertaining to watch the rhetorical strategies in action, they serve a serious philosophical purpose in his genealogy of the Enlightenment. Again, the key is the critique of "culture" and civilization.

Strauss did *not* claim that science and religion are merely two worldviews among others (Nietzsche) or that science is based on a religious belief (Spengler). Instead, he sought to trace modern science to the belief in civilization. In his claim that it is "precisely a new belief rather than the new knowledge that justifies the Enlightenment,"[56] the expression "new belief" refers to the belief in the ideal of civilization. With this move, the binary of belief and knowledge has been successfully disentangled from its symmetric attribution to religion and science. Strauss thereby avoided the antimodern relativistic talking point that science is a belief just as religion is. Instead, he argued that both modern science and the Enlightenment rest on the belief in the ideal of civilization.

This reversal serves as a preparation for the long paragraph close to the end of the introduction, a four-page tour de force in which Strauss breathlessly, without a pause, condensed some of his lasting ideas in a way that is notoriously difficult to disentangle. In a first step, he invalidated the Enlightenment interpretation of the quarrel between orthodoxy and Enlightenment by showing that it rests on the unwarranted premises of modern civilization and culture. The Enlightenment, as it came to be seen, was just a short epoch between the consolidation of modern reason and the beginning of its self-destruction. In a second step, he countered with the "Jewish tradition," claiming that the orthodox notion of *apikorsut* (Epicureanism) provided a more accurate understanding of the Enlightenment critique of religion. We have seen a similar strategy in the first two paragraphs, where Strauss had compared modern rationalism with Maimonidean rationalism. With the same freedom that was possible only on posthistoricist grounds, he now compared the philosophy of culture with rabbinical Judaism, claiming that the latter had a better answer: "The Jewish tradition gives a more adequate answer than the philosophy of culture to the question of the original ideal of the Enlightenment. The Jewish tradition characterized defection from the Law, rebellion against the Law, in most, if not all, cases as Epicureanism."[57]

The evocation of Epicureanism as the source and motivation of the modern critique of religion refers back to Strauss's *Spinoza's Critique of Religion* (1930), but only in conjunction with the critique of civilization did the motive play out its full potential. The Epicurean as understood by the Jewish tradition is the *apikoros* (also *apikores*, *epicoros*), a Tannaitic notion for the heretic who does not have a share in the world to come (Mishna *Sanhedrin* 10:1; *Avot* 2:14). The role model was Elisha ben Abuya, called *acher* (the Other), a rabbi and scholar of Greek philosophy in the Tannaitic period who was led to apostasy likely by Hellenic thought. *Apikorsut* was often used as a derogative term for "Hellenism," and being "Greek" became synonymous with rebellion. The term also implied that the rebellion against the law was driven by pleasure seeking, but for the most part, the intricate connection between *apikorsut* and the philosophy of Epicurus was lost on the Jewish tradition.

Modern Jewish thought has come to recast the *apikoros* as a Jewish hero. For Isaac Deutscher, the *apikoros* is the highest representative of a hidden Jewish tradition, in which the dissociation from Judaism is the quintessence of Judaism itself. The main figures in Deutscher's brief history of the "non-Jewish Jew" are modern revolutionaries such as Spinoza, Marx, Rosa Luxemburg, Trotsky, and Freud, all of whom followed the example of Elisha ben Abuya: "They all went beyond the boundaries of Jewry. They all . . . found Jewry too narrow, too archaic, and too constricting. They all looked for ideals and fulfilment beyond it, and they represent the sum and substance of much that is greatest in modern thought, the sum and substance of the most profound upheavals that have taken place in philosophy, sociology, economics, and politics in the last three centuries." Deutscher's point is that these Jews, in going beyond the boundaries of Judaism, represented the very essence of Judaism: "[T]hey were very Jewish indeed. They had in themselves something of the quintessence of Jewish life and of the Jewish intellect."[58] Similar histories of post-Jewish Judaism were offered by Hannah Arendt and George Steiner,[59] and Judith Butler's recent appropriation of "Jewish values" against the strawman claim that "any and all criticism of the State of Israel is effectively anti-Semitic"[60] is merely a late offshoot of this modern Jewish historiographical tradition. Most likely, then, the Jewish heretic first comes to be known today as a metaphor of resistance against an oppressive Jewish religious and political community.

Strauss had come to the opposite conclusion. As he maintained, the odd notion of the *apikoros* and the underlying interpretation of Epicureanism was correct. As he explained in 1930 to Gerhard Krüger: "The Enlightenment owes its victory not to the scientific refutation of the claims of revealed religion. It owes its victory to a certain *will,* which one may characterize *cum grano salis* as Epicurean. *This* will seems to be no justification of the Enlightenment against revealed religion to me." Strauss traced how the argument against revealed religion was based on an act of the will. At the same time, however, he also needed to justify his own disbelief before the tribunal of the Jewish tradition. As he continued: "The nearest answer was given to me by the Jewish tradition itself, which characterized the heretic as such as Epicurean." With the pejorative rabbinic notion of the Jewish Epicurean in mind, Strauss reread the philosophical sources to be able to point out the close connection between Epicureanism and the Enlightenment: "'First and foremost' heresy was indeed of 'Epicurean' providence."[61] The corresponding quote in *Philosophy and Law* runs as follows:

> Whatever facts, impressions or suspicions led the rabbis to this characterization, this description of defection, it is corroborated by historical investigation of the original Epicureanism. Epicurus is truly the classic of the critique of religion. Like no other, his whole philosophy presupposes the fear of superhuman forces and of death as the danger threatening the happiness and repose of man; indeed, this philosophy is hardly anything but the classical means of allaying the fear of divinity (Numen) and death by showing them to be "empty of content."[62]

Epicureanism, the advice not to fear God for the sake of tranquility, was hedonistic. As such, it was the opposite of the law-abiding life of orthodoxy. In Strauss's view, then, the notion of the *apikoros* described the pleasure-seeking Jew who threw off the yoke of the law in order to find his "happy peace"[63]—a variation on the apolitical German Jew seeking to find his comfort in the gentile world. But Strauss also needed to describe and justify his own defection from the law. The traditional Jewish notion of "rebellion against the Law" may have been "adequate," but that did not make rebellion against the law despicable in any case. Hence, the Straussian *apikoros* retained a deep ambiguity.

In a third step, Strauss outlined how the Epicurean critique had undergone a fundamental change in the age of the Enlightenment. The idea was spelled out more bluntly in the Spinoza Preface: "modern unbelief is . . . no longer Epicurean."[64] In the first chapter of *Spinoza's Critique of Religion* Strauss had shown that Epicureanism was the most important source for the seventeenth-century critique of religion.[65] The Enlightenment critique of religion, in the eighteenth century, understood Epicureanism on the basis of the modern concept of civilization: the "happy peace" is to be achieved by way of the subjection of nature. The "delusion" of religion is to be fought not because it is terrible but because it is a delusion.[66]

In a fourth step, Strauss claimed that this conception had been "overcome" by another conception. The ensuing argument is not only the weakest link in the entire paragraph; it is also the point where the fundamental ambiguity of the introduction—which is highly characteristic of the complicated legacy of *Philosophy and Law*—confused even his closest friends and colleagues. Strauss had demonstrated up to here why the modern critique of religion was untenable, so how did he come to deliver an even stronger and much more devastating critique of religion now? And whereas

Karl Löwith had concluded from the text that Strauss was an orthodox Jew,[67] Gershom Scholem understood the ensuing remarks as "an unfeigned and copiously argued (if completely ludicrous) affirmation of atheism as the most important Jewish watchword."[68] But who was right? Can Strauss even be located on one side or another? Scholem was certainly correct to note that the signpost that could not be overlooked was the "affirmation of atheism," but was it Strauss's actual position? Löwith, too, was correct in his assessment that some orthodox fervor lived on in Strauss's philosophical project, although his position hardly qualifies as orthodox.

In any case, Scholem was right to note that the case was ludicrously argued. We can see this in the subsidiary argument on how the original Enlightenment conception had been "overcome." It is supposed to make the ensuing turnaround in the text appear as if it were a logical conclusion derived from the first three steps in the paragraph. As should be noted, the mere *historical* fact that one conception has been "overcome" by another is little relevant by Strauss's own standards. The parenthetical "of course" (*wie sich versteht*) does not correspond to any matter of course in the text: "This 'crude' conception has long since been 'overcome,' of course, by a conception which completely exposes the self-proclaiming and self-betraying [*die sich ankündigende und verratende*] tendency in the transformation of Epicureanism into the Enlightenment."[69]

To assume that the argument is perfectly spelled out, we would need to imagine Strauss as a Hegelian: the original thesis of Epicureanism would have been "sublated" (*aufgehoben*) by the Enlightenment antithesis, and the Enlightenment conception would have been sublated and "overcome" by another conception, namely, by Nietzsche's radicalization of the Enlightenment. But Strauss indicated that the Hegelian dialectic was what he had least in mind. This can be traced from the subsequent distinction between two different post-Enlightenment "harmonizations" of the Enlightenment and orthodoxy—the moderate Enlightenment and "especially . . . the post-Enlightenment synthesis" on the one hand, and an atheist position that "refuses . . . to represent itself as a 'synthesis'" on the other.[70] The nearly unintelligible opposition between two different ways of harmonization—a synthesis and a nonsynthesis—refers to Hegel and the post-Hegelian philosophies of religion of the mid-nineteenth century on the one hand, and the Nietzschean response on the other. The new, nonsynthetic post-Enlightenment conception, for which he appears to take a side here, is meant to be Nietzschean. As Strauss continued:

> The latest and purest expression of this [tendency] is that the religious ideas are rejected not because they are terrifying but because they are desirable, because they are comforting: religion is not a tool which man has forged for dark reasons in order to torment himself, to make life unnecessarily difficult, but rather a way out chosen for obvious reasons, in order to escape the terror and the hopelessness of life, which cannot be eradicated by any progress of civilization, in order to make his life easier.[71]

The great challenge of this and the following quotes is the ambiguity between a Straussian and a Nietzschean perspective, or the question of voice. Perhaps Strauss merely channels the voice of Nietzsche, presenting him as the latest turn of the modern Enlightenment and its critique of religion to motivate the return to the medieval enlightenment? Or was he still a Nietzschean by 1935? Perhaps he even remained so (at least covertly), despite his turn to premodern philosophizing? Without a coherent argument regarding Strauss's stance on Nietzsche, the end of Strauss's introduction remains, in the last resort, unintelligible. And yet the current stalemate of scholarly arguments and counterarguments suggests that the deep ambiguity of Strauss's words precludes a satisfying answer. One must study the heavily contested chapter ending closely in order to come to a more precise understanding. As Straussians know, it is indispensible to examine the propositional content and the references, but one must also account for the setting, changes in the argument and style, and possible "watchwords." Strauss continued:

> A new kind of fortitude, which forbids itself every flight from the horror of life into comforting delusion . . . reveals itself eventually as the ultimate and purest ground for the rebellion against the tradition of the revelation. This new fortitude, being the willingness to look man's forsakenness in its face, being the courage to welcome the terrible truth, being toughness against the inclination of man to deceive himself about his situation, is probity.[72]

At this point, a change has occurred in the text. Whereas Strauss had thus far described the quarrel between orthodoxy and the Enlightenment from above, he now articulated a specific posture within the quarrel. Most of all, the tone is remarkably affirmative: Strauss now channels Nietzsche's heroism (fortitude, *Tapferkeit*; courage, *Mut*; toughness, *Härte*) and switches into a moral language. The heroic tone, but also the rare emphasis on the "new" indicate that the position is not his own. In general, emphasis on "the new" is a negative watchword in Strauss's writings, often suggesting that the respective position cannot be identified with his own.

The more difficult part is the apparent affirmation of "probity" (*Redlichkeit*). This is certainly an important watchword, and it was likely to be understood by Strauss's contemporary readers as a self-portrait. After all, Strauss was widely known among his colleagues for his probity. But the notion also has a more specific resonance that stems from Nietzsche's *Beyond Good and Evil*. Nietzsche described probity as "the only [virtue] we have left," but he sensed that it could degenerate into vanity and dullness.[73] Strauss followed this lead, but he also deviated from Nietzsche in some respects. Most notably, Nietzsche appears to equate probity with the love of truth (*Wahrheitsliebe*),[74] whereas Strauss sharply distinguished between the two. The place of this discussion is a long footnote placed after the quote above, replete with four rather oblique references.[75] This footnote explicates the difference between a critical and a dogmatic form of "atheism from probity." As Strauss argued, probity as a critical trait is a companion of the love of truth, whereas probity as a dogmatic premise stands in opposition to the love of truth. The ensuing passage in the main text continues along this line of argument. After he had successfully disentangled probity from science, Strauss reintroduced it as a means to resist mediation:

> It is probity, "intellectual probity," that bids us reject all attempts to "mediate" between the Enlightenment and orthodoxy—both those of the moderate Enlightenment and especially those of the post-Enlightenment synthesis—not only as inadequate, but also and especially as without probity; it forces the alternative "Enlightenment or orthodoxy" and, since it believes it finds the deepest unprobity in the principles of the tradition itself, it bids us to renounce the very word "God."[76]

Not only the tone has changed in these passages. The quarrel between orthodoxy and atheism is also being fought out on a different playground: the military battle has turned into a moral contest, in which minor differences in the moral motivation decide about right and wrong in an inextricably complex matrix of positions and counterpositions:

> This atheism with a good conscience, or even with a bad conscience, differs precisely by its conscientiousness, its morality, from the conscienceless atheism at which the past shuddered; the "Epicurean," who became an "idealist" in the persecutions of the sixteenth and seventeenth centuries, who, instead of being willing to "live in hiding" safely, learned to fight and die for honor and truth, finally becomes the "atheist" who rejects for reasons of conscience the belief in God.[77]

Hence, the legitimacy of atheism is dependent upon its "probity," its "conscientiousness." The Nietzschean atheist rejects the belief in God "for reasons of conscience," whereas the Enlightenment unbeliever did not know what he was doing. In the next step, Strauss used a strategy that resembles the "non-Jewish Jew" thesis to some extent, arguing that the Nietzschean "conscientious" rejection of God stands in the tradition of the Bible itself. The Nietzschean atheist is a Biblical atheist, "who rejects for reasons of conscience the belief in God. Thus it becomes clear that this atheism . . . is a descendant of the tradition grounded in the Bible: it accepts the thesis, the negation of the Enlightenment, on the basis of a way of thinking which became possible only through the Bible."[78]

With the notion of Biblical atheism,[79] Strauss challenged the widespread view of Nietzsche as a radical destroyer of religion ("God is dead"), presenting him as the latest and most radical representative of biblical morality instead. Despite many ambiguities and changes in his overall stance on Nietzsche, this teaching regarding Nietzsche's position on religion and atheism is consistent. As he wrote in his late essay on *Beyond Good and Evil*, Nietzsche was the forerunner of "an atheistic or . . . non-theistic religiosity" that only came to light after the death of God. The entire doctrine of *Beyond Good and Evil* was "in a manner a vindication of God."[80]

From here Strauss could also explicate the difference between Biblical atheism and the "non-Jewish Jew"-type atheism. As he wrote on the contemporary atheists anticipated by Nietzsche: "These religious atheists, this new breed of atheists cannot be deceptively and deceivingly appeased as people like Engels by the prospect of a most glorious future, of the realm of freedom."[81] In other words, the new atheistic religiosity founded by Nietzsche contained an antidote to the Marxian and Freudian type of atheism, which is founded upon the premises of progressivism (and hence, on unwarranted hopes, which amounted to the "conscienceless atheism" described in *Philosophy and Law*).

We might question whether Nietzschean atheism is indeed that much different from Marxian and Freudian atheism, or whether their critique of religion is not actually founded on rather similar premises—in particular, on the premise of what Strauss called "the human roots of the belief in God."[82] But whether we agree with this position or not, Strauss saw Nietzschean atheism as a departure from the modern critique of religion and as the beginning of something new, which became discernible only in his own time. The long paragraph in *Philosophy and Law* concluded:

> This atheism, the heir and judge of the belief in revelation, of the centuries-old, millennia-old struggle between belief and unbelief, and finally of the short-lived but by no means therefore inconsequential romantic longing for the lost belief, confronting orthodoxy in complex sophistication formed out of gratitude, rebellion, longing and indifference, and also in simple probity, is according to its own claim as capable of an original understanding of the human roots of the belief in God as no earlier, no less complex-simple philosophy ever was. The last word and the ultimate justification of the Enlightenment is the atheism stemming from probity, which overcomes orthodoxy radically by understanding it radically, free of both the polemical bitterness of the Enlightenment and the equivocal reverence of romanticism.[83]

With their breathless reasoning and the affirmative tone, these two sentences undoubtedly serve as the rhetorical highpoint of Strauss's introduction. Commentators often do not seem to read any farther, as if the conclusion of the long paragraph held the key to the introduction—if not the book—as a whole. The quote therefore has a history of its own in Strauss scholarship. What, after all, is his own position on the "atheism from intellectual probity"?

David Janssens has argued that the paragraph marks Strauss's "farewell to the atheism from probity."[84] He based this understanding on the fact that Strauss translated and incorporated the crucial quote above almost unchanged into the Spinoza Preface, but with one important qualification. As Strauss added to the quote in 1965: "Yet this claim however eloquently raised can not deceive one about the fact that its basis is an act of will, of belief, and, being based on belief, is fatal to any philosophy."[85] Janssens concluded that this qualification was already implied in *Philosophy and Law*, although it was not stated there. As Robert Miner pointed out, the assumption that Strauss held the position of 1962 already in 1935 is unwarranted, and furthermore, there is no direct criticism of probity in *Philosophy and Law*. Miner rightfully concluded that Strauss "did not . . . make a clear break with Nietzsche."[86] But of course that did not make Strauss a Nietzschean,[87] nor did it refute the thesis on Strauss's farewell to probity. Both interpretations therefore have their strengths and weaknesses. Overall, however, the position of Janssens is correct. One must merely restate it somewhat differently and without the subsidiary argument. The introduction to *Philosophy and Law* does indeed mark Strauss's "farewell to the atheism from probity," but this farewell remained ambiguous, both in the introduction and in Strauss's writings after 1935. Miner is correct that there never was "a clear break" with Nietzsche, but there was no necessity to break with Nietzsche altogether, as in a public denounciation. It is time to move beyond the question of whether Strauss was *for* or *against* Nietzsche.

In general, the high importance ascribed by scholars to the question of whether Strauss was a Nietzschean stems from the uneasy position of Nietzsche and Nietzscheanism in the continuum of German philosophy and politics (see Part III below). But there is a more specific line of thought pertaining to the quarrel between orthodoxy and the Enlightenment, and especially to his alleged atheistic standpoint in the quarrel. Namely, it raises the question of the meaning and purpose of philosophy. In *Philosophy and Law* the question is particularly virulent. Situated in the intermediary stage between "no longer" (the early works) and "not yet" (allegedly the philosophy of exoteric writing), the book cannot easily be located in a larger continuum of Strauss's work. With its multiple layers and philosophical contexts, it almost precludes a thorough interpretation. Presenting Strauss as a covert Nietzschean hence provides an easy way out of a scholarly impasse. The "Nietzschean" reading of Leo Strauss almost inevitably leads to the conclusion that *Philosophy and Law* is an exoteric book. Under this premise, the entire turn to medieval rationalism was a means to divert from the prevalence of an ongoing Nietzschean project. If Strauss was a Nietzschean, all talk of reason and revelation is exoteric, devised to deflect from the fact that he has abandoned philosophy for intellectual probity. As Stanley Rosen summarized: Strauss "was not a philosopher as he himself defined the term."[88]

"Probity" is the term that seems to capture this postphilosophical conception of philosophy. According to the "Nietzschean" reading, then, probity marks Strauss's farewell to the love of truth *viz.* philosophy (hence the emphasis on his alleged sophistry). But neither Nietzsche nor Strauss saw probity and love of truth as being exclusive, and neither saw probity as a universal trait or a new paradigm that would replace the love of truth.

As Strauss wrote in his late Nietzsche essay, "[P]robity is an end rather than a beginning."[89] This hesitation was well founded in Nietzsche, who counted both terms among the "false old finery, debris, and gold dust of unconscious human vanity."[90]

To bid farewell to atheism from probity, then, Strauss did not need to break with Nietzsche altogether, for Nietzsche saw the limits of probity clearly. Nietzsche's solution was to couple probity with the vision of the overman—a guide into the unknown future that would simultaneously restore a sense of human nature from an irretrievable past. This solution was not viable for Strauss, who had no stake in a philosophy of the future. True to probity, he declared the situation to be "unsoluble" instead.[91]

The last three paragraphs of the introduction contain a precise outline of this insolubility. And most importantly, they explicate why a return from Nietzsche to Maimonides is necessary. The dramatic setting of the introduction places the entire quarrel between orthodoxy and the Enlightenment in a discourse on the need to return to Maimonides: the text begins and ends with Maimonides. The transition from the long paragraph on probity is created by a sentence that replaces the opposition between orthodoxy and the Enlightenment with the opposition between orthodoxy and atheism. It is followed by the statement that the situation is "unsoluble." This sentence marks another transition, for Strauss all of a sudden "returns" to Judaism (albeit only in speech, and not yet in deed). Unlike in the long previous paragraph, Strauss speaks with his own voice here, and he clearly speaks as a Jew:

> The situation thus formed, the present situation, appears to be insoluble for the Jew who cannot be orthodox and who must consider purely political Zionism, the only "solution to the Jewish problem" possible on the basis of atheism, as a resolution that is indeed highly honorable but not, in earnest and in the long run, adequate.[92]

The statement is not just a matter of self-assurance. Strauss certainly thought that the point where he stood was characteristic for the overall situation of modern Jewry, or at least for enlightened Western Jewry in its uneasy position between orthodoxy, assimilation, and Zionism. As we saw above, the perplexed Jew of 1935 as described by Strauss differed in one decisive respect from his counterpart, the "non-Jewish Jew." Both agreed on "the need for an enlightened Judaism."[93] But they differed regarding the question of progress or return. Whereas the non-Jewish Jew ultimately found his Jewishness in adherence to a progressive political cause, the Straussian Jew sought to return to Judaism. Strauss showed him a way to do so based upon the highest principles of the Enlightenment.

Following from this paragraph, the imaginary readers of *Philosophy and Law* are the undecided—those who seek to establish a more meaningful relationship to the Jewish tradition while remaining true to the principles of the Jewish Enlightenment, and who thereby find themselves entangled in the force field of religion, politics, and culture. When Strauss insists on the insolubility of the situation, he advises them not to make any compromises between the two conflicting claims of religion and politics. The Nietzschean "atheism from intellectual probity" is useful for this task to reject all syntheses and compromises, but Nietzsche could not provide a solution. A Nietzschean solution was particularly inappropriate for the Jew as described by Strauss. Nietzscheanism, then, was the last, most radical consequence of modern philosophical thought, but it could not be "applied" to the Jewish condition. The "overman" in particular was of little use for the Jewish condition.[94]

The paradoxical purpose of the "atheism from probity" thesis, then, is to motivate the return to Maimonides. Atheism from probity captured a particular moment in the history of the quarrel between philosophy and revelation, but this moment had already vanished in 1935. Nietzsche may have provided the closest approximation to a modern solution, but the problem could not be solved by way of a modern solution. Therefore, Strauss instructed his imaginary readers to make a change in perspective and consider the possibility that the situation is insoluble only "as long as one clings to the modern premises." Hence, the entire discourse on orthodoxy and the Enlightenment, and the indefatigable insistence on the insolubility of the conflict between the two, serves as a preparation for the turn to medieval philosophy: "One sees oneself induced . . . to apply for aid to the medieval Enlightenment, the Enlightenment of Maimonides."[95]

With the imaginary reader of *Philosophy and Law* in mind, then, the book must be understood as a new guide for the perplexed that seeks to lure the Nietzsche-trained enlightened Jew of 1935 away from Nietzsche and introduce him to Maimonides's *Guide of the Perplexed*. But such a readership no longer existed in 1935. Strauss evoked the imaginary reader one last time solely to "motivate" the publication of his philosophical and scholarly endeavor, not to justify it before a Jewish public. The last two paragraphs accordingly switch back to a more scholarly tone. The first of the two paragraphs raises a number of rhetorical questions, which are meant to anticipate some of the objections to the proposed return to Maimonides. The latter paragraph, being just as "rhetorical" as the former, also serves as a bridge from the introduction to the first chapter. It suggests that the situation may be solved by returning to the "leading idea of the medieval Enlightenment," namely, "the idea of law."[96]

8

Leo Strauss and Julius Guttmann on the History of Jewish Philosophy

Strauss's Initial Argument
(*Philosophy and Law*, chapter 1, part 1)

The chapter on Julius Guttmann's *Philosophie des Judentums*[1] had initially been composed without any apparent addressee or purpose, but in the overall structure and argument of the book it serves a clear and transparent purpose. To understand the chapter, we must see it both as a text in its own right and with regard to its place in the book. This endeavor is impeded by the fact that the text is extraordinarily complex. Its challenges to textual understanding are so great that most commentators discussed only the first two out of five parts. The usual difficulties of identifying the voice in the text are particularly grave here. Strauss often assumed Guttmann's voice to summarize and clarify his position. He also used Guttmann's words on Hermann Cohen, including quotes from Cohen, to present Guttmann as a part of the same problem he described, hence adding a third voice in the text. Furthermore, the chapter is replete with hidden references that can be misunderstood as reflecting his own position. Last but not least, the text is highly ironic. In short, the chapter—with its multiple voices and layers of irony and wit—can be extremely confusing. Strauss employed a number of textual strategies to draw Guttmann into a cat-and-mouse game,[2] which subsequently forced him to rebuild his position. These strategies are indispensible for understanding the argument and the action of the chapter—much more so than the harsh, polemical tone that strikes many readers.

Within the overall structure and argument of the book, the first chapter has many characteristics of a second introduction to medieval philosophy. After the introduction had outlined the contemporary conflict between "reason" and "revelation" (substituted by Enlightenment and orthodoxy, then atheism and orthodoxy) as a preparation for the study of medieval rationalism, the first chapter serves as the "methodological" introduction to medieval thought. For although it involves harsh criticisms of scientific methodologies, it also carefully outlines and exemplifies a methodology of political philosophizing. Strauss broadly understood methodology as "the manner of treatment" of political things,[3] but there is also a certain direction in his methodological arguments: their purpose is to *lead* from the seemingly evident premises to the premises of political thinking. For this reason, Strauss was immensely occupied with the starting point, or the proper way to begin, and the way to proceed from there. The most obvious starting point for his contemporaries, he suggested, was to understand the respective matter in terms of "culture," but its original meaning needed to be understood in "political" terms. The purpose of the "methodological" introduction, then, is to lead from a cultural understanding to a political understanding of medieval Jewish philosophy.

In order to follow this directional argument in the text, one must pay attention to a nearly unknown systematic discussion, which runs through virtually all of Strauss's works on medieval Jewish philosophy. The topic of that discussion is the place of a doctrine within the division of philosophy or science. Major philosophical insights are often described with regard to a seemingly insignificant shift in the systematic disposition of a concept or doctrine. Not coincidentally, Strauss's discovery in Avicenna's prophetology that became a key quote for *Philosophy and Law* pertains to the "classification of the sciences," namely, the question of the place of prophetology in that classification.[4] This "technical" work on the place of a doctrine within the division of philosophy or science is an indispensable guide to the inner workings of Strauss's philosophical work before and after his turn to exotericism. As it were, it is also the only way to discern where he actually stood in *Philosophy and Law*. A second source for his occupation with the division of philosophy was his early acquaintance with neo-Kantian philosophy and the debate on the place of religion in the system of philosophy (as outlined in Part I above). The two sources come together for the first time in the Guttmann critique.

The overall strategy at the beginning of the first chapter is to situate Guttmann's study within the framework of neo-Kantian philosophy of religion, and then to show how this framework is in conflict with the subject matter of medieval Jewish philosophy. Strauss was well aware that Guttmann had sought to move away from neo-Kantianism: he traced the remnants of a neo-Kantian paradigm that had vanished from the surface but lived on in the tacit presuppositions of Guttmann's endeavor. Furthermore, Strauss detected a departure from Guttmann's earlier study *Religion und Wissenschaft im mittelalterlichen und im modernen Denken* (1922), in which the neo-Kantian imprint was much more visible. In other words, he sensed a fundamental tension in the outline of the book and responded to a modification in Guttmann's position. As he summarized the task of *Die Philosophie des Judentums*, it was "the historical exposition of the philosophical problem . . . of the 'methodological value of religion.'"[5] Guttmann thereby sought to combine two different approaches—the modern philosophy of religion and the history of Jewish philosophy—into a philosophical *Problemgeschichte* (problem-history).

The problem of the "methodological value of religion" is of Cohenian and hence neo-Kantian origin. It presupposes the orientation toward modern science, with its division into logic, ethics, and aesthetics, and claims that religion would render a contribution to the scientific constitution of the cultural world. Guttmann sought to combine this systematic approach with an approach that is suitable for the historian of philosophy. The problem-historical task, then, was to show how the history of Jewish philosophy—and in particular medieval Jewish philosophy—testifies to the development of the systematic question.[6] But religion as understood in medieval Jewish philosophy was resistant to becoming a part of a common philosophic-scientific culture, because the medieval world conceived of Judaism—in Guttmann's own words—as "a total, all-embracing culture based on religion." As he noted:

> Jewish philosophy . . . is religious philosophy in a sense peculiar to the monotheistic revealed religions which, because of their claim to truth and by virtue of their spiritual depth, could confront philosophy as an autonomous spiritual power. Armed with the authority of a supernatural revelation, religion lays claim to an unconditioned truth of its own, and thereby becomes a problem for philosophy.[7]

Facing the claim to "unconditioned truth" raised by religion, Guttmann concluded that there exist "two types of truth" (*Wahrheitsgebiete*; literally: domains of truth): a philosophic one and a religious one. In other words, he acknowledged the "unconditioned" claims to truth posed by philosophy *and* by religion, but at the same time he conditioned these claims by relegating them to "types" or "domains" of truth. At this point in the short introduction (which was moved to the beginning of the first chapter in the English translation) the deep conflict in the methodological disposition of the book becomes blatantly visible. The two types of truth left Guttmann with two options. The first was to follow the philosophy of Judaism to the point of culmination in neo-Kantian philosophy of culture. The other was to argue for a reconciliation of philosophy and religion. The German text expresses the deep conflict between the two approaches, as well as the attempt to mitigate this conflict by way of a nearly incomprehensible "at first, however" (*zunächst aber*):

> The ultimate result of the work dedicated to the relation between these two domains of truth are the modern attempts to determine the methodological value of religion. At first, however, religion and philosophy are not to be methodologically separated from each other, but reconciled with each other in content.[8]

It was this quote from which Strauss concluded that Guttmann's project was "the historical exposition of the philosophical problem . . . of the 'methodological value of religion.'" He thereby assumed that both parts of the quote serve a methodological purpose, so that they reflect Guttmann's approach toward the philosophy of Judaism. This conclusion is unwarranted, for both parts were historical. But the misunderstanding is well founded in Guttmann's phrasing. The first part of the quote, with its grammatical reference to "the modern attempts," alludes to the model of Hermann Cohen and his successors—including Guttmann himself in his earlier work—who sought to place religion within the systematics of culture by clarifying the methodological distinctiveness of religion vis-à-vis science. The second part of the quote refers to a different model, according to which philosophy and religion are to be coordinated and reconciled. This is the model of medieval Islamic and Jewish philosophy.

The two sentences were completely reconstructed in the English translation (which is based on Guttmann's own Hebrew edition of his study). Some details in the English text testify to the fact that he modified and clarified the quote—and there may be speculation on whether this was a response to Strauss:

> In order to determine the relationships between these two types of truth, philosophers have tried to clarify, from a methodological point of view, the distinctiveness of religion. This is a modern development; earlier periods did not attempt to differentiate between the methods of philosophy and religion, but sought to reconcile the contents of their teachings.[9]

The reconstructed quote is far more symmetrical. First, it casts the conflict between the two models as the difference between "a modern development" and "earlier periods," that is, between modern and medieval philosophy. Second, it links this temporal difference to the distinction between method and content. And third, it combines the modern/medieval divide with the methodological opposition between the differentiation and the reconciliation of philosophy and religion. While the German text, with its ambiguous and largely incomprehensible "*zunächst einmal,*" had suggested that the coordination and reconciliation of philosophy and religion would be necessary preparatory work for the Cohenian project (the latter being "the ultimate result" of the reconciliatory work), the English text clarifies that the coordination characterizes the premodern mutuality of philosophy and religion. Facing these two different structural dispositions for the philosophy of religion, Guttmann argued that the second disposition is closer to the peculiarities of Judaism and Jewish philosophy, and he emphasized the preponderance of religion over philosophy in the premodern period: "Philosophy was thus made subservient to religion; and philosophical material borrowed from the outside was treated accordingly."[10]

Guttmann's *Philosophie des Judentums* is essentially an attempt to reconcile these two approaches, despite their unmitigated clash in the introduction. Paradoxically, however, the reconciliation leads to a mutual oppression of philosophy and religion. In a "philosophy of Judaism," Judaism is the subject matter and content, while its peculiar form is largely irrelevant. Philosophy is relegated to being a method; there is no place, and no freedom, for philosophy beyond its methodological role in "the interpretation and justification of the Jewish religion."[11] This definition of Jewish philosophy serves the clear purpose of highlighting the "philosophies of Judaism" in the narrower sense against the broader and more ambiguous notion of modern "Jewish philosophy," in which the so-called Jewish contributions to European philosophy are often included, too, so that the term *Jewish* might solely refer to the philosophers' religious or ethnic origins. The emphasis on the Jewish religion as the content of Jewish philosophy therefore helps to avoid the semantic expansion of "Jewishness" in modern Jewish thought. The downside of this narrow approach, however, is that it often cedes the philosophical core of Jewish philosophy to European thought, whereas the respective works display an inextricable connection between "Jewish" and "European" thought: Maimonides or Hermann Cohen may have been Jewish philosophers, but they were not primarily "philosophers of Judaism." In the first place, they were philosophers. The *Guide of the Perplexed* is a book on the human comprehension of the divine, and Cohen's *Religion of Reason out of the Sources of Judaism* is a systematic exposition of religion that not accidentally draws upon the sources of Judaism, but it is expressly not limited to a philosophy of Judaism.[12] Guttmann's alternative to the expansion of Jewishness is a classic example of throwing out the baby with the bathwater.

As to the emphasis on the claims of religion vis-à-vis philosophy, by 1933 Guttmann had certainly moved away from his earlier occupation with "spheres," "fields," or "domains" of culture. It is therefore not clear from the outset how Guttmann qualifies as a covert neo-Kantian philosopher of culture in Strauss's eyes, since he had apparently sought to move away from his earlier neo-Kantian leanings.[13] Upon closer reading, Strauss's brief discussion, still at the beginning of the first chapter, of Guttmann's *Religion und Wissenschaft im mittelalterlichen und im modernen Denken* (1922) is very precise regarding this theoretical shift:

> At the end of this work, in express reference to Kant on the one hand and *Schleiermacher* on the other, he identifies as the task of "philosophy of religion" "the analysis of the religious consciousness" in its "autonomy . . . over against knowledge and morality" (66 f.), or more precisely, "the definition of religion as against all other areas of subject matter and consciousness, the elaboration of the specifically religious world and its truth" (R 69). Since he defines the problem of "philosophy of religion" in this way, he seems to view the task of philosophy in general as the understanding of "*culture*" articulated into its various "domains."[14]

As Strauss argued, Guttmann shows an "unmistakable inclination towards philosophy of culture" in his earlier work, while he nevertheless prefers "more formal and hence less prejudicial expressions" such as "field," "sphere," or "domain" over the term *culture*. This conclusion is highly favorable and clearly an understatement. In fact, the formal terms spotted by Strauss are an integral part of the neo-Kantian philosophy of culture. Hence, the strategy to credit Guttmann with the insight "that religion cannot be rightly understood in the framework of the concept of 'culture'" is highly tongue-in-cheek, but it was also the starting point for rephrasing the conflict in the methodological disposition of Guttmann's book in terms of religion, culture, and the political. The following quote describes the force field created by this conceptual triangle:

> Philosophy of culture understands by "culture" the "spontaneous product" of the human spirit—but religion in its proper sense does not have this character (R 65); and besides, the other "domains of validity" allow of being conceived as "partial domains of truth"—but religion raises the claim to universality (R 70). The claim to universality on the part of "culture," which in its own view rests on spontaneous production, seems to be opposed by the claim to universality on the part of religion, which in its own view is not produced by man but *given* to him. . . . Guttmann . . . finds himself driven to a remarkable distancing from philosophy of culture by the fact of religion as such, which thereby proves to be one crux of philosophy of culture.[15]

The metaphor of the "crux," or crossroad, as the meeting point of culture and religion is noteworthy here. The crux is not merely a paradox, an ambiguity or a moment of decision. The metaphor indicates not that there is a choice to be made but that the matter cannot be decided. Whatever the choice, Guttmann could not extricate himself from the grip of the religio-political problem. And as *Philosophy and Law* demonstrates, the religio-political problem was inextricable due to the "crux" of culturalism. The "crux" announces a major revision of a theoretical paradigm, not an individual decision in a time of crisis. Here, the scope of Strauss's text surpasses the occasion of Guttmann by far. The "crux" of philosophy of culture is that it can understand religion only as a spontaneous product of the human mind (and hence as *one* product of the human mind among others); but religion—as well as "the political"—cannot be located within the framework of culture, because religion and the political are not spontaneous products of the human mind. The "crux" of philosophy of culture, then, consists in the unclear relation of culture to "*the* facts that transcend 'culture' or, to speak more precisely, the *original* facts."[16]

But the example of Guttmann was also well chosen by Strauss to mark the imminent revision of the neo-Kantian model. Guttmann may have sought to move away from neo-Kantianism, but had he been successful? Upon closer reading, it rather seems that the more he tried, the deeper he got entangled in a force field he could no longer understand.

At the time Guttmann wrote the study, neo-Kantianism had largely been discredited, so that only a few adherents openly professed to the school. Some abandoned the theoretical framework and sought to find a more immediate access to "reality," however conceived; others tried to save it by fusing it with phenomenology, which seemed much more exciting at that time; still others undertook rather cosmetic changes by moving the terminology into the background. Guttmann combined all three options. He increasingly came to acknowledge the notion of revelation, namely, the immediate reality of God addressing himself to man; he sought to articulate religious experience in terms of Husserlian phenomenology; and he still expressed these insights within the framework of the neo-Kantian philosophy of culture. The latter may indeed be less obvious in *Die Philosophie des Judentums*, but a brief survey of the ways in which the book employs the term *culture* will aptly demonstrate that this leaning had by no means vanished.

The predominant use of the term is unspecific. "Culture" refers to the surrounding societies or civilizations in which Jews lived.[17] But as in his earlier text, Guttmann also referred to the Jewish religion in the Middle Ages as "a culture"—"a total, all-embracing culture based on religion."[18] The same goes for philosophy and in particular Jewish philosophy as one of the "forms of cultural activity."[19] One common feature of these heterogeneous notions of culture is their anachronism, as demonstrated in the reference to certain medieval "sections of the Jewish people whose spiritual life was not limited to the study of Bible and Talmud, but who strove for a universal ideal of intellectual culture."[20] This projection of the modern universalism of "culture" onto the Jewish Middle Ages could still be justified by the problem-historical method. Guttmann's presentation of Abravanel as a philosopher of culture, however, is way over the top. Presenting Abravanel's philosophy as "a thoroughgoing critique of culture," he employed a very wide notion of culture that apparently includes ethics, politics, history, and religion.[21] The variety of notions of culture and the unmitigated culturalism that survived in the background of the book point to the deep conflict in Guttmann's project—his attempt to return to the original conception of medieval Jewish philosophy on the one hand, and the modern concepts that informed this attempt on the other. Guttmann was drawn to the bottom of the quarrel between the ancients and the moderns.

Strauss's principal strategy was to situate Guttmann in this quarrel: Is modern philosophy really superior to medieval philosophy? The argument on Gutmann's stance changes several times over the course of the text, and Strauss playfully suggested at one point that he might have deliberately mischaracterized Guttmann's position.[22] This rhetorical pattern creates both the tension and the clear focus that are so characteristic for the first chapter despite the detailed textual analyses. The rhetorical ambiguity on where Guttmann stood is well founded in the difference between Guttmann's actual position as understood by himself and the tacit presuppositions in his methodological approach. The subsequent debate between Guttmann and Strauss is focused on the question of whether Guttmann *believed* that modern philosophy was superior to medieval philosophy, and this could easily be denied by Guttmann. According to Strauss, however, the superiority of the moderns was rather tacitly assumed by way of the remnants of the neo-Kantian paradigm in the philosophy of Judaism. Guttmann, then, did not need to believe in the superiority of the moderns over the medievals to prove Strauss's point: when he had to make a choice between culture and religion, he chose religion, but he continued to understand religion within the framework of culture.

The conflict between a covert neo-Kantian culturalism and the claims of religion sets the stage for *the* part of Strauss's chapter that has been discussed most extensively by scholars. This part, replete with references to Mendelssohn, Cohen, and the *Wissenschaft des Judentums*, reenacts the theologico-political drama of German-Jewish modernity in the medium of philosophical methodology. Throughout, Strauss used Guttmann's words to describe Guttmann as a part of the problem he described. To give a brief summary: Strauss intertwined three different criticisms into his account of a continuous loss of Jewish "substance of life" (Guttmann), fueled by an ever-growing tacit disbelief in revelation. First, the problem of the "methodological value of religion" has distorted the original conflict between religion and philosophy. "The alternative 'reason or revelation?' is . . . replaced at once, so to speak from the first moment on, by the harmonizing decision that the teachings of revelation are identical with the teachings of reason."[23] Second, modern scholarship may be capable of preserving the content of Judaism, but it cannot account for its form, namely, "its revealed character."[24] Third, once this reality of God and His revelation, transmitted by the prophets, has been tacitly denied, the philosophy of religion is relegated to the analysis of religious experience: "The Bible must no longer be understood as revealed, but as the product of the religious consciousness."[25] All in all, Guttmann failed "methodologically" to account for the reality of revelation due to the systematic constraints of his conceptual framework.

The second criticism, on the form and content of Judaism, is the least obvious here, but it is indispensable for the argument of the book. Guttmann sought to preserve the *content* of Judaism in the form of philosophy and science, thereby continuing the project of German-Jewish modernity. Strauss's approach was exactly the opposite: in his endeavor to reconstruct the premodern notion of law he was primarily concerned with the *form* of law as it was understood by the medieval philosophers. A major critical task of the first chapter is to show that the modern occupation with the content of Judaism, without regard to its original form, is subject to a fatal inner dialectic. The main proponents in Strauss's account of this dialectic are Moses Mendelssohn and Hermann Cohen, the beginning and the end of the German-Jewish "synthesis," with the *Wissenschaft des Judentums* always in the middle. Guttmann claimed in his book that Mendelssohn is "essentially closer to the Jewish tradition" than medieval Jewish philosophy,[26] despite the fact that "there remains for him no place for the truth of the historical revelation."[27] As Strauss explained this paradox, Mendelssohn retained the idea of revealed religion from the Jewish tradition that "he himself has already undermined."[28] Mendelssohn may have preserved the content of the Bible, but he surrendered its form by seeking to reconcile it with German philosophy and culture.

This reconciliation attempt set the stage for the *Wissenschaft des Judentums*, the movement that sought to preserve Judaism by way of scientific analysis, as it was formed in the 1820s in Germany. A few quotes from the textbooks of modern Jewish thought suffice to recall the tragedy of the *Wissenschaft des Judentums*—a tragedy that long preceded the rupture of the Holocaust. Overall, the establishment of the *Wissenschaft des Judentums* was perceived as a response to the forces of modernization of European Jewry. Its founding fathers were certain that Judaism as they knew it was about to vanish. As one of them, Joel Abraham List, wrote in 1819: "Behind our decision to found a society for Jews seems to be an apprehensiveness that in the future we, as individuals, will not be able to continue to live as Jews, or at least not in the way we would like to." List concluded that Judaism must no longer be conceived primarily as a religion:

> The divine, which the daughter of Heavens carries inside her breasts, does not feed us any more, and we are the victims of either hunger or surfeit. Everywhere, then, Israel rushes toward its decline.[29]

In this situation, the major task of the historical sciences was to study the cultural achievements of the Jewish people, as classically outlined by Leopold Zunz in his "Etwas über die rabbinische Literatur" ("On Rabbinic Literature," 1818). The eternal people had become "historical." This reinterpretation of Judaism was an integral part of Jewish assimilation in Europe. As Alexander Altmann noted in 1956 in a grim commentary:

> It was hoped that once one had grasped the development of the Jewish "idea" as a historical process, its essence would emerge in its unadulterated purity, freed from the encumbrances of tradition, and one had no doubt that the "refined" (*geläutert*) type of Judaism thus arrived at would splendidly fit into the world of modern Europe. One failed to see that far from tracing the historical reality of Judaism, one was guided by a preconceived idea of what Judaism ought to be in order to conform to the standards of nineteenth-century religious thought.[30]

Another notable representative of the *Wissenschaft des Judentums*, Moritz Steinschneider, said in a conversation with his pupil Gotthold Weil that the task was to provide the remnants of Judaism with a proper burial.[31] This was the emblematic quote for Gershom Scholem, who largely built his account of the *Wissenschaft des Judentums* upon the inner dialectic of German-Jewish assimilation. As he wrote in a highly dramatic piece in 1944:

> The Jew seeks to get rid of himself, and the Science of Judaism is his burial ceremony, something like a liberation from the yoke that bears on him.[32]

We must keep this catastrophic dialectic in mind to see that Strauss's cat-and-mouse game with Guttmann was utterly serious. He presented Guttmann as the latest proponent of the *Wissenschaft des Judentums* while citing the "obvious doubt" in its program that "Guttmann himself" had. Guttmann wrote: "As much as the medieval thinkers are more strongly rooted as total personalities in the Jewish tradition and way of life, and belief in the divine authority of the revelation is more self-evident to them, to the same extent do the modern thinkers, in their theoretical interpretation of Judaism, hold fast with the greater staying power to the original meaning of its central religious ideas."[33] The inverted logic of this sentence—with the consolation of theory for the loss of tradition—was an easy target for Strauss, who realized that the statement must be read the other way around: "[T]he adequate scientific knowledge of Judaism is bought at the cost of the belief in the authority of revelation."[34] But Strauss understood well that Guttmann did not think of the *Wissenschaft des Judentums* in such tragic terms: "His opinion is rather that the scientific knowledge of Judaism is precisely an act of Judaism's self-assertion. Judaism is more endangered in the modern world, by the modern world, than ever before—granted; but its scientific self-knowledge is not so much a symptom of his illness as rather the most suitable means of relieving or even curing it."[35]

As Strauss noted, the conclusion reached by Guttmann could be interpreted in opposite ways, for it was deeply paradoxical—just as the *Wissenschaft des Judentums* project itself, with its attempt to preserve Judaism as a living tradition by way of its scientific mortification, was paradoxical from the beginning. Strauss was certainly in favor of an interpretation that cast the development of the *Wissenschaft des Judentums* as a continuous loss to the "Jewish 'substance of life.'"[36] The more it advances methodologically, the more it loses the substance of Judaism.

Culture, Religion, and the Quest for a "Resolute Return" (chapter 1, part 2)

Guttmann is not merely an occasion for Strauss's narrative. He is a transitional figure that exemplifies the larger dialectic of modern Judaism in a condensed form. This transitional character is most striking at the beginning of the second part, where Strauss discussed Guttmann's interpretation of Hermann Cohen. As Guttmann's brief allusion to the Cohenian model at the beginning of *Die Philosophie des Judentums* has shown, Guttmann saw Cohen as the climax of modern Jewish philosophy, its highest degree of philosophical insight and methodological clarity. It was only natural that *Die Philosophie des Judentums* concluded with a chapter on Cohen. (Guttmann added a chapter on Franz Rosenzweig for the Hebrew and subsequent English translation.) Strauss emphasized those aspects of Guttmann's analysis in which Cohen's methodological advancement came to be seen not only as a blessing:

> Guttmann's objection against Cohen is that Cohen can no longer "affirm" the existence of God "in its absolute reality:" on Cohen's premises, even the existence of God must "find its logical place within the posits of consciousness" (346). "The methodological foundations of his system prevent" Cohen, even in his later period, when he was essentially closer to Judaism than before, "from conceiving of God as a reality" (361, cf. also 351). This inability is the more surprising since it is after all in Cohen, far more than in Mendelssohn and, particularly, far more than in the medieval philosophers, that the content of Judaism comes into prominence.[37]

For the most part, this argument repeats earlier criticisms of the characteristic turn in the philosophy of religion from metaphysics to epistemology, and from the cosmos to consciousness. Following this turn, the memory of God's creation of the world is gradually overwritten by the notion of the creation of man. The purpose of this rehearsal of earlier criticisms is clarified only by Strauss's ensuing argument on existentialism. This long and partly skewed argument has retained a strange afterlife in Strauss scholarship, resulting most frequently in the claim that Strauss himself is an "existentialist."[38] Jacob Klein knew Strauss better, but he felt that the part on existentialism is foreign to the course of the text (*Fremdkörper*).[39] Both interpretations miss a simple and much more obvious point. Strauss included the reference to existentialism to reverse a commonly held opinion, namely, that Cohen's inability to "conceive of God as a reality" was due to his idealism. As we saw above, this interpretation had been put forward most vigorously by Franz Rosenzweig. Rosenzweig claimed that Cohen could not articulate the peculiarity of religion due to the methodological constraints of his philosophical system, and in particular because this system was founded on the idealistic notion of consciousness.[40]

Strauss's argument on existentialism in *Philosophy and Law* starts with a clear rebuttal of Rosenzweig's thesis: "The difficulty [to conceive of God as a reality] becomes no less, but even greater, as soon as 'consciousness' is replaced by 'existence,' by 'man.'"[41] To summarize the further course of this argument: If the idealistic "consciousness" is replaced by the "existence" of "man," the reality of God is merely internalized. The doctrine of creation in particular—including nonhuman as well as human nature—can no longer be understood in its original meaning and is increasingly being understood as the creation of man. As Strauss concluded, idealism is superior to existentialism because it preserves at least the memory of the doctrine of creation. We must disregard the oblique references to the theologian Friedrich Gogarten here, which have apparently distracted some readers, and turn to the second, more open and programmatic rebuttal of Rosenzweig that concluded the section on existentialism: "It is not the *natural progression* from idealistic philosophy to a '*new* thinking,' but rather the *resolute return* [*gewaltsame Rückschritt*] from the newest thinking to the *old* thinking, that can put an end to our present-day difficulty."[42]

The express rejection of the "new thinking"—*the* programmatic term of Rosenzweig's philosophy[43]—clarifies the purpose of Strauss's odd discourse on existentialism: it replaced the inner-modern difference between idealism and existentialism (and, more specifically, Rosenzweig's assumption of a "progression" from idealism to existentialism) by the distinction between the modern philosophy of religion and "its earlier version,"[44] namely, medieval Islamic and Jewish philosophy. This methodological consideration completes Strauss's narrative on the flight of Jewish modernity.

Introducing Exotericism (chapter 1, part 3)

The third part of the first chapter is the point where most commentators on the Strauss-Guttmann exchange can no longer follow the argument. The characteristic difficulty of the third part of the first chapter stems from the interplay between the continued criticism of Guttmann and some inconspicuous announcements of Strauss's own thesis on medieval Jewish philosophy. The criticism of Guttmann is largely repetitive at this point, written as if to exhaust the reader by dwelling on Guttmann's alleged failures just a bit too long. But in the course of these repetitions Strauss developed his crucial argument.

Strauss no longer claimed now that Guttmann unambiguously asserts the superiority of the moderns over the ancients. To recall the course of events thus far: He had maintained in the first part that "Guttmann's argument for the superiority of modern over medieval philosophy . . . is the intellectual bond that ties together his . . . analyses." At the end of the second part, he made the opposite claim that "Guttmann acknowledges the Jewish tradition, and thus a non-modern, pre-modern court, as the judge of modern thought, in this way demonstrating most clearly his insight into the essential inadequacy of modern thought."[45] Strauss's rhetorical trick in the latter quote is to disguise his own position (including the highly typical setting of a "pre-modern court" in which modernity is being tried) as a reflection of Guttmann's true intentions. This rhetorical attribution serves a clear purpose. The ambiguity between two equally hyperbolic representations situates Guttmann within a tension from which he cannot extricate himself. It lays the groundwork for Strauss's final statement of Guttmann's position, according to which Guttmann asserts "not *the,* but only a *certain* superiority of modern philosophy over medieval [philosophy]."[46] Modern philosophy preserves the inner truth of belief, but it cannot preserve the reality of God, and hence it abandons the relationship between inner and outer. An obvious Guttmannian conclusion from this situation is that modern and medieval philosophy are to supplement each other.[47] Medieval philosophy provides the content of Judaism, and modern philosophy provides the form by which the content is to be understood. Guttmann acknowledges the superiority of medieval philosophy with regard to its content, but he tacitly denies its superiority with regard to its form, that is to say, its revealed character.

At this point, at last, Strauss provided a first glimpse of his own teaching on medieval philosophy. His thesis is built around a quote from Guttmann:

> Medieval philosophy stands incomparably closer to Judaism than modern philosophy. For at least "the formal recognition of the authority of the revelation is a self-evident presupposition even for the most radical thinkers of the Jewish Middle Ages insofar as they wish to remain Jews."[48]

The notion of form and "formal recognition" is a key here. Strauss suggested that Guttmann had not understood his own statement because he had not taken it "literally" enough. The task was to read it "quite literally."[49] The interplay between a discussion of Guttmann's quote and an explanation of his own philosophical project has made it difficult for commentators to find the crucial argument. Strauss explained:

> Not only must every medieval philosopher take revelation into *consideration*—expressly or at least tacitly, sincerely or at least outwardly—in his treatment of all important questions; even more, for all medieval philosophers, "so long as they wish to

remain Jews," at least "the formal recognition of the authority of revelation" is a "self-evident *presupposition.*" This statement is to be understood quite literally. It means first of all: there may be debate about what must be considered the *content* of revelation; there may thus be debate about the createdness or eternity of matter, about whether immortality belongs to the soul or only to the intellect, about the eternal perdurance or future destruction of the present world, etc. etc.; but no debate is possible about the reality of the revelation and about the obligation to obey it. And it also means: the recognition of the authority of the revelation is "*self-evident.*"[50]

The quote responds to the common understanding that the recognition of revelation in medieval Jewish philosophy was *only* formal—namely, that it was exoteric, whereas *esoterically* they were philosophers only. Strauss rejected this understanding. To be sure, he even emphasized at the beginning of the second chapter the possibility that "one rationalist or another did not intend the legal foundation of philosophy straightforwardly, but wrote only to allay the suspicions *of others.*"[51] As he pointed out, however, the question of whether a medieval philosopher considered revelation *sincerely* or only *outwardly* was irrelevant: the mere formal recognition of revelation turned revelation into a systematic presupposition of philosophy. "This presupposition precedes all philosophizing: it is not laid as a foundation by human thought, but it is imposed beforehand upon human thought."[52] No matter whether the medieval philosophers "really" believed in revelation or merely accepted its premise for the sake of the social order or out of fear for persecution: by recognizing revelation at least in the most formal and most insincere way, they made revelation itself a formal or systematic presupposition of philosophy.

Strauss emphasized this new understanding at several places in the book. He had learned from his correspondence with Gershom Scholem how easily the point could be misunderstood. When Scholem read the manuscript of the Guttmann review in 1933, he objected that the medieval philosophers' belief in revelation was merely conventional: "It seems to me that you overestimate the philosophers' conventional considerations in their sincerity and mostly in their systematic relevance here."[53] Strauss conceded that the philosophers may have been insincere, but he claimed that their notion of revelation was nevertheless of great systematic concern:

I fully agree with you that the falâsifa's "belief in revelation" is not entirely credible, and that, as you say, their commitment to revelation is based on conventional considerations. But unlike you I believe that this belief is nevertheless—despite its insincerity—of substantial systematic relevance.[54]

It should be added that Scholem's view is itself fairly conventional. The emphasis on the conventional character of revelation in medieval Jewish philosophy is an integral part of the exotericism thesis as it is expressly rejected by Strauss. In the teaching of *Philosophy and Law* the exotericism thesis represents the conventional wisdom of the historian of medieval religion, whereas the task of the political philosopher was to insist on the "systematic relevance" of revelation despite exotericism.[55] Even if the belief in revelation was *merely* exoteric, it left its imprints on the systematic disposition of medieval philosophy. This point was also lost on Guttmann, who took Strauss's proposition as an early indication of the teaching in *Persecution and the Art of Writing*. Seeking to locate the difference between *Philosophy and Law* and Strauss's later teaching, he wrote: "This possibility [i.e., that "one rationalist or another did not intend the legal foundation of philosophy straightforwardly, but wrote only to allay the suspicion of *others*"] has apparently become a certainty to him now."[56] This misconstruction of the link between the two writings was foundational for Guttmann's obvious difficulties to come to terms with *Philosophy and Law*.

There is a crucial difference in their response to *Philosophy and Law* between Scholem and Guttmann, the two representatives of Jewish philosophy (Kabbalistic and rationalistic) at the Hebrew University. Whereas Scholem found the exotericism thesis exciting, for Guttmann it was a scandal. And whereas the thesis resonated well with Scholem's own view on subterranean strands in Jewish thought, for Guttmann it was irreconcilable both with his democratic political taste and his view on Jewish assimilation. Both Scholem and Guttmann misunderstood Strauss's actual position, but they did so in ways that were diametrically opposed to another.

Unlike Scholem, Guttmann knew that the exotericism thesis represented an older understanding of Islamic and Jewish medieval philosophy, and that Strauss's objections to this understanding were crucial for his book: "According to an older view the Islamic Aristotelians, or at least the last and most radical of them, Ibn Rošd, were freethinkers who viewed Islam as a religion for the masses but did not seriously believe in its divine origin."[57] This "older view," to be sure, had been proposed by none other than Guttmann himself, albeit with a heavy dose of moral outrage against the medieval contempt for the multitude. He shunned Maimonides for his elitism and "intellectualism,"[58] and he was appalled to find that the notion of the double truth in Isaac Albalag "was meant to camouflage a philosophic radicalism which did not want to subordinate itself to the authority of revelation." At the peak of his moral indignation he proclaimed: "It is clear what judgment we must make as to . . . Albalag's form of the doctrine of double truth!"[59]

Medieval exotericism was not only at odds with Guttmann's democratic taste; it was also in conflict with his view on the politics of Jewish philosophy in a non-Jewish society. The deep contempt for the alleged elitism of medieval philosophy also stemmed from German Jewry's own uneasy position in society, and hence the necessity to accommodate Judaism to non-Jewish Europeans. German Jews held on to this goal even at a time when the failure of Jewish emancipation and assimilation in Germany became increasingly difficult to deny.

Guttmann was not the foremost spokesman for this understanding, but as the great representative of the *Wissenschaft des Judentums* in 1933 he certainly had a share in its untimely defense. The purpose of his book was to point out the unique contribution of Jewish thought to the European sciences, and hence to encourage German Jewry to hold on to this heritage.[60] It is written upon the premise that recognition of the extraordinary cultural achievements of European Jewry would foster their acceptance. In other words, it was devised as a contribution to the ongoing project of Jewish assimilation. The problem with this longing for a largely asymmetric symbiosis between Jews on the one hand and Germans or Europeans on the other was not simply that it did not work; it did not need to be proven wrong by National Socialism. By the mid-1930s, Judaism had already been subject to a long process of self-remodeling—a liberal reinterpretation that sought to accommodate Judaism to European sentiments. Guttmann's remodeling of Judaism along the lines of Kant and Schleiermacher was only the latest outgrowth of what Strauss grimly called "the betrayal of the Biblical heritage for the sake of an alien 'piety.'"[61]

The medieval doctrine of the "double truth" did not sit well with this project of accommodation. Exotericism in medieval thought was as much a scandal for assimilated German Jews in the twentieth century as the notion of Jewish chosenness had been in the nineteenth century. Both could not simply be explained away, but they could be reinterpreted. And just as Jewish chosenness could be accommodated to modern Jewish tastes by reinterpreting it as an ethical mission, the esoteric/exoteric divide could be reinterpreted as the double truth of modern science and religion. In this notion of the double truth, the social distinction between the elite and the masses was no longer openly visible. And just like the reinterpretation of chosenness as an ethical mission, the reinterpretation of exotericism into the double truth of science and religion turned the embarrassing facts of the Jewish tradition into a Jewish "contribution" to European science and culture.[62]

This tragic history of German-Jewish thought before and after 1933 and its impact on the inner workings of philosophical concepts helps us to understand the nature and the limitation of Guttmann's response to Strauss. Guttmann noticed the principal difference between *Philosophy and Law* and Strauss's later teaching, but he nevertheless sought to understand *Philosophy and Law* as a precursor of the later teaching. Thus, he failed to recognize that *Philosophy and Law* is essentially anti-exoteric, and therefore he missed the argument on the legal foundation of philosophy.

According to Strauss, the medieval Jewish philosophers must consider and recognize revelation "at least tacitly," simply because revelation is the problem of medieval philosophy.[63] Strauss's findings merely indicate the situation of medieval philosophy. Compared to Greek philosophy, this situation had changed from the ground up not only due to the reality of revelation, but also with the tradition of authoritative writings on revelation.[64] As Strauss cited from his favorite Maimonides quote, the three reasons assembled by Alexander of Aphrodisias for the natural difficulties of philosophizing needed to be supplemented by the addition of a fourth, a historical reason, namely, "the habituation to texts of unconditional authority: the fact that a tradition based on revelation was introduced into the world of philosophy added to the *natural* difficulties of philosophizing, which are given with the 'cave'-existence of man, the *historical* difficulty."[65] Strauss added that the modern Enlightenment sought to interpret away this situation by relegating the historical difficulty to a "prejudice."[66] To describe the situation of medieval philosophy, therefore, also served to indicate the fundamental change in the relationship between philosophy and society in modernity.

Refuting Exotericism (chapter 2)

Strauss put great emphasis on the demonstration that the historical difficulty of philosophizing was well recognized throughout Islamic and Jewish philosophy, despite the most tremendous internal differences between the respective figures. Furthermore, the most radical philosophers among them expressed this understanding most clearly. Strauss chose Averroes, Maimonides, and Gersonides as his witnesses. His argument on the legal foundation of philosophy is largely built upon Averroes (Ibn Rushd), in particular on his *Decisive Treatise* (*Fasl-al-maqâl*). To sum up the analysis of Averroes's position: "Philosophy stands *under the law*, but in a way that it is *commanded* by the law."[67] It is not only commanded as one among many human activities. For unlike other activities, the purpose of philosophy is identical with the purpose of the law; philosophy and law cannot be in conflict with another because "truth does not disagree with truth" (Averroes), and both stem from God, the creator of the law and of reason.[68] However, philosophy and law can speak differently of the same thing. In this case, the law is in need of interpretation. Philosophers (and that is, *only* philosophers) are authorized to understand the law figuratively. Inasmuch as they are not bound by the literal sense of the law, philosophy is *free* before the law. In dogmatically relevant questions, however, there are errors of legal interpretation that would constitute disavowal (unbelief) or innovation (heresy). In this sense philosophy is *bound* by the law.[69] "Philosophy owes its authorization, its freedom, to the law; *its freedom depends upon its bondage*. Philosophy is not sovereign. The beginning of philosophy is not the beginning simply; the law has the first place."[70]

Guttmann attested that Strauss's analysis of the *Decisive Treatise* is excellent, but he was in doubt whether his overall conclusions for medieval Jewish philosophy were justified.[71] Indeed, Strauss had built his overall argument on the medievals largely upon the *Decisive Treatise*, and that made doubts as to his textual basis inevitable. But the text was not chosen at random. As it were, the *Decisive Treatise* is not a theologico-philosophical treatise but a legal opinion (*fatwa*) on the question of whether philosophizing was permitted by the Qur'an. This extraphilosophical, legal character of the *Decisive Treatise* serves Strauss's argument well, for it reflects and exemplifies the condition of philosophizing under the law.

Now, Strauss sought to demonstrate that both Maimonides and Gersonides understood the relationship between philosophy and law in a similar way, despite their otherwise great differences. To summarize his argument: Maimonides is in fundamental agreement with Averroes regarding the legal commandment to philosophize; if philosophy contradicts the literal sense, one must interpret the literal sense; the interpretation must be kept secret from the nonphilosophers. Maimonides assumed that the human intellect has a limit which it cannot cross, therefore the right of interpretation is limited. Those teachings of revelation that man cannot comprehend and demonstrate philosophically are not to be rejected. Regarding the problem of creation, science can weaken the argument for the eternity of the world or to make the creation of the world probable without being able to demonstrate it: "[I]t must finally leave the question unanswered and accept the solution presented by revelation."[72] At last, Gersonides (Levi ben Gershon or Gershom), in his *Milkhamot Ha-Shem* (Wars of the Lord), radicalizes the freedom of philosophy against Maimonides but thereby paradoxically reaffirms that "the restriction of philosophy . . . underlies philosophy."[73]

One can hardly overemphasize the insignificance of Gersonides for the argument of *Philosophy and Law*. Gersonides had initially been the main subject of the study when Strauss was still employed by the Akademie für die Wissenschaft des Judentums. Strauss explained the origin of his project and its eventual modification in a letter to Cyrus Adler from September 30, 1933:

> After the composition of my Spinoza book I had started an analysis on behalf of the Academy for the Science of Judaism of Gersonides' Milkhamot Hashem. I began by investigating Gersonides' doctrine of prophecy (Milkhamot treatise II and supercommentary on Aristotle de divinatione). The investigation of his sources led me via Maimonides back to the Islamic philosophers, whose precise consideration—I studied them partly in the Arabic manuscripts—led me to discern the connection between the medieval Jewish and Islamic doctrine of prophecy with Plato's State and Laws, which in my view has not been sufficiently recognized and evaluated thus far.[74]

Strauss started this project as a "pure study work,"[75] but soon he was led to the much more exciting works of Maimonides and Averroes instead. Already the manuscript "Die Lehre des R. Lewi ben Gershom," completed in September 1930, established that the teaching of Gersonides must be seen in conjunction with Maimonides and Averroes:

> His teaching stands in fact between philosophy (Aristotelianism in neoplatonic interpretation) and law. What does this in-between position mean? It is an attempt to transpose philosophy into the world dominated by the law and the law into the world dominated by philosophy. This mutual transposition from one

world into another presents itself as a foundation in a manner of foundation that is appropriate for this world. Therefore we have to consider: 1. the legal foundation of philosophy and 2. the philosophic foundation of the law.[76]

Philosophy and Law cited the *Milkhamot Ha-Shem* as a mere confirmation of Maimonides's teaching, which was largely a confirmation of Averroes's teaching. This transposition of his initial subject matter (the prophetology of Gersonides) into the framework of *Philosophy and Law* demonstrates the "freedom of philosophizing" in action, fought out against the scholarly authority of Julius Guttmann. At the end of the first chapter, Strauss alluded to the close link between Gersonides and Guttmann when he quipped that Gersonides was the only medieval thinker who would count as a "rationalist with belief in revelation."[77] If Maimonides was the "natural model" of rationalism, Gersonides clearly marked its deterioration.

Strauss had now established the agreement between the three representatives of Islamic and Jewish (i.e., non-Christian) medieval philosophy: philosophy is commanded by the law, free before the law, and bound by the authority of the law. In other words, all three agree about the key paradox that *Philosophy and Law* seeks to recover and explicate: "The freedom of philosophy depends upon its bondage."[78] The paradoxical thesis must be read with regard to the larger contrast between medieval and modern thought. Its purpose is to question the self-sufficiency of human reason. By *presupposing* the law, the Islamic and Jewish philosophers of the Middle Ages are continuously referred to something beyond human reason. As Strauss wrote on Gersonides: "The Torah, like the world, is a work of infinite wisdom and grace and thus is knowable to the finite intellect only to a small extent; the Torah itself is a *world, in* which man lives, to the understanding of which he should apply himself according to his powers, but which always contains *more* of wisdom and goodness than man can observe."[79] At the same time, the insufficiency of human reason is the ultimate justification of philosophy; for if human reason were entirely sufficient, there would be no need to philosophize.

Theoretical Difficulties (chapter 1, part 3 continued)

With Strauss's emphasis on the "formal recognition" of revelation we are in the midst of a debate on the status of revelation: Was revelation relevant for Strauss *solely* in a formal respect or did he also take the content of revelation into consideration? The answer has many ramifications for the understanding of Strauss's medievalism *and* of his actual position in the "ever-continuing"[80] quarrel between reason and revelation. If revelation is only a formal presupposition, it does not pose a serious challenge to philosophy. This answer is particularly attractive for those who are less concerned with the Jewish content of *Philosophy and Law* (although the claim stems from none other than Guttmann).[81] If revelation is relevant for philosophy with all its content and tradition, philosophy may not be epistemically sufficient unless it becomes "Jewish philosophy."

As it were, the complementarity of the two interpretations points to a conflict in Strauss's own doctrine. The thesis on the legal foundation of philosophy is the strategic point where the larger separation between philosophy and Jewish philosophy is at stake. Following Strauss's doctrine, then, continental philosophy must take into account its Jewish part and portion and turn to the relationship between philosophy and religion as a principal topic of investigation. At the same time, Jewish philosophy must become philosophy. Thus, Strauss provides *the* present-day justification of why the larger separation between the two discourses needs to be revised.

The deep conflict between philosophy and Jewish philosophy—the latter with its commitment at least to the *problem* of revelation, the former with its disdain for extraphilosophical reasons—can be located in the inconspicuous question of how a formal presupposition can be binding. This conflict may be stated as follows: if the medieval philosophers recognize the revealed law "at least" in the formal respect, isn't this recognition *merely* formal? And would a mere formal recognition nevertheless be binding to the philosopher? These questions are closely linked to the question of what "recognition" and "presupposition" mean. We must therefore turn to the course of the argument in the third part of the first chapter, following the Maimonides quote and Strauss's ensuing commentary.

According to this commentary, the presupposition refers to the historical fact of revelation, that is, to the fact that a tradition of revelation entered into the philosophical world, thus forcing philosophy to take this fact into account. Strauss referred to this "situation" also as "the reality of revelation" in medieval philosophy.[82] This "reality" does not demand more than *formal* recognition, and Strauss emphasized that the content of revelation is subject to debate. But he also claimed that "no debate is possible about the reality of the revelation and about the obligation to obey to it." This claim changed the meaning of "reality." In the next step Strauss claimed that the authority of revelation is "self-evident." Even as the philosophers seek to explain revelation philosophically and historically, these explanations only confirm what has already been established by the reality of revelation, and this reality is not dependent on philosophical recognition. As Strauss claimed, this reality is known immediately: "[I]n spite of and because of the mediating tradition, it is known immediately. That the revelation is real is *seen* by the seeing Jew in the superhuman wisdom and justice of the Torah, is *seen* by the seeing Muslim in the superhuman beauty of the Qur'an."[83] This visibility and immediate knowability of the revelation is rather different from its tacit presupposition. But not only the notion of "reality" changes in the course of this section. The same goes for the precedence and hence the presupposition of the revelation. In the last part of the argument, Strauss repeated the claim of the first part that "the recognition of the authority of the revelation is a *presupposition* of philosophizing as such," but the meaning of the term *presupposition* has changed from a philosophical recognition in form to a religious imposition in content: "This presupposition precedes all philosophizing: it is not laid as a foundation by human thought, but it is imposed beforehand upon human thought."[84]

As Guttmann duly noted, this entire train of thought flips over.[85] And this occurs at a point where the obscurity in the notion of "presupposition" could no longer be hidden. Revelation can be presupposed either systematically or by unquestioned belief, and Strauss's words seem to be devised to conceal this essential difference. The systematic presupposition, and hence formal recognition, of revelation cannot establish the unquestionable authority of the revealed law. The law precedes all philosophizing only inasmuch as it constitutes the formal presupposition upon which all philosophizing is predicated.

Strauss later resolved this conflict by emphasizing the exoteric character of the presupposition. It may seem that this resolve came somewhat too easily, and the position in *Philosophy and Law* appears to be stronger, even as—or precisely because—the problem becomes so easily visible here. In any case, the obscurity is not a mere blunder. Strauss combined the two sources of premodern legal authority into the notion of a comprehensive law in order to contrast it with modern philosophy. But this reappropriation of the law was a hypermodern endeavor, and so Strauss inevitably ran into the deep conflict within the notion of law: in order to be comprehensive, the law needed to be imposed and presupposed. In order to allow for the freedom of philosophizing, this presupposition needed to be solely formal and/or historical. The obscurity in Strauss's notion of the law at this point stems from its chimerical character as a philosophical presupposition and a religious imposition. It lived upon the double connotation of philosophical freedom and religious compulsion.

Strauss had good reason to bury the conflict in the notion of "presupposition" in his breathless reasoning. It was created by his own sharp contrast between premodern and modern thought. As if to confirm this prevalence of a polemical contrast in the project of *Philosophy and Law*, he concluded the third part of the first chapter by emphasizing the difference between the medieval understanding of religion as law and the modern understanding of religion as a "field of culture."[86] But can the medieval notion of law be reconstructed as a contrast to the world of man and his culture? Strauss needed to appeal to medieval philosophy to find a way out of the impasse. He sought to resolve the contradiction in the fifth part of his argument by stating that philosophizing is commanded by the law: "Since the recognition of the authority of the revelation is *prior* to philosophizing and since the revelation lays claim to man *totally*, philosophizing is now possible only as *commanded* by the revealed law. . . . The one God obliges the men suited to it, by a clear, unequivocal, simple command of His revealed law, to philosophize."[87]

The statement generalized an argument by Averroes, who maintained that "these laws" (i.e., the religious laws) "summon to speculation, which leads to knowledge of the truth."[88] Strauss sought to provide this argument with a new justification. But neither the reason that the recognition of revelation is *prior* to philosophizing nor the fact that revelation makes a claim to universality provides a sufficient explanation for this commandment to philosophize. Strauss was on safer grounds when he described the "new *situation* of philosophizing" in the Middle Ages as the result of the emergence of a tradition of writings on revelation. In this situation, philosophers faced a new problem: "Their 'exoteric' writings have not so much the function of 'persuading' or 'urging' men to philosophize as the function of showing, by dint of '*legal speculation*,' that philosophizing is a duty, that it is in accord, in its form and in its content, with the meaning of the revelation."[89]

As has been noted, the quote mentions exotericism for the first time in Strauss's published writings.[90] However, it has little to do with the doctrine of writing "between the lines" in *Persecution and the Art of Writing*. As noted above, exotericism is the conventional wisdom in *Philosophy and Law*, and Strauss sought to provide this wisdom with a nonconventional foundation and limit the scope of its validity. As Strauss had explained in 1931, the esoteric character of medieval philosophy—the obligation to keep it secret, the prohibition against communicating it, and hence the need for exoteric writing—is not due to the rebellion against the law. It is *because* medieval philosophy stands under the law.[91]

In the quote above, the term *exoteric* refers to the *form* of the *Decisive Treatise*, namely, to the fact that Averroes opined for the obligation to philosophize in a legal tractate (*fatwa*). A defense of philosophy in a philosophical tractate would not have convinced anyone other than the philosophers; the argument in favor of philosophy had to be made in a form of writing addressed to nonphilosophers. Hence, the *Decisive Treatise* was "exoteric" inasmuch as it was written in an extraphilosophical literary genre, the *fatwa*. The *fatwa* was the most authoritative literary form, so Islamic philosophers such as Averroes used this form for their defense of philosophy. At least in form, the "legal foundation of philosophy," that is, "the demonstration that the men suited to philosophizing are obligated and thus authorized to philosophize by the revealed law,"[92] had to be carried out by way of a legal discourse, not a philosophical one.

This literary form of the *fatwa*, however, was also well suited for a legal twist in the argument in favor of philosophy. The medievals sought to justify philosophy by way of a clever defense: they argued not only that philosophy is in agreement with the revealed law but also that it is *commanded* by the law. This commandment to philosophize was to be established in the legal discourse, not philosophically. Hence, philosophy is referred to an extraphilosophical genre and literary form to maintain its own necessity. The legal defense of philosophy creates a formal precedence, not an absolute authority, of the law. But this formal precedence of the law suffices to secure the freedom of philosophizing before the law.

Altogether, the "medieval" argument of *Philosophy and Law* is ripe with contradictions. Strauss did not attempt to solve these contradictions on the basis of a strong exotericism thesis, although this strategy would have provided an easy way out. What he did instead in the fourth part of the first chapter is an important element of the book.

Maimonides's Critique of Reason (chapter 1, part 4)

At this point, Strauss had established that philosophizing is commanded and thus authorized by the law. The core of medieval Jewish philosophy had thus become accessible again: that philosophizing is accountable to revelation, that it is a duty vis-à-vis revelation to philosophize, and that philosophy is in accord with revelation. Now Strauss presented the paradoxical claim that from this "legal foundation of philosophy" there arises the "philosophic foundation of the law."[93]

The argument intertwines several paradoxes: First, Strauss demonstrated that the command and authorization of philosophizing by the law secures the freedom of philosophy before the law: "philosophizing as authorized by the law enjoys full freedom, is wholly or nearly as free as if it stood under no law."[94] Second, as philosophy enjoys its freedom under the law, it makes revelation its theme. Revelation thereby becomes one philosophical topic among others, and not the first or most important one. This point explains how the content of revelation becomes relevant for philosophy despite the preponderance of its form. Philosophy presupposes the revelation in form, but by making revelation a philosophical topic among others, its content also becomes a subject matter of philosophy. Philosophy is free to interpret the content of revelation, and therefore the possibility of "Jewish philosophy" in the sense of a "philosophy of Judaism" arises. At this point, the project of Guttmann has found a legitimate, albeit limited, place within the larger framework of *Philosophy and Law*. But third, as one theme of philosophy among others, the law becomes "a part . . . of the philosophic structure [*Lehrgebäude*]."[95]

From this last argument it seems that, after the "philosophic foundation of the law" has arisen from the "legal foundation of philosophy," the latter makes a reentry into the former. As a part of the philosophical structure, the law attains a systematic significance in philosophy itself. Therefore, this significance is not limited to the law becoming one topic of philosophy, or to the emergence of "philosophy of law" as a subdivision of philosophy. Speaking in terms of the prior Cohenian discourse on the systematic place of religion: although—or precisely because—the law is not the most important topic of philosophy, it attains a systematic omnipresence in the whole of philosophy. Fourth and last, this inconspicuous systematic omnipresence of the law ultimately safeguards the rationality of philosophy. If the overall purpose of Strauss's appeal to the law is to gain an outside perspective on modern philosophy, this is the point where the outside enters the inside to facilitate a principal modification in the foundation of philosophy. Such a modification is implied in the following remarks, which clarify the overall purpose of *Philosophy and Law* more than any other in the book:

> In the philosophic foundation of the law, the presupposition of philosophizing comes under discussion itself, so that in a certain

way it is made questionable. . . . The philosophic foundation of the law is the only place in the structure of medieval philosophy where the presupposition of (medieval) philosophizing becomes the theme of philosophy. Therefore one may say that the philosophic foundation of the law is nothing less than the philosophic basis of medieval philosophy.[96]

The primary purpose of Strauss's appeal to the law, then, was to clarify the status of philosophy. The double effect is that philosophy is provided with a radical foundation and that it is "made questionable." According to Strauss, philosophical reason must account for its own premise and its own necessity to be rational. We begin to see the contours of the idiosyncratic philosophical project of *Philosophy and Law* at this point: Strauss explicated the purpose of the appeal to the law to clarify the legitimacy and necessity of philosophy. As he later explained, the question "Why philosophy?" is raised by medieval philosophy "by justifying philosophy or science before the tribunal of the law, of the Torah. This most fundamental question of philosophy, the question of its own legitimacy and necessity, is no longer a question for modern philosophy."[97] While modern philosophy no longer took the challenge, medieval philosophy continually referred to the law and thereby retained its radical foundation. This is why, according to Strauss, medieval rationalism was superior to modern rationalism.[98]

It seems that this clarification of the legitimacy and necessity of philosophy was a breakthrough point for Strauss, who emphasized that several key problems could now be posed differently. Most notably, he felt that he could now describe the actual teaching of medieval philosophy according to Guttmann's "philosophy of religion," and in particular, the purpose of revelation in this teaching. In Guttmann's *Die Philosophie des Judentums*, that teaching had been described as "rationalism with belief in revelation" (*offenbarungsgläubiger Rationalismus*).[99] Strauss sensed that this notion was a key to Guttmann's endeavor, but it also seemed to codify an entire medievalist tradition of the *Wissenschaft des Judentums*. It had to be shattered by the blows of a hammer to arrive at a new answer.

Strauss's three-page analysis is a high point of his critique. To summarize: for a rationalism with belief in revelation there is no excess of revelation over the sphere of reason. Nothing in the content of revelation transcends reason. The content is identical with reason, and reason is capable of knowing this content. There is no conflict between reason and revelation. The primary purpose of revelation, then, is "pedagogic": it makes the truth accessible to those who cannot attain it by way of thinking. Revelation is particularly indispensable for the uneducated masses, who are incapable of coming to know the truths of philosophy; but to the philosopher it does not reveal anything he could not grasp on his own.[100] Strauss was careful to point out that this position—which loosely resembles the politicized understanding of Straussian "exotericism" in the anti-Straussian imagination today—is the "classical answer" as represented by Guttmann,[101] despite Guttmann's contempt for a certain version of exotericism. He commented that this position is "not only objectively untenable . . . but, above all, unintelligible in itself."[102] It was certainly the view he wanted to overcome by way of *Philosophy and Law*, and his case is particularly strong at this point.

Guttmann's view was untenable because it failed to account for the philosophers' interest in the revelation: If the purpose of revelation is primarily "pedagogical," that is, to guide the masses, why should it concern the proud Islamic and Jewish philosophers of the Middle Ages? Why should the rationalist "with belief in revelation" actually believe in the fact of revelation without any serious interest in it? Strauss's argument points to a weak spot in Guttmann's position, but his critical insight is also a key to his own understanding of medieval and modern rationalism: "There can be an *interest* in the revelation only if there is a *need* for the revelation. The philosopher needs the revelation if he knows that his capacity for knowledge is in principle *inadequate* to know *the* truth."[103] This insight into the limitation of human reason provided a basis for an understanding of the conflict between reason and revelation (qua philosophy and the law) that is in principle superior to the solution sketched in the introduction of *Philosophy and Law*.

The starting point is the epistemic and moral (i.e., theoretical and practical) difference between philosopher and prophet. Whereas Guttmann had admitted only a "difference in *degree*," Strauss maintained an "essential difference" between the two.[104] Philosophy is dependent on revelation because, according to Maimonides, man can only know the "lower world" or "*his* world," whereas clear knowledge of the "upper world"—the world of God and the angels—is restricted to the prophets. This limitation of reason is captured in a description from the *Guide* that was apparently an appropriation of Plato's allegory of the cave. As Strauss summarized:

> The highest objects of knowledge are secrets from us; only occasionally does the truth shine on us, so that we suppose it is day; but it is at once withdrawn again from our view by matter and

because of our matter-bound life. We live in a deep dark night, only occasionally illumined by flashes of lightning. Since therefore man's intellect has a limit necessarily given with nature, which it cannot cross, man is obliged for the glory of his Lord to halt at this limit and to subject himself to the revealed doctrines that he cannot comprehend and demonstrate.[105]

Strauss had thereby characterized Maimonides's position on why the philosopher is in need of revelation: the scope of philosophy is too limited to know the whole, and human reason is fundamentally insufficient. Commentators have downplayed the significance of the insufficiency thesis. It has seemed like a traditional remnant, a leftover from an older view in Jewish medievalism, as if Strauss had stood in his own way here.[106] But actually the thesis, as it is based on Maimonides's distinction between the "upper world" and the "lower world," is a keystone for Strauss's critique of reason in *Philosophy and Law*. As he explained in the third chapter: "The terms 'upper' and 'lower' world express not only a spatial relationship but also a difference of rank. The upper world is the world higher in rank; it is inaccessible to human knowledge not only because of its spatial distance but also because of its high rank."[107]

At this point in the book, Strauss had found a clear procedure to settle the conflict between reason and revelation. As stated above, this procedure is remarkably different from the procedure at the end of the introductory chapter, although it is not altogether different. In both cases, the conflict is settled by reason—"this is self-evident for a rationalist,"[108] medieval or modern. But reason operates in a different way. In the introduction, reason embarks on a path of "radically understanding" the claims of revelation, embodied by the Biblical atheist who claims to be "the heir and judge of the belief in revelation."[109] In contrast, Maimonidean reason primarily limits the scope of its own jurisdiction: "Maimonides *demonstrates* [*beweist*] that reason has a limit and must therefore accept the suprarational doctrines of revelation without being able to understand or demonstrate them."[110] The radical understanding of revelation (the thesis of the introductory chapter) is replaced by the radical insight into the limits of radical understanding.

As Strauss explained the doctrine of Maimonides, the limitation of reason does not mean that knowledge of the "upper world" is wholly inaccessible to the philosopher, so that philosophy could know only parts of the whole. In a strict sense the philosopher knows only the "lower" world. The upper world comes to be known to him "as to all man," namely, through revelation.

> Thus all the truth necessary for his life is wholly accessible to man through reason *and* revelation: through reason *his* world becomes known, in itself and in relation to the "upper world" that is inaccessible to him, while through revelation he comes to know those truths transcending rational knowledge that he needs for his life.[111]

In principle, revelation is addressed to all men, not specifically to the philosopher, but it becomes accessible to reason only after lengthy preparation. The philosopher is authorized and obliged by revelation to gain knowledge of the human world, which is protected from those who are not suited to philosophizing. Strauss turned this esoteric presupposition of medieval Islamic and Jewish philosophy into a justification for the philosophers' obligation to philosophize, and this obligation is the strongest antidote to all-out esotericism: "The man suited to philosophizing, and only he, is authorized and even obligated by the revelation to gain knowledge of the human world that is in principle accessible to human reason."[112] Furthermore, revelation does not teach man anything about things whose knowledge he can attain by himself.[113] Hence, the limitation of knowledge of the human world comes together with a self-limitation of revelation vis-à-vis reason.

Strauss went so far as to assume "an essential excess of revealed truth over rational truth"[114] as a precaution against the self-sufficiency of reason. This assumption did not require actual belief in revelation. It sufficed to follow its implications for the critique of reason—or at least it seemed so in 1935. As we shall see below, in hindsight the claim created a wide array of problems for Strauss. Most notably it seemed to contain an odor of Christian scholasticism he had sought to avoid. In *Philosophy and Law*, the claim that revelation essentially exceeds reason serves to invalidate the opposing claim of Julius Guttmann, for whom the revealed truth is fundamentally identical with the rational truth.[115] But as Strauss conceded, this restatement on the nonidentity of reason and revelation does not yet render Guttmann's "rationalism with belief in revelation" impossible, it merely limits its field of application.

Strauss had discerned the principal weakness of this "rationalism with belief in revelation," namely, its failure to explain what interest the philosopher has in revelation, but this demonstration was not sufficient. To disprove Guttmann's account of revelation he needed to find a comprehensive new interpretation that would no longer view revelation within the horizon of the philosophy of religion. He needed to start again by asking for the meaning and purpose of revelation, and his answer was that this meaning and purpose was *political*. This is the topic of the last part of the Guttmann critique, the fifth part of the first chapter, which must be read together with the third chapter.

Introducing the Scholarly Argument (chapter 1, part 5)

Strauss started from the systematic place of prophetology in the disposition of science. Prophetology had hitherto been understood as a part of psychology, but as he sought to demonstrate, it could only be properly understood as a part of politics, even as politics stands at the last place in the system of science.[116] It is useful to keep this systematic starting point in mind in order not to misunderstand Strauss's claim that the philosopher "is in need of the law."[117] After all, Guttmann suggested in his late reply that this claim expressed a pitiable longing for authoritarian rule, born out of an existential need.[118] Strauss was familiar with the difference between a need and a fact. As he explained in *Natural Right and History*: "A wish is not a fact. Even by proving that a certain view is indispensable for living well, one proves merely that the view in question is a salutary myth: one does not prove it to be true."[119] Strauss certainly thought that the law was to be more than a "salutary myth." But did he therefore seek to "prove it to be true"?

In fact, there was no reason to prove the law to be true, because *Philosophy and Law* does not seek to reestablish its premodern authority in modernity. The phrase in the book that seems to contradict this understanding most directly actually serves to prove it: The contention that "the Islamic and Jewish philosophers of the Middle Ages . . . are guided by the *primary, ancient* idea of *law* as a unified, total regimen of human life"[120] could be read as if Strauss sought to *reestablish* such a "unified, total regimen" as an authoritarian philosophico-theological order. He would have to prove the law to be true to establish its unquestionable authority, because such legal authority could not be founded upon a "wish" or a "need" for the law. At the very least, he would have to argue that the law is implied in our moral actions and our political judgment; the fact of the law has only been obscured and forgotten by modern liberalism, but actually the law is true because it is *real*. The problem with this interpretation is simply that it is not supported by the text. Strauss showed that the medievals presupposed and justified the law, but does this warrant the inference that he thought the moderns should do the same? Is there any support for Guttmann's shortcut to the introduction, with its completely different historical setting and conceptual framework? Furthermore, was the notion of "the law" but a crude mix of Platonism and Jewish medievalism?

Three important qualifications suggest otherwise, and they all point to the *historical* thesis of *Philosophy and Law* on the medieval Islamic and Jewish philosophers. First, they "are pupils of *Plato*," that is, they sought to reconcile their Platonism with the claims of revelation. This is the major thesis regarding the sources of medieval Islamic and Jewish philosophy. Second, "they are . . . not pupils of Christians."[121] This difference is crucial with regard to the conflict between reason and revelation: whereas Christian thought made philosophy subservient to theology from early on, in Judaism and Islam the relationship remained fragile. Third, the medieval Islamic and Jewish philosophers understood Plato in light of the revealed law. Platonism was hence modified with regard to the new reality of revelation. Thus, medieval Islamic and Jewish philosophy suggests a particular interpretation of Platonic political philosophy, which not only places the *Nomoi* before the *Politeia* but also understands the *Nomoi* by way of its medieval reinterpretation and modification. Hence, the project of *Philosophy and Law* was also a genealogical effort to uncover why the political tradition of Plato's *Nomoi* had been lost to modernity. It had been overwritten by Christian natural law; the modern opposition to Christian natural law, then, had caused the abandonment of the law altogether.

One need not subscribe to this genealogy in detail to see that the argument is primarily a *historical* one. In the course of this historical argument, Strauss spelled out a *systematic* argument on the place of prophetology in the division of philosophy, explaining the relocation of medieval prophetology from psychology to politics. The *political* argument of *Philosophy and Law* can only be understood on the basis of the historical *and* the systematic argument. Direct political interpretations of Strauss's book evade both the historical and the systematic argument, and hence they inevitably misconstrue the political argument. To come to a better understanding of Strauss's political perspective, we must study the course of the fifth part of the first chapter. To do so, we must first study the third chapter. This highly exegetic chapter is difficult to comprehend for nonmedievalists. But many of the remote details are important with regard to Strauss's philosophical and political thesis. We must understand the scholarly theses of the third chapter to see more precisely the purpose of the condensed version in the fifth part of the first chapter. Only then can we hope to be able to understand the book as a book.

The Scholarly Argument (chapter 3)

The third chapter is, again, divided into five parts or subchapters. After a brief introduction and overview in the first part, the second part starts with a clarification of the term *medieval religious Enlightenment,* as opposed to the modern Enlightenment. As Strauss explained, Maimonides and his Islamic predecessors were precisely *not* Enlighteners in the modern sense because they maintained "the *esoteric* character of philosophy." This esoteric character was due to the prevailing idea of the theoretical life, combined by the medievals with the assumption of revelation. They sought to protect philosophy from the nonphilosophers. The modern Enlightenment, in contrast, was "exoteric": its philosophical teachings were directed toward the outside, and they "propagated" their teachings to spread light and educate the multitude. Strauss used the esoteric/exoteric distinction in a remarkably different way here (medieval philosophy is esoteric, whereas modern philosophy is exoteric) than in *Persecution and the Art of Writing* (medieval philosophy is esoteric and hence uses exoteric writing to protect its esoteric truth, whereas modern philosophy abandoned both). This version of medieval "esotericism" merely restates a matter of course: The medievals were necessarily "esoteric" because they were not moderns, which is to say, they did not seek to educate the multitude.[122]

The statement on esotericism serves a clear purpose in this specific textual situation: It prepares for a better understanding of the character and the end of revelation in its relationship to philosophy. As Strauss explained: "Maimonides's position . . . maintains the Greek ideal of the life of *theory,* as classically explicated by Aristotle at the end of the *Nicomachean Ethics,* on the assumption of the *revelation.*"[123]

Under this condition, Maimonides faced the paradox that revelation is binding *and* that man's highest pursuit is to live the life of theory. To combine these two allegiances, he argued that the highest end of revelation consists in leading men to philosophizing, in education toward the theoretical life. Strauss cited this thesis on the highest end of revelation as the ultimate justification of why philosophizing is authorized and commanded by the law, and he suggested that this legal commandment constitutes the freedom of philosophy to interpret the law: "Philosophy, *free on the basis of this authorization,* takes for its subject matter all that is. Thus the revelation itself, like all that is, becomes its subject matter. It is in prophetology that the revelation, as the *law* given by God through a *prophet,* becomes a subject matter of philosophy."[124]

This tersely written third section of the second part repeats the problem of how exactly the legal foundation of philosophy and the philosophic foundation of the law coincide or meet. The "dialectical" explanation in the third part of the first chapter was not entirely satisfying. Strauss needed to locate the meeting point in a more precise understanding of revelation. The crucial issue was the notion of prophecy, that is, the means through which God carries out the act of revelation. Strauss's initial concern here was to reinterpret the revelation as a *natural* fact, not as a miraculous, divinatory act. Since God entrusts the prophet with carrying out the deed, revelation becomes a *human* matter, and hence the philosophers are free to explain prophecy from the nature of man. In a second step, Strauss argued that this explanation of prophecy was presupposed—with a minor modification—by Maimonides because he was influenced by the *falâsifa*. These Islamic Aristotelians taught that the prophet is a suitably endowed and prepared man who possesses the perfect intellect, morals, and imaginative faculty. As Strauss explained, these conditions are necessary if the end of prophecy is the perfection of man through the life of theory. Prophecy presupposes the perfection of the intellect, and therefore the prophet "must at least be *also* a philosopher."[125]

In a third step, Strauss described the essential difference between prophet and philosopher, and here the esoteric presupposition of medieval philosophy comes into play: whereas revelation is addressed to all, the theoretical life is suitable only for the few. The truth of revelation must therefore be communicated to the multitude in accordance with their level of comprehension. It must be communicated in a figurative way. In addition to a perfect intellect, then, the prophet must also possess a perfect imagination.[126] The prophet must be *also* a philosopher, but he must be *more* than a philosopher. His perfect imagination safeguards his unconditional superiority over the philosopher.[127] In the further course of the second part of the third chapter, Strauss argued that this understanding is inevitable despite the critique of imagination throughout the *Guide,* and he described the "rank-ordering of men" according to Maimonidean prophetology. Following this description, there is a crucial difference between prophet and philosopher *and* between the highest prophet Moses and the other prophets. The highest type of prophet has prophecy at his disposal at any time, receives the prophecy calmly and steadily, and is morally perfect.[128]

The third part of the third chapter outlines why this interpretation of Maimonidean prophetology is insufficient and must be supplemented by a different strand. The missing link is that, beyond its function in the figurative representation of theoretical insights, prophecy also has the purpose of knowing the future by way of imagination. It is only at this point, and in order to elucidate the relationship between these two different purposes of prophecy, that Strauss turned to a comparison between the prophetologies of Maimonides and the *falâsifa,* especially Alfarabi and Avicenna. He discussed some minor differences at length (particularly with regard to miracles) only to emphasize the fundamental agreement.[129] Speaking in terms of Alfarabi's doctrine, the two fundamentally different activities involved in prophecy—the figurative representation of theoretical insights and knowledge of the future—represent the prophet's possession of theoretical and practical knowledge. Prophetic knowledge of the future pertains to the practical intellect, represented by the imagination. Theoretical knowledge is knowledge of those intelligibles whose sensible representation is reserved to prophecy. In itself, theoretical knowledge is not concerned with the task of representation for the multitude but only with the prior intellectual apprehension. "Prophecy is therefore a union of theoretical and practical perfection (and also a heightening of each of these perfections beyond the measure attainable by non-prophets)."[130]

This basic course of the argument on Maimonides's prophetology in the second and third part of the third chapter does not yet clarify the purpose of Strauss's detailed analyses, but it is indispensible in order to understand the fourth part. In this long and highly condensed part, Strauss argued for a political interpretation of medieval prophetology and presented the historical thesis that, in political matters, the medieval Islamic and Jewish Aristotelians were covert Platonists. Even as the book may not have a clear center, this part—introducing Strauss's all-time favorite Avicenna quote—leads into the heart of *Philosophy and Law.*

Strauss started again from prophecy as the coming together of theoretical and practical knowledge, of intellect and imagination. The sole reliance on the intellect is appropriate for the philosopher, whereas the sole reliance on the imagination turns man into a politician, veridian dreamer, soothsayer, or sorcerer. If the prophet combines both faculties—so argued Strauss—he is a philosopher, statesman, seer, and (possibly) miracle worker in one. At the same time, the question arises as to whether these different functions are equivalent or whether there is a difference in rank between them: "Is mantics or politics the supreme function of the prophet?"[131] Strauss had occasionally downplayed the mantic function of prophecy, and he retained the prophet's ability to work miracles mostly for systematic purposes. The supreme function of prophecy needed to be political, and only this political function would explain the purpose and the final end of prophecy: "Why does the human race depend on prophets?"[132]

Maimonides's answer as channeled in a chain of syllogisms by Strauss can be summarized as follows: Men need a governor to regulate their affairs, in particular a legislator (as opposed to the ruler); legislation can be directed toward the bodily or the spiritual perfection of man; the specific perfection of man is spiritual perfection and, more precisely, the perfection of the intellect; the law directed to the specific perfection of man is a divine law, proclaimed by the prophet. The prophet proclaims a law directed to the specific perfection of man; but the purpose of law is to make living together possible; therefore, the prophet is the founder of a society directed to the specific perfection of man. He is the founder of the perfect society. To be able to found the perfect society, the Maimonidean prophet cannot be a philosopher only: he must be philosopher, statesman, and seer (and possibly miracle worker) in one, and not only a philosopher.

In a next step, Strauss sought to prove his thesis that the purpose of prophecy is political. We must be careful not to misconstrue this assertion, which has sometimes been understood as a politicization of medieval philosophy. As should be noted, Strauss built his argument on a parallel in the teachings of Maimonides and Avicenna[133] and added a quote from Avicenna's *On the Parts of the Sciences* on the place of prophecy in the division of the sciences. This quote was none other than his ground-breaking discovery in the Prussian State Library around 1929 that he later singled out as *the* cause for a fundamental reorientation.[134] As he recalled in a late autobiographical statement:

> One day, when reading in a Latin translation Avicenna's treatise *On the Division of Sciences*, I came across this sentence (I quote from memory): the standard work on prophecy and revelation is Plato's *Laws*. Then I began to begin to understand Maimonides's prophetology and eventually, I believe, the whole *Guide of the Perplexed*.[135]

Strauss also quoted the phrase in a number of other writings,[136] and used it as a motto for his late *Nomoi* commentary, *The Argument and the Action of Plato's Laws*: "[T]he treatment of prophecy and the Divine Law is contained in . . . the *Laws*."[137] The long version in *Philosophy and Law* runs as follows:

> Of this, what has to do with kingship is contained in the book of Plato and of Aristotle on the state, and what has to do with *prophecy* and the *religious law* is contained in both of their books on the *laws* . . . this part of practical philosophy (viz. politics) has as its subject matter the existence of prophecy and the dependence of the human race, for its existence, stability, and propagation, on the religious law. Politics deals both with all the religious laws collectively and with the specific characters of the individual religious laws by nation and epoch; it deals with the difference between divine prophecy and all invalid pretensions.[138]

As mentioned before, Strauss used the quote as supplementary evidence for his thesis on the political purpose of prophecy. He started from the place of prophetology in the division of the sciences. If prophecy and the law are treated as a part of practical philosophy rather than psychology, then the political purpose overrides the mantic purpose. This systematic argument alone is not particularly strong, especially because Strauss could not explain away the fact that prophecy is *also* treated in psychology.[139] The political interpretation of prophecy found much stronger support in the historical thesis founded upon the same Avicenna quote. In Strauss's construction, this quote contains a (philologically contentious) reference to Plato and Aristotle, followed by the proposition, "What has to do with *prophecy* and the *religious law* is contained in both of their books on the *laws*."[140] How did Strauss get from there to the short version, quoted from memory in 1970, that "the standard work on prophecy and revelation is Plato's *Laws*"? And why did he choose this short version as a motto for his late *Nomoi* commentary? In other words: What was so important about it?

The purpose of the quote is identical with the main scholarly thesis of the third chapter. Strauss sought to create a link between medieval prophetology and Plato's *Nomoi*: "*The prophet is the founder of the ideal state*. The classical model of the ideal state is the *Platonic* state. . . . The prophet is the founder of the Platonic state; the prophet carried out what Plato called for."[141] The double outcome of this link was a philosophical rediscovery of medieval prophetology by way of its political interpretation *and* a new understanding of Plato's *Nomoi* as the principal text of political philosophy.[142] This intricate connection ultimately seemed to allow for a radical harmonization of philosophy and revelation that would surpass all modern syntheses.

To maintain this fragile link between Plato and the prophets, Strauss needed to remove a few obstacles. The prime obstacle was Aristotle, who was mentioned in the quote together with Plato. Strauss briefly mentioned that Avicenna could have known Aristotle's *Politics* only by name, because it had never been translated into Arabic.[143] In his subsequent writings on medieval Islamic and Jewish philosophy, Strauss further generalized the matter of translations to emphasize the fundamental characteristics of Islamic and Jewish medieval thought as opposed to Christian scholasticism.[144] In short: the medieval Islamic and Jewish philosophers were Aristotelians in all respects but the political (and hence also in their prophetology). Because they could not read Aristotle's *Politics*, they resorted to Plato instead.

Another obstacle is the apparent oscillation in Strauss's references to Plato between the *Nomoi*, the *Politeia*, or both combined. The internal difference between the books was the topic, not only of many later writings,[145] but also of the end of the first chapter, where Strauss strongly emphasized the *Nomoi* against the preponderance of the *Politeia*. The Platonic argument of the third chapter is largely built upon a combination of both writings—the Platonic state, the philosopher-king, and the Platonic laws provide the philosophical framework in which the medieval Islamic and Jewish philosophers understood prophecy, supplemented by the recognition of the fact of revelation.[146]

A third obstacle, their precise relationship to the position of Plato, is the topic of the fifth and last part of the third chapter. "They understand [*rezipieren*] Platonic politics from an un-Platonic premise—the premise of the revelation."[147] Hence, they took for granted a binding, divine law proclaimed by a prophet. Paradoxically, this law authorized them to philosophize, and philosophy as authorized by the law makes the law a topic among others. The philosophers answer the question now posed by the law within the Platonic horizon.

At last, the Platonic framework was modified to account for the fact of revelation, and the primordial and binding character of revelation even implied the "*critique* of Plato."[148] This modification ultimately confirms that *Philosophy and Law* cannot be understood in terms of hard "exotericism," which would render any serious modification of philosophy through revelation impossible or unnecessary. After all, the exotericism thesis is based on the understanding that the medieval philosophers were philosophers only, whereas their commitment to the revelation was merely conventional. Strauss's point cannot be reconciled with this understanding: "What Plato *called* for—that philosophy stand under a higher court, under the state, under the *law*—is *fulfilled* in the age of the belief in revelation. . . . The Platonism of these philosophers is given with their *situation,* with their standing in fact under the law. Since they stand in fact under the law, they admittedly no longer need, like Plato, to *seek* the law, the state, to *inquire* into it: the binding and absolutely perfect regimen of human life is *given* to them by a prophet. Hence they are, as authorized by the law, free to philosophize in Aristotelian freedom: they can *therefore* aristotelize."[149]

Strauss embedded these closing theses in a brief discussion of Hermann Cohen, who had maintained that Maimonides was "in deeper harmony with Plato than with Aristotle."[150] At first this discussion seems little relevant for understanding the scholarly argument of the third chapter, like a mere allusion to the scholarly context of his lecture "Cohen and Maimonides" (1931). Here, Cohen was called upon "to open up for us the access to Rambam."[151] In other words, Cohen was indispensible both as a guide into the *Guide of the Perplexed* and a continuous reference point for a new, post-Cohenian interpretation of Maimonides. Why did Strauss import this discourse into *Philosophy and Law*, and particularly into the third chapter, where Cohen seems to have no bearing on the exposition of the scholarly argument? Strauss had announced his thesis on Cohen's understanding of Maimonides as a Platonist in the last sentence of the first chapter, and he certainly found it important—but important for what?

As it turns out, this discussion is the only place in the third chapter where Strauss explicated the philosophical significance of the scholarly argument and its place in *Philosophy and Law*. This significance is located precisely at the border of Judaism and philosophy. The thesis runs as follows: "Hermann *Cohen* claimed that Maimonides, at least, was a Platonist. We adopt this claim as our own, but on the basis of a consideration which completely diverges in detail from Cohen's grounds."[152] As Strauss explained, Cohen's exposition of the link between Maimonides and Plato was "untenable in detail" and based on "a misconstruction of the historical evidence,"[153] but thereby his guiding insight remained unaffected. In Cohen's words: "All honor to the God of Aristotle; but truly he is not the God of Israel."[154]

Strauss, surprisingly, subscribed to these words without reservation. As he maintained: "For this reason a Jew as Jew cannot be an Aristotelian; for him the matter can never at any time be left at the primacy of theory; he cannot assert this primacy unconditionally and unreservedly; if he asserts it, he must restrict it in some way, so that ultimately he calls it into question through this restriction."[155] The reference to Cohen's link between Maimonides and Plato serves to prepare for a radical harmonization of philosophy and Judaism. The need for such a radical harmonization had been postulated in the introduction, but only on the basis of his historical thesis could Strauss outline how it was to be done: Judaism could not be harmonized with Aristotelianism, but on the basis of Plato's *Nomoi,* Jews were free to aristotelize, to philosophize.[156]

This historical thesis is highly important when it comes to the question of how to combine Judaism and philosophy (commonly referred to as "Jewish philosophy"). To name some of the ramifications, Jewish philosophy must turn to Plato to find the philosophical (unbelieving) foundation of the belief in revelation.[157] It must therefore turn to the medieval Islamic and Jewish Aristotelians to find a Platonic tradition that is genuinely philosophical and yet grounded in the irreducible reality of revelation. The consequence is not that philosophy must "believe" in revelation or bow to its unconditional claim to obedience. The continuous reference to revelation pushes philosophy to acknowledge its own epistemic limitation concerning the highest knowledge.

The purpose of the enigmatic Cohen reference, then, was to transpose the scholarly findings on medieval Platonism back into the problem of Judaism and philosophy, or the task of Jewish philosophy. Strauss thereby answered the question that, according to Jacob Klein, had remained open in the introduction: *Where* would Maimonidean rationalism lead?[158]

A further peculiarity of *Philosophy and Law* is that Strauss linked these programmatic lines on the relationship between Judaism and philosophy with an emphatic turn to political philosophy. Following Cohen's lead, he explained the essential difference between Plato and Aristotle with regard to their respective stances on theory, understood as the highest perfection of man: "Aristotle sets it completely free; or rather, he leaves it in its natural freedom. Plato, on the other hand, *does not permit* the philosophers . . . the life of philosophizing as an abiding in the contemplation of the truth. He 'compels' them to care for the others and to guard them, in order that the state may really be a state, a true state (*Rep.* 519–520C). . . . Even the philosopher as such stands under the state, is answerable for himself before the state; he is not simply sovereign."[159] As Strauss suggested, Plato's *demand* to place philosophy under a higher court was *fulfilled* in medieval philosophy: "With all their freedom in the pursuit of knowledge, the philosophers of this era are conscious at every moment for their answerability for the law and before the law: they justify their philosophizing before the bar of the law; they derive from the law their *authorization* to philosophize as a legal *duty* to philosophize."[160]

The responsibility of philosophy toward society has a different meaning here than in *Persecution and the Art of Writing*. This difference of meaning is in accordance with the difference in the relationship between philosophy and revelation: According to *Philosophy and Law*, philosophy acknowledges its own limitation vis-à-vis the revelation, and hence it becomes free *before* and *under* the law. According to the teaching of *Persecution and the Art of Writing*, philosophy accepts the doctrines of revelation exoterically, as an outer limitation, and hence secures its freedom *from* the law. Far from being a mere precursor of the later doctrine, then, *Philosophy and Law* provides a unique and—despite its difficult presentation—coherent solution as to the relationship between philosophy and revelation; and hence it forces us to rethink the social and political responsibility of philosophy.

Strauss's Conclusions (chapter 1, part 5)

From here we are now in a position to understand the purpose and meaning of the fifth and last part of the first chapter. It is partly a summary and complement to the third chapter, partly the *finale grande* of the Guttmann critique and the methodological discourse on the historical and systematic task of Jewish philosophy. Overall, this part presents itself as the attempt to solidify the *political* over the religio-philosophical interpretation of revelation. As Strauss argued, in Guttmann's version the truths communicated by revelation are in principle accessible also to human reason; therefore, revelation ultimately has "a merely popular pedagogical significance. The society-founding, *state-founding* meaning of revelation becomes in Guttmann a secondary end."[161] Strauss added that "this misconstruction of the leading idea of medieval philosophy follows from Guttmann's modern formulation of the question,"[162] and he emphasized once again the dependence of this formulation upon Schleiermacher's philosophy of religion. The problem of this approach was not only its modern design but also that it led to a Christian reinterpretation of Islamic and Jewish thought.[163] In other words, it misconstrued the idea of revealed law as a matter of religious consciousness and belief, whereas the original idea of the law was the foundation for the ideal state, and hence a political matter. This ideal state was the Platonic state. Hence, the prophet was the medieval reinterpretation of the Platonic philosopher-king.

But here Strauss needed to explain two last difficulties: following this Platonic interpretation, the notion of law is not the original achievement of medieval thought but only a modification of Plato's philosophy, and furthermore, it was only one topic among others in medieval philosophy. Strauss sought to turn these objections into the strongest argument for the centrality of the law. This argument comes in three parts. First, no matter whether the legal foundation of philosophy is only one teaching among others, it is *the* systematic place in medieval philosophy where the presupposition of philosophizing is clarified. Second, this place was marked by Plato—the philosophers answered a Platonic question within a Platonic framework. "Ultimately they differ from Plato only in this, though decisively in this: for them the founder of the ideal state is not a possible philosopher-king to be awaited in the future, but an actual prophet who existed in the past. That is, they modify Plato's answer in the light of the revelation that has now actually occurred."[164] Third, the law is but one topic among many because it is *given* through the revelation and must therefore not be *sought*. It is no longer questionable but must only be *understood*. And since Plato's demand has been fulfilled, it is a matter of course that medieval philosophy is not as penetrating as original Platonic political philosophy. Strauss concluded that this insight into the fundamental dependence on Plato allows for "a coherent and original interpretation" of the teachings of medieval Islamic and Jewish philosophy,[165] and such a coherent interpretation was possible only on the basis of a reconstruction of the idea of a *rational* and *divine* law.

Strauss could have ended here, but apparently he felt he needed to resume the methodological discourse once again in order to make the results more comprehensible. In a last step, therefore, he gave a long and somewhat surprising outline of the necessary direction of historical study. Stretching over more than two pages, the path he sketched in six steps led all the way from Plato's *Nomoi* to—Moses Mendelssohn.

First, the radical interpretation of the Islamic philosophers and their Jewish pupils must start with the *Nomoi,* seen under the premise that Plato here *points* to revelation. If Strauss had presented Nietzsche as the epitome of an atheistic religiosity in the first chapter, it is clear at this point that his true natural model of such a religiosity is Plato's Socrates. The course of *Philosophy of Law* therefore also marks a shift from Nietzschean nonbelief toward Socratic nonbelief, negotiating the relationship between philosophy and revelation in the force field of atheistic religiosity *before* and *after* revelation. If Nietzsche was an end point, Socrates was a new beginning.

Second, one needs to investigate the modifications of Platonic politics in Hellenistic thought, when the notion of the philosopher-king was transformed into the notion of the prophet. This intermediate step is to be understood in accordance with the interpretation of Epicureanism toward the end of the introduction. Third, one must understand the prophetology of the Islamic Aristotelians in order to be able to interpret—fourth—the prophetology of Maimonides. Here, Strauss added the task of explaining why the political orientation is less explicit in Maimonides than in the prophetology of his Islamic predecessors. As he suggested, this was due to the fact that for Maimonides, revelation also conveyed teachings that were not sufficiently reassured by reason. Fifth, one needs to study Gersonides to trace the "decay of Platonism" and the ensuing reduction of prophetology to its mantic function. Due to the radicalization of the idea of providence in Gersonides, the notion of law and the ideal state loses its meaning here. As Strauss explained the ensuing paradox of Gersonides's teaching, the Platonic ideal state needed not be established by men or by the prophets, because the existing world ruled by providence *is* already the ideal state; thereby Gersonides anticipates a modern theopolitics that seeks to limit state power in the name of providence. Sixth, from here, Mendelssohn's doctrine of revelation presents itself as the questionable endeavor to radicalize the belief in providence and restore the Platonic-medieval idea of law under this premise.[166]

Strauss could easily have continued here with Hermann Cohen as the seventh step and Julius Guttmann as the eighth and last; and the chapter does indeed close with Cohen and Guttmann. He could as well have started all over again at the beginning of the chapter. The brief discussion of Moses Mendelssohn only marks the point where the Jewish law enters into the philosophical discourse of modernity. Hence, the narrative on the flight of the Jewish notion of law and its hypermodern restoration has come full circle here. The "critical dissection"[167] of Guttmann's critique of religion has been a necessary precondition of this endeavor.

9

A Complex Afterlife

Julius Guttmann, the "Jewish Thomism" Affair, and the Turn to Exotericism

Building a Straw Man: Guttmann's Reply

There must have been something deeply disturbing in Strauss's words for Guttmann, despite his friendly response to the critique and his unwavering support for its publication. He shared this type of response with others who were scrutinized in Strauss's early works, most notably, Martin Buber and Carl Schmitt. Just like Schmitt, Guttmann was extraordinarily open to the challenge posed to him. And just as Schmitt had reportedly ventured that Strauss could see through him like an X-ray,[1] the critique of *Die Philosophie des Judentums* resonated deeply in Guttmann, so much so that he sought to modify his position in some respect. Initially, he wrote several letters to Strauss to defend his position, and the two henceforth maintained a correspondence until 1949. He also composed a review article on *Philosophy and Law*, which was found incomplete among his unpublished works after his death in 1950.[2] It was eventually published with the title "Philosophie der Religion oder Philosophie des Gesetzes?" in 1974. Moreover, Strauss made a brief appearance in the revised Hebrew edition (*Ha filosofia shel ha-yahadut*, posthumously published 1951), on which the English translation is based. These sources suggest that Guttmann was occupied with Strauss's critique virtually until his death.[3]

This occupation stands in sharp contrast to Strauss, who never entered into a debate with Guttmann on *Philosophy and Law* to defend his critique. In his letters from 1934–35 he repeatedly assured Guttmann that he could not reply to his remarks at the present.[4] This type of response is unusual for Strauss, who did not hesitate to openly state his case in the correspondences with Krüger, Scholem, or Kojève. Even in the respective years of 1934 and 1935—a time of restless work and disquiet for Strauss—he found the time for elaborate letters from England, but he never did so when it came to Guttmann. This is unfortunate for the fact that a thorough explanation of *Philosophie und Gesetz* to Guttmann would have made an excellent guide to the premises of the book for today's readers. Such an explanation may not be entirely reliable or authoritative, but it would certainly be helpful. What caused Strauss to be silent?

There is little reason to assume that he abstained from a debate so as not to reveal to Guttmann his new insights on the "exoteric" Maimonides. *If* he had already arrived at these insights, he could have easily concealed them in a statement on the matter. To use the exotericism model as an explanation for Strauss's silence, then, is self-refuting. Moreover, Strauss did explain his exotericism thesis on Maimonides and Xenophon to Guttmann in a letter from May 20, 1949.[5]

A partial explanation is that Guttmann's objections were of little importance for Strauss. This scenario is not refuted by a remark on Guttmann in a letter to Scholem: "I am of the opinion that G.'s critique is still highly relevant."[6] The remark testifies to Strauss's deep respect for Guttmann, and yet the obvious question is: relevant for what? To quote from an earlier letter to Guttmann—which had to do with the delay in the publication of his Spinoza book—a debate on *Philosophy and Law* no longer provided any "factual gains" (*sachliche Ertrag*) for him: it did no longer yield any new insights on the subject matter of his studies.[7] It is also doubtful whether Strauss considered Guttmann a relevant interlocutor in the first place. We may put greater trust in the judgment of Jacob Klein, who suggested that Guttmann would not understand the critique anyway.[8]

Guttmann's unfinished reply to *Philosophy and Law* shows the great effort he made to understand the project. It is thorough and guided by the will to enter into a serious debate on the matter. Written in the spirit of a nineteenth-century scholar attempting to fend off a modernist attack, it lacks both the bitterness over Strauss's radicalism and the pretension of superiority over his former employee. Overall, it is written in the spirit of a sober and fair scholarly argument, although not without irony and polemical edge. And yet its scope is limited, and Guttmann faced serious problems in his reply, up to the point where he could defend his philosophical and scholarly project only by way of extraordinarily *rhetorical* arguments. No one else has voiced these rhetorical arguments with greater honesty and scholarly elegance than Guttmann. It is all the more necessary to see their flaws and their characteristic misrepresentations of Strauss's position, because they point to some of the enduring problems in the interpretation of *Philosophy and Law*. In other words: more than Schmitt had ever done, Guttmann "accepted Strauss's challenge,"[9] but the crucial question is how he sought to master it, and whether he did master it.

There is a tendency among Strauss scholars to exaggerate the scope and magnitude of Guttmann's counterarguments, as if they provided the long-awaited key to Strauss's impenetrable text.[10] In reality, a philosophical defense of *Philosophy and Law* has nothing to fear from Guttmann's critique. It is nevertheless valuable to trace some of the misunderstandings of *Philosophy and Law* that persist until today. Caught between attraction and repulsion, Guttmann's reply is exemplary for the difficult legacy of *Philosophy and Law*. Even beyond its direct impact on a number of current Strauss scholars, it prefigures many of the persistent difficulties of interpretation and the corresponding cover-up strategies. To begin with, apart from early reviews, all commentaries on *Philosophy and Law* were written on the premise that Strauss no longer stood where he had stood in 1935. No matter the extent to which commentators were familiar with Strauss's subsequent development, they knew that he had moved away from the position of *Philosophy and Law*. Hence, they sought to find a clue to the book in his later writings, particularly in *Persecution and the Art of Writing*. In one way or another, and without knowing of it, they all followed the path of Guttmann's unpublished reply.

Guttmann wrote on the condition that his remarks would be preliminary until Strauss would clarify his position on exotericism. He had learned from Paul Kraus that Strauss had changed his position after *Philosophy and Law*,[11] but he did not know where exactly Strauss stood. As we have seen, he inevitably ran into the problem of whether *Philosophy and Law* was a precursor of the "exoteric" Strauss. But where did Strauss stand in 1935? On this point Guttmann was unable to follow the argument of the book.

Guttmann's representation of Strauss's position is based on three characteristic fallacies of interpretation, which are still present in current Strauss scholarship. First, scholars attempt to understand *Philosophy and Law* as an early indication of the "exoteric" Strauss,[12] but Strauss's position in the book is anti-exoteric. Second, they seek to understand Strauss's thesis on the law in medieval Jewish philosophy in light of the closing pages of the introduction, so as to evade the historical argument; and third, they appeal to the author's personal motivations to evade the philosophical argument.[13] On this basis, at last, Guttmann misrepresented Strauss's political philosophy as an all-out politicization of philosophy.

Guttmann reframed Strauss's interpretation of Islamic and Jewish philosophy in a three-step argument. First, he explicated Strauss's starting point that "the medieval thinkers understand revelation as the revelation of a law, namely, a political law." Second, he declared this to be common knowledge, but third, he depicted the radical consequence of the claim allegedly made by Strauss "that the medieval understanding of revelation can only be comprehended by way of the political problem, and that the whole content of revelation is to be subjected to this viewpoint."[14] As Guttmann pointed out, the thesis on the primacy of law stood in sharp opposition to the dominant viewpoint, according to which the main purpose of revelation in medieval prophecy was the communication of metaphysical truths. He understood well that Strauss did not altogether refute this viewpoint but merely sought to provide it with a radical political foundation; but in the course of the text he more and more shifted toward the claim that Strauss sought to place "the whole content of revelation under the idea of law."[15]

This claim is a critical junction in Guttmann's reply. Henceforth, he switched between two different strategies. One was to argue that the primacy of law in medieval philosophy was merely a matter of course, the other was to reframe it as an all-out politicization. And whereas the first served to downplay Strauss's interpretation, the point of the second was to question his motives. Overall, the second strategy found greater resonance in the further course of the text. From the allegation of an undue politicization of medieval philosophy, Guttmann was led to seek for help in the introduction and appeal to Strauss's personal motivations: "The philosophical convictions upon which this judgment is based are those of existential philosophy. From here, the human meaning of metaphysics becomes its actual meaning, and the revelation can be brought to an original understanding only as a total order of human life."[16] Guttmann sought help in particular from the closing pages of Strauss's introduction, claiming that the appeal to the law expressed his existential longing for irrational authority. Medieval rationalism would not provide him with anything beyond the proof "that man is in need of the law," because his longing for "authoritarian guidance of life" can only be satisfied by the strict authority of revelation.[17]

Commentators are in disagreement whether the claim is a bit over the top and should not be taken seriously, or whether it is a faithful representation of Strauss's radical inclinations. But as a matter of fact, it is fundamentally flawed, and Guttmann had departed the discourse of scholarly argument here. Alas, it was a cornerstone of his defense against Strauss. Guttmann used this defense both in his counterreview and in *Philosophies of Judaism*, providing it with the authority of a sober scholarly argument. It is all the more important to note that this defense rests on a straw man argument. Another strategy was to argue that Strauss had not consulted *all* medieval philosophers—a variation on the "infinite variety" mother argument of relativism. Guttmann coupled this argument with the absolutistic claim that Strauss had therefore missed *the* "ultimate" purpose of prophecy: "The ultimate and essential purpose of human existence, what makes man a man, is beyond the world of community and completely beyond the political community and cannot be understood from there."[18]

At this point Guttmann revealed his own proclivity toward strong binary concepts, such as the contrast between a world of politics and a world of metaphysical truth (which is *completely beyond* politics). In his *Philosophies of Judaism*, he wrote in a comment on Strauss: "Maimonides did not regard the political law as the sole purpose of divine revelation."[19] The exaggerated argument (the *sole* purpose) is another straw man, for Strauss had not made this claim, and he did not use these binary concepts. He argued for a systematic relocation of the philosophical problem of revelation from metaphysics to politics, for he held that the political problem would bring the foundation of medieval philosophy to the light. But this relocation did not entail a radical alternative between politics and metaphysics, it was solely about the question of how to begin:

> The interpretation of medieval Jewish philosophy beginning from Platonic politics . . . does not have to lose sight of the metaphysical problems that stand in the foreground for the medieval philosophers themselves. And in this procedure . . . actually offers the only guarantee of understanding their proper, that is their human, meaning. If, on the other hand, one begins from the metaphysical problems, one misses . . . the political problem, in which is concealed nothing less than the foundation of philosophy, the philosophic elucidation of the presupposition of philosophizing.[20]

Starting from the political problem did not invalidate the metaphysical problems altogether, it rather served to put them in perspective. This is also confirmed by the fact that Strauss explicitly posed the problem of prophecy with regard to the difference "from all that is merely political."[21]

In the last resort, Guttmann's strategy of framing Strauss as a proponent of radical politicization driven by a need for "authoritarian guidance" is a tit-for-tat response to the cat and mouse game he had been played with. But his hermeneutic and philosophical strategies were far more limited in comparison. His reply is based on a combination of straw man arguments. The last straw man is the conclusion that Strauss could not expect any help from medieval rationalism if he could only prove that man is in need of a law.[22] If Strauss's position were really as weak as it appears in Guttmann's reply, then the entire turn to political philosophy would amount to a mere politicization of philosophy. But in what sense is the philosopher "in need of the law"?[23] What is the reason why "man, as a political being, can live only under a law"?[24] If properly supplied with the qualification "as a political being," the claim is little contentious and hardly qualifies as a defense of authoritarian rule. According to the doctrine of *Philosophy and Law*, the law must be directed toward the specific perfection of man, and ultimately toward the perfect society, or the ideal state.[25] Strauss further balanced this view by maintaining that this society exists only in speech, thereby distinguishing his recovery of the law from all political programs. It is difficult to imagine a less "authoritarian" political explanation of the medieval Islamic and Jewish notion of law.

Guttmann sought to place the notion of law in medieval philosophy within the setting of Strauss's introduction. This was part of his strategy to explain it as a matter of existential psychology. With his imputation of a "need for authoritarian guidance of life,"[26] he became a major reference for those contemporary readers who seek to cast Strauss's notion of law as a quest for an authoritarian theopolitical order. Guttmann went even further than most contemporary readers by deducing this quest out of an existential "need," thereby leading almost to the point of ridicule against Strauss. Once he had missed the systematic argument on the law in medieval philosophy, he could not make sense of the historical argument any other way than by appealing to Strauss's personal motives. But the strategy to see the reason for a theoretical problem in the personal motives of the author is the epitome of a hermeneutic weakness. Guttmann misunderstood the "need for a law" because he could not account for the factuality of law.

In November 1972 Strauss wrote to Scholem "that Guttmann in a manner retracted his critique in the Hebrew (or English) translation of his history of philosophy in Judaism; he seems to have realized that I am somewhat more flexible or slippery than he originally thought."[27] One can easily follow from the English translation what Strauss had in mind. The claim is only partly correct, but it leads in the right direction: at one point Guttmann basically conceded everything to Strauss's interpretation, but then he immediately built up his straw man again to save his own scholarly project:

> In his concept of the Torah, Maimonides followed the doctrines of the Islamic Aristotelians concerning the nature of prophecy. The purpose of the prophetic mission was legislation, the establishment of political laws. This theory is based on the view that man can live only in society, and that life in society requires laws which determine relationships between man and man. According to Maimonides, however, a perfect legislation requires prophetic inspiration. Legislation thus becomes the main function of the prophet, and all his other activities are subordinate to this. The prophet here fulfills the task which Plato had assigned to the philosopher, and the Islamic philosophers were, in fact, very much indebted to Plato's ideas concerning the foundation of the ideal state by philosophers. This conception of prophecy gained support from a peculiar characteristic shared by Islam and Judaism; both contained a divine law, which included political law as well. Maimonides, too, adopted this doctrine. The purpose of the Torah is to order social life, and both its political laws and moral commandments are directed to this end, educating the individual and making him fit to live with the rest of society.[28]

Guttmann's statement explicates the standpoint of *Philosophy and Law* in a clear, downright orthodox fashion. This marks a significant advancement from his unfinished reply as far as his ongoing quarrel with Strauss's book is concerned, but it is far from clear why he chose to incorporate it into the book. For, immediately following this passage, Guttmann hastened—without any mediating formula or even a new paragraph—to restate his argument on the metaphysical purpose of revelation, followed by a long footnote against Strauss. As he claimed:

> It seems to me incorrect to interpret the basic meaning of divine revelation, especially in regard to Maimonides, to be the disclosure of political laws and ordinances. Even less can I agree with

Strauss' hypothesis that one must set the political interpretation of prophecy as the foundation stone for the understanding of the whole of medieval philosophy. . . . [T]he relation of reason to revelation also cannot be understood from this "political" viewpoint.[29]

Needless to say, the two positions are entirely irreconcilable. More than his unfinished reply did, *Philosophies of Judaism* shows how Guttmann was caught between attraction and repulsion, unable to come to terms with the meaning and the purpose of Strauss's political interpretation of medieval prophetology. His reaction unwillingly confirms Strauss's initial thesis on the "crux" of philosophy of culture:[30] the "crux" of Guttmann's religio-philosophical approach indicated not a difficult choice but a problem that could not be solved.

Guttmann had seen a small chance to save his philosophico-historical project by discrediting Strauss's interpretation, just as Strauss had formulated his own project by discrediting Guttmann's interpretation. Even as Guttmann's argumentative and rhetorical means seem too limited to decisively challenge Strauss, his reply is built on similar epistemic premises of radical interpretation, based on an act of the will. This type of thought is postfoundational: it is no longer founded on a stable ontological order, corresponding to a stable and finite set of signs to describe this order. Such thought cannot account for the veracity of its own premises, it can only perform them. In particular, it must seek to replace or invalidate another interpretation. Such thought must inevitably be radical, although its presentation must seek to be moderate. In this sense, both Strauss and Guttmann are proponents of radical interpretation, although it is more openly visible in Strauss, whereas it is rather concealed in Guttmann.

Guttmann's interpretation feeds upon the authority of modern Jewish scholarship as professed by the *Wissenschaft des Judentums*, against which Strauss's interpretation was directed in the first place. But the *Wissenschaft des Judentums* approach could no longer provide a stable standard of timeless scholarship, as its proponents had envisioned it would. It rested on an act of the will, too—the will to provide Judaism with a proper burial. This burial was conceived as a prerequisite for bringing to light the cultural value of Judaism, so that the Jews would be accepted into Western European societies. After the historical collapse of this program, any defense of the corresponding scholarly project inevitably became postfoundational and radical—it could only seek to discredit those who openly sought to do away with the foundation of the *Wissenschaft des Judentums* when this foundation had ceased to provide a stable standard of scholarship. Guttmann's reply is a first-rate document of these historical shifts, and this is due both to his extraordinary openness to the challenge of *Philosophy and Law* and to the limitations of his critique. But these limitations do not make *Philosophy and Law* invulnerable to criticism. Strauss ran into severe problems, too, and he saw these problems more clearly than most of his critics.

"Jewish Thomism"

In June 1952, two years after the death of Guttmann, Scholem reported to Strauss that the incomplete manuscript of Guttmann's reply had been found among his papers.[31] Strauss's reply, written on June 22, 1952, is extraordinarily significant because it connects three seemingly unrelated aspects that are emblematic for the complex afterlife of *Philosophy and Law*. The statement must be read in full to see the intricate connection:

> I knew from Guttmann himself about the reply he had begun. He wrote me several years ago (it may be 8–10 years already) that he had ceased to work on the reply because I had given up the standpoint I had held in *Philosophie und Gesetz*. That is correct insofar as I publicly agreed to G.'s thesis about the identity of reason and revelation in the M.A., but my earlier rejection is "sublated" in my current agreement: I have moved, so to speak, contrary to G.'s moderate rationalism, on the path via a Jewish Thomism to radical "rationalism," am now therefore on the right wing (for the right is truth, the left is *sinister,* as no one knows better than you), whereas I stood on the left wing in *Philosophie und Gesetz*: Guttmann ever in the middle. (I am *now* attempting to reach a moderate "rationalism," but one that, I am afraid, would be even less acceptable to G. than my two earlier positions.) Be that as it may, I am of the opinion that G.'s critique is still highly relevant.[32]

The quote interlinks a late restatement on Guttmann, the much-quoted "Jewish Thomism" phrase, and a retrospective view on the genesis of his exotericism thesis. Furthermore, it provides this constellation with a rather unusual political attribution. The catchphrase in the quote is certainly

"Jewish Thomism," used as a retrospective characterization of *Philosophy and Law*. The phrase alone has retained a vivid afterlife in Strauss scholarship.[33] But it is both narrower in its specific meaning and more important for the subsequent development of Strauss's philosophy than has been hitherto acknowledged. This can be traced from a number of subsequent statements—most notably in his *Persecution and the Art of Writing* and the 1961 introduction to Alexander Altmann—but also from a peculiar strand in late medieval Maimonideanism. Apparently without any knowledge of Strauss, the term *Jewish Thomism* has been coined again in 1976 by Josef (Giuseppe) Sermoneta to describe the position of Italian Jewish Thomists, namely Hillel ben Samuel (Hillel of Verona, ca. 1220–1295) and Judah Romano (1280–1325), who interpreted the *Guide* without subscribing to the Averroist viewpoint of their predominantly French contemporaries. They were therereby influenced by Thomas Aquinas.[34]

Strauss knew Hillel ben Samuel at least from Isaac Husik's *History of Mediaeval Jewish Philosophy*, and his distinction between prophet, philosopher, and statesman/magician in the *Guide* was apparently prefigured by Hillel.[35] The overall problem to which the "Jewish Thomism" phrase responds, then, is the understanding of Maimonides's philosophy in its relationship to Christianity—a topic that virtually ran through *Philosophy and Law* but remained unresolved for Strauss in one decisive respect. The passage in *Philosophy and Law* where the possibility of a "Jewish Thomism" arose is as follows:

> Maimonides undoubtedly establishes an essential excess of revealed truth over rational truth. . . . Hence Guttmann's assertion that the identity of the revealed truth with the rational truth is the prevailing doctrine in medieval Jewish philosophy does not accord with the facts.[36]

Later, Strauss saw the open flank in this interpretation. It was the "excess of revealed truth over rational truth" that opened up the possibility of understanding Maimonides along the lines of Thomas Aquinas. After all, this excess of revelation over reason was the epitome of Thomas's teaching: According to Thomas Aquinas, "It was necessary for the salvation of man that certain truths which exceed human reason should be made known to him by divine revelation" (*Summa Theologica*, question 1, article 1).

Furthermore, if Maimonides was understood along these lines, then he could also be viewed as a Jewish equivalent of Thomas Aquinas. He would then be the key authority for Judaism in the same way Thomas Aquinas was the key authority for Christianity.[37] Strauss's rejection of this idea in *Persecution and the Art of Writing* is a direct response to the thesis of *Philosophy and Law*, adopted by Strauss from Hermann Cohen, that Maimonides is the "'classic of rationalism' in Judaism," "the true natural model, the standard [of rationalism] to be carefully protected from any distortion."[38] In hindsight, this program seemed to turn Maimonides into a Jewish scholastic—a keeper of the Jewish faith in revelation against the claims of philosophy, and a proponent of philosophy as the handmaiden of theology. This proximity was most pertinently addressed in another statement connecting Guttmann, Maimonides, and Thomas Aquinas, namely, in Strauss's 1961 spoken introduction for Alexander Altmann:

> Julius Guttmann had suggested roughly the following interpretation, if not of Jewish medieval philosophy as a whole, at least of the leading figure, Maimonides, and some others. Namely, that according to this man, the teachings of revelation are fundamentally identical with the teachings of reason. Guttmann of course supplied this with many qualifications, but in the main this was his assertion. I think that Professor Altmann is satisfied that this is an untenable position. The immediate consequence which one could draw from this change of outlook would be to say that these great Jewish thinkers, say especially Maimonides, is a Jewish equivalence of Thomas Aquinas: there is an *excess* of revelation beyond the teaching of reason. But here again I believe that Professor Altmann is distinguished from quite a few other scholars in the field [by the fact] that he does not take this view, for the simple reason that Maimonides cannot be the Jewish Aquinas, that is, Jewish scholasticism cannot be Christian scholasticism, because Judaism is not Christianity. The essential difference between Judaism and Christianity will lead to the consequence that there is an essential difference also—if even formally—between their theologies.[39]

Coupled with the reference to Guttmann, the statement on the essential difference between Judaism and Christianity serves a clear purpose. Even in its utmost simplification, the notion that "Maimonides cannot be the Jewish Aquinas, that is, Jewish scholasticism cannot be Christian scholasticism, because Judaism is not Christianity" is a late rebuke of his own thesis in *Philosophy and Law*. Most notably, the description fits his own earlier polemics against Guttmann much better than Guttmann's position itself. Regardless of whether the thesis on the excess of revelation over reason was viable, it seemed to put Maimonides in too close a proximity to Christian scholasticism. And no matter how hard Strauss had sought to evade the scholastic interpretation of Maimonides, this proximity seemed to suggest that he had failed in a decisive respect.

We must be careful to note that this failure was Strauss's own perception, and there may be debate on whether the problem was as severe as Strauss thought. In particular, the excess of revelation over reason—and hence the insufficiency of human reason—did not necessarily amount to a covert Christian interpretation of reason and revelation. But Strauss did make this link in his later thought. As should be added, it had no direct impact on the public afterlife of *Philosophy and Law*, but it was extremely important for Strauss's theoretical construction of the reason/revelation divide, and hence for the inner history of his work after 1935. The traces in his subsequent works showing the growing discontent with his interpretation of Maimonides in *Philosophy and Law* have a clear focus here, and the 1952 statement on "Jewish Thomism" seems to connect the various dots most visibly.

There are a few other aspects in the quote that need to be addressed to arrive at a satisfying interpretation. The commitment "to 'radical' rationalism" refers to Strauss's position on medieval Jewish philosophy as it had developed in the meantime. Most importantly, he had come to present Maimonides as the most radical Jewish proponent of exoteric writing. Reason and revelation had indeed been brought into a paradoxical identity here, but this identity was exactly the opposite of what Guttmann had had in mind. Hence, it was certainly warranted to put "rationalism" in quotation marks. The political attribution of the two positions is playful, drawing upon the Latin adjectives *sinister* (or *sinistro*) and *dextro* for left and right.[40] But in what sense was the position of *Philosophy and Law* on the left wing, and the position of *Persecution and the Art of Writing* on the right? Strauss had a knack for asymmetric attributions of these political terms,[41] but perhaps he was not merely playful here. The position of *Philosophy and Law* could be understood as a left-wing "Jewish Thomism" because Strauss seemed to employ Maimonides to justify his "atheism from probity"; after all, an atheist position as the heir of the Jewish tradition has been the basic axiom of the Jewish Left. As we have seen above, Strauss dissociated his commitment to "atheism from probity" from the Jewish Left in a rather deconstructive fashion, but this had apparently not settled the matter for him.

The playful political attribution notwithstanding, the most important part is the addition "Guttmann ever in the middle." It strongly suggests that Strauss's subsequent development after *Philosophy and Law* was largely caused by his polemics against Guttmann, in particular against his perceived Protestant leanings. At last Strauss's words suggest that his emphasis on the "exoteric" Maimonides (or his switch from the "Italian" to the "French" interpretation of Maimonides) was rather an intermediate stage in his development than a discovery of his true teaching, thereby flying in the face of many of his most devoted disciples. To repeat: "I am *now* attempting to reach a moderate 'rationalism,' but one that, I am afraid, would be even less acceptable to G. than my two earlier positions."

By 1952 Strauss had embarked on a path that was remarkably different from the teaching of *Persecution and the Art of Writing*. In particular, he sought to arrive at a different understanding of reason and revelation that eventually came to its most authoritative formulation in "Jerusalem and Athens" (see Part V below). Altogether the conclusion seems inevitable that the "Jewish Thomism" phrase refers to an unresolved problem, which Strauss himself saw clearly (and maybe perceived too strongly). From here we are in a much better position to see *why* Strauss saw himself compelled to turn from the position of *Philosophy and Law* to the "radical 'rationalism'" of *Persecution and the Art of Writing*. This turn, too, was a response to a perceived failure.

"Returning" to Maimonides: Strauss's Turn to Exotericism

If *Philosophy and Law* is the greatest stumbling block in current Strauss scholarship, the transition from *Philosophy and Law* to the philosophy of exoteric writing is where the difficulties become most blatantly visible. Current interpretations of Strauss's turn to exotericism often struggle to describe the precise relationship between *Philosophy and Law* and Strauss's teaching after 1935. To arrive at a new, more precise interpretation of Strauss's turn to exotericism, we must follow up on the break with *Philosophy and Law* and reassess the predominant focus in Strauss scholarship on the influence of Farabi and the ensuing changes in Strauss's hermeneutic techniques.

As Strauss wrote on the *falâsifa* in a letter to Paul Kraus from May 1936, "their belief in revelation has become completely dubitable to me."[42] And whereas he had previously understood Maimonides as a gentle Jewish modification of the *falâsifa,* he henceforth emphasized his full agreement with his Islamic predecessors. The change of mind came with a stronger emphasis on the influence of Farabi, the great tenth-century Muslim philosopher, upon Maimonides; and soon Strauss began to see some peculiar Farabian techniques of writing in other philosophers, too. From here one can trace the spectacular self-interpretation of Strauss's turn to exotericism as it is documented in his correspondence with Jacob Klein and Norbert Nahum Glatzer in February 1938. This turn led him to the conclusion "that Maimonides in his beliefs was absolutely no Jew"—he was a philosopher, namely, "an 'Averroist,'" and hence a nonbeliever in the guise of a moderate rationalist seeking to accommodate reason and revelation. This discovery, Strauss believed, would strip Judaism of its foundation, for after all, Maimonides *was* the foundation of Judaism. "When I explode this bomb in a few years," he wrote to Klein, "a great battle will erupt."[43]

These quotes testify to the dramatic changes in Strauss's intellectual outlook after the publication of *Philosophy and Law*. But they cannot explain *why* Strauss thought he needed to turn his understanding of Maimonides upside down. Commentators therefore often feel compelled to mischaracterize *Philosophy and Law* as a "traditional" interpretation of medieval philosophy and the subsequent teaching as a "radical" one—as if Strauss had all of a sudden, without any determinable inner or outer reason, turned his scholarly project upside down.

Strauss was certainly bound to move on from the position sketched in his 1935 book, which had brought the subject matter of Maimonidean rationalism into an irresolvable tension. The teaching of *Philosophy and Law* was not a fixed position: in the first place, it was an exercise in bringing together two heterogeneous theoretical strands—standing under the law and thereby being free to philosophize. Both the solution and the argumentative and rhetorical means employed by Strauss were no less "hypermodern" and "radical" than the position codified in *Persecution and the Art of Writing*. In a way, it was a much more radical harmonization of reason and revelation: it brought the two irreconcilable claims into a fragile balance, whereas the esoteric/exoteric divide seemed to radically subordinate revelation to reason.

But *Philosophy and Law* had left an open flank, which was marked by the close proximity of Maimonides to Thomas Aquinas, and therefore the proximity of Strauss's own interpretation to a tradition that was informed by Christian scholasticism—or so Strauss thought in retrospect. He subsequently sought to close this flank by moving Maimonides closer to his Islamic predecessors. In particular, he was drawn to Farabi and Averroes, the radical rationalists among them, to eliminate the notion of an "essential excess of revealed truth over rational truth." Here, he discovered some of the interpretative techniques that were formative for his large-scale rediscovery of exoteric writing.

Scholars have drawn far-reaching consequences from this influence. Daniel Tanguay has spelled out these consequences most vocally. According to Tanguay, *Philosophy and Law* cannot be properly understood because it merely "represents an intermediate stage in Strauss's understanding of the theologico-political problem." It can only be understood in light of, and hence as a precursor to, the doctrine of exoteric writing. This later teaching "does not always appear with absolute clarity in *Philosophy and Law*," for Strauss "still hesitates to interpret Maimonides altogether" through the Farabian framework, whereas he freed himself "from this hesitation" after 1935. The influence of al-Farabi, then, led Strauss "from a rather traditional interpretation of prophetology . . . to a radical understanding of it."[44] On second thought, the notion that Strauss had simply "not yet" arrived at those later insights one might think of as particularly important or genuinely Straussian is of little explanatory value. Moreover, the view that the 1935 position is merely traditional—or at best stuck halfway between traditional and "radical"—is itself based on a rather traditional reading of *Philosophy and Law*.

At last, this view seems to misconceive the nature of theoretical innovations in general, and Strauss's own proclivity toward radical reorientations and changes in particular. Theoretical innovations usually occur at a point when an older paradigm appears to be exhausted. They come as a response to a perceived theoretical weakness, an imagined failure, of the older teaching. Strauss had a knack for radical changes in his theoretical outlook. In his own perception, his new teachings always seemed to offer a powerful tool to reorganize the entire field of his previous studies. But adding to this self-perception, he also had his own theory on the transition from one doctrine to another. In the transition to a new doctrine, older insights are inevitably forgotten, so that the transition does not necessarily bring about a progress "but merely a change from one type of limitation to another type."[45] One must merely apply this teaching to his own transition from one doctrine to another in order to avoid the notion of reorientation as progress.

But the predominant reading of *Philosophy and Law* as a mere precursor to the genuine, "exoteric" Strauss is not just based on a problematic notion of progress. It also misconceives a key argument of the book, namely, its anti-exotericism. We must briefly return to the question of the purpose of exotericism in *Philosophy and Law* and seek to draw a proper conclusion here. The initial problem is that Strauss first refuted exotericism and then presented the esoteric Maimonides. Upon superficial reading, this would be a blatant contradiction, arousing suspicion that the treatment of exotericism in *Philosophy and Law* is itself exoteric. But Strauss did not reject exotericism altogether; he argued that it is rather unimportant. We must keep in mind here that the esotericism thesis was the common view among scholars of Islamic and Jewish medieval philosophy at the time. The fact that most of the medieval philosophers (including Maimonides, but not Gersonides) restricted the freedom of philosophizing before the law to those suited to philosophizing was a matter of course. We find this thesis in Isaac Husik's *History of Mediaeval Jewish Philosophy* (1916)[46] as well as in Guttmann's *Philosophie des Judentums*, even as medieval esotericism was at odds with his democratic taste and his politics of revelation.

Strauss could not simply reject this canonic understanding of medieval philosophy: that philosophizing was limited to those suitable for philosophizing, and forbidden to the multitude, was evident. The crucial question was how this notion pertained to the reason/revelation divide. To restate Strauss's argument in *Philosophy and Law*: Even if philosophy was esoteric, the commitment to revelation was not merely exoteric. As we saw above, this reinterpretation can be traced both in the arguments and in the place of these arguments in *Philosophy and Law*. After the first appearance of exotericism emphasized the philosophers' "accountability" (and not paying lip service) to the revealed law, the most straightforward statement in the second chapter on the exotericism of Maimonides confirms this tendency. Not by coincidence, this statement occurs not in the part on Maimonides but in the discussion of Gersonides, who refuted esotericism.

Strauss started from the question of why Maimonides did not explain the metaphysical teachings in a clear and coherent fashion. As he explained, Maimonides limited the transparency of his presentation because it was prohibited by the law to openly express the secrets of the Torah *and* because metaphysical truths, being less accessible to the insufficient human mind than the subject matters of the other sciences, can only be expressed in similitudes and riddles; but since similitudes and riddles are unsuitable to scientific treatises, scientific speech must become obscure and brief.[47] Gersonides, propagating the sufficiency of human reason, had no use for presenting metaphysical truths in an obscure fashion, and he argued against the understanding that the open communication of metaphysical truths is forbidden.[48]

The purpose for Strauss to rehearse these arguments was to highlight Gersonides's anti-esotericism by contrasting it with Maimonides' esotericism.

In this contrast, Maimonides represented the "moderate" rationalism, while the anti-esoteric Gersonides held a "far more 'radical' view developed . . . in an explicit polemic against Maimonides."[49] The contrast served to emphasize that the medieval Jewish philosophers *presupposed* the law, *regardless* of whether they subscribed to esotericism or not. The teaching of the second chapter, then, is as follows: no matter how severe the differences between the doctrines of Averroes, Maimonides, and Gersonides—including their different standpoints on esotericism—they all presupposed the law as the indubitable, unquestionable foundation of philosophizing.

As we saw above, Strauss also emphasized esotericism in the third chapter to maintain that the medievals were not moderns, because they did not seek to educate the multitude to rational knowledge: "Again and again they enjoin upon the philosophers the duty of *keeping secret* from the multitude the rationally known truth; for them . . . the *esoteric* character of philosophy was unconditionally established."[50] This line does not contradict the anti-exoteric argument of *Philosophy and Law*, either. It has a precise function within the overall argument on medieval prophetology and, hence, a limited scope. As Strauss maintained, the medieval enlightenment is esoteric because it is based on the Aristotelian ideal of the theoretical life, modified in accordance with revelation. Maimonides maintained that revelation is simply binding *and* that the highest pursuit of man is to live a life of theory. This paradox is possible on the grounds that the theoretical life is the ultimate end of revelation. As the argument goes, then, it is revelation itself and its unconditional validity that requires the philosopher to keep the philosophical truth secret. The esoteric character of philosophy is therefore not in conflict with the unconditional presupposition of revelation. The restatement on "the *esoteric* character of philosophy" serves an anti-exoteric purpose.

To add to this anti-exoteric purpose of esotericism in the text, *Philosophy and Law* itself is not an exoteric book. Not only did Strauss explain everything in the open, despite some difficulties in his presentation; he did not even address his work to any particular readership. Therefore, it is difficult to argue that Strauss simply had not yet mastered the art of writing "between the lines," so that he unwillingly expressed his opinions too openly. There is no evidence that he even attempted to do so, and without any imaginary reader in mind—apart from his close acquaintances, from whom he needed not hide his "true" opinions—there is no reason why he should have.

The quest for exotericism emerges with the expectation that two types of readers will read the text. But *Philosophy and Law* is not addressed to a twofold readership. It was written in the historical vacuum of German-Jewish scholarship between the closing of its former institutions in Germany and its reestablishment in the countries of exile and the respective academic environments. German censors unanimously allowed the continued publication of "Jewish" books in "Jewish" publishing houses under the condition that they were not addressed to non-Jewish Germans.[51] The fateful separation between Jewish philosophy and philosophy before 1933, in which a "Jewish" philosophical work found little resonance beyond the world of Jewish scholarship, was supplemented by the dwindling of a German-Jewish academic readership between 1933 and 1938, up to the point when there were practically no more addressees except for a few fellow exiles. That did not keep authors from writing some of their most daring works during that period.

In the case of *Philosophy and Law*, these outer circumstances of its publication have left a deep imprint on the book itself: it was written without any external purpose or intended audience. In a way, it was more daring and experimental than Strauss's writings before and after the historical vacuum of the mid-1930s. Its often hermetic outlook testifies to the fact that German-Jewish philosophy of the interwar period and thereafter was hardly ever exposed to the challenge of argument and counterargument. It was replete with references to a scholarly world that was ceasing to exist. This discourse was soon to be assumed in various places all over the world, most notably in France, England, the United States, and at the Hebrew University of Jerusalem. But despite this reconstruction process, the enigmatic works written between 1933 and 1938 have often remained in the historical vacuum between "no longer" and "not yet." The fateful separation between philosophy and Jewish philosophy cemented this vacuum. The case of *Philosophy and Law* aptly demonstrates why this situation has only recently begun to change: it seemed "too philosophical" for Jewish scholarship and "too Jewish" for philosophy. But *Philosophy and Law* is a unique philosophical work, a "world" of its own. It must be understood both upon its own premises *and* as a part of the historical vacuum in which it emerged. Such an understanding will also help to see more precisely what happened *after* 1935 in Strauss's works.

If esotericism was the conventional viewpoint in German-Jewish medievalism around 1935, Strauss's "rediscovery" of exotericism from 1937–38 onward is likely to be more than a repetition of the decayed esotericism he had refuted in his earlier work.[52] It was something new—but what exactly was so new about it? The first innovation that likely comes to the reader's attention is a change in the strategies of textual understanding. Most visibly, Strauss seemed to be concerned more than hitherto with textual surfaces, or with the literary character of philosophical writings. As he later explained: "Subtle allusions are perhaps more important than the doctrine developed in an explicit manner."[53]

The systematic preoccupation did not vanish altogether. In part, systematic considerations were put forward as a means to a more literal reading, and Strauss still built his arguments with regard to the place of a doctrine in the division of philosophy. But he began to pay greater attention to minor deviations from the traditional division, in particular from other statements by the same author on this division. We may say that Strauss gradually began to read systematic considerations on the division of philosophy more literally, and less systematically. A passage in his "Some Remarks on the Political Science of Maimonides and Farabi" (1936) shows this new attention toward the seemingly insignificant details of the division of philosophy in Maimonides:

> That he divides philosophy into speculative philosophy and practical philosophy, that he calls the latter political or human philosophy, that he divides it into ethics, economic, and politics properly speaking, all this is well explained by the Aristotelian tradition, whose influence on his thought is known. But here are the facts which strike the present-day reader: (1) Maimonides does not mention happiness [*félicité*] when speaking of ethics, [but] he does so only when speaking of politics properly so-called; (2) he begins by dividing practical or political philosophy into four parts but, later on, he distinguishes among only three: the distinction between the governance of the city on the one hand, and the governance of the great nation or nations on the other, made with such clarity at first, appears to be of no consequence; why then is it made?; (3) without any prior justification, Maimonides attributes to politics strictly speaking the treatment of the "divine matters."[54]

The larger point of this analysis is that the deviations from the "normal" division of philosophy are exoteric: they hide and yet communicate an esoteric message. As Strauss made clear, this Maimonidean technique was due to the influence of Farabi, who was Maimonides's immediate source: "Farabi also sometimes divides practical or political (*madaniyya*) philosophy into ethics (*kholqiyya*) and philosophy of government (*siyasiyya*). But this division does not correspond to his guiding idea."[55] Strauss drew two consequences from this discrepancy: first, the preponderance of politics over ethics, and second, the subordination of divine matters to politics. Third, he thereby established that on this Farabian basis, Maimonides subjects the study of the Torah to political science. This demonstration of the political purpose of a doctrine was basically the same task as in *Philosophy and Law*, but the means for this demonstration had changed.

Another example of both the changes and the continuity in Strauss's "exoteric" interpretation of Maimonides can be found in "On Abravanel's Philosophical Tendency and Political Teaching" (1937). As the course of the text shows, its exoteric argument has a specific purpose that pertained to the overall task to outline an extramodern critique of modernity: it was a signpost to ensure that Maimonides would not be translated back into modern categories.

Strauss introduced the idea as follows: Maimonides seeks to harmonize the Jewish tradition and the philosophical tradition by the concept of law, understood in the sense of Plato's *Laws*—a perfect law that leads to the study of philosophy and that is based on philosophical truth. Maimonides demonstrates, first, that Judaism is such a philosophical law, and second, that those Jewish beliefs that are of an unphilosophical nature are *necessary* for political reasons. Thus, the Jewish law "has two different meanings: an exterior, literal meaning, addressed to the vulgar, which expresses both the philosophical and the necessary beliefs, and a secret meaning of a purely philosophical nature."[56] Strauss had thereby established that the Jewish law as understood by Maimonides has an exoteric and an esoteric side, but he wanted to show that the whole *Guide of the Perplexed* was structured along this divide. He argued that Maimonides ingeniously "imitated" the double character of the law in his philosophical interpretation: Maimonides did not explicitly distinguish between true and necessary beliefs so as not to endanger the acceptance of the necessary beliefs by the vulgar; thus, he made this distinction visible only in allusions, in compositional features and rhetorical gestures, all of which are accessible only to philosophers. To quote the catchphrase of Straussian exotericism: "Thus not only the law itself, but also Maimonides' philosophical interpretation of the law, has two different meanings: a literal meaning, addressed to the more unphilosophic reader of philosophic education, and a secret meaning, addressed to true philosophers, which is purely philosophical."[57] The *Guide of the Perplexed* can therefore be subject to either a "radical" or a "moderate" interpretation, the latter resting upon Maimonides's expressions of beliefs, the former aiming at the philosophical consistency of his work.

Strauss's exposition of the exoteric character of the *Guide* serves a clear rhetorical purpose in the article. It highlights by contrast what the title refers to as the "philosophical tendency" of Abravanel. The rhetorical contrast between Maimonides, the greatest medieval Jewish philosopher, and Abravanel, the last medieval Jewish philosopher and adherent of Maimonides, could hardly be more powerful: Whereas Maimonides's teaching is deeply ambiguous, Abravanel reads the *Guide*—and particularly its discussion of the creation of the world—literally. In his defense of the Jewish tradition Abravanel remains "unphilosophic" and, one is tempted to say, a little bit goofy.[58] With his "catastrophic" messianism, Abravanel stands at the beginning of modernity, in which the Messiah and the prophets are understood in "unpolitical" terms. His political teaching remains "essentially unpolitical."[59] Its core is a rare combination of the critique of civilization in §42 of Seneca's nineteenth letter with the first chapters of Genesis, so that the natural life of man is projected onto the life of Israel in the desert.[60] A firm believer in miracles, Abravanel is a proponent of "antirationalism" and depreciates political philosophy. He is deeply influenced by Christian political thought, but he is also a humanist who uses his learning to confirm—or rather construct—his traditionalist views. Strauss goes so far as to characterize Abravanel, albeit "with due caution," as an early adherent of historicism.[61]

Strauss wrote the article not long after the publication of *Philosophy and Law*. With the stark contrast between Maimonides and Abravanel, it also served to guarantee that his philosophical exposition of medieval Jewish thought would not be translated back into modern philosophical categories. Hence, the thematic analysis of Abravanel's teaching primarily exemplified a methodological concern. Julius Guttmann had voiced a similar analysis of Abravanel's political teaching, but he seemed to disgrace it by embedding it into his anachronistic account of Abravanel's "critique of culture."[62] Strauss did not differ much in substance from Guttmann, but he described the matter without the modern category of culture in order not to systematically miscast Abravanel's teaching. With the inconspicuous difference, he also facilitated a reentry of the subject matter (Abravanel's teaching) into the methodology (ancients versus moderns). Consequently, he cast Abravanel as the first of the moderns rather than the last of the medievals.

Beyond its scholarly merits in the field of medieval Jewish thought, the article, with its typical argument on a literal reading of the text in which the true meaning of the text is diametrically opposed by the literal reading, has a clear purpose in Strauss's larger philosophical and hermeneutical project. It addresses the modes of transformation that play out in the force field of seemingly similar doctrines, in which small shifts in the epistemic presuppositions turn the earlier doctrine into its opposite. Hence, the transitional, seemingly random article deserves to be understood as an essential part of his overall project to regain the political horizon of a problem or a doctrine.

By July 1938, Strauss had come to the conclusion that the *Guide* had accomplished what Nietzsche's *Zarathustra* meant to do—it was a parody of the Bible.[63] From here onward he both radicalized his notion of exotericism and widened its scope beyond the field of medieval scholarship. The lasting document of this process is the book *Persecution and the Art of Writing* (1952), which has captured the minds of Straussians and anti-Straussians alike. The latter are particularly at odds with the difference drawn between the few and the multitude, and therefore its alleged antidemocratic elitism.[64] At least in the wider public perception, the teaching of Leo Strauss is often identified with exotericism altogether, despite the fact that it marks only a certain phase in his scholarly life. It is hardly an exaggeration to say that exoteric writing is the *exoteric* political dimension of Straussian political philosophy.

Few are those who do *not* believe from the outset that Strauss himself was an exoteric writer and that an esoteric dimension is hidden in his texts. W. H. F. Altman suggests that Strauss "tells us between the lines that he too must be read between the lines," but it remains unclear which divinatory powers helped him to arrive at this insight.[65] Most likely, "exotericists" will quote Strauss's claim that "one writes as one reads,"[66] but hence they merely evade the proof that his statements on premodern exoteric writers necessarily and continually (not coincidentally) refer to himself, too.

To the extent that Strauss is an exoteric writer, exotericism is largely a matter of course. The notion of exoteric writing has a clear, limited function in his philosophical project, but it is neither his overall theme nor his major achievement. A *soft* version of exotericism remained, owing to the basic fact that Strauss, as well as many other philosophers, addressed different audiences differently; but his own initial excitement over the discovery of a strong version wore off soon. By the time Strauss published his "exoteric" articles from the early 1940s as a book in 1952, he was already moving away from the "radical 'rationalism'" of these articles to a "moderate rationalism."[67] In the same year, he gave the lecture "Progress or Return?," in which exotericism is little relevant, just as little as for his subsequent writings on Plato and the Bible as the most important texts of Western civilization.

Nevertheless, exotericism is extremely important in Strauss's political philosophy. One must merely seek to locate more precisely its meaning and scope. To state a few considerations in the form of antitheses: Exotericism has certain weaknesses as a hermeneutic theory, but it is a powerful tool for reorganizing the field of the history of philosophy. It is not the overall theme of Strauss's political philosophy, but it provided it with a clear focus and, more importantly, with an addressee, both of which it had previously lacked. The political dimension of exotericism is not the protection of the philosophical truth from the multitude, but the education of the potential philosophers toward philosophy.

There is little disagreement today on the basic notion that many great philosophers of the past were not in a position to speak their mind, so that they were compelled to write "between the lines."[68] The greater uncertainty is on the ways to discern exoteric writing in a text, the scope of the corresponding philosophical and historical program, and the meaning and purpose of Straussian exotericism in a liberal democracy. To start with the latter, Strauss cited the example of Spinoza to point out that exotericism "is reconcilable with the democratic creed,"[69] but overall he was little concerned by the allegation that it was undemocratic. There is a simple reason why: he conceived of the political aspect of exotericism rather indirectly, and not in terms of a social hierarchy. It was located in the classrooms in political science and humanities departments, where Strauss taught students how to read carefully—and that was his most important legacy.[70]

Strauss loved those students who loved to read carefully, and he deplored the idle readers. The "lazy reader" had been a target in an early article already,[71] but exotericism put him and his counterpart, the careful reader, in the center of a theory of education toward philosophy. In a way, this know-it-all type was the extension of the Nietzschean "last man" into the scholarly world of the university. Hence, Strauss targeted "the complacency" of modern readers "with which they claim to know what the great thinkers thought, to admit that the thought of the past is much more enigmatic than it is generally held to be."[72] However, he did conceive lazy reading not so much as a matter of degeneration of liberal education but as an everlasting human possibility. He was in full agreement with Plato's *Seventh Letter* that the important distinction regarding the suitability to philosophizing is not between the elites and the multitude, but between genuine philosophers and pseudo-philosophers—those imposters who superficially speak the language of philosophy in order to secure their nonphilosophical advantages.

The focus on exoteric writing provided Strauss with a powerful tool to distinguish between potential philosophers who love to think and unphilosophic readers of philosophic education who repeat the opinions of their respective peer groups. The essential criterion was the capability for attentive reading. With this guiding distinction, Strauss had indeed moved the political question of exotericism away from a social hierarchy, for the suitability for careful reading did not, in principle, correspond to any social distinction.

Today, the legacy of Straussian exotericism is more ambiguous, owing to the fact that his notion of exotericism can easily be appropriated by the very "lazy reader." An example must suffice here. As Strauss explained the typical procedure of exoteric writing, the author would initially write in a very technical and somewhat boring manner until he reached the core, "the center" of his argument; only here "would he write three or four sentences in that terse and lively style which is apt to arrest the attention of young men who love to think."[73] Later on in the book, he held that statements such as these are most likely to occur "somewhere in the middle, i.e., in places least exposed to the curiosity of superficial readers."[74] References to "the middle of the book" have given way to a disproportionate preoccupation of Strauss scholars with the middle of his texts. If Strauss were hinting that the middle of his book must contain exoteric writing, one would merely need to look up the middle to find the secret teaching. As a rule, this would of course deprive exotericism of its exoteric character, and provide even the laziest reader with a convenient tool to decipher Strauss's hidden intentions. All too often, the search for the center, from which all other parts could be accessed and deciphered, seems to excuse the reader from a thorough understanding of the argument and the action of a text. The case of *Philosophy and Law* is the most virulent example of this simplification on the part of Strauss readers.

Strauss knew this type of reader. In the course of his programmatic essay on exotericism, he carefully outlined some of the basic rules of reading between the lines, because he knew that the matter needed to be approached with the necessary precaution. Exoteric reading, or reading between the lines, could easily degenerate into a kind of conspiracy theory, in which the rules of scholarly exactness no longer seemed to apply. But the point of reading between the lines was to *increase* scholarly exactness, not to give up on it. Strauss sought to entice the reader to careful reading. There is a catalogue of rules in the text that seems to cite all the conventional tropes of exactness, with one exception that is strikingly unconventional:

> Reading between the lines is strictly prohibited in all cases where it would be less exact than not doing so. Only such reading between the lines as starts from an exact consideration of the explicit statements of the author is legitimate. The context in

A Complex Afterlife 159

which a statement occurs, and the literary character of the whole work as well as its plan, must be perfectly understood before an interpretation of the statement can reasonably claim to be adequate or even correct. One is not entitled to delete a passage, nor to emend its text, before one has fully considered all reasonable possibilities of understanding the passage as it stands—one of these possibilities being that the passage may be ironic. If a master of the art of writing commits such blunders as would shame an intelligent high school boy, it is reasonable to assume that they are intentional, especially if the author discusses, however incidentally, the possibility of intentional blunders in writing. The views of an author of a drama or dialogue must not, without previous proof, be identical with the views expressed by one or more of his characters, or with those agreed upon by all his characters or by his attractive characters. The real opinion of an author is not necessarily identical with that which he expresses in the largest number of passages.[75]

There is a shift in the description from the rules of certainty and caution for reading between the lines to the principles of reading between the lines. This shift occurs in the discussion of "blunders"—to be more precise, the discussion of blunders disrupts the series of rules of certainty and caution. It is followed by a highly conventional and rather boring elaboration on the difference between the author's views and those of his characters, which indeed could "shame an intelligent high school boy." Apparently Strauss meant to "perform" the task he had ascribed to the great writers of the past here. Any careful reader must wonder at this point: Is the interspersing of the rule on blunders a blunder in the rhetorical composition of the rules? Or is it an exoteric message hinting at some esoteric truth? Did Strauss intend to make the reader believe that he was himself an exoteric writer? Was he playful here, and if he was, what kind of game did he play?

As it stands, there is no definitive answer to these questions, but the matter forces the attentive reader to read again and turn his attention to hitherto neglected details. He may stumble upon the fact that the strikingly unconventional rule is the fifth one, whereas Strauss has nurtured the suspicion that the exoteric phrase would be in the middle, namely, in the fourth out of seven rules. Maybe, then, the exoteric teaching has been relocated from the fifth to the fourth place. But upon further consideration, it would be more feasible to assume that the unconventional fifth rule was devised to distract from the fourth. According to the fourth thesis one must consider that the text is to be understood exactly as it stands—only that the whole thing may be completely ironic. In other words, maybe Strauss was playing his readers for fools here, but even this is a mere possibility. In the end, one must consider that the passage may be meant exactly as it is written. Careful reading must therefore not result in the discernment of an exoteric message—it could as well result in a "plain" reading of the passage in question. But perhaps this the precise meaning of exoteric writing: it is directed to careful readers only, who love to read and think. Lazy readers, who often cannot even tell what his texts are about, would not notice anyway that something does not add up here.

Part III

"German Nihilism" and the
Intellectual Origins of National Socialism

10

Genealogies of National Socialism

"German Nihilism" (1941) may seem too occasional to warrant a long commentary. The text was edited from a lecture manuscript for a talk at the New School for Social Research, which Strauss did not intend to publish.[1] But since its posthumous publication in 1999, it has attracted a growing number of readers who seek to discern the actual political content of Strauss's political philosophy. For, as Susan Shell noted, the text provides "Strauss's first extended public statement as a U.S. citizen on contemporary politics."[2] But "German Nihilism" is also a firsthand report on culture and politics in post–World War I Germany, combining intimate knowledge of the intellectual situation with a new evaluation of key concepts from the Weimar Republic. Strauss created an idiosyncratic and somewhat uncanny account of the rise of some "young nihilists" that preceded the National Socialists in Germany, appealing to the audience to understand their sincere motives and suggesting that their liberal teachers had a share in their radicalization and, ultimately, in the rise of National Socialism. Thus, "German Nihilism" is currently perhaps the most controversial Strauss text. In more extreme cases it has been alleged that, rather than analyzing National Socialism, Strauss himself was a secret National Socialist.[3] Discussing a controversial topic in a controversial manner, the text offers ample opportunity for commentators to reveal "the real scandal" of his political philosophy.[4] As they suspect, Strauss's discourse is a Trojan horse of reactionary German *Kulturkritik* serving the most sinister political purposes.

One does not need to be led by apologetic motives to remind those readers of one basic Straussian insight: "One cannot refute what one has not *thoroughly* understood."[5] A new interpretation of "German Nihilism" cannot ignore these prior interpretations for the deep political resonance they have created. In the first place, however, the text must be read more closely. "German Nihilism" should be read with respect to three intertwined contexts: It must be read with regard to the discussions of the New School for Social Research, where Strauss delivered the "German Nihilism" lecture in February 1941, and of the subsequent Study Group on Germany. It should also be placed in the wider intellectual debate on the intellectual origins of so-called Hitlerism, National Socialism, and eventually the Holocaust. The New School discussions of 1940–41 were part of a wider discourse at the time, and this discourse merely extended the lines of discussion on German philosophy and politics around 1915. Finally, "German Nihilism" must be read in the context of Strauss's philosophy, especially with regard to Strauss's specific understanding of "culture" and "civilization." After all, the chief characteristic of the German nihilists, according to Strauss, is their rejection of civilization and their love for culture.[6] There seems to be a peculiar conceptual strategy at work here, and this strategy is a key to Strauss's stance on German *Kulturkritik* and his actual position on National Socialism.

Readers who are unfamiliar with these three contexts are likely to be drawn to the critique of liberalism in "German Nihilism." From here, the actual political content of the text seems easy to guess. Strauss appearantly wanted to provide an alternative to the predominantly progressive accounts of the intellectual origins of National Socialism. To a certain extent the text can indeed be understood as an antiliberal counterhistory to the current liberal interpretations. But Strauss's main point is philosophical—it is an argument about the meaning and purpose of philosophy in its relationship to politics and society. Strauss also exemplified a philosophical manner of treatment of his subject matter. Treating a political topic in a political, public manner, he emphasized and exemplified the perspective of the political philosopher. Strauss sought to instill a deep suspicion against the identification of philosophy with its political meaning, that is, with its public or exoteric side. The overall strategy, then, was to defend philosophy without denying its political responsibility. He argued for, and demonstrated in his manner of treatment, an irresolvable tension between philosophy and politics.

To provide some further context: At the time he composed "German Nihilism," in the year 1941, Strauss published his article "Persecution and the Art of Writing" in *Social Research*. This text introduced the doctrine of "writing between the lines," which he had originally developed in his post–*Philosophy and Law* studies on Maimonides, to a broader social science readership. The temporal proximity suggests some inner connection between the two texts. Superficial reasoning is likely to conclude that the topic of writing between the lines must be contained in "German Nihilism" too and, furthermore, that Strauss adapted the principle of writing between the lines to the composition of his lecture. It appears, then, that "German Nihilism" is an exoteric speech. But the case that Strauss *practiced* writing between the lines in "German Nihilism" is difficult to make. In particular, there is a far more obvious thematic semblance between the two writings, which is completely in the open. Both address the tension between the political or popular view and the philosophical view, and both express this tension with regard to two kinds of readers: superficial readers and philosophic readers. Both texts are ultimately parables of liberal education. Strauss's proposition in *Persecution and the Art of Writing* that education is "the only answer"[7] to the problem of the relationship between philosophy and politics is also a guiding theme in "German Nihilism."

A Brief Outline of the Genre

The topic of Strauss's text is commonly known as the "German problem." It is related to, but not to be confused with, the historiographical debates on the German *Sonderweg* (literally, special path) or the *Schuldfrage* (the question of collective war guilt). It is related to the *Sonderweg* theories for the general question: Why is Germany different? But whereas *Sonderweg* theories sought to trace the differences to the peculiar historical and social circumstances in which Germany belatedly evolved into a nation-state, "German problem" theories were far more concerned with German philosophy. That also shifted the question of political responsibility. Whereas the post–World War II *Schuldfrage* pertained to the German people, German problem theories focused on the responsibility of German philosophers. In this narrower sense, the "German problem" is often referred to as the "German spirit" theory. The question revolves around the alleged intellectual origins of German militarism, National Socialism, and, ultimately, the Holocaust. Genealogical efforts were made to trace the origins of the Nazi creed in the great formations of the German mind or spirit. Therefore, the "German spirit" theory is but one example of the "German problem" species, but it is the most persistent of its kind and has provoked the most controversial and inconclusive debates. The respective texts deserve to be read with a great amount of skepticism, but not with outright refutation.

Strauss has been known among historians of the genre for his famous "reductio ad Hitlerum" line in *Natural Right and History*, which refers to the genre as a "fallacy": "A view is not refuted by the fact that it happens to have been shared by Hitler."[8] But the problem is certainly more serious for Strauss's own project than these ironic remarks seem to suggest. It is inseparably connected with his stance on that part of German philosophy that had been affiliated—whether justifiably or not—with National Socialism. In other words, it is intertwined with one of his life themes, viz., his relationship to Nietzsche and Heidegger.

The recurring theme of the genealogies of National Socialism is put forth in the basic propositional form of *from x to Hitler*. Genealogists of National Socialism believed that Luther, Kant, Hegel, Schelling, Nietzsche, or other German thinkers had this or that impact on, or serve as the intellectual origins of, National Socialism. "German Nihilism" is Strauss's principal contribution to the genre, although it is by no means typical for the genre.

At this point, a clarification of the terms *genealogy* and *genre* is called for. As to "genealogy," the genre contains a characteristic reversal of the historical perspective: The basic form *from x to Hitler* is actually reversed to *from Hitler back to x*. The key elements of "Hitlerism," so the story goes, can already be detected in *x*. The principle was perhaps best described by Karl Popper. Trying to understand Hitler and Stalin, Popper "searched for traces of evidence in history; from Hitler back to Plato: the first great political ideologue, who thought in classes and races and suggested concentration camps. And I went from Stalin back to Marx."[9] This perspective distinguishes the genealogies of National Socialism from ordinary historical research, although the line between the two is often vague. In a way, history had always been read backward, that is, from the perspective of the present, but genealogists of National Socialism turned this natural condition of the historian into a major principle of their studies.

As to the notion of "genre," it is only to a certain extent metaphorical, although the genealogies of National Socialism do not comply with the definition of a literary genre. While some might prefer the notion of a "discourse," the genre stretches across various discourses and contextual situations. Even as these discourses and contexts often overlap, they usually ignore each another, thus existing more or less peacefully side by side. The genealogies of National Socialism do not have a linear history, nor are they defined in a coherent textual body. But even the briefest historical sketch of the genre cannot overlook the recurrence of a certain pattern of argument, a method (genealogy), a literary form (the tractate), and a set of metaphors that pose as methodological reflection. These common features recur in spite of the most severe internal disputes on arguments, concepts, methods, and forms. Reading through a number of those half-forgotten writings, it is surprising to see that the theories basically seem to face the same problems. Furthermore, they all provide extremely unsatisfying answers, but even the most unsatisfying answers employ certain patterns of argument and critique that are characteristic of the genre as a whole. No matter what the individual solutions were, they all played out German philosophy on the battlefield of politics and culture.

Many historians up to the present agree that, because Germany did not have a political revolution, its revolutionary energy was absorbed into the cultural realm. After all, it has been said, only the Germans had a national theatre before they had a nation-state.[10] This historical peculiarity gave birth to the speculative trait in German thought, with its ambiguous reputation of being intellectually productive and politically dangerous at the same time.[11] As far as they were serious historians of philosophy and theology, genealogists of this peculiarity faced a paradoxical task: seeing the history of German philosophy from its purported endpoint in Hitler, they sought to trace the political events of the time in the philosophical tradition, that is to say, in the sphere of culture. This supreme feature of the genealogies of National Socialism had an unfortunate side effect: as much as they emphasized the apolitical character of German thought, in the last resort their analyses remained apolitical, too. For the most part they did not principally transcend the type of thought they opposed.

Wolf Lepenies described the outlines of the genre in an ironic retrospect on *The Seduction of Culture in German History*. Arguing against "a strange indifference to politics" and a compensatory overemphasis on culture as the two chief characteristics of modern German intellectual history, he showed how genealogies often reproduced those characteristics they meant to analyze. For Lepenies, "attempts to construe causal links between the sphere of politics and the spiritual realm have not been convincing—regardless of whether individuals such as Luther, Kant, Schelling and Nietzsche or intellectual movements such as idealism or romanticism were seen as the beginning of a road that inevitably, with Hitler, turned out to be a dead end."[12]

But the genealogists' opponents fared little better. To deny any connection between German philosophy and politics, as Hannah Arendt did,[13] does not lead out of the impasse. It may be justified in a polemical argument against the genealogists, but as a principal stance on the German problem it remains indefensible. In other cases, the denial led straight into the "other

Germany" fallacy, according to which the German intellectual tradition had remained unharmed by National Socialism. The most outspoken proponent of this view was Friedrich Meinecke, who suggested in 1946 that one could just continue with the glory of German culture of Goethe and Mozart.[14]

It is easy today to ridicule the methodological fallacies of the genealogies of National Socialism, but their principal concern was entirely legitimate and sound. It is difficult today to imagine the urgency of writing genealogies "in a moment of danger" (Walter Benjamin),[15] but at the time they were widely seen as a major task of philosophical reflection. Not coincidentally, the genre reached its heyday around 1940–41, at a time when Hitler might well have won the war, and it decisively changed its course in 1943 when that prospect had changed. The early 1940s must be regarded as an "extreme" situation in which culture all of a sudden gained a political significance hitherto unknown. The general questions had often been discussed before, but in the extreme situation they gained a new reality and announced an epistemic shift.

However, scholarly habits and intellectual attitudes are persistent even in "extreme" situations. For the most part, larger epistemic shifts were in the air, but in the last resort they did not take place. The predominant attitude in the overall literature was to integrate the new political views into the older theoretical framework, albeit with some modifications. There are a number of assumptions that typically stood in the way of a sound analysis as their authors had imagined it in the first place.

Cassirer's *The Myth of the State* is not a typical work of, and does not fully belong to, the genealogies of National Socialism, but it expresses one typical assumption most vigorously—the assumption of conventional history of ideas: to understand the political myths of the twentieth century, we must first provide a general theory of the emergence of myth, then we can study the history of philosophy and its stance on myth, beginning with the pre-Socratics. In short: "We must begin with the beginning."[16] Cassirer was therefore in great trouble when he sought to account for the radical break of National Socialism with the world of ideas as he knew it.

Another typical assumption was held by some of the émigré scholars at the New School (particularly, but not only, those of the first generation), as well by members of the Institute for Social Research over at Columbia University. As they believed, the "German spirit" theory was overrated, and the rise of National Socialism needed to be explained in terms of socioeconomic history. The New School discussions did not endorse a *hard* version of this explanation, which was openly dismissed by Albert Salomon for its failure to address "the political frame in which economic conflicts reach revolutionary strength."[17] Arguing against the "Nazi-capitalist conspiracy" thesis proposed by Ernst Fraenkel's *The Dual State* (1941), Erich Hula held that "the Marxist interpretation of National Socialism" would "confuse rather than clarify the issues that are at stake in the struggle against that system."[18] The socioeconomic paradigm was stronger at the Institute for Social Research. Franz Neumann's *Behemoth* (1942) and Horkheimer and Adorno's *Dialectic of Enlightenment* (1944/1947) are the most visible contributions to the genre from the group that later came to be known as the Frankfurt School. At one point, the Institute for Social Research attempted to secure a grant by way of a research project on the topic ("The Collapse of German Democracy and the Expansion of National Socialism," September 1940). The socioeconomic explanation of National Socialism was attractive for all those who sought to reconcile their Marxist or social democratic creed with the new reality that was played out in the force field of politics and culture. Strauss therefore referred to these scholars as "half-Marxists."[19]

Another danger was to identify the political significance of philosophy too easily. It often resulted in a misunderstanding of the nature of philosophical ideas. The unhindered politicization of philosophy is most visible in post–World War II intellectual disputes that evoked the atrocities of the Holocaust in an argument over the methodology of the social sciences. But the danger was inherent in the genealogies from the beginning, as can be traced in those early genealogies that were built upon American pragmatism.

The genre was first established around the outbreak of World War I, when the political and military battles in Europe were accompanied by an intellectual battle that must be seen today as an early and formative example of the so-called culture wars. Even the term *culture war* emerged in this context.[20] The purpose of a multitude of predominantly English writings was to trace the intellectual origins of German militarism, which was then proven to be rooted in the German soul or national character rather than in political constellations of any kind. The French had their most outspoken analyst of German militarism, and later of National Socialism, in Edmond Vermeil.[21] The British debate was largely focused on Nietzsche. "The accusation [that Nietzsche brought on the war of 1914] was made in many forms and in many different organs, from *The Times* to popular broadsheets. The English were most vocal, with the French much less certain that Nietzsche was worth blaming when there were plenty of live Germans to attack. In the first few months of the war, Nietzsche, Treitschke and von Bernhardi were linked together in British propaganda as mainly responsible for working the

Germans, leaders and led alike, up to an immoral lust for conquest never yet seen on this earth."[22]

Often these were indeed works of propaganda (just as their German counterparts wrote works of propaganda in favor of the war against civilization and commerce), but often they were too easily dismissed as mere propaganda. For all those involved, German culture had become a force field of political ideas. Some of the best and most lasting works were written during such a Benjaminian "moment of danger," a moment in which a new constellation of culture and politics "flashes up"[23] and obtains a new intensity. Anachronistic studies written during the interwar period, which were not located in that force field (such as Helmuth Plessner's *Das Schicksal deutschen Geistes im Ausgang seiner bürgerlichen Epoche*, 1935; republished in 1959 as *Die verspätete Nation*), rarely gained the same intensity.

Also during World War I, American philosophers George Santayana and John Dewey published their pioneer works on German philosophy, which were both republished during World War II. The discussions of 1940–41 largely renewed and extended the lines of a genre that had been established around 1914–15. In other words, analyses of the roots of "Hitlerism" written in the early 1940s were often built upon the older model of German "militarism." The British had their most vocal proponent of this endeavor in the political field in Robert Vansittart.[24]

There were not only periods but also places in which the discussions reached their highest intensity. The Graduate Faculty of the New School for Social Research with its "Study Group on Germany" was a key institution. With the founding of the "University in Exile," the New School provided a safe haven for a number of refugee scholars from Germany and Austria. New arrivals joined a group of prior immigrants, primarily economists and political scientists from Kiel, Vienna, and Berlin. The Study Group was a crosspoint of various German intellectual traditions. For example, Erich Hula was a political scientist and student of Hans Kelsen; Adolph Lowe and Eduard Heimann were social economists (Heimann belonged to the Paul Tillich circle of religious socialists); Salomon and Carl Mayer were sociologists (with Mayer putting special emphasis on the sociology of religion); Felix Kaufmann was a philosopher of law and former member of the Vienna Circle, who was well versed in Husserlian phenomenology and mathematics; and Kurt Riezler was a former diplomat and a philosopher who, as the curator, had brought a number of illustrious scholars to the University of Frankfurt between 1927 and 1933.

Despite their grave theoretical differences, most of these German and Austrian scholars shared a sense of German *Bildung,* a tradition of learning that had largely vanished from the German soil around 1941 and that many of these scholars sought to continue. Apart from Leo Strauss, the Study Group was completed by the American (Silesian-born) philosopher Horace M. Kallen, who had studied with Santayana and Dewey and originated the notion of cultural pluralism. All these different scholars were united under the New School idea of a progressive social science, with Strauss being the most dissenting member in this respect.

The Study Group marked, at least temporarily, a significant shift in the New School focus from the socioeconomic history of Germany toward German intellectual history. "They called themselves the Study Group on Germany," Rutkoff and Scott wrote in their landmark study on the history of the New School, "and organized themselves along the lines of the policy committees that had existed in the Kiel institute. . . . The study group met regularly for nearly nine months to . . . address the question of German national character, and its members presented papers which, despite their diversity, dealt with the historical and philosophical implications of the 'crisis of European liberalism.' Relatively unconcerned with the exact means by which Hitler had come to power, they asked instead whether or not Hitler and Nazism should be understood as something intrinsic to the German national character."[25] This shift was certainly due to the "moment of danger," but it was also conceived as a modest contribution to the war effort, and especially to the effort of winning peace, by the politically engaged social scientists of the New School. Alvin Johnson, the New School's president, outlined this understanding in his *Social Research* article "War and the Scholar" (1942). The scholar, he wrote, "will stand, unabashed, for the principle that the rules of civilization . . . are prior to the bomber and the poison gas, and will survive beyond them. The scholar will wake up, as the shock of war becomes incorporated into the standard of living, and assert, humbly and boldly: I will persist in scholarship as usual. I offer myself for the winning of the war, so far as you can use me; but you can certainly use me for the winning of the peace."[26]

This persistence in "scholarship as usual" should not be confused with resistance to facing the new political reality, or with a failure to understand the traditions from which these scholars had emerged in the light of that new reality. The Study Group discussed key texts such as Heinrich Heine's *On the History of Religion and Philosophy in Germany,* George Santayana's *Egotism in German Philosophy*, or John Dewey's *German Philosophy and Politics*, as well as recent literature on the subject such as Hermann Rauschning's *The Revolution of Nihilism*. The latter was the reading portion for the session of February 26, 1941, when Strauss delivered his "German Nihilism" lecture.

"There were factions within the group," Rutkoff and Scott reported, "Adolph Lowe and Eduard Heimann arguing that German society was fundamentally antagonistic to liberal doctrines and Horace Kallen and Kurt Riezler claiming that the spirit of German liberalism, which had shown itself during the Enlightenment, had been crushed by historical events."[27] Kaufmann and Strauss objected to the understanding of National Socialism as an heir of German philosophy, while Kallen (following Dewey) emphasized the contrast to the liberal Anglo-American model of philosophy—a typical difference between the analyses of German émigré scholars and their American counterparts. American philosophers (Santayana, Dewey, Kallen) understood German philosophy in light of pragmatism, whereas most Germans sought to find an inside-outside perspective on the philosophical traditions with which they had grown up. However, fault lines emerged not only between Americans and Germans, but also between various refugee scholars and scholarly groups. A generation of émigré philosophers, social scientists, and intellectuals was forced to see the German intellectual tradition from which they had emerged with different eyes, and often their genealogical efforts marked an important step in their adaptation to the new academic and political environment. In one way or another, they all came to revaluate the political significance of German thought in the United States.

The Cases of Lutheranism and Romanticism

There are four German traditions or movements that are frequently referred to as the intellectual origins of German militarism and Hitlerism, sometimes in more or less viable combinations: Lutheranism, German Idealism, Romanticism, and Nietzscheanism. Broadly speaking, Lutheranism stands for authoritarianism, German Idealism for totalitarianism, Romanticism for nationalism and irrationalism, and Nietzscheanism for nihilism. Accounts of these four movements often overlap, and all too often they attempt to discern the principle of *one* of these movements in the overall course of German thought. However, the wide impact of these studies stemmed not so much from the complex analyses but from the catchy titles and phrases in the form of *from x to Hitler*.

The proposition *from Luther to Hitler* is closely associated with the wartime studies of William McGovern and Reinhold Niebuhr. McGovern sought to outline the origin and development of fascism as a global conflict between liberalism and fascism. Evoking the horrors of a possible "Fascist-Nazi victory in Europe" that would also affect and potentially overthrow the liberal order in America and England, he switched between an analysis of National Socialism as a distinctly German phenomenon and a description of fascism as a global possibility. With this model, the book combines profound analyses of political ideas with an odd mixture of overly sharp contrasts and a curious lack of differentiation. Starting from a definition of fascism as "authoritarianism plus etatism,"[28] McGovern found its earliest precursor in the Reformation, and he traced the authoritarian mindset through Bodin and Hobbes, de Maistre and Burke, Kant and his English disciples, as well as Fichte and Hegel. To explain the course of the nineteenth and twentieth centuries he switched from "authoritarianism" to the new criterion of "absolutism." In short, McGovern's odd project of a "history of Fascist-Nazi political philosophy" had a clear focus neither on Germany nor on the theological origins of fascism.

In both respects, he took a different path than the theologian Reinhold Niebuhr, who understood the conflict between Germany and the West as "a conflict between pessimistic and optimistic corruptions of Christianity." According to Niebuhr, Luther was pessimistic regarding the social and political world and its government, and this was due to the sinfulness of man, and he was optimistic that the law of love and the absolute ethic of the Sermon would provide a sufficient basis for individual life in this world.[29] Now, German fascism was based upon Luther's pessimism, whereas American religiosity was optimistic. Niebuhr's distinction between pessimism and optimism, with its clear preference for American religiosity, was asymmetric and remained to a large extent metapolitical. But it clearly marked the place in Luther's doctrine where proponents of the *from Luther to Hitler* thesis located the interconnection between politics and religion.

In-depth discussions usually found the political vantage point of Lutheranism in "authoritarianism." According to this view, Luther's theological pessimism informed his view of all social and political affairs, particularly affairs of the state. The state is the necessary byproduct of man's sinful nature, repressing the dangers of chaos and destruction that stem from sin. A remedy against anarchy and a safeguard of worldly peace, the state is fundamentally good and cannot be judged by any higher law. Carl Mayer summarized the political implications as follows: "The place accorded to the state in the whole texture of individual and social life appears to be such as to lead, sooner or later, to a theory of its omnipotence. . . . The idea of autonomy of the political order, if taken radically, excludes the establishment of any moral principle, for instance the idea of justice by which political life may be judged from without or above. The conclusion is therefore that the Lutheran doctrine of the state, stripped of its theological context, has all the elements upon which the theory of authoritarian and totalitarian government is founded."[30]

As opposed to the other three culprits, Luther was rarely evoked as the *sole* progenitor of National Socialism. In most cases he was seen as the *earliest* manifestation of a principle that can also be discerned in later intellectual formations.[31] For example, Niebuhr asserted that Hegel, the Romantics, and Nietzsche contributed to the rise of National Socialism as well as Luther. An exception to this rule was Peter Wiener's *Martin Luther: Hitler's Spiritual Ancestor* (1945), which presented Luther as "a political demagogue" and an "evil" man.[32] Wiener acknowledged that Luther could not possibly be the sole source of the current war, and yet he found Lutherans and Lutheranism in virtually every other expression of German thought: "In whatever I have read of Germany's history of religion, philosophy, and politics, everywhere I have found and encountered, open or in disguise, that evil spirit which we are fighting at the moment: the spirit of immorality, Herrenvolk, irrationalism, antisemitism, mysticism, nationalism, étatism, and so forth—the spirit of Martin Luther."[33] Another example, to be found not in philosophy but in its strange transposition into the sphere of political organizations and committees, is a UNESCO document from 1949, in which one Dr. Verkade created a direct link between Lutheranism and the policies of the Wehrmacht.[34]

For the most part, starting with Luther led genealogists to argue that a protestant streak in modern German thought had made Germans prone to the seduction of unlimited state authority. But the evocation of the Protestant origins of National Socialism had a wider appeal. It could also be used as a subsidiary argument for the claim that German Idealism is a distinctly German phenomenon, as opposed to the understanding of philosophical idealism as a European phenomenon. References to Luther could serve to create a prehistory of the philosophical origins of National Socialism. The task was to describe some fundamental, incredibly ancient and longstanding principle that somehow came to play out its full destructive potential in the present. Contributions to the genre could easily become a part of a genealogical race, in which subsequent scholars sought to outplay their colleagues by extending the lines back from Hitler to German philosophy even farther. This logic of extension ultimately led away from German thought, back to Plato and Homer.

In general, getting from Luther to Hitler required some sort of a secularization thesis. But it was difficult to explain why and how secularization led to National Socialism, and often the arguments were not convincing. Just like the problem they sought to address, the genealogists themselves were situated in the very force field of politics, religion, and culture, and this made coherent arguments difficult to build. As Helmuth Plessner showed in his study *Das Schicksal deutschen Geistes im Ausgang seiner bürgerlichen Epoche* (1935, later published as *Die verspätete Nation*, 1959), German culture itself was secularized Lutheranism, acquiring a religious function in the process of secularization. The secular religion of culture, Plessner argued, became the foundation of German nationalism.[35]

Plessner wrote his large-scale study long before World War II and the heyday of the genealogies of National Socialism in 1940–41. Henceforth, it became increasingly difficult to make this argument when it came to Nazi policies. Could the extermination camps still be understood as an expression of secular culture? The genealogies of National Socialism show their double face here. Their explanations point to an epistemic state of exception, in which older explanations were quickly vanquished by the atrocious new realities. But, hence, they also point to an epistemic limitation. Such limitations—the natural byproducts of writing "in a moment of danger"—can be seen not only in the case of Lutheranism. The debate on Romanticism is similarly constricted.

Eric Voegelin referred to the genealogies of National Socialism as "the gallery of nefarious figures from Herder to Hitler."[36] Surprisingly, however, Herder is rarely mentioned in these studies. The occupation with the Romantics was widely focused on those who could possibly serve as proto-Hitlers, but not on those who also laid the ground for the modern concept of culture (which was predominant also in the United States). Romanticism, with Herder being the great mastermind, was notorious for the invention of the *Volk* (people) as a nation with a distinct culture. This invention prompted the notion of the German people as an ethnic unit with a common origin, language, and culture; but it also gave birth to the understanding that the products of the mind (philosophy, literature, art) reflect the spirit of the German people. Herder's original notion of culture had given birth to the two predominant notions of culture in the twentieth century: culture as understood with regard to the autonomy of man and the products of the human mind, and culture as understood in cultural anthropology, which had long been absorbed into American thought. It is remarkably difficult to find a notion of romantic culturalism in the genealogies of National Socialism. For the most part, genealogists stood under the spell of the very culturalism they sought to analyze. But some genealogists did notice the connection between Romanticism and current notions of the *Volk,* the homogeneous ethnic community envisioned by National Socialists. Rohan Butler began his wartime study *The Roots of National Socialism* (1941) with an attack on Herder, and his conclusion was that "the community of the folk runs from Hitler right back to Herder."[37]

The genealogical preoccupation with Romanticism is closely associated with the name of Paul Viereck, who in 1941 provided a large-scale study on the path that led "from Wagner and the German Romantics to Hitler."[38] The guiding principle of his investigation was the "metapolitical" character of German thought. Whereas Western civilization was "compounded of three separate heritages: rationalism, classicism, Christianity," Nazism stood for the opposition to these three heritages: "for force against reason, for romanticism, for tribal paganism."[39] Focusing on what Ernst Troeltsch had called "a queer mixture of mysticism and brutality" in German thought,[40] he sought to demonstrate how German metapolitics translates into political action. One key tool for this translation was for Viereck "the magic word 'Kultur.'" In his account, *Kultur* was a code word for the German preoccupation with a mystique of instinctive wisdom and superiority of the blood.

> It became a rationalization of barbarism, an overcompensation for the inferiority complex of feeling less "Romanized" than the Mediterranean world. It became an easy way to side-step the challenge of sanity, reason, and logic; in fact, a deliberate revolt not only against reason but against all moral and political restraints, a revolt against humanity, against universals, against internationalism on behalf of Volk and mother nature.[41]

Viereck's account of German thought, which set modern Germans back into their Germanic tribal past, reached from Father Jahn via Fichte and Hegel to Houston Stewart Chamberlain, Alfred Rosenberg, and Hitler; but the main target was certainly Richard Wagner, "the most important single fountainhead of current Nazi ideology."[42] Viereck discussed Wagner's writings at length, but he hardly even mentioned the music.

Romanticism was also the main target of Thomas Mann's analysis of National Socialism. Mann, the novelist who had fled Germany for the United States in 1933, is a key reference when scholars seek to describe how German exiles learned to see German *Kultur* from a political standpoint. Indeed, he left behind much of the apolitical culturalism that was formative for his earlier *Betrachtungen eines Unpolitischen* (1918; *Reflections of a Nonpolitical Man*).[43] But the tension between culture and politics is still clearly visible in his wartime reflections on Germany. Mann's comments on Viereck's *Metapolitics* read as if they reenacted the principle of "two souls in one breast." Just as Viereck did, he rejected this classical trope on the German mind, but it nevertheless resonated in his thought. In particular, it showed when he sought to reconcile his love for Wagner's music with his notion of its deep connection with National Socialism. Mann agreed with Viereck that Wagner's work is paradigmatic for the German spirit. He expressed his "very nearly complete approval" of Viereck's study at the beginning, but in the course of his comments he added two qualifications that suggest nearly complete disapproval. On the one hand, he missed "a sense of nuance" in Viereck's account of Wagner, particularly "the nuances of love, of passionate personal familiarity with this artistry, which is, after all, admirable and gifted beyond measure."[44] On the other hand, he added to Viereck's analysis that Wagner's metapolitical radicalism was apparent not only in his writings but in his music as well. This idea that music itself can be deciphered with regard to its mytho-political outlook was unfamiliar to many American readers at the time. Mann's claim fed upon a deep familiarity with the music, but he developed it further on the theoretical background of Theodor W. Adorno, who had a knack for discerning the course of history from the tiniest details in a written piece of music (and with whom Mann was working for his novel *Doktor Faustus*).[45] Restating once again his love for the music, Mann nevertheless unambiguously declared that its metapolitical element "must be beaten" in order to establish a new order in Europe.[46]

German Idealism: Santayana, Dewey, and Beyond

The alleged connection between National Socialism and German Idealism, particularly Kant and Hegel, is most closely associated with the names of George Santayana and John Dewey. Both wrote their works on German philosophy at the outset of World War I and republished them at the high point of World War II. The two studies have much in common, in particular the critique of idealism from a pragmatist standpoint. But they were also wide apart in their overall perspective and their specific arguments.

Santayana's interpretation of German philosophy is not so much an analysis as an appeal to like-minded readers. Claiming the position of a "layman," "an outsider, with no professorial pretensions," he set out to describe "the aroma of German philosophy that has reached my nostrils. If the reader has smelled something of this kind, so much the better: we shall then understand each other."[47] The statement suggests that German philosophy cannot be properly understood by way of conceptual analysis,[48] for its true nature is revealed through the somatic reaction of the layman and his feelings aroused in the act of reading. "Under its obscure and fluctuating tenets," Santayana recalled his experiences with German metaphysics, "I felt something sinister at work, something at once hollow and aggressive."[49] This double characterization—*hollow and aggressive*—resonated in many subsequent attempts to locate the intersection between German philosophy and German politics, particularly in those which sought to trace the anomalies of German politics to idealism.

But even as Santayana retained an outside perspective on German philosophy to see its political significance, he knew that in order to provide a convincing interpretation of German philosophy he needed to outline its premises and its historical development. In short, he needed to be both outside and inside. The most concise statement on his premises reads as follows:

> The great characteristic of German philosophy is that it is deliberately subjective and limits itself to the articulation of self-consciousness. The whole world appears there, but at a certain remove; it is viewed and accepted merely as an idea framed in consciousness, according to principles fetched from the most personal and subjective parts of the mind, such as duty, will, or the grammar of thought. . . . Its fundamental conviction is that there are no existing things except imagined ones.[50]

The idea that "egotism" and "subjectivism" are the chief characteristics of German philosophy makes Santayana susceptible to subsuming all German thought under the notion of idealism. Protestantism, and Romanticism, Goethe's *Faust* and Ibsen's *Peer Gynt*, Kant as well as Nietzsche—they all represent the same transcendental mindset, which "regards mental life as groundless and all-inclusive, and denies that a material world exists, except as an idea necessarily bred in the mind."[51]

Santayana's pioneer study set the tone and style for many studies to come, but the philosophical means at his disposal were too limited to uproot idealistic thought. In the end his case amounted to the claim that "the whole transcendental philosophy . . . is false, and nothing but a selfish perspective hypostasized."[52] The statement was a gentle rebuff to John Dewey, who, according to Santayana, "skillfully avoids complicating his survey with any account of the transcendental theory of knowledge." To emphasize the major difference between Dewey's and his own account of German philosophy, Santayana stressed that the transcendental theory "is the foundation of everything in this philosophy, and until it is radically abandoned we shall hardly emerge from the moral quicksand to which it leads."[53] But can transcendentalism be "radically abandoned" by merely declaring that it is "false"? It took the effort of John Dewey's *German Philosophy and Politics* to decisively change the tone of discussion on German thought and politics.[54]

Whereas Santayana had conveyed a few observations to the like-minded, Dewey meant to say the truth about German philosophy and present it in a coherent and comprehensive interpretation. And whereas Santayana had lumped together virtually all German philosophy, literature, and music under the category of idealism, Dewey had a clear target in Kantian idealism. Kant was simply "the philosopher of Germany."[55] Dewey briefly touched upon Luther, but only to mention that Lutheranism played a role in the formation of Kant's thought. He was also certain that Nietzsche's influence upon German thought was insignificant in comparison with Kant—a view for which he was complimented by Oscar Levy, the German-Jewish Nietzschean who compiled the first English edition of Nietzsche's works.[56] Kant was the key reference for what Dewey called the "two worlds" of German thought: a world of science and a world of morals, "two realms, one outer, physical and necessary, the other inner, ideal and free."[57] Whereas the inner world was a realm of freedom and idealism, the outer world represented mechanism, efficiency, and organization. German civilization was characterized by the "combination of self-conscious idealism with unsurpassed technical efficiency and organization in the varied fields of action."[58] For Dewey, the German mind always favored the inner, while its mechanistic outer called for a deontological ethics; these ethics served as a blueprint for the authoritarian mindset that came into its own in German politics.

Dewey's exposition did not state whether German politics was a perpetuation or a perversion of Kantian philosophy, but he was certainly in favor of the perpetuation thesis. He described how the teachings of Kant infiltrated into popular attitudes and habits, where they developed their political significance; but he did not sufficiently address the question of whether they were still the same Kantian teachings after this transposition. He did not explain the precise relationship between philosophy and politics in his 1915 book, and his new preface to the 1942 edition, which applied his earlier stance to the new reality of "Hitlerism," did little to clarify his stance. Invoking all kind of correlations, which partly exclude each other, Dewey indiscriminately assumed a "one-to-one correspondence," "a prepared soil and a highly favorable climate of opinion," "a kind of pre-established harmony" or a "coadaptation."[59] These descriptions were little more than metaphorical attempts to circumscribe what was simply evident for him.

Dewey must be regarded as a main target for Strauss in his concern with the genealogies of National Socialism.[60] Strauss was particularly concerned with the general relationship between philosophy and politics in Dewey's genealogy. His criticism may in part belong to the long history of a mutual misunderstanding of pragmatism and German thought, but he added a few points that were underrepresented elsewhere. To understand these points, it is helpful to start from the principle of pragmatism that all philosophical thought should be viewed in light of its practical use. For Dewey, philosophy played a crucial role in the making of a better society. As Robert Horwitz gently put it in the Straussian *History of Political Philosophy*, Dewey's philosophy is characterized by "the attempt to further the realization of democracy in every sphere of life. . . . Dewey's philosophy is politically programmatic, which is to say that it addresses itself to what it regards as the true end of philosophy, progress."[61] In other words, Dewey subordinated philosophy to a particular political cause.

This political agenda is visible from the outset in his study on German philosophy. Dewey chose an entirely different starting point from Santayana's. As he asserted, German philosophy serves as his "illustrative material," providing an "illustration of the mutual relationship of philosophy and practical social affairs."[62] German philosophy merely illustrates his general opinion on the social context of philosophical ideas, but he could also have picked Plato. The purpose of this philosophical rhetoric is to downplay Dewey's deep discontent with German philosophy. The tone was entirely different where he complained that "there is no people so hostile to the spirit of a pragmatic philosophy," or where he wondered why positivism, materialism, and utilitarianism did not gain traction in Germany.[63] He occasionally referred to the brutality of war, but the gravest danger he saw stemming from Germany was the belief in an absolute. The notion that there are some kind of transtemporal and transcontextual ideas and values—this being the core of "idealism," according to Dewey—was the true and principle enemy of pragmatism. Hence, Kantian philosophy was the comprehensive, universal interpretation of human affairs that Dewey needed to invalidate if he wanted to prove that pragmatism was truly comprehensive and universal.

But proofs of this sort are hard to come by, and Dewey eventually settled for a strategy from the playbook of philosophical rhetoric instead. In his closing statement he emphasized the difference "between a theory which is pinned to a belief in an Absolute beyond history and behind experience, and one which is frankly experimental. For any philosophy which is not consistently experimental will always traffic in absolutes no matter in how disguised a form."[64] To provide this stark contrast with a political marker, he ventured that "philosophical absolutism" may be practically as dangerous as "political absolutism." The outcome is that any philosophy but pragmatism is politically dangerous. Following these statements, Dewey's book was a contribution to a "culture war" on the meaning and purpose of philosophy. It did not provide a solution to the problem as Dewey had imagined it—that the Germans turn from idealism to pragmatism and join the experiment of creating a free and universal democratic society. He gave a large-scale counterinterpretation to German philosophy from a pragmatist standpoint, but this interpretation did not form a comprehensive and universal account that would decisively invalidate the idealistic understanding of German philosophy. During World War II, a contemporary critic of Dewey's approach, idealist philosopher and "negative pragmatist" William Ernest Hocking, retorted by asking "whether the German government is not at the present more faithfully following the experimental prescription":

> It is trying its own theories to see how they work. It believes firmly that its methods are the methods that succeed; and it believes so not because of anything that Kant taught, but because of the way in which it has recently been interpreting history, led by its series of economic historians from Marx . . . to Lamprecht and Schmoller. . . . It is radically experimental or pragmatic, which is what *Realpolitik* essentially means.

Hocking simply applied Dewey's interpretation to Dewey himself. He saw German philosophy in the same force field of idealism and experimentalism, but he came to the opposite conclusion. "Germany's course," he asserted, "might be defined as experimentalism without the Kantian corrective."[65] Dewey's grim rejoinder is remarkable for the way it weakens his own case:

> I have not said that the behaviour of the rulers of Germany was dictated by an idealistic philosophy. I meant (and said) that it was a *Realpolitik*—highly pragmatic if you please. . . . But the prevalence of an idealistic philosophy . . . has disguised from the mass of the German people . . . the real nature of the enterprise in which they are engaged.[66]

The statement suggests that if not the rulers, then at least the masses were idealists. This would mean that German politics acted upon the principles of pragmatism, whereas the German people understood these actions in terms of philosophical idealism. Idealism, then, is the opiate of the German masses, whereas the rulers have risen to the principles of *Realpolitik* (which they, however, did not really understand, according to Dewey). But the enterprise of German politics was hardly disguised by the philosophy of German Idealism. The prevalent ideologies may have been partly shaped by German Idealism, but they had lost any meaningful connection with the philosophical framework of idealism. If applied to the 1940s and the *völkische* ideology, Hocking was more likely right that this framework would rather have acted as a corrective to the ideas of National Socialism than as a concealment of National Socialist policies.

But rather than reenacting the arguments and counterarguments, we must seek to see more clearly the philosophical principles upon which Dewey's investigation is based. After all, his task was to clarify "the mutual relationship of philosophy and practical social affairs."[67] The most concise theoretical exposition of his stance in *German Philosophy and Politics* reads as follows:

> There are no such things as pure ideas or pure reason. Every living thought represents a gesture made toward the world, an attitude taken to some practical situation in which we are implicated. Most of these gestures are ephemeral; they reveal the state of him who makes them rather than effect a significant alteration of conditions. But at some times they are congenial to a situation in which men in masses are acting and suffering. They supply a model for the attitudes of others; they condense into a dramatic type of action. They then form what we call the "great" systems of thought.[68]

It is difficult to find a twentieth-century philosopher (perhaps with the exception of Hermann Cohen) who would disagree with the claim that "there are no such things as pure ideas or pure reason." The more serious question was how the "gesture" or "attitude" of an idea could be adequately deciphered. And would this be possible upon the model of pragmatism? Dewey apparently had no doubts that pragmatism was perfectly capable of deciphering German philosophy, while German philosophy had completely misunderstood itself. His claim to superiority stems from his ability to translate philosophical ideas into a "practical situation," while the idealists had mistaken them for being "pure." One must pay greater attention to the precise relationship between philosophical thought and the "dramatic type of action" modeled upon its gesture, as well as the techniques and the methodological fallacies involved in the act of translation, to see the fundamental difference between Dewey and Strauss.

Strauss's hermeneutic advice is that philosophical ideas must be understood on their own terms, for these terms contain indispensible information on their practical "attitude." Pragmatism cannot accept this notion, for it is wont to assume that the link between philosophy and its cultural and political ramifications can be established much more directly. Dewey asserted "that philosophy, like politics, literature, and the plastic arts, is itself a phenomenon of human culture."[69] The proposition that philosophy—just like politics—is "a phenomenon of human culture" seems nearly self-evident: philosophizing stems from human activity, whereas Gods and brutes do not philosophize. But Dewey had something more specific in mind. His argument is based on the variety of philosophies as witnessed by the history of philosophy. For example, he noticed the differences between occidental and oriental philosophy, between the various epochs of Western philosophy, etc.[70] But most of all, he was concerned with the differences in argument and style between the various philosophies that correspond to the various national cultures of the West. Accordingly, each philosophy is a contribution to, and an expression of, a particular national culture. German philosophy contributes to and expresses the German national culture, just as American philosophy contributes to and expresses the culture of America. This cultural understanding of philosophy sits uneasily with Dewey's claim that American philosophy (i.e., pragmatism) is in principle superior to German philosophy. If philosophy reflects the culture of a particular nation, there is no reason why any "national" philosophy—given that there is such a thing—should be better than any other national philosophy. The claim to superiority stems from the presupposition that American culture is *the* true culture; it is superior because it has reached, for the first time in history, full insight into the relativity of all cultures; thus, it is capable of understanding all other cultures better than these cultures understood themselves.

At this strategic point we are in a better position to understand Strauss's reservations: he had good reasons—philosophical as well as political—*not* to subscribe to Dewey's interpretation of German philosophy and politics. Given his insistence on the latent culturalism of twentieth-century philosophy, he was well prepared to refute Dewey's claim that pragmatism could understood German philosophy better than it had understood itself. In his Dewey review, Strauss did not argue per se against any connection between German philosophy and German politics. His criticism was focused on its location in Kant, and in particular on the way in which Dewey advanced his case. He voiced his dissent with regard to one particular sentence in Dewey's book: "Surely the chief mark of distinctly German civilization is its combination of self-conscious idealism with unsurpassed technical efficiency and organization in the varied fields of action."[71] First, Strauss argued that Dewey's claim is based on a particular German ideology of the German spirit, and not on an adequate understanding of that spirit. This argument pertains to the difference between philosophy and its public appearance. Second, Strauss held that almost the same could be said about American civilization. This argument concerns the alleged differences between civilizations. Third, Strauss maintained that the separation between the world of inner freedom and the world of civil and political life, in which subordination to authority prevails, was also advocated by Descartes and Spinoza. This argument concerns the purported difference between German and non-German philosophers.

In his conclusion, Strauss presented a more general case of political philosophy against the pragmatist understanding of politics and philosophy: "Dewey defends not simply the cause of democracy and international order, but a particular interpretation of that cause—his own philosophical doctrine." From there, Strauss questioned Dewey's equation of democracy with experimentalism and of political absolutism with philosophical absolutism. The argument consists of two counterexamples that break up this strong nexus: experimentalism can be dangerous if used by unscrupulous leaders, and the Declaration of Independence was inspired by the belief in an "absolute."[72] This appeal to the founding of American democracy was a brilliant endpoint for Strauss's review, for in effect it undermined the opposition between the "German" and "American" understanding of philosophy and politics. But Strauss's somewhat ironic anti-anti-absolutism is not merely a rhetorical gesture. The appeal to a transnational and transcultural principle points to a universalist streak in Strauss's own thought. Given his occupation with natural right and his lifelong refutation of all kinds of particularisms—the particularism of nations, peoples, or cultures—it is no wonder that the Declaration of Independence had a deep resonance in his political thought.[73] Strauss's argument with Dewey, then, is not an argument between two particularistic understandings of philosophy (i.e., "American" and "German" philosophy). It is an argument on the precise understanding of the very universalism to which both philosophers subscribed.

Nietzsche and National Socialism

Eric Voegelin's sarcastic opening remark in his wartime article on Nietzsche was that "Nietzsche has the distinction of being the only philosopher who ever has been considered the major cause of a world war."[74] Compared with those who held that Luther, Kant, or the Romantics were responsible for the rise of Hitler, those who saw Nietzsche as a progenitor of fascism and National Socialism were often disproportionally fervent in their anti-Nietzscheanism. But outer evidence such as the fact that both Mussolini and Hitler considered themselves Nietzscheans did little to strengthen their case. After all, Mussolini was also an adherent of William James, the founding father of pragmatism, whereas Hitler knew Nietzsche only at second hand. More sober commentators usually granted that Nietzsche would have despised the National Socialists as a particularly insufferable breed of the *Schlechtweggekommenen* (the misdeveloped, underprivileged), but this did little to change their minds. As to Nazi anti-Semitism, it was widely known that Nietzsche considered himself an "anti-anti-Semite," but some argued that the passages on the Jewish question were anti-Semitic anyway: "the substance is good Nazi doctrine," wrote Crane Brinton in 1941.[75]

Brinton is a particular case in the fervent anti-Nietzscheanism of the early 1940s. Even as he noted that Nietzsche had to be prepared for the German audience by a number of popular books to fit into the *völkische Weltanschauung,* he held that every detail of that Weltanschauung was already present in Nietzsche himself: Nietzsche glorified war and the soldier, his praise of Caesarian spirits anticipated the *Führerprinzip,* and he supported *Rassenhygiene.*[76]

> Nietzsche, then, fits into National Socialist needs both in what he damned and in what he praised. He damned democracy, pacifism, individualism, Christianity, humanitarianism. . . . He praised authority, the warrior spirit and practise, the stern life and

the great health, and urged upon his fellow-citizens a complete break with their bad old habits and ideas.[77]

Point for point he preached, along with a good deal else which the Nazis choose to disremember, most of the cardinal articles of the professed Nazi creed—a transvaluation of all values, the sanctity of the will to power, the right and duty of the strong to dominate, the sole right of great states to exist, a renewing, a rebirth of German and hence European society.[78]

The difference between Nietzsche himself and the Nazi use of Nietzsche boiled down to a few "suppressions" and "omissions" they had to make when quoting him.[79] Brinton was nuanced compared to Rohan Butler, for whom Nazism "was nothing less than the Nietzschean transvaluation of values, the education of Germans in Germanity, the nihilistic revolution which would not stop at smashing countries, but would wreck the very hearts of men and utterly destroy the civilization of the West."[80] As opposed to those genealogies which are occupied with Luther, the Romantics, or the German Idealists, genealogies that ran "from Nietzsche to Hitler" were not only more fervent, but also more easily satisfied with a shorter genealogical line. Ultimately, Nietzsche's philosophical radicalism remained too strange for them as to allow for a less monocausal line of German political radicalism.

But neither their fervor nor the weakness of their arguments justifies simply dismissing their case retrospectively. An intricate connection between Nietzsche and National Socialism was also maintained by some of those who had grown up with Nietzsche's thought and who thereby remained closer on philosophical grounds. Karl Löwith, who wrote his *From Hegel to Nietzsche* in 1941, noted in his autobiography:

> Even today . . . I would not know of anyone else with whom to conclude the history of German thought. . . . Nietzsche continues to be the epitome of German unreason, or what is called the German spirit. A gulf separates him from those who unscrupulously preach his message, yet he prepared the way for them that he himself did not follow. . . . Those who know Nietzsche's significance for Germany can easily find the bridge that spans the abyss between the "before" and the "after." It is indeed impossible to understand the development of Germany without this last German philosopher. His influence within the boundaries of Germany was—and still is—boundless. The

Anglo-Saxon world—even Italy and France, with d'Annunzio and Gide, will never be able to fully comprehend it, so essentially foreign to them is what draws Germans to Nietzsche. Like Luther, he is a specifically German phenomenon—radical and fatal.[81]

Löwith's stance on Nietzsche was deeply ambiguous. An uneasy interplay of attraction and repulsion was also prevalent in his 1944 article "Friedrich Nietzsche (1844–1900)." For Löwith, attempts to discharge Nietzsche from the guilt of his historical impact were as futile as the opposite attempts to charge him with direct responsibility.[82] The latter understood the deeper implications of Nietzsche's philosophy, but they did not understand the difference between the teaching and its historical impact. And the former "liked" Nietzsche but did not understand the tragedy of his greatness: "It is the privilege of great individuals to become guilty in history."[83] The center of Löwith's article was the question of "why Nietzsche is dangerous."[84] There is something in these words that resonates in Strauss's position on Nietzsche, but Strauss was even less willing to resolve the enigma of Nietzsche's thought.

Whereas Löwith's stance remained ambiguous, Strauss's was straightforwardly aporetic. This is also visible in "German Nihilism," where he sought to outline a more nuanced position on nihilism in his analysis of National Socialism. Strauss started from Rauschning's *The Revolution of Nihilism*, which was the reading portion in the General Seminar for that week, but he understood nihilism and the emergence of the "young nihilists" in terms he had learnt from §12 in Nietzsche's fragment "The European Nihilism":

> Nihilism as a symptom of the fact that those who turned out badly [*die Schlechtweggekommenen*] have no consolation left: that they destroy in order to be destroyed, that, relieved of morality, they no longer have any reason to "surrender themselves"—that they position themselves on the territory of the opposing principle and *want power* for themselves, too, by *forcing* the powerful to be their executioners. This is the European form of Buddhism: *doing no,* after all existence has lost its "sense."[85]

The "young nihilists" are Nietzscheans just like Strauss was a Nietzschean, according to his own testimony, between around 1921 and 1929, when he was "dominated and fascinated" by Nietzsche to such an extent that "I believed every word of what I understood from him."[86] It should be noted, however, that Strauss himself was the opposite of a "nihilist"—not a proponent of absolute values, to be sure, but a seeker for "a *known* and *stable* standard"[87] by which one would be able to distinguish between good and bad or right and wrong. (Part IV of this study explores some of his difficulties in maintaining such a standard.) This quest for a standard is a clear vantage point in "German Nihilism." Strauss turned to Nietzsche to understand the nihilistic sentiment and open up a horizon beyond nihilism. As he suggested, he had liberated himself from the spell of Nietzscheanism "through years of hard and independent thinking," so that he was no longer susceptible to the nihilists' doubts he knew from his "own experience."[88] The assumption that Strauss's position matches with the young nihilists is premature.

No other philosopher, he declared in "German Nihilism," "was more responsible for the emergence of German nihilism than was Nietzsche. The relation of Nietzsche to the German Nazi revolution is comparable to the relation of Rousseau to the French revolution. That is to say: by interpreting Nietzsche in the light of the German revolution, one is very unjust to Nietzsche, but one is not *absolutely* unjust."[89] Nietzsche is clearly the most important of the four intellectual sources of National Socialism for Strauss, the only serious contender for the title of the intellectual progenitor of the Nazis.[90]

Two Interpretations of German Philosophy and Politics

At this point, we have attained a first idea of Strauss's discontent with the genealogies of National Socialism. In order to understand his precise position, we must seek to better understand the immediate context in which it was developed, namely, the discussions at the New School for Social Research and in some related articles in the journal *Social Research*. The debate between Carl Mayer and Carl Landauer, in particular, leads right into the heart of the matter. It shows that Strauss's emphasis on the problematic relationship between philosophy and politics was well founded in that intellectual context.

Carl Mayer's judgment of the intellectual origins of National Socialism oscillates between various assumptions and positions, in effect laying bare the methodological snares of the genealogies of National Socialism more faithfully than virtually everyone else. His article "On the Intellectual Origins of National Socialism" therefore deserves to be read with greatest care. Mayer's initial discussion of the four intellectual origins of National Socialism, in the first part of the article, gives the appearance that he found all these historical deductions more or less convincing. To sum up: The Lutheran doctrine of the state contains all the elements upon which the theory of authoritarian and totalitarian government is founded; the Hegelian notion of the state justifies the idea of the *Machtstaat*; Romanticism is a source of National Socialism with regard to the advancement of irrationalism and nationalism; and Nietzsche laid the philosophical basis of National Socialism with his doctrine of radical nihilism.[91] Only two minor qualifications indicate that his actual position is almost the opposite. As he asserted: "[T]he Lutheran doctrine, *stripped of its theological context*, has all the elements upon which the theory of the authoritarian and totalitarian government is founded." And Hegel "interprets the state in terms which, *divorced of their philosophic connotation*, mean simply state omnipotence."[92]

Mayer did not add such qualifications to his discussion of the Romantics and Nietzsche, but he provided a theory in the second part of his article that applies to all four intellectual movements. The keyword here is the notion of "context," which he understood as the place of an idea within the whole of a doctrine. As Mayer saw, ideas become accessible to political use only when they have been stripped of their philosophical context and meaning. Their political impact is most likely not based on the actual doctrines. In many cases it rather rests on a misunderstanding or, most likely, on the type of half-knowledge that is said to be a dangerous thing:

> To begin with, Lutheran Protestantism is a Christian theology. Its logical structure as well as its problems and concepts and interpretations are shaped by this fact. This means that sin, grace, redemption, faith are the fundamental realities, and that the interpretation of life and the world proceeds in terms of these realities. . . . German idealistic philosophy can be called a world of reason. Its fundamental concept is that of reason. . . . Schelling and Hegel attach extraordinary importance to state and power; but power and state are to them not the ultimate reality but rather a fact that must be brought into the framework of, and interpreted according to, a philosophy of reason. As far as Hegel in particular is concerned . . . the true character of his political philosophy emerges only if it is read in the light of the whole of his ideas. . . . [O]ne would fall short of the truth if one were to try to show that romanticism is an effort to abandon reason altogether. Romanticism is rather an attempt . . . to find what is believed to be the true relationship between nature and history on the one hand and reason . . . on the other, and by doing so to

> arrive at a higher principle which includes both. . . . Nietzsche's philosophy is not a mere nihilism. . . . [H]is philosophy of power is . . . not meant to be a brutal and cynical glorification of force. . . . As Nietzsche is opposed to socialism and nationalism, so he is opposed to the state. His philosophy of power may lend itself to the vindication of a political theory of totalitarianism, but in itself it is not that.[93]

Henceforth, Mayer discussed the Nazi "denial of everything" for which these four doctrines stand. From here he brought his point home that there is "a fundamental gulf" between the alleged intellectual origins of National Socialism and National Socialism itself. The methodological insight at which he aimed to arrive is a distinction between original "systems of thought themselves" and the intellectual movements into which they transform: "The original motives and intentions from which a thought receives its real life become largely lost, and what remains are the diluted and adulterated concepts, the outworn formulae, the commonplaces, the empty shells." In conclusion, Mayer proposed that the four doctrines do have a certain relationship to National Socialism, whereas they cannot be cited as its intellectual origin.[94]

Mayer's distinction between original thought and its "vulgarization"[95] appeared somewhat backward in the overall climate of intellectual history in the early 1940s, in which the "systems of thought" were identified with their purported political meaning rather easily. Accordingly, philosophical works must be understood on their own terms in order to discern their political meaning. Their true political "gesture" cannot be discerned from solitary ideas and concepts, without regard to their place in the whole of a doctrine.

Mayer took yet another turn in the third part of his article, speaking out on what *he* believed to be the intellectual origins of National Socialism: "nihilism, nationalism and authoritarian socialism."[96] He still maintained the separation between original thought and its vulgarization, but now he sought to reconcile it with the idea he had so vehemently refuted in the second part of his article: that some intellectual sources "created the moral-intellectual climate in which the tenets of National Socialism became possible."[97] As the saying goes, he wanted to have his cake and eat it too. It is not surprising that Carl Landauer, in his short "Comment on Mayer's Analysis of National Socialism," held that Mayer had "not gone far enough" in his criticism of the genre.[98]

Landauer, a social democratic economist who had been working at the University of California in Berkeley since 1934, basically tore apart the theory that National Socialism was directly rooted in German philosophy and theology. Acknowledging the "great temptation" to create such a link, he suggested that "a simple test" should be applied to propositions of this kind: "When some similarity between the Nazi creed and German philosophy has been stated, one should search the literature of other nations for comparisons with Nazism." Landauer cited the example of Thomas Carlyle. Carlyle's writings are replete with utterances "that sound like an exposition of some of the fundamental Nazi tenets," and yet Carlyle is not suspected of being a Nazi pioneer. "The method that leads to an absurd result in the English case," Landauer concluded, "should not be relied upon in the German."[99]

As to Landauer's larger perspective, he held that National Socialism was "only part of a larger movement," of fascism, and that the fascist movement "is represented by individuals and groups the world over." Fascism represented merely one "late offshoot" of the antirationalist wave that swept across Europe between 1895 and 1914. In his emphasis on the transnational character of the movement Landauer's analysis bore some similarity to McGovern's *From Luther to Hitler*. But whereas McGovern had lumped (German) National Socialism and (international) fascism together to create the monstrous image of a transtemporal and transnational "Fascist-Nazi" mindset, Landauer explored the transnational elements of German fascism itself.

There is an obvious downside to Landauer's position: it could not explain why fascism played out differently in Germany than anywhere else and how it developed its "extreme character" there. At this point Landauer found no other way out than to resort to the older New School model of socioeconomic history, although this did not quite match with his analysis of antirationalism: "It seems to me that the social and economic conditions of the 1920's and 1930's, together with the outward events of German history after 1871, furnish a full answer."[100] Similar points were made by Hannah Arendt in 1945.[101] Strauss's late reply to this type of argument was that "there were other liberal democracies which were and remained strong although they had to contend with the same difficulties."[102]

Being written after Strauss's "German Nihilism" lecture, Mayer's and Landauer's analyses did not "influence" Strauss's interpretation of National Socialism (it is more likely that Strauss actually edited the manuscripts for *Social Research*); but they nevertheless provide a proper contextual basis for a more precise understanding of his lecture. With the variety of topics and arguments they offered, we are in the midst of the controversy of which "German Nihilism" was a part.

11

Strauss's Argument

The outer formal structure of Strauss's "German Nihilism" lecture is not very helpful with regard to its argument. There are two tables of contents, which partly contradict each other. The first table of contents divides the lecture into nine parts, whereas the second divides it into three chapters with fourteen parts altogether. The actual lecture manuscript is divided into twelve parts. These divisions were apparently helpful in the process of composition, but they bear no relevance for the inner structure of the argument. The text offers two different narratives, the first stretching over parts 1 through 11, the second making a brief appearance only in part 12.

At the beginning, Strauss distinguished between nihilism and National Socialism as but one form of nihilism; between nihilism and its underlying non-nihilistic motive; and between absolute nihilism and limited nihilism (the desire for the destruction of everything, including oneself, versus the desire for the destruction of something specific). Strauss dismissed the claim that German nihilism is absolute nihilism, arguing that it would merely provide a symptomatology of mental diseases. Instead, he suggested a little test. Matching the test proposed by Landauer both in simplicity and selectivity, its scope reaches beyond a refutation of the absolute-nihilism thesis. As he ventured, even if that thesis were to be correct it could not explain "why that desire took on the form, not of the mood called *fin de siècle* or of alcoholism, but of militarism."[1] Accordingly, genealogies of National Socialism must be able to explain, first, how a cultural discontent took on a political form, and second, why it took on the particular political form of militarism and fascism. This test should also be applied to Strauss himself, who opted for a limited-nihilism thesis: German nihilism was "a desire for the destruction of something *specific*: of *modern* civilization."[2]

Now, to reconcile this position with the Nietzschean view that the nihilists simply "destroy to be destroyed," he introduced the notion that "limited nihilism *becomes* an *almost* absolute nihilism." The difference between an absolute and a limited, near-absolute nihilism is, admittedly, technical, but Strauss needed both notions of nihilism to maintain his position. He needed the absolute-nihilism thesis to explain both the magnitude and the inarticulateness of the nihilists' passionate rejection. And he needed the limited-nihilism thesis (the thesis that German nihilism was limited nihilism) to maintain that their fundamental convictions were sound and led by moral motives: they desired "to destroy the present world and its potentialities," but they did so out of morality, for the "love of morality."[3] This double position, which is almost impossible to maintain, creates the philosophical tension and political ambiguity that is so characteristic of Strauss's "German Nihilism" lecture.

The subsequent analysis of *why* the German nihilists sought to destroy modern civilization retains this tension. The hypothesis is that nihilism originated from "a moral protest" against modern civilization, "a sense of responsibility for endangered morality."[4] This emphasis initially appears to be a defense of German nihilism. Since the text does not offer any term for the assumed *original*, not-yet-nihilistic form of nihilism, we may tentatively refer to the phenomenon as proto-nihilism. There are two explanations for the proto-nihilistic protest that eventually evolved into German nihilism, their common denominator being the moral emphasis of their protest. The first explanation is derived from Henri Bergson's distinction between the closed and the open society. The moral protest is directed against the ideology of the open society.

> Moral life, it is asserted, means *serious* life. Seriousness, and the ceremonial of seriousness—the flag and the oath to the flag—, are the distinctive features of the *closed* society, of the society which by its very nature, is constantly confronted with, and basically oriented toward, the *Ernstfall,* the serious moment, M-day, *war*. Only life in such a *tense* atmosphere, only a life which is based on constant awareness of the *sacrifices* to which it owes its existence, and of the necessity, the *duty* of sacrifice of life and all worldly goods, is truly human: the sublime is unknown to the open society.[5]

This explanation does not entirely fit into Strauss's overall narrative, particularly because it does not match with the characterization of the young nihilists later in the text. It is even doubtful how this position could eventually evolve into a nihilistic position. Several catchwords (the moral life as the *serious* life, the *Ernstfall* as the possibility of war, the sacrifice of life) suggest that Strauss meant to characterize the position of Carl Schmitt. Another hint to Schmitt is given in the proposition that the prospect of the open society rests on a notion of progress that is "largely fictitious or merely verbal," for the postpolitical language of liberalism and its alleged hypocrisy was indeed Schmitt's main target. If this link to Schmitt is correct, it allows for a more precise understanding of the alleged "love of morality." For it is dubious how Strauss's emphasis on the moral character of proto-nihilism could serve as its defense. The emphasis on morality, rather, indicates the limits of this type of protest. As Strauss had argued in the "Notes on Carl Schmitt," it was the moral surplus of his doctrine that had made it impossible for Schmitt to find a horizon beyond liberalism. In the same vein, Strauss showed in 1941 that the German nihilists remained entangled in what they opposed.

There is a major obstacle in Strauss scholarship to a precise understanding of the "love of morality." It concerns the current attempts to identify his own position, his voice in the text. More than in any other of his writings Strauss often did not draw a clear rhetorical line in "German Nihilism" between his own views and his summaries of other people's views. The Strauss-as-a-secret-Nazi narrative, in particular, rests on the notion that his position matches with the position of the young nihilists.[6] But the the quote above suggests precisely the opposite. Strauss continued with the words "Let us pursue this argument a little further," and twice he inserted "it is asserted."[7] These phrases suggest that the tacit identification of Strauss with the German nihilists cannot be maintained.

Another indication is the use of irony. One cannot help but notice the irony in Strauss's paradox of a *serious nihilist*. Perhaps this paradox is a first demonstration of what he later called "the dualism of play and seriousness."[8] The serious aspect is the notion of a moral protest without a goal: The German nihilists are serious without knowing what to be serious about—*dead serious*, as the colloquial phrase goes. The moral surplus of their protest makes their political beliefs and their potential actions all the more dangerous. Straussian political philosophy teaches that seriousness must be mated with knowledge of what is good.[9]

There is a second explanation of nihilism, which takes the matter into a somewhat different direction. Here, Strauss refers to a transnational and transepochal tradition of the "passionate protest," for which Glaucon, Rousseau, and Nietzsche are the main examples. As he maintained, their protest is "neither nihilistic nor entirely unsound." The reference to Glaucon and his "passionate protest against the city of pigs, in the name of noble virtue"[10] is the least obvious and the most illuminating in this genealogical line. Broadly speaking, the inclusion of Glaucon indicates that Strauss meant to take the matter out of the modern battlefield in general and the battlefield of German thought in particular. The "passionate protest," then, is rather an eternal possibility for the morally outraged youths. But the meaning of Glaucon's protest against the "healthy city" in Plato's *Republic* is more specific. Strauss had second thoughts about the assertion that his protest is uttered "in the name of noble virtue."

Following *The City and Man*, Glaucon's protest was initially prompted "by his desire for luxury, for 'having more,' for the thrills of war and destruction."[11] His desire for luxury first comes to sight as the desire for meat. "Glaucon is characterized by the fact that he cannot distinguish between his desire for dinner and his desire for virtue. (He is the one who calls the healthy city the city of pigs. In this respect too he does not quite know what he says. The healthy city is virtually the city without pigs. Cf 370d-e and 373c.)"[12] The healthy city is the prepolitical city in its original innocence and harmony, in which each man gets as much as he needs. It is characterized by the fact that no animals are being killed. The inhabitants of the healthy city are vegetarians, and hence the city is called "the city without pigs." For Glaucon, the inhabitants of the healthy city are themselves pigs because they "feast without relishes," that is, they *eat* like pigs: their diet consists of plants and roots. The lack of meat in their diet indicates their lack of virtue: they miss both the sophistication and the hardness of will necessary for the ideal republic. Following the action of Plato's dialogue, Strauss showed how Glaucon is led by Socrates to undergo a change of heart:

> The spirit of luxury and gain is replaced by the spirit of discipline and selfless service. Glaucon's education in this respect is part of the education to moderation which is effected by the conversation reported in the *Republic* as a whole.[13]

This reference point helps to better understand the philosophical program of Strauss's "German Nihilism." It suggests that his education of the German nihilists is a repetition of Socrates's education of Glaucon. "German Nihilism," then, is to a certain extent a repetition of Plato's *Republic*. The common theme is the education of young radicals to moderation. The German nihilists were to undergo a transformation from the nihilistic rejection of civilization to the qualified embrace of civilization, just as Glaucon underwent a transformation from protest to real virtue.

Strauss's two explanations of the proto-nihilistic protest are united by his assertion that it stems from "a love of morality," and in both explanations he strongly emphasized that the protest is not yet nihilistic. But he left open how exactly proto-nihilism had turned into nihilism. The text seems to suggest that there are two different *degrees* of nihilism: "It was the *same* passion . . . in a much more passionate and infinitely less intelligent form."[14] This ambiguity can to a large degree be resolved on the condition that the German nihilists were not nihilistic from the beginning. Instead, their moral protest *became* nihilistic through its affiliation with progressivism. This argument is sustainable to the extent that German nihilism was not initially *motivated* by anticommunism, which is *also* suggested by Strauss. To untangle all these rhetorical strategies and subsidiary arguments, we must follow the text more closely. Eventually, even the most apparent contradictions are instrumental with regard to Strauss's central philosophical point.

German Nihilism as Anticommunism

Strauss's text proceeds to the point when German nihilism is actually born, at a time preceding the revolution of 1918–19. That time saw the emergence of communism both as an institutionalized, comprehensive doctrine and a major political force. According to Strauss, it was "the time when certain people asserted that the conflicts inherent in the present situation would necessarily lead to a revolution, accompanying or following another World War—a rising of the proletariat and of the proletarianized strata of society which would usher in the withering of the State, the classless society, the abolition of all exploitation and injustice, the era of final peace. It was this prospect at least as much as the desperate present, which led to nihilism. The prospect of a pacified planet, without rulers and ruled, of a planetary society devoted to production and consumption only, to the production and consumption of spiritual as well as material merchandise, was positively horrifying to quite a few very intelligent and very decent, if very young, Germans."[15]

According to this view—which is not congruent with another explanation later in the text—German nihilism is basically anticommunism. This was also the premise in the two tables of content at the beginning of the text: "German nihilism is . . . the passionate reaction of a certain type of young atheist to the communist ideal."[16] Superficially speaking, this is the place in the lecture where Strauss seems to come closest to a Nazi position—for isn't the claim that Nazism is merely a response to communism (or Judaism, capitalism, etc.) a key element of the Nazi ideology? Didn't socialism, too, claim that the proletarian revolution would be a response to the rising of fascism? Must not Strauss's stance inevitably be understood as a defense of National Socialism?

The actual sources for his argument suggest otherwise. To a large extent, it was modeled upon Emil Lederer's *State of the Masses*, a study on modern dictatorship that was widely known among Study Group members.[17] Lederer urged that, in light of recent political experiences, the "utopian and somewhat empty" idea of a classless society should be revised, for "the psychological conditions of an unstratified modern people [cannot] be other than those of a crowd."[18] The greatest, most imminent danger, Lederer held, "is enslavement of ourselves by ourselves, by the destruction of our best guarantee of freedom, the existence of social groups."[19] As he suggested, the coming of the classless society had been simply taken for granted, because the general trend, if not the details, seemed to point in this direction. The problem was that the classless society turned out to be a mass state. Under these conditions, a "dictatorship of the proletariat . . . must rest upon terrorism and must be the monopoly of power by a political party, that is, by its leading gang. It will, by necessity, destroy society and subjugate everyone. . . . The dictatorship of the proletariat . . . must in our times transform the population into masses and create a mass-state, just as fascist dictatorships do."[20] The dream of mankind had turned into another dictatorial nightmare. The mass-state, Lederer wrote, was "inimical to reason and destructive of civilization."[21]

Lederer wrote these lines to save socialism from itself. His task was to transform its utopian streak into a "realistic" socialism. Trying to safeguard the socialist creed of "planned production," he argued that such social and economic planning is possible only "on a democratic basis."[22] In other words, *State of the Masses* made the case for social democracy. Strauss did not follow Lederer in this respect. Instead, he sought to describe the nihilistic reaction to the communist ideal more closely. He combined Lederer's lesson on the transformation of the classless society into a totalitarian dictatorship with a different set of ideas, which belonged to the pool of relatively stable motifs he used across various texts and contexts. Its core is the notion of the world-state and its purported counternarrative, Nietzsche's story of the "last man." Assuring that the nihilists were not concerned with their own "economic and social position," he explained their anticommunism in terms that resembled the discourse of *Kulturkritik* with its uneasy combination of culture and politics:

> What they hated, was the very prospect of a world in which everyone would be happy and satisfied, in which everyone would have his little pleasure by day and his little pleasure by night, a world in which no great heart could beat and no great soul could breathe, a world without real, unmetaphoric, sacrifice, i.e. a world without blood, sweat, and tears. What to the communists appeared to be the fulfilment of *the* dream of mankind, appeared to those young Germans as the greatest debasement of humanity, as the coming of the end of humanity, as the arrival of the latest man.[23]

The discourse of *Kulturkritik* is the habitat in which the Nietzschean "last man" (or "latest man") lived to provide an image of the "most contemptible man."[24] Again, Strauss did not simply subscribe to the view he presented. He coupled the Nietzschean image with a reference to Winston Churchill's "Blood, sweat, and tears" speech,[25] and he repeated this mating of Nietzsche and Churchill at the end of the text. As we shall see below, this move serves to redefine the difference between culture and civilization: Strauss transformed *Kulturkritik* into a defense of civilization. At this point, the contrast between Nietzsche and Churchill demonstrates that "the *same* passion" can express itself in different forms. In Nietzschean terms, the passion expresses itself within the sphere of culture, the discourse of *Kulturkritik*, which had nurtured the nihilistic desire to destroy modern civilization. In Churchillian terms, that passion expresses itself as a spirited defense of Western civilization. Strauss ultimately sided with Churchill against Germany, with British "prudence and moderation" against German radicalism and romantic nostalgia.[26]

Seen from that endpoint, the overall tone of defense and the emphasis on the nihilists' sincere motifs becomes more and more questionable. In particular, it does not seem to match with the course of the argument. Nevertheless, it has a precise, albeit limited, function in the text. The basis of the nihilists' opposition to communism is their tacit acceptance of a communist key presupposition:

> They simply took over the communist thesis that the proletarian revolution and proletarian dictatorship is necessary, if civilisation is not to perish. But they insisted rather more than the communists on the conditional character of the communist prediction (*if* civilisation is not to perish). That condition left room for *choice*: they chose what according to the communists was the only alternative to communism.[27]

The radical alternative between socialism or barbarism had been proposed most vigorously by Rosa Luxemburg. In the so-called Junius Pamphlet (1915) she wrote that World War I and the coming period of wars would bring about a reversion to barbarism:

> Thus we stand today, as Friedrich Engels prophesied more than a generation ago, before the awful proposition: Either the triumph of imperialism and the destruction of all culture, and, as in ancient Rome, depopulation, desolation, degeneration, a vast cemetery; or, the victory of Socialism, that is, the conscious struggle of the international proletariat against imperialism, against its methods, against war. This is the dilemma of world history, its inevitable choice, whose scales are trembling in the balance, awaiting the decision of the proletariat.[28]

History has reached an absolute moment in which the future course of mankind is decided. The regression into barbarism is not just some behavior that is inhumane or unjust, but a threat to civilization as such, a possible end to civilization. The future will either bring the global victory of war and death or else socialism will put an end to all this. Only socialism can prevent the "destruction of all culture."

In hindsight, fascism and communism had an equal share in the dissemination of war and death in the twentieth century. The more immediate reaction of those people whom Strauss had in mind in "German Nihilism," however, was to take the socialist alternative seriously but to emphasize its downsides. They granted that the future was bound to bring about the classless society, but they denied that this option was preferable to the prospect of war and death. In short: if the alternative was either socialism or barbarism, the nihilists chose barbarism as the lesser evil. But hereby they had conceded that there was a fundamental alternative between socialism or barbarism. As Strauss argued, they could not evade the alternative because they had tacitly accepted the historical prediction upon which it was based: "Unfortunately, all rational argument they knew of, was *historical* argument, or more precisely: statements about the probable future, *predictions*, which were based on the analysis of the past, and above all, of the present."[29] In other words, they were historicists in disguise—progressives with the opposite polarity. Strauss saw the fallacy of the nihilists in the fact that they stuck to communism's *historical* argument regarding the probable future. Even as they opposed communism, they remained entangled with the communist thesis of "history" and "progress."

Strauss was apparently convinced that this emphasis on the covert historicism was his major insight concerning the political events of the time, even as virtually no one else seemed to buy into the idea. "Historicism" is also the title of the lecture he delivered at the New School in 1941, this time in the Study Group. Arguing for a broad definition of historicism, he declared that democrats, fascists, and communists alike were covert historicists.[30] Already his 1940 lecture at Syracuse University, "The Living Issues of German Postwar Philosophy," had in large part been devoted to the topic.[31] As to the German nihilists, Strauss linked their covert historicism to their failure to become truly radical, using a line of argument he had rehearsed in his "Notes on Carl Schmitt": Just as Schmitt turned out to be a liberal "with the opposite polarity,"[32] the nihilists were progressives with the opposite polarity. And their political radicalism was just the flip side of their nonradical philosophizing. Hence, they remained within the horizon of what they opposed.

It is useful to compare this genuinely Straussian viewpoint on nihilism with his description of nihilism "from the point of view of the nihilists themselves." Appealing with a rhetoric of radical understanding "to the highest duty of the scholar, truthfulness or justice," Strauss embarked on a long journey through the nihilists' phraseology:

> "Nihilism," they would say, is a slogan used by those who do not understand the new. . . . How can a reasonable man expect an adequate expression of the ideal of a new epoch at its beginning, considering that the owl of Minerva starts its flight when the sun is setting? The Nazis? Hitler? The less is said about him, the better. He will soon be forgotten. He is merely the rather contemptible *tool* of "History": the midwife who assists at the birth of a new epoch, of a new spirit; and a midwife usually understands nothing of the genius at whose birth she assists; she is not even supposed to be a competent gynaecologist. A new

reality is in the making; it is transforming the whole world; in the meantime there is: nothing, but—a fertile nothing. The Nazis are as unsubstantial as clouds; the sky is hidden at present by those clouds which announce a devastating storm, but at the same time the long-needed rain which will bring new life to the dried up soil; and (here I am almost quoting) do not lose hope; what appears to you the end of the world, is merely the end of an epoch, of the epoch which began in 1517 or so.[33]

This long quote has posed a great obstacle for commentators. It is the point where W. H. F. Altman—whose interpretive ambition surpasses all other commentators of "German Nihilism"—can no longer follow the text. According to Altman's overall narrative, Strauss was learning the art of writing "between the lines" at the time he composed his lecture (the same year he published his article "Persecution and the Art of Writing"); he sought to place a hidden message to his followers in the phrases above; but since his command of exoteric writing was not yet sufficient, he unwillingly expressed his real opinion too openly; hence, the quote reveals the secret teaching of "German Nihilism." This teaching can be explained in a single sentence: "Strauss hails National Socialism as 'a new epoch at its beginning.'"[34]

The principal fallacy is to misattribute the voice in the text to Strauss. Strauss's quote is replete with notions from the arsenal of historical thought that allegedly had a share in the rise of nihilism and eventually National Socialism. The synthetic summary is meant to characterize the position of the conservative revolutionaries who openly despised Hitler but initially saw him as a welcome ally, or a useful tool, in the fight against the liberalism of the Weimar Republic. Strauss let the audience know that he was speaking *from the point of view of the nihilists themselves,* that he was *almost quoting* them, mimicking what *they would say*. Stressing their covert historicism, he showed that they were a part of the problem, not its solution. The emphasis on "history" and on "the new" (*a new epoch at its beginning, a new spirit, a new reality*) narrows down the scope of this problem. As he suggested, it was the progressive belief in a "new epoch," for which National Socialism would merely be a necessary interlude, which made the conservative revolutionaries prone to complicity with National Socialism. Strauss's subsequent comment brings this point home:

> I frankly confess, I do not see how those can resist the voice of that siren who expect the answer to the first and the last

question from "History," from the future *as such*; who mistake analysis of the present or past or future for philosophy; who believe in a progress toward a goal which is itself progressive and therefore undefinable.[35]

The fallacy of the conservative revolutionaries was that they took over the communist notion of a coming revolution, thereby importing the communist analysis of the present (the *situation*) and their prediction about the future (the *new epoch*). "History" and "progress" were the presuppositions of their thought, borrowed from communism, which made them susceptible to underestimating the danger of Hitler.

One may question the scope of that thesis for good reasons. Strauss may stretch the fact that virtually all political movements were entangled in the snares of "history" and "progress" a bit too far here. And yet his analyses were entirely correct as far as his main personnel, especially Ernst Jünger, were concerned. Jünger, who is mentioned several times in the text, strongly emphasized the coming of a new epoch. Strauss referred to his essay on pain, where Jünger announced the imminent coming of "a last . . . phase of nihilism, which is characterized by the fact that new orders have largely advanced already, while the *values* that correspond to these orders have not yet become visible."[36] The new epoch would be marked by man's ability to endure pain, and pain would serve as the ultimate moral and epistemic standard. Jünger was certainly a good example for the latent progressivism of reactionary thought. The same goes for Oswald Spengler, another German nihilist named in the text.[37]

But ultimately, Strauss's point is philosophical in nature: it leads to the point where philosophy itself is at stake. Strauss spelled out this argument more visibly in his "Restatement" on Xenophon's *Hiero*, on the occasion of his debate with Alexandre Kojève on the universal and homogeneous state at the end of history. Strauss carried over some of his arguments from "German Nihilism" and elaborated on them rhetorically, but the pattern of argument on the prospect of a "nihilistic revolution" against the world state remained virtually unchanged. It shows that he had a clear idea of how to find a way out of the impasse between proponents and opponents of the world state. That state, he wrote, is "the state in which the basis of man's humanity withers away, or in which man loses his humanity. It is the state of Nietzsche's 'last man.'"[38] Evoking the dreadful image of an anticommunist/fascist counterrevolution against the world state and the coming of the Nietzschean "last man," Strauss showed that this prospect was inevitable only as long as one accepts Kojève's premise—the Hegelian-Marxist premise of *work* and *recognition*. Proponents and opponents of the universal and homogeneous state believed that its coming was inescapable, because they were all committed to the Hegelian-Marxist premise. There may be debate as to whether this argument is as strong as Strauss believed. But it is the place in the text where he prepared his audience for the truly radical alternative. This alternative would settle the political argument between fascists and communists: the possible conversion to philosophy.

> But perhaps it is not war nor work but thinking that constitutes the humanity of man. Perhaps it is not recognition . . . but wisdom that is the end of man. Perhaps the universal and homogeneous state is legitimated by the fact that its coming is the necessary condition for the coming of wisdom . . . if the final state is to satisfy the deepest longing of the human soul, every human being must be capable of becoming wise.[39]

In other words, both the progressives and the nihilists could become philosophers. This conversion to philosophy is also the vanishing point of "German Nihilism." The possibility of becoming a philosopher also has a broader political implication here: It shows that there is a way to live a "moral life" that would *not* be complicit in the political catastrophes of the twentieth century.

Strauss, of course, had in mind a particular type of philosophy to serve as a bulwark against nihilism, culturalism, historicism, communism, and fascism at the same time. Only Platonic political philosophy reborn would provide a standard beyond "history" and "progress." As Strauss explained, the conservative revolutionaries who are nihilists, historicists, and progressives at the same time "are not guided by a *known* and *stable* standard: by a standard which is stable and not changeable, and which is known and not merely believed."[40] He advocated for a stable notion of reason against which all historical change could be measured. Commentators are likely to understand this "standard" as a reactionary resurgence of Platonism; but as *Philosophy and Law* has shown, it is well thought out. And whereas *Philosophy and Law* developed the notion of a nonchangeable standard of reason via Maimonides and Plato, "German Nihilism" plays it out right in the field of modern thought. The setting is the distinction between culture and civilization in the last two sections of the text.

Strauss's discussion of culture and civilization marks a turnaround in the understanding of a controversial topic. According to an older view in early twentieth-century Germany and onward, Western man lived in an age of decline, of *mere* civilization as opposed to culture. Civilization was first and foremost a debasement of culture. This perception played a decisive role in the pre–World War I discourse on the alleged superiority of the German people over the Western nations. For many genealogists of National Socialism, it also had a strong impact on the political anomalies of modern German history. Strauss dismissed the view as resulting from "romantic judgment,"[41] from an uncanny longing for the tribal past. The occupation with the natural basis of the Germanic *Volk*, which was still prevalent when "culture" was played out against "civilization," was not his greatest concern in his overall critique of culture, but it certainly added to his discontent. The main line at this point is: a nihilist rejects the principles of civilization while he might appreciate culture. Many nihilists love culture despite their contempt for civilization; even the "champion of nihilism," Adolf Hitler, was "famous for his love of art" but had nothing to do with the search for truth.[42]

Strauss objected to the concept of culture here that it does not specify what is to be cultivated—it could be blood and soil as well as the human mind. This argument refers to the emergence of the modern notion of culture in the late seventeenth century. Until then, the term *culture* predominantly referred to the cultivation of the soul (*cultura animi*); henceforth, it became autonomous and referred to all products and practices of the human mind. The reference to the Nazi creed of "blood and soil" points to the consequence of this modern notion of culture—its peculiar double feature of relativism and particularism. The relativistic consequence is that, without further qualification, everything becomes "cultural," even the products and practices of National Socialism. The particularistic consequence is the notion of a *German* culture, people, or race.[43]

Strauss unanimously opted for "civilization" for the reason that the notion is neither relativistic nor particularistic: It is incommensurate with particularism because it refers to man as man, and it is nonrelativistic because it relates to man as a political being. As he explained, it "designates at once the process of making man a citizen, and not a slave; an inhabitant of cities, and not a rustic; a lover of peace, and not of war; a polite being, and not a ruffian."[44] In the terminology of "German Nihilism," culture is an aesthetic notion, and civilization is a political notion. Civilization is a reflection of culture in terms of its political and ethical basis: "By civilization, we understand the conscious culture of humanity, i.e. of that which makes a human being a human being, i.e. the conscious culture of reason."[45]

On this basis, Strauss proposed a stripped-down, radically simplified notion of human reason, which follows up on the prior debate on the systematic division of philosophy (see part I above): "Human reason is active, above all, in two ways: as regulating human conduct, and as attempting to understand whatever can be understood by man; as practical reason, and as theoretical reason. The pillars of civilization are therefore morals and science, and both united."[46] Against the Kantian triad of logic, ethics and, aesthetics, which had been re-erected within the neo-Kantian philosophy of culture, Strauss proposed a definition of reason within a framework of civilization. Civilization rests on the two "pillars" of science and morals. Both are referred to each other, because science without morals becomes cynical, and morals without science becomes superstitious and fanatic. Aesthetics and art are "deliberately" excluded from this definition.[47]

With the Kantian framework in mind, the obvious question is what brings morals and science together once the triad of science, morals, and aesthetic judgment has been torn apart. After all, the faculty of judgment was cited by Kant specifically to bring morals and science together after reason had separated the two from each another. The solution in "German Nihilism" is as follows: if culture is replaced by civilization, the place of aesthetics in the systematic disposition of philosophy is occupied by political philosophy. And whereas aesthetics belongs to the cultural understanding of reason, political philosophy unites morals and science within a civilizational understanding of reason. Aesthetic judgment is replaced by political judgment. But there is also a fundamental systematic difference between aesthetics and political philosophy, for the latter does not constitute a "domain" of its own; it does not add a third pillar to the two pillars of civilization.

This orientation toward morals and science—the two pillars of civilization—comes closest to "a *known* and *stable* standard." In the teaching of "German Nihilism," this standard would strengthen the "resistance to nihilism."[48] The conversion to philosophy is therefore not a conversion to a particular program of philosophy (namely, Straussian philosophy) or a mere leap into premodern philosophy (Platonic philosophy unrefined). Strauss outlined a broader program of education toward reason, with its two pillars in practical and theoretical philosophy, united by a *civilizational* and hence *political* understanding of philosophy. What results and insights follow from such education is in principle open. But in any case, it needed to facilitate a genuine conversion, rather than a gradual shift, to philosophy.

A Parable of Liberal Education

The vanishing point of a possible conversion to philosophy helps to understand why such a large portion of "German Nihilism" is devoted to education—in fact, the text is to a great extent a parable of liberal education. This also explains why so many of Strauss's arguments are *directional* arguments: they are intended to show and exemplify a way out of an impasse by *leading* to philosophy. The rhetoric of radical understanding has a precise meaning within the context of education toward philosophy. As the saying goes, Strauss wanted to start from where the nihilists stood, so that he could draw them into philosophy. To quote his own words, he wanted to give an answer that "would have impressed the young nihilists if they had heard it."[49] It must remain open here how the orientation toward morals and science could have truly "impressed" the young nihilists. But whether or not the program of education toward philosophy is realistic, it is in principle not apologetic.[50]

The topic of education first comes to sight where the text emphasizes the German nihilists' adolescence. The repeated statement that they are young suggests in the first place that they are not philosophers. The statement that they are "very intelligent and very decent"[51] indicates that they could become philosophers. In the terminology of *Persecution and the Art of Writing*, they are "the puppies" of the philosophical breed, "the young men who might become philosophers: the potential philosophers are to be led step by step from the popular views which are indispensible for all practical and political purposes to the truth which is merely and purely theoretical."[52] Educating these young men toward philosophy would effect the mating of their radicalism with moderation.[53] Their adolescent passion would be directed toward wisdom, so that their inarticulate protest against civilization would eventually be replaced by a qualified embrace of Western civilization.

Strauss's emphasis on the nihilists' adolescence comes with a swipe against the liberal teachers of the interwar period. He ventured that the progressive thinkers of the Weimar Republic had contributed to the rise of German nihilism because they could not give a meaningful answer to the young radicals' questions. According to this view, the liberal defenders of culture had a share in the rise of National Socialism: deeply rooted in their progressive beliefs, they merely refuted the destructive aspirations of their pupils rather than trying to understand their radicalism: "They believed to have refuted the No by refuting the Yes, i.e. the inconsistent, if not silly, positive assertions of the young men. . . . And many opponents did not even *try* to understand the ardent passion underlying the negation of the present world and its potentialities. As a consequence, the very refutations confirmed the nihilists in their belief." The liberal belief in modern civilization and its infinite progress had turned into a prejudice and become apologetic and defensive.[54]

This part of Strauss's narrative has occasionally been singled out for its alleged polemical content, in particular because it appears to match at least in part with his description of Ernst Cassirer.[55] But the case against Strauss is not very strong here. The weakness of liberal democracy in the late Weimar Republic is well known, and the same goes for the weakness of liberal philosophy and education. The proposition that certain dogmatic elements of liberalism contributed to the young antiliberals becoming more radical is principally sound. We may compare this stance to the position of Walter Benjamin, who was similarly convinced that progressivism was complicit in the rise of fascism. As he argued, fascism benefited from a liberal misrepresentation of history as progress. The problem with the conformist Social Democrats was that they opposed fascism "in the name of progress as a historical norm."[56] They presupposed a progress of humanity proper (not just a relative progress in human ability and knowledge) and expected it to be infinite and inevitable. As Michael Bernstein commented:

> Benjamin became convinced that Social Democratic policies, old-fashioned narrative historiography, and a belief in the attainability of social progress were in fact three directly linked manifestations of a single evil. In his view, it was precisely these three ideas that had prepared the philosophical path for fascism's success, and each of them needed to be categorically resisted. It is difficult to imagine a more disastrously self-isolating position in the embattled circumstances of the 1930s, but Benjamin clung to it with increasing stubbornness, even as its untenability became more evident with every Nazi victory.[57]

Benjamin's position may have been untenable, but others fared little better. The same goes for Strauss. Neither Benjamin nor Strauss claimed that the progressivists were actually Nazis, or that a straight line led from Cassirer to Hitler. Their shortcomings are not altogether different from those of their liberal counterparts. In one way or another, everyone involved understood the rise of National Socialism in the light of their own theoretical and political imprints, thereby combining blindness and insight in ever-new ways. No one could have fully grasped in real time how the horrors of National Socialism unfolded. Seen from the perspective of full knowledge about the extermination camps, most contributions to the overall debate were more or less grotesque misunderstandings of the situation. In retrospect, then, that debate was an intellectual battlefield on which a variety of problems and solutions were played and fought out, but it was *the* battlefield in which all participants revealed their intellectual imprints and prejudices most openly. Seen within the context of that larger debate, there is little to object to in Strauss's claim that the crisis of liberal education shared some responsibility for the rise of National Socialism, but it is only a minor variation on the surface of opinions regarding the intellectual origins of National Socialism.

A Second Narrative on German Philosophy and Politics

To sum up Strauss's argument thus far: His first explanation for the rise of German nihilism was that it stemmed from anticommunism, and it led him to discern the nihilists' covert historicism. He reversed the relationship between culture and civilization and reaffirmed the understanding of morals and science as the two "pillars" of civilization. Suggesting the young nihilists' possible conversion to philosophy, he held that the progressives had a share in the process in which German nihilism turned into National Socialism.

Now, there is a second line of thought in the text, according to which German nihilism stems from German militarism. The ensuing genealogy is remarkably different from the first, although nihilism and militarism may otherwise have much in common. Both reject peace, and particularly the idea of eternal peace, in favor of war; both passionately respond to modern civilization, combining the initial moral motivation of their protest with the insufficiency of their mere reaction; and both are a *response* to the ideal of the revolution. In general, Strauss reframed developments in German thought as a response to respective developments in Western (English or French) thought. Again, the argument is in principle not apologetic, and Strauss also stressed that the response was inappropriate, albeit understandable. Moreover, it is entirely consistent with his overall understanding of the history of philosophy, in particular of modern philosophy. Each time, a teaching is forced to rebuild itself to counter the attack of another teaching, and each time, the rebuilding causes previous insights to be forgotten. There is a clear historiographical pattern in Strauss's work through the ambiguities of philosophy and politics.

As to the genealogy of German "militarism," scholars have often stressed the fact that the German nation or German civilization is *younger*, or came later, than the Western nations. This was the main thesis of Plessner's *Die verspätete Nation*. Strauss appeared to advocate this view in his lecture "The Living Issues of German Postwar Philosophy" (1940), holding that "the Germans are, strictly speaking, less civilized than the English and the French, i.e., they are to a lesser degree citizens, *free* citizens."[58] One year later, he may still have thought that the Germans were less civilized, but he had come to doubt the explanatory value of this diagnosis. He refuted it by way of a simple counterexample: other nations, particularly the Slavonic nations, were even younger than Germany, but they did not embark on the same path of militarism and nihilism.[59]

Strauss concluded that the discussion should be shifted from the "prehistory" of German civilization to the encounter of modern German civilization with the Enlightenment. To follow through the narrative on the German revolt against the Enlightenment: the ideal of modern civilization as conceived in the seventeenth and eighteenth centuries originated in England and France. Its tendency was to *lower the standards* of moral conduct against the classical notion of virtue. This "lowering of the standards"[60]—a chief characteristic of modernity for Strauss—came together with a shift from duties to rights, with the notion of enlightened self-interest, with putting political utility in the place of honesty, and with solving the conflict between private and common interest by way of industry and trade. The high point of German civilization and culture between 1760 and 1830 was reached by way of a *reaction* to this ideal of civilization and its perceived debasement of morality. The German reaction to the Enlightenment spirit laid the intellectual foundation for German militarism: German philosophers insisted on old-fashioned noble morality as opposed to self-interest, and on duty and honesty as opposed to utility; they emphasized self-sacrifice and self-denial against the fusion of the self with the spirit of commerce. But they overemphasized these virtues to such an extent that they neglected happiness, the natural aim of man. Being radical in their opposition to the Enlightenment, they were driven toward one particular virtue in which the contrast between nobility and utility and between duty and self-interest was visible most clearly, namely, courage. Courage, the military virtue per se, is the only virtue that is not rewarded, that does not pay off, as seen in the example of self-sacrifice on the battlefield. "Courage is the only unambiguously unutilitarian virtue." Thus, the German philosophers defended pre-Enlightenment morality but thereby came to overstress the military virtue.[61]

To continue with Strauss's narrative, a decisive turnaround occurred in the second half of the nineteenth century. Up until then, German philosophy had understood itself as a synthesis of premodern and modern thought, but now it became clear that such a synthesis was untenable. This was due to the emergence of positivism. Faced with the impossible task of maintaining the synthesis against the positivistic creed, the German philosophers "saw no way out except to purify German thought completely from the influence of the ideas of modern civilization, and to return to the pre-modern ideal. National Socialism is the most famous, because the most vulgar, example of such a return to a pre-modern ideal."[62]

We have traveled a long way on the road that, according to Strauss, led from eighteenth-century German philosophy to Hitler. The first part of the argument is written exactly along the lines of his opening statement in "The Living Issues of German Postwar Philosophy" (1940): "Both the intellectual glory and the political misery of the Germans may be traced back to one and the same cause. . . . German philosophy *implies* a more or less radical criticism of the very idea of civilisation and especially of modern civilization—a criticism disastrous in the political field, but necessary in the philosophical, in the theoretical field."[63] The second part of the argument shows why such a clear-cut separation between philosophy and politics was unsustainable. It also raises the question of whether the development of German militarism can indeed be properly understood as a response—no matter how insufficient—to French and English thought. Strauss thereby seems to neglect the fact that the turn to scientism in Germany also had its roots in German thought.

However, the argument has a specific function in the text, and its explanatory value largely follows from this function. We must keep in mind here that the genealogy of German militarism is but one out of two genealogical explanations given by Strauss, which partly refute each other. According to the first explanation, German nihilism was a passionate response to communism, whereas in the second explanation it was a response to the Enlightenment ideal of civilization. In moving through a variety of explanations and contradictions, "German Nihilism" performs its own argument in the action of the text.

Strauss did not entirely refute any connection between German philosophy and politics; he argued for a more complex, and in the last resort aporetic, view of the relationship. He had started in 1940 from the assumption that the course of German philosophy was "disastrous in the political field but necessary in the philosophical, in the theoretical field."[64] Accordingly, the antipolitical or metapolitical radicalism marked "both the intellectual glory and the political misery" of German thought. It was beneficial for its insistence on nature as opposed to civilization, but it ended in misery by seeking nature either in the Teutonic past or in classical antiquity.[65] German philosophers laid bare the natural foundations of civilization, but their opposition was articulated in the very terms of what they opposed. Again, their radicalism turned out not to be radical enough. "German Nihilism," written a year later, shows that such a separation could not be maintained. The text's original contribution to the genealogies of National Socialism, then, is the demonstration that the relationship between philosophy and politics remains aporetic. This aporetic stance is also the hallmark of Strauss's later statements on Nietzsche and Heidegger. They combine a certain aporetic subversion of arguments with a clear and continuous reference to common sense:

> Everyone who had read his first great book and did not overlook the wood for the trees could see the kinship in temper and direction between Heidegger's thought and the Nazis. . . . The case of Heidegger reminds to a certain extent of the case of Nietzsche. Nietzsche, naturally would not have sided with Hitler. Yet there is an undeniable kinship between Nietzsche's thought and fascism.[66]

Another example from a later text concerns the facts of Heidegger's involvement with National Socialism:

> We cannot help holding these facts against Heidegger. Moreover, one is bound to misunderstand Heidegger's thought radically if one does not see their intimate connection with the core of his philosophic thought. Nevertheless, they afford too small a basis for the proper understanding of his thought.[67]

The aporetic stance in these quotes demonstrates and exemplifies the limits of reasoning when it comes to the relationship between German philosophy and German politics. The tension is mimetically reproduced in a spoken introduction to Nietzsche in 1971:

> Nietzsche produced the climate in which Fascism and Hitlerism could emerge. One must not be squeamish about admitting this dubious paternity. One must emphasize it. Every fool can see and has seen that Nietzsche abhorred the things for which Hitler in particular stood and to which he owed his success.[68]

Last but not least, the Straussian trademark aporia on Heidegger as a "great thinker" belongs to this context: "Only a great thinker could help us in our intellectual plight. But here is the great trouble: the only great thinker in our time is Heidegger."[69]

Strauss did not deny any connection between German philosophy and German politics, but he was careful not to unriddle that connection by way of a simple argument. His position is free from the ambivalent reverence that characterizes Löwith's position on Heidegger. It refutes the politicization of philosophy—the "reductio ad Hitlerum"—as well as the "other Germany" thesis, according to which the German philosophers have nothing to do with the course of German politics.[70] His paradoxical stance, then, simply expresses the aporia inherent in the genealogies of National Socialism right from the beginning. In one sense or another, every statement on the matter was a part of the problem and not a proper solution.

Conclusion

Looking back at the genealogies of German philosophy, we are advised to maintain a categorical historiographical difference between National Socialism and the Holocaust. The knowledge of mass annihilation of European Jewry fundamentally altered the genre, for it became far more difficult to trace mass annihilation to German philosophy than it had been with National Socialism in general, not speaking of the much wider genealogical effort to trace the roots of "militarism."

This is not to argue that National Socialism had nothing to do with the Holocaust, for the Holocaust clearly followed (albeit not necessarily) from the principles of National Socialism. A categorical difference can be maintained only with regard to the retrospective understanding of the political events in light of their presumed intellectual origins. In *this* respect, the succession of German militarism, National Socialism, and the Holocaust is *not* a gradual escalation of one and the same principle of some German national character that was miraculously preserved in the great formations of German philosophy. The more the horror of German politics unfolded, the less it could be explained from the history of German thought.

With the gradual awareness of the horrors of National Socialism—coinciding with the increasing certainty that Germany was losing the war—a fundamental change within the genre occurred in 1942–43. Attention shifted from the concern with the intellectual roots of National Socialism toward the policies of postwar reeducation in Germany. At the New School, the collective research work was reorganized in the winter of 1942–43. The discussion changed its course and saw, among other things, a return of economic planning. Adolph Lowe contributed an eighty-page paper outlining the task for the political and economic integration of postwar Europe to reconstruct Germany by means of economic planning: "Europe should not be abandoned to the blind and erratic forces of the marketplace." The search for the intellectual origins of National Socialism was replaced by topics such as "totalitarian methods of state intervention, women's place in the German labor force, the demise of small business in Germany, the decline of working-class living standards, and resource allocation under the Nazis."[71] Leo Strauss, too, contributed a paper to the question of reeducation, which was published under the title "The Re-Education of Axis Countries Concerning the Jews."[72] Overall, New School members were not too influential in the policies of reeducation, unlike some of their colleagues over at the Institute for Social Research, such as Franz Neumann.

The shift from the intellectual origins of National Socialism to the more practical matters of future reeducation was one part of the change. Another pertained to the remaining discourse on the roots of National Socialism. While many scholars left the genealogical discourse altogether, those who still sought to trace the horrors of National Socialism through the history of German thought often resorted to longer historical lines. Particularly on the margins of that discourse, a variety of odd genealogies were put forth, often reaching back as far as to the origins of Western thought. Two preeminent genealogists of National Socialism, Karl R. Popper and Theodor W. Adorno, went as far as to evoke Homer and Plato. While Popper embarked upon a path all the way back "from Hitler back to Plato,"[73] Adorno read the *Odyssey* as an allegory of one historical principle that led from Homer to Hitler.[74]

The examples of Popper and Adorno were not chosen at random. The two philosophers were the main participants in the so-called positivist dispute in the 1960s.[75] The respective methodological debates contain some metaphorical references to National Socialism and the persecution of the Jews. This occasion also furthered the process in which key texts of Western thought were swallowed into the antitotalitarian mood of the postwar era. Overall, however, Popper and Adorno are but two examples of how the genealogies of National Socialism retained a strange afterlife in contemporary thought. Evoking the imaginary endpoint of Hitler, the genealogies of National Socialism also provided a convenient way to dispose of a thinker whom one did not much like. For example, Nietzsche was a main target in the genealogies of Georg Lukács and, later, Jürgen Habermas.[76]

These late ramifications of the genealogical discourse notwithstanding, the purpose of revisiting the genre is not so much to defend German philosophy against its uncanny affiliation with politics. Most of all, it is necessary to acquaint oneself with the genre in order to break with the pattern that evokes a philosopher as a precursor, ideologue, or hidden sympathizer of National Socialism. (Needless to say perhaps, this holds true only for genuine philosophers and not for the actual Nazi thinkers such as Baeumler or Rosenberg.) Not coincidentally, apart from the notorious Heidegger, the philosopher who has recently been linked to this ideology is Leo Strauss. Read without regard to the philosophical framework in which they are situated, his wartime analyses of pre–World War II German philosophy and politics—written in a "moment of danger"—appear as a partly crude and borderline-apologetic defense of the conservative revolutionaries who preceded National Socialism. Upon closer inspection, however, these analyses are part of a philosophical program in which all political motives become part of a program of education toward philosophy, in which the young radicals of a generation—the "puppies," as Strauss came to call them—moderate their views due to their exposure to philosophy.

Strauss's wartime statements call for a careful reading with regard to the intricate relationship between philosophy and politics. His "German Nihilism" lecture in particular, if seen within the larger context of the genealogies of National Socialism, helps to develop a more precise notion of the nature of philosophical ideas. The inner-philosophical chain of influence and tradition follows a different logic than the course of national politics. And whereas each philosophy is rooted within its specific time and place, one may not overlook its transcultural and transtemporal dimension—in Strauss's words, its claim to universality (even as the validity of this claim may, retrospectively, be limited to a specific situation). To read the long-forgotten texts, as well as those texts that have become a bone of contention in the culture wars of the present, is necessary because many of the methodological pitfalls of the genealogies of National Socialism are still lurking when we attempt to clarify the relationship between philosophy and politics today.

Part IV

Strauss on Modern Relativism

12

From "Culture" to "Cultures"

Émigré Scholars, the Rise of Cultural Anthropology, and the Americanization of Leo Strauss

It is remarkable how easily Strauss seemed to adapt his scholarly project, which was so deeply rooted in the German philosophical tradition, to the new context of American social science. He established within the American social sciences a certain attitude and style of uncompromising German *Gelehrsamkeit*,[1] but he also spoke the language of social science debates (albeit with a heavy philosophical accent). Intellectual historians have long noted this self-adaptation, but they needed to reconcile it with their view of the continuity in his thought, namely, with the "Weimar Jew" narrative.[2] According to this narrative, Strauss outwardly adapted well to the American social sciences, but in his philosophical and political views he always remained a Weimar Jew, projecting the intellectual constellation of post-assimilationist Jewry in the late Weimar Republic onto the situation of postwar America. For some of his rather outspoken critics, he used his extraordinary rhetorical talent to hold on to the political views he held in Germany but to express them in a language that suited the situation of post–World War II America, hiding his Weimar Jew mindset behind the language of democracy and liberal education. For those who subscribe to this viewpoint, Strauss represents both the theoretical imagination and the political danger of what Steven Aschheim has aptly termed the "cult of Weimar."[3]

The problem with this half-canonical interpretation is that it cannot account for the profound changes in Strauss's theoretical framework *after* Weimar. We come to a different conclusion if we focus on a set of theoretical writings on modern social science, which contain Strauss's own discussions of the intellectual migration from Germany to the United States. These texts form a microcosm in which a variety of theoretical problems and historical experiences were played out. The concept of culture with its transformations is a key concept here. Strauss did not merely apply his critique of "culture" to American social sciences, he traced the prior migration of the concept into the American discourse and its transformation. His own intellectual transition is to be detected in a shift of his critical attention from "culture" to "cultures."

This seemingly small modification led him to recalibrate his critique in several respects: First, it was more clearly than before directed against "relativism." Second, it was primarily targeted against the field of cultural anthropology, which was the paradigmatic form of a mixed German-American relativism prior to the influx of émigré scholars from Nazi Germany. And third, it was transposed into a framework in which the tension between historicism and positivism was the foremost theoretical concern.

When Strauss faced American social science, the transformation of German culturalism into American social science had already taken place. The decisive turnaround had occurred in the mid-1930s, when the academic discipline of cultural anthropology emerged as a major cultural force beyond academia. In the 1930s, as the anthropologists A. L. Kroeber and Clyde Kluckhohn put it, "the idea of culture, in the technical anthropological sense," became "one of the key notions of contemporary American thought."[4] The transmitter was Ruth Benedict's *Patterns of Culture* (1934). As Warren Susman noted in his landmark study on what he called the "culture of the thirties": "Obviously, the idea of culture was anything but new in the 1930s, but there is a special sense in which the idea became widespread in the period."[5] Until then, the predominant notion of culture was based on Matthew Arnold's *Culture and Anarchy* (1869). For Arnold it was "the love of perfection" that was nurtured and preserved in culture.[6] Its material basis was high culture, especially the arts. But for the most part it was an "inward operation," such as in reading books, which came to be regarded as the very life and essence of culture.[7] Conceived in such a way, culture fostered the comprehensive development of man's highest faculties. It was the realm of the universal striving for "sweetness and light" (i.e., beauty and intelligence).[8] By the 1930s, this view of culture had come to be regarded as outdated. Susman explains:

> The remarkable popularity of Ruth Benedict's *Patterns of Culture* (1934)—surely one of the most widely read works of profes-

sional anthropology ever published in the United States—provides us with a symbolic landmark. Its impact was significant; but more important, her analysis of the possibility of different cultural patterns and the way such patterns shape and account for individual behavior was part of a more general discovery of the idea itself, the sense of awareness of what it means to *be* a culture. . . . It is not too extreme to propose that it was during the Thirties that the idea of culture was domesticated, with important consequences. Americans then began thinking in terms of patterns of behavior and belief, values and life-styles, symbols and meanings.[9]

The quote recaptures the amazement over the new "idea of culture" that arose in the 1930s: the smell of a new beginning, the conviction that previous theories of culture had all missed the most important point. But it also provides a sense of the eventual disappointment over the solutions. The new idea of culture was built upon a notion of cultures, or of *a* culture in express opposition to culture in the singular. This notion was not entirely new, and it had been preceded in Germany, too. It had its roots in the *Völkerpsychologie* of Wilhelm von Humboldt, in his followers Heymann Steinthal and Moritz Lazarus, and in Oswald Spengler's *Decline of the West* with its idea of a continuous rise and decline of cultures or civilizations. Cultural anthropologists in the 1930s knew these writings and studied them with different degrees of reverence and repulsion. But all of a sudden the philosophical and wider cultural implications of the idea of cultures seemed boundless and unheard of. Grace de Laguna explained these implications in a seminal article published in 1942:

As the anthropologist conceives it, a culture is an integrated individual whole. It is a complex of all that belongs to a common way of life. On its material side it includes, for example, dwellings and their mode of construction, tools and techniques, articles of food, modes of dress, etc. Equally constitutive of a culture are the form of social organization, language and myth, religious ceremonial and belief, moral standards and ideals, and all common modes of thought. All these fall into a distinctive pattern characteristic of the particular culture. All these traits, both material and immaterial, are mutually dependent and interrelated. Every culture is thus a more or less functional whole, a going concern, self-sustaining and self-perpetuating. There is an implicit nominalism in modern anthropological thought: it is the individual cultures which are real, while culture tends to be regarded as an abstraction.[10]

De Laguna's account of the wholeness of cultures was groundbreaking in her emphasis on the materiality and modality of culture. But most importantly, she followed Ruth Benedict in her emphasis on a certain "pattern" that runs through all forms of social life. Oddly enough, it was this purely formal and hence remarkably abstract notion of "patterns" that came to be seen as exceptionally *real*. This new idea of culture fundamentally changed the way in which Americans understood themselves. As Susan Hegeman noted, cultural anthropology taught people in America "to understand themselves as participating in a distinctive 'American' culture, and to see this culture as a set of patterns, values, and beliefs roughly comparable to those of other cultures. . . . 'Culture' may have hit home to many Americans, but it left them thinking about themselves and their allegiances in a newly relational, contextual, and often critical way."[11] The latter point is particularly important. Cultural anthropology may have taught Americans to see themselves as a part of "American culture," but this lesson came together with a new "openness" to other cultures. The new science of culture fostered a sense of otherness by teaching people to respect all other cultures and behavioral patterns. Not by coincidence, this new cultural awareness came into being at a time when the social sciences were particularly strong, with their impact reaching beyond the confines of a specialized discourse and into the broader public sphere. The creation of a purely *relational* and, to a hitherto unknown degree, *critical* individual was a major goal of progressive social science. Clearly, a new man was in the making.

The new understanding of culture in the 1930s was not fostered by cultural anthropology alone. Another source of culturalism in America at the time was the influx of German-speaking émigré scholars (and, to some extent, writers and artists). They played an important (and often neglected) role in the culturalization of America, although they also subverted the newly found notion of a distinct American culture. These émigré scholars, many of whom were Jewish, had grown up with the tension between universalism and particularism in the force field of culture, religion and the political. Hence, they had their own, often complicated story with "American" culture. And yet they had a large share in the way that "culture" came to be understood in the United States.

In Germany, three thousand scholars were dismissed from their academic positions in 1933 and after, most of them Jews or socialists or both. Two thousand of them fled Germany, with the United States the prime destination. While the overall immigration to the United States reached slightly more than one-fourth of the emigration from Nazi-controlled countries (130,000 out of 500,000), two-thirds of the refugee scholars made their way to the United States. A main reason for the relatively high number was the combination of comparably good job chances and a thriving academic community. Immigration became increasingly difficult from 1938 onward, with many restrictions imposed on those stranded in various parts of Europe; but the United States was one of the few countries that still accepted Jewish refugees at all.[12]

The impact of German-speaking émigré scholars is most obvious in the field of social science. In psychology, émigré scholars introduced Gestalt theory (Max Wertheimer) or social psychology (Kurt Lewin) and initiated the turn to the psychological foundations of fascism and anti-Semitism. That turn was closely linked to the influx of German and Austrian sociologists, for example, of the groups that came to be known as the Frankfurt School and the Vienna Circle. Political scientists such as Franz Neumann, Ernst Fraenkel, Franz Borkenau, and Hannah Arendt seem to provide the best example of the scholarly influx of German émigrés. Combining their recent political experiences with penetrating scientific analysis, political scientists from Germany (who for the most part *became* political scientists in America) exerted a profound change in their profession in the United States.[13]

The viewpoint summed up here is often embedded into a larger narrative on the happy encounter of German and American scholarship in unhappy circumstances. According to this narrative, German scholars overcame their "Teutonic" patterns of thought in the United States and became citizens of the world while American academia, in turn, overcame its nativist provincialism by way of the German influx. But not everyone was happy with the political and cultural influx of German scholars from the 1930s onward: the fusion of American and German scholarship was not in every respect a success. A fine example of the "curious logic"[14] of the intellectual migration is provided by the case of philosophy. The impact of German-speaking refugee scholars on the philosophical discipline tended to zero. Their lasting influence played out over a variety of academic fields and, most notably, in the larger cultural discourse that was largely formed in the 1960s and onward. Here, they emerged as the icons of a German-Jewish tradition that had never really been "at home" in the overall

German academic world before 1933.[15] German émigrés provided many of the keywords that originated in philosophy, sociology, or psychology, only to become formative for the wider intellectual sphere, and subsequently for everyday culture, in America.

This background helps to understand a particular Straussian discourse on the cultural influx of German thought. The "German connection" was a topic in Allan Bloom's best-selling book *The Closing of the American Mind* (1987). According to Bloom, it was the German émigrés who initiated the lapse of the American mind into relativism, with their concepts having become catchwords in everyday language of the United States. Bloom located this influx particularly in the films of Woody Allen, whose intellectual outlook he traced back via David Riesman and Erich Fromm to Martin Heidegger and Nietzsche: "There is now an entirely new language of good and evil, originating in an attempt to get 'beyond good and evil' and preventing us from talking with any conviction about good and evil anymore." That "new language of value relativism," he wrote, served as a "great release from the perpetual tyranny of good and evil."[16] As Bloom conceived the matter, it was all about the "popularization" of German philosophy in the United States.

> Words such as "charisma," "life-style," "commitment," "identity" and many others, all of which can easily be traced to Nietzsche [!], are now practically American slang, although they, and the things to which they refer, would have been incomprehensible to our fathers, not to speak of our Founding Fathers.
>
> The self-understanding of hippies, yippies, yuppies, panthers, prelates and presidents has unconsciously been formed by German thought of a half-century earlier . . . the new American life-style has become a Disneyland version of the Weimar Republic for the whole family.[17]

The Strauss-as-a-Weimar-Jew narrative rests on the premise that words such as these, written by a Straussian, match with his own stance. It seems, then, as if he transposed the reactionary discourse of German *Kulturkritik* to America.[18] But Strauss had little to do with that discourse, and he was not involved in the quarrels of Bloom. Most notably, Strauss was not at all concerned with the influx of émigré scholars, a group to which he himself belonged. His sole concern was the prior migration of ideas. His disdain with the influx of German ideas into the American discourse found its strongest expression in the diatribe in *Natural Right and History* that "it would not be the first time that a nation, defeated on the battlefield and, as it were, annihilated as a political being, has deprived its conquerors of the most sublime fruit of victory by imposing on them the yoke of its own thought."[19]

Strauss followed Ernst Troeltsch's assertion that the abandonment of natural right in Germany had led to relativism,[20] and he argued that the same goes now for Western thought in general. Undoubtedly, for Strauss modern relativism had originated in Germany and set foot in the American discourse via influential books such as Spengler's *Decline of the West*. In his imagination, modern relativism stood on the twin pillars of historicism and positivism, and these had been brought to America via the teachings of Oswald Spengler and Max Weber. The American work that combined these teachings most seamlessly was Ruth Benedict's *Patterns of Culture*.

Compared with Bloom, Strauss understood the problem in a longer historical timeframe. But he also maintained a more ambiguous stance on the German tradition. His argument in "The Living Issues of German Postwar Philosophy" (1940) was that this tradition with its emphasis on the critique of civilization was "disastrous in the political field but necessary in the philosophical, in the theoretical field."[21] In "German Nihilism" (1941), he demonstrated why such a separation between the political and the philosophical fields was untenable. But most of all, Strauss was solely concerned with the migration of ideas, particularly with the idea of culture, upon which both historicism and positivism were based to a large degree. Cultural anthropology was certainly a good example for this prior migration of ideas, having originated in German *Völkerpsychologie* and being transformed into a teaching that was widely perceived as being genuinely "American." Strauss saw that the anthropological discourse combined the two seemingly opposed characteristics of cultural relativism and absolutism.

13

Cannibalism

Leo Strauss and Cultural Anthropology

Cultural anthropology was not the only school of social science with which Strauss wrestled. He also discussed Max Weber at length, studied the behavioralists and quarreled with some of his fellow immigrants from Germany in political science departments in the United States. But cultural anthropology combined various traits that perfectly seemed to capture the spirit of the social sciences in the U.S.: it represented both the old and the new, the German origins and the American transformation, the coming together of historicism and positivism and, ultimately, the mating of relativism and absolutism.

Strauss did not write at length on cultural anthropology, but he gave a number of hints both in his major works and in his unpublished lectures. Cultural anthropology was a focal point in his theoretical imagination when he discussed the relativism of American social science. He placed one prominent hint in *Natural Right and History*, at the beginning of the first chapter, where he singled out anthropology as a proponent of the view that the experience of history proves the impossibility of natural right:

> The attack on natural right in the name of history takes, in most cases, the following form: natural right claims to be a right that is discernible by human reason and is universally acknowledged; but history (including anthropology) teaches us that no such right exists; instead of the supposed uniformity, we find an indefinite variety of notions of right or justice.[1]

This explicit inclusion, carefully hidden in brackets so as not to confirm the centrality of the move, is certainly an understatement: in twentieth-century social science, anthropology is not one among many fields that promote the idea of a variety of notions of right. Even if the general idea had been invented before, cultural anthropology was its chief promoter and provided it with a normative pretension hitherto unknown. As Edward Westermarck summed up the argument in *Origin and Development of the Moral Ideas*: "A mode of conduct which among one people is condemned as wrong is among another people viewed with indifference or regarded as praiseworthy or enjoined as a duty."[2] But it was not only this mother argument itself, but also its application to some extreme cases of life and death that turned cultural anthropology into a vanguard of relativism. Westermarck, for example, applied his insight to the ethics of killing one's own parents: "What appears to most of us as an atrocious practice," he wrote in 1932, "may really be an act of kindness, and is commonly approved or even insisted on, by the old people themselves."[3] He also named infanticide, incest, and cannibalism as examples of the cultural variability of moral judgments.[4]

In general, cultural anthropologists proved to be extremely open to practices such as cannibalism, human sacrifice, and genital mutilation (female circumcision). A fine example of this openness can be found in Jomo Kenyatta's *Facing Mount Kenya* (1938). Kenyatta, who was a student of Bronislaw Malinowski at the London School of Economics, argued that the initiation rites of the Gikuyu are "parts of an integrated culture" from which "no single part is detachable." He thereby meant to defend particularly the custom of female circumcision. Whereas "a good many Europeans" saw this as "nothing but a 'horrible' and 'painful' practice, suitable only to barbarians," he argued that it was "the most important custom among the Gikuyu," and "its abolition would prevent them from perpetuating that spirit of collectivism and national solidarity which they have been able to maintain from time immemorial."[5]

The case of genital mutilation as a "cultural" practice is still a topic of the twenty-first century, although its justification has somewhat shifted from culture to religion. The classical example is cannibalism. It has "played a big role in the history of Westerners' or Europeans' conceptions of 'the other' and thus in their self-reflection since the sixteenth century,"[6] with numerous references to the practice in modern popular culture. It also served as an important and serious reference point for thinking about good and evil. With the rise of cultural anthropology in the 1930s it also became a test case for liberals to reflect upon the principles and possible limits of liberalism (and for conservatives to lambaste the liberals for their lenient judgment). The fact that cannibalistic practices still prevailed seemed to provide an extreme case, which brought to light some of the most intricate moral and theoretical problems of judgment in the force field of politics and culture.

Strauss's references to cannibalism are legendary, but they have been understood too broadly. The context of his view on cultural anthropology helps to arrive at a more precise understanding of their meaning and purpose. The most prominent quote, still at the beginning of *Natural Right and History*, runs as follows:

> All societies have their ideals, cannibal societies no less than civilized ones. If the principles are sufficiently justified by the fact that they are accepted by a society, the principles of cannibalism are as defensible and sound as those of civilized life. From this point of view . . . nothing except dull and stale habit could prevent us from placidly accepting a change in the direction of cannibalism.[7]

According to the doctrine of cultural anthropology, all ideals and values are relative to a social group or culture. In effect, all ideals and values are justified by the fact that they are accepted by a social group or culture. There may be preferences or choices for the civilized life, but there is no principal reason why cannibalism should *not* be practiced. Most of all, there is no criterion by which civilization should be judged superior to the social life of those tribes which practice cannibalism. As Strauss explained with regard to Rousseau: "If the ultimate criterion of justice becomes the general will, i.e., the will of a free society, cannibalism is as just as its opposite. Every institution hallowed by a folk-mind has to be regarded as sacred."[8]

Strauss was primarily concerned with the epistemic and moral inability of modern reason—operating under the premises of historicism and positivism—"to take a stand for civilization against cannibalism." As to historicism, he explained:

> The relativist asserts that objectively civilization is not superior to cannibalism, for the case in favor of civilization can be matched by an equally strong or an equally weak case in favor of cannibalism. The fact that we are opposed to cannibalism is due entirely to our historical situation. But historical situations

> change necessarily into other historical situations. A historical situation productive of the belief in civilization may give way to a historical situation productive of belief in cannibalism. Since the relativist holds that civilization is not intrinsically superior to cannibalism, he will placidly accept the change of civilized society into cannibal society.[9]

Strauss continued that, under the premise of positivism, the very distinction between civilization and cannibalism came to be regarded as an inappropriate value judgment. "The use of the terms 'civilizations' or 'cultures' by scientific anthropology presupposes the abolition of the distinction between civilization and barbarism and therewith, in particular, the abolition of the distinction between civilization and cannibalism."[10]

This quote is from a forgotten section of Strauss's "Relativism" article that refers to Arnold Brecht,[11] a former colleague of Strauss at the New School who had sought to rebuff the cannibalism thesis in his book *Political Theory* (1959). Brecht was one among a number of political scientists at the time who wanted to have his cake and eat it too: he proposed some mild form of relativism that would avoid the relativistic consequences.[12] He attacked Strauss with an argument that both denied and affirmed scientific relativism. As he claimed, civilization *may* indeed be superior to cannibalism, but we cannot *know* scientifically that it is. On this basis he insinuated that Strauss's cannibalism thesis was flawed: "Where and when has a scientific relativist ever asserted as a fact that civilization is *not* superior to cannibalism?"[13] Brecht was familiar with the topic in general: he did not need to be told that the science of cultural anthropology had come into being. His claim that Strauss's statement "is in conflict with the facts"[14] easily turns against itself, and Strauss was at no loss to point out the inconsistencies of Brecht's reasoning.[15]

A textbook example of a scientific relativist asserting as a fact that cannibalism was superior to civilization is Ruth Benedict. In her early manuscript "The Uses of Cannibalism" (1925), she made the case for the praxis with unmatched bluntness. Seeking to do justice "to the reasonableness of cannibalism," she set out to explore the "excellent motives" behind it. Her description of the "ethical use" of cannibalism for the well-being of mankind is replete with positive emotional qualifiers:

> Especially it has been proven to foster the feeling of solidarity within the group and of antipathy toward the alien, providing

an incomparable means of gratifying with deep emotion the hatred of one's enemy. Indeed, all the noblest emotions have been found not only compatible with it, but reinforced by its practice. . . . Cannibalism has proved also to be extraordinarily well qualified to provide the excitement of an ultimate aggression.[16]

For Benedict, cannibalistic practices had a specific purpose for the society: they "satisfied the craving for violence," offering a channel for violence where Western societies could only go to war. Faced with this alternative, she combined her florid depictions of cannibalistic folk life with sober cost-benefit analysis: "When a modest feast had been secured, the fires were lighted, and the angry passion which uncurbed might have killed a hundred enemies was humanely employed in the disposal of a few."[17] Hence, cannibalism was not only "harmless" and "comparatively innocent,"[18] it was also a viable alternative to modern civilization with its proclivity toward war. Cannibalism was superior to civilization because it fostered emotional bonds, whereas modern Western societies were marked by a "breakdown of emotional satisfaction."[19] Drawing upon examples from the Indians of Vancouver Island and the Maoris of New Zealand, Benedict suggested "to see in all this a hopeful device for the re-establishment of an emotional complex which shows every sign of disintegration among us. It is obvious that something must be done, and no suggestion seems more hopeful than this drawn from the Maoris of New Zealand."[20] In a strict sense, Benedict's 1925 article, with its strong preference for cannibalism, was not relativistic. The overall sentiment was not that Westerners should not judge this practice but that Western societies should embrace it for their own well-being. This sentiment had moved into the background in her *Patterns of Culture* (1934), with its striking claim that Westerners should not condemn cannibalism because "standards . . . range in different societies."[21]

Strauss referred to this book over a span of many years in his seminars at the University of Chicago, as can be traced from the transcripts that have successively become available. As he jokingly told his audience in a 1963 seminar on the *Gorgias*, he frequently quoted the book "because it is the only book of cultural anthropology which I have ever read [laughter]."[22] In conjunction with the reference to anthropology at the beginning of *Natural Right and History*, the remark testifies to the enduring importance of Benedict's book for Strauss. Another reason he named for his frequent references was the high probability that some of his students "may have read it,"[23] because *Patterns of Culture* was on college reading lists at the time.

As a rule of thumb, when Strauss spoke of social science relativism he had cultural anthropology on his mind, and his view of cultural anthropology was shaped by Benedict's *Patterns of Culture*.

Two remarks in his unpublished 1956 lecture "Historicism and Modern Relativism" illustrate how he saw the book. As he explained, Benedict's approach amounted to a rare combination of positivism and historicism, for which Dewey and Spengler served as a *pars pro toto*. Hence, it exemplified the intertwining of the American and the German heritage in the new social science:

> Historicism admits that it is impossible to understand without evaluating but it denies that there are timeless values. Positivism says it is possible to reach universally valid knowledge, objective knowledge, but only of facts. And it is possible to understand facts without evaluating. Now in actual practice, the two things which I distinguish as positivism and historicism overlap. Under the influence of German historicism, American social science has embodied certain of these principles which came originally from Germany—you only have to read the preface of Benedict, I almost said Benedict Arnold, of Ruth Benedict's Patterns of Culture, to see that she makes it clear. There is an American heritage of Dewey and there is Spengler. Only the marriage, the mating of these very heterogeneous beings, Dewey and Spengler produce this kind of anthropology.[24]

The setting of Strauss's reference to Benedict at the beginning of his "Historicism and Modern Relativism" seminar is an explication of the term *comprehensive view*, which is a translation of the German term *Weltanschauung*. Individuals could as well have a *Weltanschauung*, a particular way of seeing the world; but most of all the term refers to a group or an epoch however conceived. As Strauss explained, the notion of a "comprehensive view" involved the idea that every society or culture and every historical epoch is characterized by certain fundamental premises, which cannot be questioned or set aside. It has also been called the "climate of opinion" of an age, which can never be fully grasped,[25] or the "horizon . . . within which knowledge is possible."[26] The notion that "cultures" (as opposed to "culture") are constituted by such a "comprehensive view" is the theme of the second quote that involves Ruth Benedict.

> For example . . . for the Greeks: that there is the cosmos, an ordered whole, the world in which we live, and within this cosmos there are human associations of various kinds and the polis is the highest. That would, in the popular notion, be part of the comprehensive view of Greek life or for the Middle Ages we would say the truth of Christianity, the truth of the ecclesiastical order established in the Middle Ages, the peculiar relation of Church and Empire and the feudal order. This would be the comprehensive view keeping the society as a whole together.

Strauss emphasized that this understanding was open to various objections:

> If I take the Greek example there are quite a few people who did not believe in the eternity of the visible universe. There were quite a few Greeks who regarded the polis as something very questionable. And so they are very doubtful, these general remarks.

Strauss further explained the matter by way of a comparison between Spengler and Benedict. The outcome is that Spengler's notion of a "comprehensive view" was open to a rational discourse, while Benedict's "patterns of culture" were beyond any possible critical discussion:

> Spengler is of course the most famous example of a presentation of such comprehensive views. In American literature I know only of Ruth Benedict's *Patterns of Culture*. If you say Pattern of Culture, whatever that may mean, that is more or less the same as what I meant by comprehensive view. Only when you speak of a comprehensive view you emphasize those presuppositions which can be expressed in propositional form. But when you speak of Patterns of Culture that is not necessarily the case. Every culture, if there are such things, is based on certain ultimate premises which people do not question and which they cannot question without becoming completely lost. Now, secondly, these absolute presuppositions differ from culture to culture, from epoch to epoch, but not in such a way that you can say one set of absolute presuppositions is true and the others are untrue. They just are unevident assumptions which cannot be criticized from any point of view.[27]

Benedict was a pupil of Franz Boas, the founder of cultural anthropology, who had emigrated from Germany to the United States in 1887. Boas established a new pattern of inquiry that was founded upon the respect for cultural diversity and otherness. In the United States, he and his pupils played a significant role in challenging the predominant anthropological paradigm of racial difference—a challenge that had a significant impact on the American discourse on National Socialism in the 1930s and 1940s.[28]

Boas slipped into the "Historicism and Modern Relativism" seminar as well, though only by way of a fallacy of memory. When Strauss mentioned the preface of *Patterns of Culture*, he apparently misattributed it to Benedict, but the preface had been contributed by Boas. Benedict had worked as Boas's field assistant for some time, and the two had developed a close friendship.[29] But Boas had some reservations about the book, particularly about the German influences. He had written the preface for personal reasons,[30] but the three-page text is ambiguous. Whereas Boas had sought to move away from the German origins of cultural anthropology, Ruth Benedict had immersed herself deeply in Nietzsche, Spengler, and Dilthey to explore the relationship between individual and culture.[31] According to Boas, this approach required "a deep penetration into the genius of the culture." He also referred to this "genius" of a culture as its "configuration" or its "dominant character." He emphasized how the methodological approach served a relativistic agenda, concluding that the knowledge of this "character" of a culture shall provide a new perspective on traits that "seem to us as abnormal attitudes when viewed from the standpoint of our civilization. The relativity of what is considered social or asocial, normal or abnormal, is seen in a new light."[32] These words were what Strauss had in mind when he evoked *Patterns of Culture* to explain the notion of a "comprehensive view."

Although he hardly knew the debates and theoretical conflicts within the school of cultural anthropology, his emphasis on the problematic interplay between American and German influences was highly perceptive. At the same time, the strong link between Ruth Benedict on the one hand and Spengler and Dewey on the other seems to set a certain limit to Strauss's understanding of Benedict's relativism, for there are elements in cultural anthropology that could no longer be understood within the framework of historicism and positivism. Strauss saw these elements, but he described them only at random, and not with full theoretical clarity. To understand these elements *and* the way Strauss saw them, it is useful to acquaint ourselves further with *Patterns of Culture* and its proposition that "standards . . . range in different societies."[33]

Benedict's observation was that regarding "the matter of taking life," not all peoples agree in condemnation: "It may be that those are killed who steal a fowl, or who cut their upper teeth first, or who are born on a Wednesday."[34] The task for the anthropologist was to set aside any "preferential weighting" for a particular culture, especially for one's own.[35] This proposition had far-reaching political implications. Benedict paid great attention to the way in which modern discriminations were being imposed on primitive societies. Her particular focus was on the basic political discrimination between "us" and "them": "Anthropology was by definition impossible as long as the distinctions between ourselves and the primitive, ourselves and the barbarian, ourselves and the pagan, held sway over people's minds."[36] According to this view, the discrimination of "us" and "them" is a peculiar standard of Western societies, and this standard must be suspended in order to understand non-Western societies. Cultural anthropology teaches that "our" categories of interpretation are not to be imposed on primitive societies, because they are alien to these societies.

But Benedict also needed to account for the fact that the discrimination between "us" and "them" is an elementary trait of primitive societies as well. Her observation was that many primitive societies do not have a specific term for "human beings" but only the tribal names by which these primitive people know themselves. "Outside of the closed group there are no human beings. . . . Primitive man never looked out over the world and saw 'mankind' as a group and felt his common cause with his species. . . . The first and important distinction was between his own human group and those beyond the pale."[37] How could this observation be reconciled with the claim that "us" and "them" are Western concepts? Would it be possible to maintain a difference between the "good" discrimination of "us" and "them" in primitive societies and the "bad" discrimination of "us" and "them" in Western societies? Benedict's solution was to describe the discrimination as a continuous cultural trait while criticizing modern man for the continuity. As she suggested, he should have learned better in the meantime: "If we carry on the primitive tradition in this matter, we have far less excuse than savage tribes."[38] The notion that modern man would owe the anthropologist an excuse for his behavior is odd. Hadn't the anthropologist set aside any "preferential weighting" and dedicated herself to the impartial study of cultural differences? Why should the "political" distinction she described in primitive cultures no longer be viable in complex societies?

As it were, Benedict did not abandon the distinction between "ourselves" and "the primitive," she merely reversed it. And despite the claim to a nonpreferential approach, her preferences were merely the opposite of the previous preferences. She abandoned the view that "we" are superior to "them," but she nevertheless criticized "us" for not being superior to "them." Claims such as these were obviously grounded in a moral judgment of modern Western society and a deep moral preference for "otherness." But this procedure was at odds with the staunch universalism to which Benedict, just as did her fellow cultural anthropologists, subscribed. Benedict may be the symbolic landmark for the spread of cultural anthropology in America, but she is not a singular case in the formation of the anthropological worldview. This view consists of a set of ideas that can be traced through various writings and contexts of the profession. These ideas were expressed more or less clearly on different occasions and in different contexts, but they form a clear and coherent worldview.

Melville J. Herskovits ran into similar problems of "us" and "them" in his analysis of what he called ethnocentrism, or the view "that one's own way of life is to be preferred to all others." When Herskovits noted that the ethnocentric discrimination between "us" and "them" is prevalent in Western and non-Western societies alike, he *almost* came to the conclusion that this discrimination is universal. But he also believed in the fundamental moral difference between Western and non-Western man. Therefore, he added a number of qualifications. First, he distinguished between a tacit presupposition and a verbal proposition: "Outside the stream of Euroamerican culture, particularly among nonliterate peoples, [ethnocentrism] is taken for granted rather than phrased in any precise terms." The second qualification was that taking ethnocentrism for granted is fine, while making ethnocentric propositions is not: as Herskovits sought to argue, a "serious problem" arises "when, as in Euroamerican culture, ethnocentrism is rationalized and made the basis of programs of action."[39] Non-Western ethnocentrism was natural and hence morally good, while Western ethnocentrism was nonnatural ("rationalized") and hence morally bad. Just as in the case of Ruth Benedict, the older view was not abandoned but merely reversed. Cultural anthropologists needed the distinction between "us" and "them" for their own project. They merely provided it with the opposite moral value, and ultimately with a moral surplus hitherto unknown.

Seen from the perspective of the twenty-first century, the anthropological worldview has become "historical," but it has also retained a vivid afterlife. It is both familiar and strange. But is it as dangerous as its critics believe? One lesson of the older debates is that cultural relativism did *not* lead to "complete chaos," as Strauss quipped.[40] He qualified this claim by adding "if it were acted upon," and this clause leads closer in the right direction. Indeed, the reason why cultural relativism did not lead to "complete chaos" is not that it is actually harmless, but that it is not being acted upon. The staunchest relativists are usually staunch absolutists as well,[41] believing firmly in the absolute validity of the relativistic truth.

Strauss described this phenomenon in his *Historicism and Modern Relativism* seminar. There is a question and answer period in which he gave a longer sketch of the new kind of relativism, particularly with regard to the problem of superiority. Due to a change of tape the transcription is incomplete, so that the immediate point of departure is not quite clear:

> This realization of the equality of all cultures distinguished modern western society from all other cultures. The superiority which is denied in the thesis is, in fact, asserted. . . . It allows us to regard every society, every culture as equally high. . . . But the point is that all other cultures and all other societies regarded themselves superior to all others or to many others. The insight into the equality of all cultures is the outcome of modern science, or however you might call it, modern history alone. Therefore in the assertion of the equality of modern scientific culture there is implied the assertion of the superiority of modern scientific culture which made us see that. In other words . . . up to now all other cultures have been parochial, now we have become nonparochial. But parochialism means to say that the others are wrong, are narrow, but they make, of course, the same assertion. They say the other cultures are all parochial; we are nonparochial. In the decisive respect, we are superior . . . we find this on the every day level. . . . An absolute truth is asserted, but the possibility of an absolute truth is denied.[42]

From his random remarks, it seems that Strauss was undecided about whether there was something new in the new cultural anthropology or whether it was, rather, a continuation of older theoretical traditions. His overall emphasis is that it was old—a late offshoot of the drama of science and culture in the modern age—and cultural relativism seemed to be a mere continuation of historical relativism. For the most part, *Patterns of Culture* seemed to be an endpoint, not the beginning of something new. On other occasions, he appeared to see Benedict's book as a landmark for the beginning of a new culturalism.

Another example, in the opening pages of "Jerusalem and Athens," traces how the praise of pluralism turns into a new kind of monism. Following the description, the decisive element of the new type of relativism was its "moral posture," and this posture had created the peculiar blend of universalism and particularism:

> However much the science of all cultures may protest its innocence of all preferences or evaluations, it fosters a specific moral posture. Since it requires openness to all cultures, it fosters universal tolerance and the exhilaration deriving from the beholding of the diversity; it necessarily affects all cultures that it can still affect by contributing to their transformation in one and the same direction; it willy-nilly brings about a shift of emphasis from the particular to the universal: by asserting, if only implicitly, the rightness of pluralism, it asserts that pluralism is *the* right way; it asserts the monism of universal tolerance and respect for diversity; for by virtue of being an ism, pluralism is a monism.[43]

Strauss's random, sometimes enigmatic remarks on what he called "the science of all cultures" become readable in the wider context of the theoretical discourse on relativism in the 1950s and 1960s. This critique of cultural anthropology will also be helpful to decipher a key topic within that discourse, namely, the critique of reason in the social sciences.

14

Irrationalism and the Remnants of the Social Question

The cannibalism thesis is part of a more generalized diagnosis of modern reason, with a particular view on scientific reasoning and its political ramifications. The argument runs as follows: Just as social science cannot make a principled argument for civilization against cannibalism, it is incapable of taking a stand for democracy against tyranny; it therefore becomes complicit with tyrannical political regimes;[1] this openness toward tyranny has its basis in the very understanding of science. As Strauss stated, scientific reason had become "instrumental."[2] To quote the famous passage at the beginning of *Natural Right and History* at length:

> According to our social science, we can be or become wise in all matters of secondary importance, but we have to be resigned to utter ignorance in the most important respect: we cannot have any knowledge regarding the ultimate principles of our choices, i.e., regarding their soundness or unsoundness; our ultimate principles have no other support than our arbitrary and hence blind preferences. We are then in the position of beings who are sane and sober when engaged in trivial business and who gamble like madmen when confronted with serious issues—retail sanity and wholesale madness.[3]

Retail sanity and wholesale madness has become the catchphrase of the Straussian discourse on social science relativism, and it has even left its traces in popular culture. However, Strauss was not concerned with madness but with irrationality. He had convinced himself early on that rationality had become irrational.[4] If reason cannot account for the ultimate principles of human choices, he thought, these choices are blind and subject to an irrational decision. On this basis, he concluded, it would be equally as permissible to act in accordance with the meanest self-interest as to act in accordance with moral values. But even if man is willing to act in accordance with moral values, reason cannot tell him how to choose among a variety of ends:

> The choice among attainable ends may be made *en pleine connaissance de cause*, i.e., in full clarity about the likely consequences of the choice; it cannot in itself be rational. Reason can tell us which means are conducive to which ends; it cannot tell us which attainable ends are to be preferred to other attainable ends. Reason cannot even tell us that we ought to choose attainable ends . . . it cannot tell [us] that [we] ought to act rationally or that acting irrationally is acting badly or basely.[5]

Straussians have often taken this analysis as a one-of-a-kind and thoroughly authoritative exposition of modern social science. But its scope and magnitude is much more limited; and Strauss was by no means the only thinker of his time offering an all-out criticism of social science relativism, nor was he the first to use the irrationality charge in this context. To see the singularity and the enduring importance of his analysis, one must follow a few historical references. For even if Straussians were to be right that his analysis is the best one, it did not come out of nowhere. Strauss had translated a discussion in German philosophy of the early twentieth century into an entirely different temporal and spatial context, and that prior discussion structured his own discourse on relativism. He was thereby in surprisingly close proximity to Georg Lukács, whom he briefly discussed in the article "Relativism." In Lukács, the link between the older discussion and the new post–World War II playing field is more easily traceable via influences and conceptual dependencies. But Strauss as well as Lukács discussed the irrationalism of reason in terms that had been set out around 1910 in the debate in southwestern neo-Kantianism on the problem of irrationality. Stated in the shortest possible form, it was supposed that rationality as understood in the natural sciences is concerned with general laws and their validity, so it can account only for the form of individual objects and events, not for their content. This understanding was formed in a reinterpretation of late

German Idealism. Wilhelm Windelband had explained the general discovery with regard to Schelling:

> The new in this movement is not the knowledge that the rational consciousness always has ultimately something for its content, which it simply finds present within itself, without being able to give any account of it. . . . The new was, that this which could not be comprehended by the reason, and which resisted its work, was now also to be thought as something *irrational*.[6]

Windelband and Heinrich Rickert built an early theory of the humanities upon this discovery. The task of the humanities was to account for this irrational individual content, whereas the natural sciences accounted for the general laws. The discourse in southwestern neo-Kantianism on the limits of the natural sciences is still visible in Strauss's account of reason in the social sciences—after all, they were modeled upon the natural sciences, as Strauss often criticized.[7] A direct link between southwestern neo-Kantianism and Strauss's *Natural Right and History* was Max Weber, who was closely associated with the school and considered himself a pupil of Rickert in methodological questions. In Weber's assumption of "a *hiatus irrationalis* between the concretely and individually given reality and the concepts and laws that come into being by way of abstraction from the individual,"[8] the impact is directly visible. But Weber had his own way of interpreting the matter. Overall, he understood irrationality as incalculability or noninterpretability.[9] Strauss traced how Weber combined the influence of "certain neo-Kantians" and their understanding of science with the thesis of the historical school regarding the essential variety of social and cultural orders, none of which can claim to be the right order.[10] From this intricate combination, Strauss led Weber all the way to the point where the adherence to rationality was justified solely by Weber's irrational decision.[11] The attempt to safeguard reason by fusing it with historicism had resulted in utter nihilism.[12]

The problem of irrationality was still a vibrant topic in German philosophy of the interwar period. Alfred Baeumler, who later became a notorious Nazi philosopher, devoted a major study to the problem of irrationality in Kant.[13] Major impulses at the time stemmed from Emil Lask, another southwestern neo-Kantian (but actually rather a neo-Fichtean), who had sought to further clarify the logical form of irrationality. According to Lask, rationality pertains to the form, which is the domain of validity, timelessness, and truth, while the material is fundamentally irrational. "One may call the impenetrability, incomprehensibility and intransfigurability, this 'givenness' and logical insolubility the *irrationality* of the material."[14]

This inconspicuous proposition was the template for Georg Lukács, who was directly influenced by Lask. The two had become friends in Heidelberg, and for a while Lask thought he might win Lukács for a habilitation thesis, before he came to doubt Lukács's aptitude for systematic philosophical work. In Lukács's *History and Class Consciousness* (1923), the influence of Lask is so clearly visible that his approach can be described as a neo-Kantian Marxism or a Marxian neo-Kantianism.[15] Lukács had a particularly strong sense of the philosophical problem, but compared with Lask's systematic-philosophical approach, he also had a proclivity toward sociological shortcuts. In a first step, he defined irrationality as "the impossibility of reducing contents to their rational elements," thereby restating the Laskian view. In a second step he brought the problem of irrationality into the form of an insoluble philosophical dilemma: "For either the 'irrational' content is to be wholly integrated into the conceptual system, i.e. this is to be so constructed that it can be coherently applied to everything just as if there were no irrational content or actuality. . . . In this event thought regresses to the level of a naïve, dogmatic rationalism. . . . Alternatively we are forced to concede that actuality, content, matter reaches right into the form, the structures of the forms and their interrelations and thus *into the structure of the system itself*. In that case the system must be abandoned as a system." The latter characterizes the position of Heinrich Rickert. In a third step, Lukács headed from philosophy toward the antinomies of bourgeois thought, explaining that the dogmatic problem was characteristic of an epoch "in which the bourgeois class naïvely equated its own forms of thought . . . with reality."[16]

Strauss knew this work as well as Lukács's *The Destruction of Reason* (1954; English 1980), which he discussed in "Relativism." In *The Destruction of Reason*, the terminology had changed as radically as the willingness to engage with the inner logic of philosophical problems. Most notably, Lukács was no longer concerned with irrationality: his focus was on irrationalism, which he located particularly in Nietzsche.[17] The difference reflects not only the dramatic changes in his own philosophical and political outlook but also a major shift in the overall discourse on rationality and irrationality.

In the post–World War II discourse on the collapse of reason, the focus had shifted from irrationality to irrationalism.[18] The problem of irrationality was the epistemic template for the new discourse, but when philosophers in the 1950s resorted to this template, they did so to articulate a very different problem (despite the obvious fact that both were part of a diagnosis of reason) and used different philosophical references. And, most notably, the new discourse on irrationalism was decisively shaped by World War II and the Holocaust. Strauss may be famous for his prohibition against what he called "the *reductio ad Hitlerum*," but this prohibition merely served as an antidote to the claim that post–World War I thought is "inevitably . . . darkened by the shadow of Hitler."[19] After the destruction of World War II and the extermination of European Jewry, reason could no longer be said to be in a mere crisis: it was marked by the catastrophe—or rather, it had itself become a part of the catastrophe.[20]

Strauss is in greater proximity to Lukács here than anywhere else. But at this point the parting of the ways was inevitable. With the diagnosis that scientific reason has become "formal"[21] and hence "instrumental,"[22] Strauss is also unmistakably close to Horkheimer and Adorno's *Dialectic of Enlightenment* and their diagnosis of a "formalization" or "instrumentalization of reason."[23] The decisive difference is that Strauss questioned much more fundamentally the idea of progress. While Horkheimer and Adorno—as well as Lukács—came to doubt progress facing the dialectical merging of culture and barbarism, they still clung to the Marxian notion of historical progress, which to their dismay had not yet begun. After all, history was still prehistory. Genuine history would only begin after mankind had overcome prehistory.[24]

Strauss abandoned these hopes. As he explained in *Natural Right and History*, all human thought is incomplete or limited and in need of revision. Every progress in one direction comes at the price of a retrogression in another direction. With every progress in thought, important earlier insights are forgotten. Instead of progress proper, then, thought switches from one limitation to another. It is unlikely that this condition will change radically. Each doctrine will eventually be superseded by another.[25] Now Strauss traced how his colleagues sought to overcome the limitations of human thought. Their fallacy was, to some extent or another, to conceive these limitations "in terms of social, economic, and other conditions, that is, in terms of knowable or analyzable phenomena."[26] Strauss therefore needed to account for the prevalence of certain semantic structures associated with the social question. As he noted in "Progress or Return?," the term *society* rearranged the semantic field of a political association according to the distinction between progressive and reactionary.[27] The distinctions between good and bad, right and wrong, etc. were successively overwritten by the new one. The new code that had emerged in the nineteenth century under the hegemony of the social question made the good life dependent on progress. It hence codified the understanding "that we have to choose and to do what is conducive to progress, what is in agreement with the historical trends, and that it is indecent or immoral to be squeamish in such adaptations."[28]

Strauss referred to the shock the progressivists suffered when they realized that they could "no longer claim to know that we are moving in the right direction."[29] The classical reference for this simultaneity of progressivism and doubt in progress is Friedrich Engels, who tried to reconcile his dialectical progressivism with the notion of an inevitable decay and eventual perishing of mankind. "For the history of mankind, too," he concluded, "there is not only an ascending but also a descending branch. At any rate, we still find ourselves at considerable distance from the turning-point at which the historical course of society becomes one of descent."[30] Strauss commented: "Here we see infinite progress proper is abandoned, but the grave consequences of that are evaded by a wholly incomprehensible and unjustifiable 'never mind.'"[31] Progressivism could only be maintained by deciding "just to forget about the end."[32]

These statements were already made with an eye to the situation of the "half-Marxists"[33] or "crypto-Marxists"[34] in the 1940s, who became increasingly confused by the catastrophic political events: as they could not escape the semantic traps of the social question, which had been exhausted and yet remained predominant, they proved unable to account for the dramatic political experiences. Progressivism without a solid belief in progress, Strauss suggested, lapses into relativism—or more precisely, it brings into recognition that Marxist progressivism is actually one variation of relativism.[35]

This concurrence of progressivism and relativism was the punch line of Strauss's comments on Georg Lukács. This brief discussion, starting from Lukács's critique of Weberian social science and leading to the universal advent of the Nietzschean "last man," is a rhetorical masterpiece in its own right, while one of its central premises is open to a serious objection. According to Lukács, Weber's value-free examination of facts presupposes the selection of relevant facts; this selection is guided by reference to values; the selection is arbitrary; therefore, social science is fundamentally irrational or subjective. The task of social science is not to study mere facts but to understand social phenomena in light of the social situation as a whole, or of the historical process as a whole. Lukács's overall idea was to show that this task could be fulfilled by dialectical materialism alone: "Historical and dialectical materialism is that comprehensive view in which the progressiveness and the rationally knowable lawfulness of history are expressed in the highest form, and in fact the only comprehensive view that can give a consistent philosophic foundation to progressivism and reasonableness."[36] Strauss agreed with Lukács to the extent that social science must study the particular phenomena in light of the whole. But, as he claimed, the whole is not the historical process, and history is neither progressive nor rational.

Strauss objected to Lukács's materialistic appropriation of the "comprehensive view" on the basis of a comparison between Hegel and Marx. For Hegel the progressiveness and rationality of history is based on the premise that this process is completed, while for Marx it is incomplete or has not even begun. Furthermore, Marx does not admit any transhistorical ends from which change could be judged as progress or regress. Strauss concluded: "It is therefore a question whether by turning from Western relativism to Marxism one escapes relativism."[37] His principal strategy was to show that Marxism does not reach the core of the problem of history as it was posed by modern relativism. Following the argument of Lukács, the fundamental principles or "substantive truths" of Marxism are valid only with regard to a specific historical situation that they mean to illuminate, but within these limits "they possess absolute validity."[38] As Strauss noticed, then, the substantive truths of Marxism are merely "true until further notice," until they are replaced by different truths. Marxism is hence only "a one-sided truth, a half-truth." Just as the French Revolution was right in its diagnosis of the old regime but utterly mistaken about the new one, so Marxism can be useful to detect the bad state of contemporary society, but it cannot account for the state of society after the revolutionary action of the proletariat: the new society "may be as rich in contradictions and oppressions as the old society, although its contradictions and oppressions will, of course, be entirely novel."[39]

Here, Strauss had prepared his final blow to Lukács's progressivism. He had led historical materialism to the point where it could found itself either on the grounds of historicism or as a radically nonhistorical exposition of the final truth. If it opts for historicism, it remains "relative" to its particular situation, being unable to provide a standard beyond the standards of contemporary society. Marxism must then be applied to itself, so as to reveal its being a mere variation of modern relativism. At best, then, progress is being abandoned for mere "muddling through" (*weiterwurschteln*).[40] If dialectical materialism opts for the nonhistorical final truth, it must claim an absolute moment in history, in which the realm of freedom comes into view for the first time. History will then be abandoned in the future, paradoxically in the same moment it finally begins. But most likely, Strauss held, the realm of freedom would be "the earth of 'the last man,' of the one herd without a shepherd."[41] It seems as though not even the end of history would lead out of historical relativism.

Strauss's frequent use of this pattern of critique raises the question of whether it suffices to lead each contemporary thinker to the point where he inevitably poses as a historicist. This is not so much an objection to his interpretation of Lukács, whose dramatic intellectual flight from political experience can indeed be described as the consequence of his systematic prejudice toward (and all too schematic use of) the distinction between progress and reaction, and hence a Marxist variation of historicism. But Strauss displays a very broad (maybe too broad) understanding of historicism—and, to a lesser degree, positivism—as the source of relativism. Historicism was not just a school or a doctrine among many but an assumption shared by virtually every thinker of the time. As Strauss explained in 1941 to the General Seminar at the New School, a broader definition of historicism was needed. It had to include both the nineteenth century and the twentieth, both the historical school and contextualism, and both the longing for the past and the doctrine that "everything is historical"—but it had to be much wider. It was an "all-pervasive" "trend" that stretched across virtually all contemporary philosophical schools (phenomenology, Hegelianism, Marxism, sociology of knowledge, pragmatism,[42] Nietzsche,[43] Heidegger[44]) and political orientations (democracy, communism, fascism).[45] It was synonymous with "the spirit of our time."[46] According to this view, "all human thought is historical and hence unable ever to grasp anything eternal. Whereas, according to the ancients, philosophizing means to leave the cave, according to our contemporaries all philosophizing essentially belongs to a 'historical world,' 'culture,' 'civilization,' 'Weltanschauung,' that is, to what Plato had called the cave. We shall call this view 'historicism.'"[47]

Strauss exemplified how such a broad definition can indeed facilitate a change of perspective on twentieth-century thought. Something became visible in modern thought that had never been seen before: virtually all contemporary thinkers *were* covert historicists, each in their own way. And in some way or another they had all been lured into historicism by the notion of modern culture. This finding, however, was not overly helpful when it came to building an actual argument against relativism.

15

Two Types of Relativism

The discourse on relativism in the 1950s and 1960s (and ever since) was not an orderly theoretical disputation in which the best argument wins the debate. "Relativism" is not so much a clear-cut philosophical term but rather a set of ideas stretching across a variety of academic disciplines and beyond; and more likely than by theoretical arguments, the debate is being decided by sentiments nurtured in the political and cultural world. Strauss knew that he could not altogether refute relativism, at least not without subscribing to the type of absolutism he considered to be incompatible with the civic life.[1] But he was also a child of his time in this respect: most theorists at this time proposed some qualified version of relativism in order to avoid giving in to an unqualified relativism. They all sensed that relativism had won the debate, and despite a common discontent it was difficult to imagine what would replace it.

Strauss tried several strategies. One was to steer a middle course between relativism and absolutism. This was the model of *Natural Right and History*. A second strategy was to reframe the problem of relativism as a problem of liberal thought. This is characteristic of Strauss's discussion of Isaiah Berlin in the article "Relativism." The principal fallacy of this critique is that it reprimands Berlin for a problem that cannot be solved on Straussian grounds either: resistance to an unqualified relativism seemed to require "an 'absolute' basis, but it has no basis." Straussian political philosophy, just like Berlinian liberalism, "cannot live without an absolute basis and cannot live with an absolute basis."[2] Relativism and absolutism were inseparably intertwined.

A third strategy was to pursue a nonrelativistic goal with the means of relativism—a most likely unsuccessful attempt to beat relativism with its own weapons. This strategy can be seen in "Social Science and Humanism" (1956), a casual article that explored two types of relativism. One type of relativism—the one discussed above—argues that our opposition to cannibalism is unjustified because civilization is not in principle superior to cannibalism. Opposition to cannibalism is due to our historical situation, but historical situations change. A historical situation that encourages the belief in civilization may give way to a historical situation that encourages the belief in cannibalism. The relativist denies that civilization is in principle superior to cannibalism, so he will accept the change of civilized society into cannibal society. According to Strauss, this argument refers to "a perhaps outdated version of relativism."[3] A more recent version of relativism denied the strict linkage between values and the historical situation, arguing that people can transcend their historical situation and assume different perspectives. It is characterized by "its apparent generosity and unbounded sympathy for every human position," its "openness to everything that is human."

Strauss's statement on the "perhaps outdated version of relativism" must be taken with a grain of salt, especially since his subsequent writings on relativism are chiefly concerned with that version. It seems more appropriate to assume that several versions of relativism existed simultaneously, with some of them overlapping, others being confined to their respective contexts of discussion. Perhaps this explains the anachronism in Strauss's account. He discussed relativism predominantly in social science contexts, in which the Weberian fact/value distinction was the main reference point. The new type of relativism, however, was played out in the larger field of American culture. It gained traction in the 1960s and soon recommended itself as a main intellectual foundation of the new counterculture of flower power and antibourgeois protest. From there it spread into the beliefs and attitudes of people with various backgrounds and political outlooks. Roughly thirty years after Strauss's diagnosis of a new type of relativism, Allan Bloom came to recognize this type as the predominant form of relativism. As for Strauss, the keyword was "openness." Bloom started from his observation as a teacher:

> Almost every student entering the university believes, or says he believes, that truth is relative. . . . Some are religious, some atheists; some are to the Left, some to the Right; some intend to be scientists, some humanists or professionals or businessmen; some are poor, some rich. They are unified only in their relativ-

ism and in their allegiance to equality. And the two are related in a moral intention. The relativity of truth is not a theoretical insight but a moral postulate, the condition of a free society, or so they see it. They have all been equipped with this framework early on, and it is the modern replacement for the inalienable natural rights that used to be the traditional American grounds for a free society.[4]

The primary moral impulse of these young students was their indignation over "absolutism" and intolerance. Bloom concluded his first paragraph as follows:

> Openness—and the relativism that makes it the only plausible stance in the face of various ways of life and kinds of human beings—is the great insight of our times. The true believer is the real danger. The study of history and of culture teaches that all the world was mad in the past; men always thought they were right, and that led to wars, persecutions, slavery, xenophobia, racism, and chauvinism. The point is not to correct the mistakes and really be right; rather it is not to think you are right at all.[5]

With his diagnosis of a "gradual movement from rights to openness,"[6] Bloom followed Strauss's lead more closely than he did when it came to the German origins of relativism. But his Straussian argument was also a creative adaptation of the actual argument given by Strauss, which took a surprising turn in the article "Social Science and Humanism."

For the new type of relativism, there is no reason why people should not be able to transcend their historical situation or their culture, provided that their "openness" to all expressions of human culture is genuine. According to Strauss's example, there is no reason why an Englishman should not be able to become a Japanese. What matters is the belief in certain values, but these values "cannot be traced beyond our decision or commitment." The latter statement is extraordinarily important, for it reaches far beyond the position described by Strauss and also characterizes his own position to some extent. His subsequent discussion is extremely ambiguous, which makes it difficult to discern his own voice in the text. Strauss had maintained that in the quarrel between the philosophical life and the religious life, the option for either life cannot be traced beyond the individual decision or commitment. Both options were possible, but whatever the choice, it had to be mated with a serious commitment to the philosophical or the religious cause. Strauss had opted for the philosophical life, but he remained in perpetual doubt whether or not the choice was justified beyond his individual decision and commitment. He could not ascertain that his choice was the true choice.

But there is another aspect of the quarrel. By taking a stand in the quarrel, one also takes a stand *for* the quarrel. By opting either for philosophy or for the Bible, one opts for a view that places the conflict and the choice between philosophy and the Bible in the center of human orientation. Strauss understood this view as a commitment to the roots of civilization, and it is clear that this commitment is meant to provide an antidote to the commitment to relativism. The article "Social Science and Humanism" explores the extent to which such a commitment can dissolve the rigid antithesis of relativism and absolutism. "Now, if we commit ourselves to the values of civilization, our very commitment enables and compels us to take a vigorous stand against cannibalism and prevents us from placidly accepting a change of society in the direction of cannibalism." The commitment to the values of civilization entails a defense of these values against the values of cannibalism, especially vis-à-vis those who are undecided between the values of civilization and those of cannibalism; but one cannot thereby assume that the values of civilization are valid or true. The case for civilization cannot be made by way of a rational argument: it is mere "propaganda," just as is the "equally legitimate" case for cannibalism.[7]

Two phrases suggest that the voice in the text is not Strauss's own ("according to the premise," "this notion . . . is said to be arrived at"). Judging from the further course of the text, the statement is meant to characterize some unnamed humanistic social scientists who sought to combine a perspectivistic relativism with unlimited sympathetic understanding of every human perspective. These social scientists are distinguished by their adherence to "existentialism."[8] Their sympathetic understanding is based on individual commitment and inner depth. Strauss characterized this new type of relativism as a "median" position in between the older relativism and absolutism. The article raises—and ultimately leaves open—the question of whether such a median position, or a "qualified relativism"[9] as a middle ground between full-scale relativism and absolutism, can find a solid basis. It may seem doubtful whether the question was raised earnestly, that is, whether Strauss truly considered a "qualified relativism" as a viable solution. Given his unwillingness to subscribe to "absolutism," however, Strauss had good reason to take the possibility of a "median" position seriously. To some extent, the notions of commitment and seriousness also reflected his own epistemic and moral situation as outlined in *Philosophy and Law*; and they bore many signs of a median position, despite his insistence from early on that mere commitment was not enough. It was not to be confused with a universally valid system of values.

In "Social Science and Humanism," Strauss evoked the image of such a universally valid system of values to question the notion of commitment, introducing "the Bible and Plato" in its place. But does not the adherence to the Bible and Plato rest on a commitment, too? To find orientation in the fundamental alternative between the two roots of Western civilization, it seems, one must first commit to this alternative. The alternative between the Bible and Plato may be superior to other alternatives with regard to epistemic breadth and moral clarity, but it finds little protection against the principal relativistic argument that there are multiple possible alternatives: one must already have subscribed to the view that this particular alternative is the fundamental alternative. In this situation, Strauss employed the hazardous strategy of using the relativistic argument against the relativists: he sought to secure a space for the Bible and Plato in the relativistic universe. The key quote runs as follows:

> But perhaps it is wrong to assume that all positions ultimately rest on commitments, or at any rate on commitments to specific points of view. We all remember a time when most men believed explicitly or implicitly that there is one and only one true value system of universal validity, and there are still societies and individuals who cling to this view. They too must be understood sympathetically. Would it not be too harsh and even inconsistent to deprive the Bible and Plato of a privilege which is generously accorded to every savage tribe? And will sympathetic understanding of Plato not lead us to admit that absolutism is as true as relativism?[10]

The irony and the rhetorical excess notwithstanding, this position is clearly untenable. It suggests that those who believe in the "one and only one true value system of universal validity" give up on defending its universality against relativism, settling for the minimum goal to be "understood" (and maybe accepted) by the relativists. The quest for a "qualified relativism," it seems, creates a situation in which those who "still . . . cling to this view" demand some kind of protection, similar to wildlife preservation, which would allow them to hold on to their anachronistic beliefs and behavioral patterns. Strauss is correct in his proposition that the bearers of Bible and Plato cannot be deprived of the principle accorded to a savage tribe; but thereby he has already relegated them to the status of a savage tribe. The principal issue with this attempt to argue against relativism on relativistic grounds is that it transforms any nonrelativistic position, such as the Bible-and-Plato position, into *one* position among others in a relativistic framework. "Absolutism" may indeed be "as true as relativism," but hence it is also as untrue as any relativistic position. In other words, Strauss's principal argument against relativism does not lead out of relativism.

This limitation of his argument does not make his criticism useless, and we may again wonder whether relativism can at all be refuted by way of a principal argument. To use Strauss's phrase from another context, he merely sought to "awaken a prejudice" against relativism.[11] The relativistic prejudice is countered by another prejudice, which is nonrelativistic in content but relativistic in form. While this strategy has its weaknesses, Strauss made it as as sound as possible. His writings on relativism cast doubt on many of the assumptions that seem to speak in favor of a relativistic position. He attacked not only the philosophical position but also the prephilosophic "system" of relativistic beliefs and attitudes fostered in modern culture. He targeted a comprehensive value system that seemed to make any principled distinction between right and wrong impossible. He had to cast into doubt the relativistic value system in order to "awaken a prejudice" in favor of the Bible and Plato, or Jerusalem and Athens. In other words, relativism was one comprehensive interpretation of man and the world that needed to be invalidated and replaced by another interpretation. This task, however, did not yet provide a viable defense against relativism: As Strauss knew, the new interpretation, with Jerusalem and Athens standing in the center, could be said to be mere "propaganda." From a relativistic standpoint, it was just as legitimate a position as the position in favor of "savage tribes." At least from the textual surface it may seem that his more elaborate writings on Jerusalem and Athens are written from a different epistemic standpoint: they do not position the Bible and Plato in the force field of relativism and absolutism, but they lead into a region where neither relativism nor absolutism was a principal concern of philosophizing. This impression, however, is only partly warranted, for even the smooth "Jerusalem and Athens" is replete with references to the contemporary force field of cultural relativism.

Part V

Jerusalem and Athens

16

Jerusalem and Athens or Jerusalem versus Athens?

Perhaps Leo Strauss's most lasting philosophical impact on contemporary thought plays out in the renewed discussions on reason and revelation, or Athens and Jerusalem. The article "Jerusalem and Athens" (1967), in particular, has the reputation of a principal contribution to recent debates on the return of religion, although it is not exactly clear what this contribution might actually be. Readers of all sorts sense that Strauss had something important to say, even as they might find it difficult to pinpoint it. In other words, the text has an aura that often seems to outshine its propositional content and its meaning.

To dwell on the outer appearance of "Jerusalem and Athens" a bit further, one important factor for its wide appeal is the fact that the quarrel between Jerusalem and Athens does not seem to have been decided in advance. As Pierre Manent quipped, Strauss's account was "so impartial that it seems impossible to say where he stands."[1] Unlike in many previous versions of the problem, Strauss brought Jerusalem and Athens into a highly symmetric form. This wondrous symmetry is not impeded by the fact that he spoke clearly as a philosopher; and after all, he had told Stanley Rosen that "philosophers are paid not to believe."[2] Hence, "Jerusalem and Athens" is extremely interesting also from the viewpoint of advanced theoretical construction and rhetorical strategy.

To arrive at this viewpoint, a better understanding both of the systematic structure and the historical genesis of the Jerusalem and Athens theme in Strauss's work is called for. As to the structure, there are two different ways of understanding the nexus between Jerusalem and Athens: it can be understood as Jerusalem *and* Athens and as Jerusalem *versus* Athens, and both ways are indispensible parts of Strauss's endeavor. He had divided his 1950 lecture with the same title into "Agreement" and "Conflict," suggesting that one must understand the agreement to be able to understand the conflict.[3] Henceforth, he emphasized both the "coming together" of and the fundamental "choice" between Jerusalem and Athens.[4] To see the scope and the enduring significance of "Jerusalem and Athens," we must find the point where these two seemingly exclusive possibilities meet, and why it would be unwise (and certainly against the intention of Leo Strauss) to drop one in favor of the other.

As to the genesis, it would be unwise to assume that Strauss's position remained fundamentally the same over the years. Tracing the formation of the theme of Jerusalem and Athens in his thought from its emergence in 1946 to 1967, we find a great variety in his emphasis on the problems and his manner of treatment. We must come to terms with this variety to be able to see the unique argument and action of "Jerusalem and Athens." Lastly, one must study the setting, the characters and references, and Strauss's work/play with the binary of Jerusalem (revelation) and Athens (philosophy). "Jerusalem and Athens" may not be an example of good writing, but the stylistic features and conceptual schemes employed by Strauss are extremely advanced and well thought out.

The Setting

The first thing that is likely to strike any reader upon their first encounter with "Jerusalem and Athens" is the extraordinarily festive tone of the text. Strauss had a knack for the grandiose style of public lectures, his early difficulties notwithstanding. The smooth and polished style is entirely different from his early works, as well as from those books that have gained him the reputation of an exoteric writer. "Jerusalem and Athens" gave birth to an oracular style that greatly helped his reputation as the enunciator of some distant theopolitical wisdom. "All the hopes that we entertain in the midst of the confusions and dangers of the present," he began the lecture, "are founded positively or negatively, directly or indirectly on the experiences of the past."[5]

Certainly, the past is founded upon the present, and the present is confusing and dangerous. Once the reader has settled into the festive tone, he is in grave danger of overlooking the second sentence: "Of these experiences the broadest and deepest, as far as we Western men are concerned, are indicated by the names of the two cities Jerusalem and Athens."[6] As Strauss indicates, the text is directed toward a community of "Western men"—a community of people who are in principle willing to engage with the foundational texts of Western civilization. These texts provide "Western men" with a fresh access to the foundational experiences of the West. But "Western men" must be led to a proper understanding of these texts. As we shall see below, the underlying concept of "the West" was no longer a matter of course.

With the festive tone and affirmative reference to "the West," the text poses an extraordinary challenge to many scholars of twentieth-century philosophy, who expect a philosophical text published in 1967 to be more dramatic and in some way more radical. With the rise of antiwar protests and student movements in the United States and Western Europe, that year did not seem favorable for Strauss's endeavor. If compared to other philosophical works written in close temporal proximity—for example, Theodor W. Adorno's *Negative Dialectics* and Jacques Derrida's *Of Grammatology*—one can hardly overlook a certain anachronistic aura, whereas the overall moment in 1967 was in favor of progress, if not revolution. How could Strauss philosophize like that in a moment when a new beginning seemed possible?

A partial answer is to be found in a previous article that must be read closely together with "Jerusalem and Athens." Progress, Strauss explained at the beginning of "Progress or Return?" (a talk at the Hillel House Chicago in 1952), "has become a problem": it seemed "as if progress has led us to the brink of an abyss, and it is therefore necessary to consider alternatives." Western men have taken a wrong turn, so it might be better "to stop where we are, or else, if this should be impossible, to return."[7] Spoken seven years after the end of World War II, these words are not very spectacular with regard to the diagnosis. Progress *had* become a problem for even the most hard-boiled Marxists. The surprise is in the suggestion that it might therefore be useful to "consider alternatives" to progress: whereas many of his colleagues sought to convince their audiences that the abyss of progress demanded an unabated and often radicalized commitment to the principles of *real* progress, Strauss suggested that it might be better to return to the right way.

This marvelous beginning puts much emphasis on a connotation that later moved to the background. To set aside the powerful prejudice that it is impossible to return, Strauss emphasized the religious meaning of the term, its origin in the Hebrew notion of *teshuva*. This notion of *teshuva* is still employed today when a formerly orthodox individual who had abandoned Judaism returns to the Jewish creed. The preceding break with Judaism had been carried out in the name of "progress," of a future "progress beyond Judaism."[8] The return is accompanied by an act of repentance. The dramatic model for a return to the roots of Western civilization had entirely changed in 1967, but some distant religious connotations are still at hand.

These connotations largely contribute to the perception that "Jerusalem and Athens" represents the principal alternative to the pseudo-revolutionary moment. In his judgment of this movement, Strauss was in principal agreement—despite their otherwise great philosophical and political differences—with Alexandre Kojève, who in the same year advised the protesting students in Berlin to "learn Greek." As Jacob Taubes reported:

> He gave a lecture, and you could have heard a pin drop when his listeners heard that history had now come to an end and could only be "recapitulated" in the form of a fictive "as if." These were ideas that met considerable resistance and moral disgust among adherents of progress and futurology. Kojève was notoriously fond of shock effects, renowned for enigmatic rhetoric, for statements that, spoken *ex cathedra,* were nonetheless presented simply as commentary to Hegel's *Philosophy of the Spirit*. In 1967 Kojève was at the Hotel Berliner am Dianasee surrounded by the leading student "rebels," Dutschke & Co., to whom he said, among other things, that the most important thing for them as student leaders to do would be—to learn Greek. The leaders of the SDS stood there quite perplexed. They had been ready for anything except that.[9]

Strauss was less ambiguous and playful than Kojève when it came to the political task of the moment. He straightforwardly argued for a return, and this could be understood as a reorientation, as a historical inversion, or as repentance (*teshuva*).

Another main figure who in 1967 found himself in the force field of philosophy and radical politics was Theodor W. Adorno. He had long decried the glaring disproportion between the status of philosophy and its no-longer-existent political opportunity, arguing that the moment of its realization "had been missed."[10] He had his own way of encountering the radical students in Berlin, when he was chastised for the lack of any direct political precepts in his lecture on Goethe's *Iphigenie*.[11] The "message" of his lecture was the reversion of the Enlightenment into myth, and that was far from apolitical in the heated atmosphere of June 1967. But it was certainly not the type of theoretical discourse the students wanted—they expected a theory to tell them how to set the university on fire, and a few America Houses on top of that.[12] Adorno had no doubt about the pseudo-revolutionary character of their actions, but he incessantly supported them in order to avoid giving in to their right-wing counterparts. Hence, his political position became a radical embodiment of the double negation, and this dialectical figure was increasingly difficult to maintain in the world of political action.

These few examples suffice to keep in mind that "Jerusalem and Athens" is situated in the pseudo-revolutionary moment of the late 1960s, when philosophy was drawn into the culture wars. In this moment, the pre–World War II type of Western European scholar, who in the meantime had learned to merge his German *Bildung* and *Kultur* with a more realistic view on politics, was about to be dethroned, with a new type of hyperpolitical scholar-activist replacing him. This model was not sustainable for long, eventually collapsing under the heavy weight of immoderate expectations from politics. It gave way to the emergence of "theory" as a hyperprogressive political praxis after the revolutionary moment had vanished.[13]

To be sure, the Western European scholar was not vanishing altogether. In the United States, he was about to become a cultural icon, whose radical rhetoric was understood just a tad too literally by protesting students. The embodiment of this iconic type was Herbert Marcuse. The European-trained scholar also played a role (although a more modest one) in the emergence of a counter-counterculture in the United States—a heterogeneous group of intellectuals who were turned off by the protest culture and the increasingly narrow view on culture and politics that it fostered. This was the audience for Strauss's lecture "Jerusalem and Athens" at the City College of New York. They were liberals without a dogmatic worldview. But they were liberals mugged by reality, as Irving Kristol's famous definition of neoconservatism goes.

Education "Toward Culture"

Kristol himself had been turned off by the radical students long before, after a brief stint with a Trotskyist group in New York in the early 1940s. But it was Leo Strauss who taught him to read the foundational texts of Western political thought. Strauss, he later recalled, "was from a different planet. . . . Encountering Strauss's work produced the kind of intellectual shock that is a once-in-a-lifetime experience. He turned one's intellectual universe upside down."[14] In particular, Kristol found access to Aristotle's prudent approach to politics. There, he learned not to conceive of the political task as an effort to shape society according to moral and political ideals but to begin from the world as it was.[15]

Strauss never exerted any direct political influence, but he did influence a great number of people by teaching them how to read. And by reading the great books of the Western tradition, they would become receptive to the notion of "the West." They started seeing themselves as "Western men," as bearers of Western civilization. Indirectly, then, reading became a political praxis, but this educational politics was entirely different from the way it was practiced in "theory" reading groups. It was a new form of cultural politics *before* the academic culture wars of the 1970s and onward.

As Strauss conceived it, the new counter-counterculture was all about preserving an intellectual space that seemed to vanish under the wave of radical politics. This counter-counterculture could be swallowed neither by mainstream culture nor by the predominant protest culture of the Left. It could not be integrated into a hegemonic discourse, because it was addressed only to a few, to a minority. As Hadley Arkes recalled the atmosphere in Strauss's seminars:

> It was evident that the thing that connected everyone in that room—from the Catholic priests to the young Jewish students—was the interest in standing against the world—*contra mundum*—standing against the current culture, with its variants of moral relativism.[16]

There is a beautiful passage in Anne Norton's Strauss book on Joseph Cropsey and Ralph Lerner, two former students of Strauss who passed on his spirit to a younger generation at the University of Chicago:

> To listen to them read a text was to go into a garden, into a wilderness, into an ocean and breathe. They were scandalous, they were daring, they took your breath away with their honesty. They were precise, disciplined, ascetic, reverent, heretical, blasphemous, and fearless. Nothing stopped them, nothing at all. Often it went entirely unnoticed. There would be an unfinished quotation or a pun and in it the cleverest, wittiest heresy.

There would be a discreet allusion or a simple statement, and one would find oneself at the edge of the abyss. Perhaps this is the origin of the idea of secret teachings. If so, I can tell you, there were no secret teachings; it was all done in the open.[17]

In *Liberalism Ancient and Modern*, Strauss referred to this type of liberal education as "education in culture or toward culture."[18] The expression "toward culture" signifies the *direction* of liberal education rather than its presupposition. It is primarily directed *against* culture—not only against what Strauss labeled "the horrors of mass culture"[19] but also against the prevalent culturalism that was being taught in humanities departments. In "German Nihilism," Strauss had criticized an apologetic and defensive style of liberal education, which had allegedly confirmed the young German radicals in their passionate protest against the principles of modern civilization.[20] Liberal education "through the great books," we are led to assume, would channel these radical passions by teaching the young radicals to listen to the conversation between the great minds. This experience would make them insusceptible to the dual forces of immoderate hopes in politics and irresponsible contempt for politics. Being educated "toward culture," they would become responsible members of liberal democracy while resisting the homogenizing forces of liberal democracy.

Strauss had been hired by the University of Chicago to become a pillar of the Great Books movement, which fostered liberal education by focusing exclusively on the reading of the great books of the Western tradition. As Jacob Taubes quipped on the reform facilitated by Robert Maynard Hutchins in Chicago, it was about the abolition of the soccer team and the introduction of Thomism.[21] The Great Books program of Hutchins and Mortimer Adler has been criticized for many things, all of them pertaining to its glaring untimeliness—logocentrism, moralism, hermetism, elitism, exclusion of non-Western texts, and exclusion of women.[22] Strauss is a continuous reference point for this criticism, but he had his own way of interpreting the nature and the political task of reading the great books. One distinct marker of his notion of liberal education is the complete lack of any universal pretension. As he saw it, it was "the necessary endeavor to found an aristocracy within democratic mass society."[23] This endeavor was in blatant contradiction to the egalitarian notion of education that came to predominance in the 1960s, but it also allowed for a peaceful coexistence of mass society (or mass culture, mass education) and liberal education through the great books (which is restricted to those suited to it). The latter were like the Nietzschean overmen, who coexist side by side with the last men: they lived like epicurean Gods, not attending to the others.[24] The founding of an aristocracy of readers was therefore perfectly compatible with modern democracy and mass culture.

Two Concepts of Culture: The Starting Point

"Jerusalem and Athens" does not claim to be Strauss's final word on the subject. The subtitle indicates that the text merely consists of "some preliminary reflections." Susan Orr suggested that the text is perhaps "only a guidepost with which Strauss would have us to begin to rethink the question of what should command our first allegiance—philosophy or theology, reason or faith."[25] This suggestion seems warranted only in part. Strauss certainly wanted his audience to think, but he did not demand that they make a decision. It would, rather, seem that the matter cannot be decided. The emphasis on the preliminary character, then, is not appellative but methodological: the guiding question of "Jerusalem and Athens" is *how to approach* the Bible and Greek philosophy. In a way, all of Strauss's writings are methodological, but "Jerusalem and Athens" took it to the extremes. As it developed over the course of twenty-one years, the project *became* ever more preliminary. The eventual publication is not even a well-organized text, with its two chapters being unequal not only in length but also in the style of argument. Its lasting greatness and true legacy is marked by its many layers of preliminary remarks, or methodological reflections, that surround the subject matter in rotating movements, guided by the knowledge that Jerusalem and Athens are not immediately accessible.

As the text explains, one main obstacle to a thorough understanding of Jerusalem and Athens was the prevalent notion of culture. Strauss needed to make sure that Jerusalem and Athens would not be understood within the framework of culture. By the 1960s, Strauss had two critiques of culture. One was concerned with culture as in the philosophy of culture; the other was concerned with cultures, that is, with the infinite plurality of cultures and the corresponding infinite plurality of ideas about right and wrong. These two critiques of culture had coexisted in his works before, but they seemed to have little to do with each other. "Jerusalem and Athens" was the appropriate place to bring the two critiques of culture together. It is therefore not by coincidence that both parts of the article start with a refutation of the concept of culture.

Strauss started from a synthetic description of some unnamed and rather obscure "scientific" understanding of Jerusalem and Athens. As his initial remarks illustrate, this was an allusion to the science of cultural anthropology and its problematic stance toward Western culture: "The objects to which we refer by speaking of Jerusalem and Athens are today understood by the science devoted to such objects as cultures; 'culture' is meant to be a scientific concept. According to this concept there is an indefinitely large number of cultures: n cultures."[26]

To summarize Strauss's initial train of thought: Science understands its objects, Jerusalem and Athens, as cultures—as two out of an infinite number of cultures. These cultures are regarded by the scientist as objects; he stands outside of them; all cultures are equal to him; he is objective, anxious not to distort any of them by using "culture-bound" concepts (i.e., concepts bound to one specific culture, that is, to Western culture). The objects often did not know that they are or were cultures. Those men who are said to be the contributors to past cultures did not understand themselves in terms of culture, since they were not concerned with "culture" at all; what is now called culture is the accidental result of concerns with other things than with culture, most notably with truth. The scientist believes that he understands those people better than they understood themselves.[27] Strauss asserted that this approach had been questioned by Nietzsche, whose speech "Of 1000 Goals and One" in *Thus Spoke Zarathustra* characterized the epistemic situation of modernity: "The Hebrews and the Greeks appear in this speech as two among a number of nations, not superior to the two others that are mentioned or to the 996 that are not mentioned." The overman was cited to create a superculture that would do away with the variety of cultures.[28]

The brief second chapter of "Jerusalem and Athens" opens with a discussion of the other notion of culture, represented by Hermann Cohen as the foremost proponent of the philosophy of culture. Cohen's equivalents to Athens and Jerusalem, and hence his closest approximation to the problem of reason and revelation, were Plato and the prophets. He discussed their relationship in his late lecture "The Social Ideal in Plato and the Prophets" (1918), which opens with the marvelous declaration that "Plato and the prophets are the most important sources of modern culture."[29]

That quote was certainly a gift for Strauss, who disassembled the cultural understanding of Jerusalem and Athens piece by piece. As he summarized Cohen's interpretation, the truth of Plato and the prophets is their synthesis. Plato represents the truth of science, whereas the prophets serve as the bearers of the ethical truth. Whereas the scientific truth as represented by Plato was Cohen's utmost concern, this truth needed to be supplemented by the ethical truth. For Plato there is an unchangeable human nature, so that wars and social inequalities are bound to persist; these defects of human nature must be remedied by the ethical teaching of the prophets, who are not bound to nature. Whereas scientific knowledge is concerned with the unchangeable world, the prophets represent the idea that the world is changeable. The binary of Plato and the prophets, then, is meant to indicate the possibility of a fundamental social change via the return to the two sources of culture. As Strauss concluded, the quest for a return is guided by "the modern belief in progress."[30]

There seems to be a specific constellation of progress and return at work here, and Strauss needed to disentangle it in order to show why Cohen's solution was not viable. This is the purpose of the second paragraph of the second chapter, a tour de force through a number of historical references and conceptual binaries. Strauss based his critique on a rare historical argument, drawing on the difference between pre–World War I and post–World War II Jewish thought: Cohen belonged to the world before World War I, in which the Dreyfus affair and the Russian pogroms were the worst experiences; he "had a greater faith in the power of modern Western culture to mold the fate of mankind," because "he did not experience communist Russia and Hitler Germany."[31] Strauss suggested that the disillusionment regarding culture following these political experiences compelled him to rethink the systematic relationship between Jerusalem and Athens: "We wonder whether the two ingredients of modern culture, of the modern synthesis, are not more solid than that synthesis." Initially mimicking the voice of Cohen, Strauss first spoke of the two ingredients of modern culture, then rephrased the expression as the modern synthesis, and then asked whether the ingredients are not more solid than the synthesis. The highly technical distinction between the synthesis and their pre-synthetic ingredients is made with regard to the political experiences of the twentieth century: "Catastrophes and horrors of a magnitude hitherto unknown, which we have seen and through which we have lived, were better provided for, or made intelligible, by both Plato and the prophets than by the modern belief in progress."[32]

At this point, the text is an extremely dense constellation of ever-changing binaries. First, there is the modern synthesis and its premodern ingredients. Then, all of a sudden the synthesis is being replaced by the belief in progress; once the belief in progress has been abandoned, one can see the fundamental opposition; and, at last, the difference between a synthesis and an opposition is replaced by the difference between a solution and a problem. As Strauss put it at the end of the paragraph: "We are ultimately confronted by a problem rather than by a solution."[33]

One would expect this hypermodern work with ever-changing and ever-collapsing binaries from Deleuze or Derrida; but Strauss, too, had mastered the art of building and dissolving an infinite number of antitheses. A passage in Deleuze's *Proust and Signs* captures the high art of deconstructing Jerusalem and Athens well: "Proust has his own way of experiencing the opposition of Jerusalem and Athens."[34] Deleuze described how a variety of antitheses come into being and dissolve into a multiplicity again, thereby demonstrating this "own way" in action. "He eliminates many things or many people in the course of the Search, and these form an apparently incongruous group: observers, friends, philosophers, talkers, homosexuals *à la grecque,* intellectuals. But all of them participate in the *logos,* and are with varying qualifications the characters of a single universal dialectic."[35] Strauss was capable of such conceptual work/play, too, as the paragraph cited above shows. But of course he did it with the opposite goal: he sought to return to Jerusalem and Athens as the two roots of Western civilization *without* imposing either a philosophical framework on Jerusalem or a theological one on Athens. The work/play scheme with the conceptual binaries was a part of the overall strategy to bring Jerusalem and Athens back into a tension rather than to allow one side to appropriate the other or to dissolve the binary into a multiplicity. How did Strauss do this? To see his strategies in action, we must acquaint ourselves further with the web of preliminary remarks and decipher an inconspicuous third concept of culture, which found its way into Strauss's work only by a few traces.

A Third Concept of Culture

According to the first refutation of the cultural paradigm, Jerusalem and Athens could only be understood if they were no longer misrepresented as "two cultures," namely, two out of an infinite number of cultures. Following the second refutation, Jerusalem and Athens could only be understood if they were not misrepresented as two ingredients of modern culture, so that the tension between the two would not be resolved by reference to social progress. In a way, the second refutation was about the infinite variety of cultures as well. Following Cohen's quote, Jerusalem and Athens are the most important sources of modern culture, but this implies that there might be other sources. Jerusalem and Athens are then merely two out of many sources of modern culture. Cohen did *not* draw this conclusion, and doing so would have been at odds with his aim to preserve the unity of reason. But judging from his exposition of the problem, there is no good reason why it should not be drawn. In other words, Cohen was drawn to the bottom of the problem posed by the infinite variety of cultures.

"Jerusalem and Athens" brought together these two refutations of the concept of culture for the first time. But the owl of Minerva begins its flight only when dusk begins to fall. In the meantime, a new type of culturalism had emerged. "Jerusalem and Athens," with its belated double critique of culture, was also a response to this new type of culturalism. By the mid-1960s, the indigenous "cultures" were no longer mere objects of anthropological research, they had become political entities: they had reinvented themselves as nations and aspired toward sovereignty as states. This process was flanked and fostered by a new discourse on culture, which has been come to be known as postcolonialism. The emergence of postcolonial theory brought about a fundamental shift in the matrix of culture, religion, and politics. Among other things, it provoked a renewed interest in the foundations of "the West." The return to Jerusalem and Athens as the two pillars of Western civilization is also in part a response to this new discourse.

The new reality that had emerged in the 1950s and especially in the 1960s is perfectly captured in a famous note by Emmanuel Levinas on the Bible and Greek philosophy: "I often say, though it's a dangerous thing to say publicly, that humanity consists of the Bible and the Greeks. All the rest can be translated: all the rest—all the exotic—is dance."[36] Levinas scholars have reluctantly agreed that the "notorious" statement, with its reference to exotism, "is not an exceptional lapse" in his thought, as Howard Caygill put it. One commentator wrote: "These spoken comments clearly dismiss all culture outside the Europeanized Hellenism/Hebraism axis. They are . . . racist, and bear more than a trace of the West's contempt for non-Western cultures."[37] Another commentator took it to extremes: "One cannot help noticing in Levinas's words here an unthinking complacency about his own cultural vantage point, complete with all of its presuppositions. . . . It seems likely that Levinas is not much interested in a dialogue with cultures or religions significantly different from his own. . . . He has carelessly assumed his culturally engendered givens, without paying attention to any other that might question these givens."[38] Responses such as these, fueled by a powerful prejudice, have become an integral part of Western moral sentiment. The understanding of Jerusalem and Athens, too, has been modified by the discourse of postcolonialism—after all, the overall purpose of this discourse was the flight from Eurocentric concepts and conceptual schemes.

Levinas knew this type of response already. He was aware that speaking of Jerusalem and Athens in this way was "a dangerous thing" to do.[39] In another version, ventured in an interview with Christoph von Wolzogen, Levinas already responded to the racism allegation: "I always say—but secretly—that in humanity the only serious things are the Greeks and the Bible; everything else is dancing. I think this is open to the whole world; there is no racism in it."[40] Here, Levinas sought to bring the matter into a private/public distinction. The form of the interview was not altogether appropriate for this task: it did address another person, but unlike a private correspondence it would be printed and hence made public. But the more remarkable aspect of the statement is that Levinas already expected to be called a racist. Furthermore, he let the interviewer know that he had said it before, so he probably had experienced the type of postcolonial protest as a direct response to his initial statement. Finally, he assured the interviewer that he "always" says it, thereby suggesting that he would say it again and again. The case documents a turnaround in the interplay between the new type of culturalism and the European scholar type from before World War II, who was unaffected by the hyperpolitical pretension of the culturalist discourse.

Levinas attracts this type of criticism because he has a reputation as the high representative of "otherness." Readers therefore attack him for being different from what they expected him to be. Unlike Levinas, Strauss is beyond discussion for postcolonials, although he—with his dubious reputation as a neoconservative—has all the potential to pick a fight with. The problem is simply that there is little to find in his writings. One can only trace his encounters in his writings with "nonwhite" or "non-Western" cultures, people, or texts.[41] But there Strauss does not present himself as the typical ideologue of Western superiority. He rather appears as a somewhat old-fashioned but friendly man of the 1950s and 1960s, who is principally open to the challenge but sees little that would compel him to fundamentally alter his views.

Speaking of reading the greatest books written by the greatest minds, he found a way to both address and circumvent the problem that Jerusalem and Athens could no longer be conceived as the roots of all mankind: "The greatest minds to whom we ought to listen are by no means exclusively the greatest minds of the West. It is merely an unfortunate necessity which prevents us from listening to the greatest minds of India and of China: we do not understand their languages, and we cannot learn all languages."[42] When asked about possible differences between discrimination against Jews and discrimination against Negroes, he replied with great honesty that he had never considered the matter. He added, bringing the matter down to the level of personal life experience: "I have known Jews who have had the same desire [to have someone to look down on]. I mean, every man who has 'ambition,' in the vulgar sense of the word, has this desire."[43]

On the same occasion, Strauss touched upon Western otherness when he defended his view that "Judaism cannot be understood as a culture." As he ramblingly explained: "There are folk dances, and pottery, and all that—but you cannot live on that. The substance is not culture, but divine revelation."[44] There is a close link between Strauss and Levinas with regard to the Bible and Greek philosophy: for both, everything else was mere "culture." When Strauss explained in the late 1950s that liberal education was education toward culture, he already needed to add that "culture" was meant here "in the sense of the Western tradition. Yet Western culture is only one among many cultures. By limiting ourselves to Western culture, do we not condemn liberal education to a kind of parochialism, and is not parochialism incompatible with the liberalism, the generosity, the openmindedness, of liberal education? Our notion of liberal education does not seem to fit an age which is aware of the fact that there is not *the* culture of *the* human mind, but a variety of cultures."[45]

The most pertinent passage in "Jerusalem and Athens" is a reference to *1001 Nights* (*Kitāb 'alf layla wa-layla*, also known as *Arabian Nights* or *One Thousand and One Nights*), the Arabic folk tale compilation that had long sparked the exotic imagination of Westerners. There is also an unpublished manuscript with reading notes on *1001 Nights*.[46] In "Jerusalem and Athens," Strauss coupled the reference with Nietzsche's "Of 1000 Goals and One" in *Thus Spoke Zarathustra* for a tongue-in-cheek comment on the situation posed by the variety of cultures: "We have said that according to the prevailing view there were or are *n* cultures. Let us say there were or are 1,001 cultures, thus reminding ourselves of the Arabian Nights, the 1,001 Nights; the account of cultures, if it is well done, will be a series of exciting stories, perhaps of tragedies."[47]

Strauss clearly saw the problem posed by the new concept of cultures. He sought to adjust his philosophical and scholarly project to the new reality; and he felt that this reality needed to be acknowledged in order to preserve the open-mindedness of liberal education. But he saw little that compelled him to fundamentally change his ways. For Strauss, the principal challenge to the West did not come from postcolonial movements, nations, or states. It came from the other superpower of the time, the Soviet Union, with its aspiration toward world hegemony. As he wrote in *The City and Man*, the survival of the West was endangered by the East.[48] It was also endangered by Western uncertainty over its own meaning and purpose, caused by the spread of relativism. Sure, the West seemed to be in a crisis,[49] but the emerging postcolonial discourse was merely the latest offshoot of that crisis, and by no means a very important one for a philosopher who thought in much longer historical lines.

Jerusalem *and* Athens: Western Universalism Redefined

As we saw at the beginning of "Jerusalem and Athens," Strauss addressed the lecture to a community of "Western men" or, more precisely, to a community of potential representatives of the West. This choice is far from obvious, because political philosophy is addressed to man as man, not to Western man. But just like Levinas, Strauss took it for granted that Jerusalem and Athens were universal, despite their origin in a particular tradition. The question they left for post-postcolonials, then, is as follows: How can a particular tradition—or a combination of two out of an infinite number of particular traditions—be universal? How can the foundational texts of a particular culture be valid beyond that particular culture? Was "the West" merely an ideological tool invented to suppress other cultures, or was it actually meant to be a universal concept despite its geographic, cultural, and political limitation?

The task for today is to recover the original meaning of these terms under the rubble of postcolonial theory without ignoring the foundational experiences of postcolonialism (being different, oppressed, voiceless, etc.), which have persisted until this day. The universality of the Western tradition had already been challenged by cultural anthropology, but postcolonialism seemed to have made it indefensible. A decisive factor was what Samuel Huntington referred to as "indigenization": the resurgence of non-Western cultures that had formerly had no voice, reemerging as nations and ultimately as states. It was a process of cultures becoming political (and subsequently religious), and this process turned around the relationship between the West and its Other. As Huntington explained: "The revolt against the West was originally legitimated by asserting the universality of Western values; it is now legitimated by asserting the superiority of non-Western values."[50]

Non-Western values had always persisted. It was their emergence and their assertion of superiority on a worldwide scale, particularly in the Western world itself, that made it difficult to justify the universality of the Western tradition. Any argument in favor of Western universalism inevitably became entangled in the snares of diversity and otherness.

In this situation, the defensibility of genuinely "Western" concepts depends on a renewed understanding of what they are or what they were meant to be. Here, it seems useful to make the voice of Leo Strauss audible again. Strauss was neither a typical proponent of Western superiority nor one of its self-indulgent critics. But more importantly, he reframed the question by referring to the West in nonessentialist terms as a "tension," and a way of living in this tension: "The very life of Western civilization is the life between two codes, a fundamental tension."[51]

At this point, we are again confronted with the double aspect of Jerusalem *and* Athens and Jerusalem *versus* Athens. The statement implies that the speaker takes a stand *for* the conflict, not primarily a position *in* the conflict: before making a choice, he would need to acknowledge that there is a conflict between Jerusalem and Athens. Furthermore, he would need to agree that this conflict is fundamental, whereas numerous conflicts between the proverbial 999 other goals are *not*. He must begin to see life in the fundamental tension between Jerusalem and Athens.

To take a stand for the conflict between Jerusalem and Athens means to subscribe to a notion of the West that is informed by its theological and philosophical heritage. This notion is opposed to a liberal narrative, according to which the West based its former glory solely on superior firepower. Samuel Huntington expressed the latter most sharply: "The West won the world not by the superiority of its ideas or values or religion (to which few members of other civilizations were converted) but rather by its superiority in applying organized violence. Westerners often forget that; non-Westerners never do."[52] This view certainly has all the merits of being "realistic," and yet it is perhaps not realistic enough. Most of all, it entirely disregards, or debunks, the theopolitical characteristics of Western civilization. One characteristic feature of what has been called the West is a certain ratio between the sacred and the profane, and an irresolvable tension between the two worlds. This feature has largely remained invisible under the preponderance of the secularization thesis, but it has not vanished altogether. In the twenty-first century, it has once again become apparent against the backdrop of societies in which all secular life is impregnated with theology (theocracies), as well as of societies in which all transcendence reemerges from within the secular sphere. (We may say that the paradigm of the latter is sports consumption, which has often been described as a quasi-religious act.) Both of these ways of life are in principle Western, too, but each of them is counterbalanced by the other. The Jerusalem-and-Athens paradigm provides a viable middle ground between the two. To take a stand for the conflict means then to opt for a tension in the foundation of political life between its theological and its philosophical roots and, further, for the orientation of secular life according to this tension.

Understanding the core idea of Western civilization as a "tension" between two premodern principles has a lot to offer concerning some of the twenty-first-century questions in the force field of politics, religion, and culture. Most notably, it strips the very notion of "the West" of its ideological smack. It restates Levinas's proposition that his notion of the Bible and the Greeks "is open to the whole world." As it were, the notion of "the West" can *only* be revaluated with regard to the tension between its double heritage, or its two foundational traditions. In the current resurgence of the notion of "the West," affirmative references to specific modern ingredients of Western civilization such as the "six killer apps of Western power" (science, rule of law and property rights, competition, work ethic, medicine, and consumer society)[53] inevitably remain entrapped in the ideological force field of the present. But the founding principles are likely to survive, being inscribed into the memory of Western civilization, to be reactivated at various times and in ever-changing circumstances.

It is only at this point, when the guiding principle of Jerusalem *and* Athens has become clear, that we can begin to understand the irresolvable conflict or the principal disagreement according to Strauss. It was certainly much more difficult for Strauss to do justice to the conflict than it had been to outline the agreement. And while the agreement is hardly more than a matter of historical recollection today, the conflict leads into the field of contemporary battles in the force field of culture, religion, and politics.

Jerusalem versus Athens

As Daniel Tanguay noted, "in itself" the subject matter of Jerusalem and Athens was "not new."[54] The long and illustrious history of the Jerusalem/Athens divide encompasses a variety of references from Tertullian and St. Augustine via Matthew Arnold to Leo Shestov, as well as the old rabbinical wrath against Hellenism and a number of modern-day outliers such as Erich Auerbach, Hans Kohn, and Gilles Deleuze.[55] The topic could be put forward to safeguard the belief in revelation against the challenge of reason, to ponder an infusion of transcendence into the moribund forms of modern culture, or as a reminiscence to a bygone intellectual tradition. The Christian scholastics secured a place for philosophy by turning it into a subsidiary of faith, or a "handmaiden of theology" (*ancilla theologiae*), as the classic formulation goes. Twentieth-century philosophers often sought to grant *some* meaning to theology, but to discern this meaning they were often compelled to appropriate it from the side of philosophy, society, or history. In any case, the relationship between Jerusalem and Athens was largely asymmetric. Strauss was certainly up to something when he remarked that the entire history of the West presents itself as a failed attempt to harmonize or synthesize Jerusalem and Athens.[56] There is something different in his own account here, and his resistance to mediation or harmonization is part of a larger set of conceptual strategies.

More than any other thinker concerned with the topic, Strauss brought the binary of Jerusalem and Athens into a symmetry. To do so, he employed some surprisingly advanced conceptual techniques to account for the asymmetries that arise when we speak of Jerusalem and Athens. Despite the text's initial aura of old-fashionedness, he had a knack for ever-changing and collapsing binaries, as we saw in the brief discussion of Hermann Cohen above.

The intricate connection between premodern and hypermodern thoughts is difficult to grasp and adds to the uncertainty over the position of the author. Where is Strauss when he speaks of Jerusalem and Athens? To begin with, he speaks clearly as a philosopher, but he does not seem to appropriate Jerusalem from the side of Athens. We must locate the position of the author more precisely. Is Strauss "between" Jerusalem and Athens, or moving "on the border" that separates the two?[57] Does he perhaps keep changing his position over the course of a text, or at least from one text to another? To come to a satisfying answer, we must see his occupation with the Jerusalem/Athens theme in its genesis. The symmetry in "Jerusalem and Athens" evolved over the course of many different texts and through a variety of contexts. Strauss presented his text as a mere assembly of "some preliminary reflections," but these reflections were the end product of a process spanning over more than twenty-one years—or even more than forty years if we trace the topic before the emergence of the *terms* Jerusalem and Athens.

By the late 1920s, Strauss had convinced himself that the conflict between belief and unbelief was the everlasting theme of philosophy. The new understanding is documented by the appropriation of a Goethe quote in his Freud review (1928): "The real, only and deepest theme of the history of the world and of mankind to which all other themes are subordinate remains the conflict between unbelief and belief."[58] This conflict is not necessarily connected to the other great quarrel rediscovered by Strauss about the same time, the *querelle des anciens et des modernes,* but for Strauss the two could only be understood together: the *querelle* was repeated with an eye on the conflict between Jerusalem and Athens, and Jerusalem and Athens could only be understood on the basis of a preparatory renewal of the *querelle.* One may well prefer to disregard this intricate connection or interpret it away (for example, by finding Jerusalem and Athens in the constitution of a particular modern nation), but the result will inevitably be a modification, not an elaboration, of Strauss's position.[59]

The Goethe quote could be understood in different ways. Ernst Cassirer remarked that Goethe's conception of belief and unbelief was very different from its later appropriations. "According to Goethe every productive period in human history is *ipso facto* to be regarded as a period of belief. The term has no theological not even a specific religious connotation but simply expresses the preponderance of the positive over the negative powers."[60] While Cassirer clearly downplayed the religious dimension, Strauss opted for a literal interpretation of the quote. He put great emphasis on the conflict between unbelief and belief and on its singular importance.[61] As he maintained, this battle had almost given out (*eingeschlafen,* literally: fallen asleep) at a time he characterized as the epoch of the philosophy of culture and experience (*Epoche der Kultur- und Erlebnisphilosophie*). It had been put forward by a few Protestant theologians (most notably Karl Barth), but overall it was advanced by the Jewish philosophers more than by anyone else.

As we saw, the general presupposition and problem of Jewish philosophy took on a very specific shape around 1930—a period of awakening for German-Jewish thought in its problematic interplay with German culture. Strauss's use of a Goethe quote to express the situation of Jewish philosophy shows the intricate connection between Jewish and German or European thought at the time. "Jewish philosophy" in the narrower sense (as opposed to those philosophies rather randomly written by Jews) has always been a discourse on the compatibility of Judaism and philosophy. With Strauss's discovery of exoteric writing, concerns about this compatibility largely moved into the background. The prime concern was to protect philosophy against the claims of religion. If philosophy is esoteric and the commitment to revelation is exoteric, the tension between Jerusalem and Athens is largely resolved. The esoteric/exoteric divide functions as a "theory" here, dissolving the original problem into a grand narrative of persecution and resistance qua literary forms and techniques. By 1946 Strauss was already dissatisfied with this solution. As he wrote in a personal note:

> 8–11–46 / I herewith strike out everything I have done so far—I must *really* begin from the *very* beginning. / I must once again get clear on what the real question is—and I have to change my working plans accordingly (to the extent that I am not bound by promises—courses). / Thus far I have assumed that the account of the original concept of philosophy (including the critique sketched of the modern concept of philosophy) could suffice, since for me the right and the necessity of philosophy was certain. Impressed by Kierkegaard and recalling my earlier doubts, I must raise the question once again and as sharply as possible whether the right and the necessity of philosophy are completely evident. / Since this is the case, much more important than the topic "Socrates" and "Introduction to pol(itical) philos(ophy)" becomes—*Philosophy and The Law* or (perhaps) *Philosophy or The divine guidance*.[62]

To capture the sudden recurrence of the topic in Strauss's thought, the note must be read together with his report to Karl Löwith, written four days later, on how he had "suffered shipwreck once again." It was an intellectual crisis that compelled Strauss "to begin once more from the beginning."[63] Radical doubt had returned. But something was different here. The domain of philosophy had been radical doubt in revelation, but for Strauss, the radical doubt pertained to philosophy. In other words, the problem was philosophy, not revelation. As Strauss claimed, the right and the necessity of philosophical reason could become evident only vis-à-vis revelation, and not vis-à-vis poetry or "pagan myths and laws," for example: "The Bible thus offers the only challenge to the claim of philosophy which can reasonably be made. One cannot seriously question the claim of philosophy in the name, e.g., of politics or poetry."[64]

The practical difficulty was how to reconcile the radical doubt with "working plans" and assigned courses. In a philosopher's academic workload and classes, the right and the necessity of philosophy must be presupposed. Another remarkable aspect is the attribution of the doubt to a renewed encounter with Kierkegaard. There are few references to Kierkegaard in Strauss's published works, and the overall tendency was to downplay his significance, especially in comparison to Nietzsche.[65]

From here onward, Strauss advanced the topic in a series of lectures. The first reference to a lecture under the title "Jerusalem and Athens" stems from November 1946, when Strauss presented the topic to the General Seminar of the New School for Social Research.[66] A second version from 1948 was partially preserved as an audio recording.[67] "Jerusalem and Athens" was also meant to be the second chapter of his planned book with the working title *Philosophy and the Law: Historical Essays*, which never materialized.[68]

In the same year, Strauss gave the lecture "Reason and Revelation" at the Hartford Theological Seminary, where he assumed the role of "a non-theologian" speaking to theologians. True to this dramatic setting, he staged the conflict as a hypothetical argument between a philosopher and a theologian, in which neither side can make a decisive point against the possibility of the other. Philosophy and the Bible cannot refute each other, but each would need to do so to present itself as the one thing needful. This truly insoluble situation led Strauss to state the matter as a "fundamental" alternative (as opposed to alternatives that can be resolved by way of a synthesis or a decision):

> No alternative is more fundamental than the alternative: human guidance or divine guidance. *Tertium non datur*. The alternative between philosophy and revelation cannot be evaded by any harmonization or "synthesis." For each of the two antagonists proclaims something as the one thing needful, as the only thing that ultimately counts, and the one thing needful proclaimed by the Bible is the opposite to that proclaimed by philosophy. In every attempt at harmonization, in every synthesis however impressive, one of the two opposed elements is sacrificed, more or less subtly, but in any event surely, to the other: philosophy which means to be the queen, must be made the handmaid of theology or *vice versa*.[69]

The addition of "or *vice versa*" is not altogether justified. To be sure, the task was to outline the mutual nonrefutability of philosophy and theology. And unlike later versions, the text also seeks to show why theology cannot refute philosophy.[70] And yet Strauss left no doubt that he was much more concerned with the consequences for philosophy. As he added:

> Confronted with the claim of revelation, the philosopher is . . . compelled to *refute* that claim. More than that: he must prove the *impossibility* of revelation. For if revelation is *possible*, it is possible that the philosophic enterprise is fundamentally wrong.[71]

In his early expositions of the Jerusalem/Athens theme Strauss remained true to the initial problem he had sketched in his personal note: The core was "the right and the necessity of philosophy" vis-à-vis revelation.[72] This question matched well with his earlier genealogy of how modern philosophy had attempted to secure its own possibility by eliminating the possibility of revelation and miracles.[73] In other words, "Reason and Revelation" is also a continuation of *Philosophy and Law* with different means. The principal dispute between philosopher and theologian is preserved in the third part of "Progress or Return?," Strauss's 1952 lecture for a small Jewish audience at the Hillel House Chicago, virtually in his neighborhood in Hyde Park. This closing part is a tour de force through the current arguments in favor of one side and against another, with the outcome that *all* these arguments run into severe problems sooner or later.[74]

Up to this point, Strauss had treated the matter in the form of a personal reorientation or presented the topic to small audiences. The problem made its first wider public appearance in *Natural Right and History* (1953). In the midst of a discourse on methodological issues in Weberian social science he all of a sudden faced "the real issue," namely, "religion versus irreligion," as if the previous twenty-eight pages in the chapter had merely been a necessary preparation, an act of removing some obstacles in the way.[75] The topic disappeared again in a cascade of arguments against Weberian value-free science, only to pop up again twelve pages later. Here, it initially seems particularly misplaced and not quite integrated into the text, almost as if it were copied and pasted from another text. The characterization of the conflict indeed contains hardly anything new, but the conclusion drawn by Strauss remarkably shifts the balance toward revelation and against philosophy:

> If we take a bird's-eye view of the secular struggle between philosophy and theology, we can hardly avoid the impression that neither of the two antagonists has ever succeeded in really refuting the other. All arguments in favor of revelation seem to be valid only if belief in revelation is presupposed; and all

arguments against revelation seem to be valid only if unbelief is presupposed. This state of things would appear to be but natural. Revelation is always so uncertain to unassisted reason that it can never compel the assent of unassisted reason, and man is so built that he can find his satisfaction, his bliss, in free investigation, in articulating the riddle of being. But, on the other hand, he yearns so much for a solution of that riddle and human knowledge is always so limited that the need for divine illumination cannot be denied and the possibility of revelation cannot be refuted. Now it is this state of things that seems to decide irrevocably against philosophy and in favor of revelation. Philosophy has to grant that revelation is possible. But to grant that revelation is possible means to grant that philosophy is perhaps not the one thing needful, that philosophy is perhaps something infinitely unimportant. To grant that revelation is possible means to grant that the philosophic life is not necessarily, not evidently, *the* right life. Philosophy, the life devoted to the quest for evident knowledge available to man as man, would itself rest on an unevident, arbitrary, or blind decision. This would merely confirm the thesis of faith, that there is no possibility of consistency, of a consistent and thoroughly sincere life, without belief in revelation. The mere fact that philosophy and revelation cannot refute each other would constitute the refutation of philosophy by revelation.[76]

Scholars have been at odds over this particular quote. Is this turn in favor of revelation genuine or merely rhetorical? Did Strauss make the position of revelation stronger than it actually is? And does the statement even reflect his own position? His use of cautionary expressions such as "seems to" and "perhaps" and the repeated use of "would" may indicate otherwise. But most of all, the asymmetric attribution seems unsustainable: How could the mutual nonrefutation of philosophy and revelation amount to a refutation of philosophy only? For if the mutual nonrefutability of philosophy and revelation refutes philosophy, it would also seem to refute revelation. If revelation cannot refute philosophy—the life of free investigation—then revelation is perhaps not the one thing needful, and the life of obedient love is not evidently the right life. Furthermore, the mere yearning for a conclusive solution to the riddle of being does not yet prove the way of philosophers unviable.

But the asymmetric formulation is not entirely unwarranted if we see the quote in its immediate context of Weberian social science. Strauss inserted the statement on reason and revelation to make a point about the "superficiality" of Weber's methodology.[77] First, he constructed Weber's preoccupation with the distinction between facts and values as a failed response to the challenge of revelation, and second, he cast the persistence of the possibility of revelation as the reason for Weber's despair. Third, the ensuing return to reason and revelation provided an access to reality—and "reality" is the guiding concept of the methodological discourse on Weber in *Natural Right and History*.[78] Hence, the reference to philosophy and revelation has a precise function within the chapter. The renewal of the dispute between belief and unbelief indicates and prepares for a departure from the abstractions of social science methodology and a reentry into reality. The implication of this move far surpassed the discourse on Weber for Strauss. In a way, the preoccupation with positivism and historicism, and perhaps even the entire discourse on social science relativism, had been a preparation for the one thing that really mattered: the quarrel between Jerusalem and Athens was infinitely closer to reality than historicism or the distinction between facts and values.

As noted, there is one core element in these early expositions of the Jerusalem/Athens theme that wore off later: In "Jerusalem and Athens," Strauss was much less concerned with the mutual nonrefutability of the Bible and philosophy. Other changes include the gradual transition from a dispute between philosophy and theology to a closer interpretation of the foundational texts. And thereby Strauss developed a much greater variety of perspectives and analytic strategies. This greater flexibility made "Jerusalem and Athens" much more symmetric, although it is not perfectly symmetric. Despite the reduction to two clear and coherent principles, the early formulations of the problem had remained asymmetric throughout.

Dissolving the Binary

After devoting four paragraphs to a demonstration of why Jerusalem and Athens cannot be understood as two "cultures," Strauss made a fresh start by pointing to a word that occurs both in the Bible and in Greek philosophy: wisdom. The purpose was to find a common reference point that originated in the Bible and the great works of the Greeks themselves. The last criticism against cultural anthropology had been directed against its dependence "on a conceptual framework that is alien" to the phenomena "and therefore necessarily distorts them."[79] Culturalism pretended to understand its objects better than they understood themselves. The task was to understand them exactly as they understood themselves. It is doubtful whether Strauss ever understood a teaching or an author *exactly* as they understood themselves. Often, he articulated their intentions and presuppositions much more radically than they could. It suffices to say that he made a great effort to articulate the self-understanding of Jerusalem and Athens and their respective notions of wisdom.[80] This endeavor allowed him to account for his own position within the asymmetric juxtaposition:

> Not only the Greek philosophers but the Greek poets as well were considered to be wise men, and the Torah is said in the Torah to be "your wisdom in the eyes of the nations." We must then try to understand the difference between biblical wisdom and Greek wisdom. We see at once that each of the two claims to be true wisdom, thus denying to the other its claim to be wisdom in the strict and highest sense. According to the Bible, the beginning of wisdom is fear of the Lord; according to the Greek philosophers, the beginning of wisdom is wonder. We are thus compelled from the very beginning to make a choice, to take a stand. Where then do we stand? We are confronted with the incompatible claims of Jerusalem and Athens to our allegiance. We are open to both and willing to listen to each. We ourselves are not wise but we wish to become wise. We are seekers for wisdom, *philosophoi*.[81]

The claim that the incompatibility of Jerusalem and Athens compels the reader or listener "to make a choice" is somewhat misleading. As a matter of fact, the problem of Jerusalem and Athens could hardly be solved by making a choice for the philosophical *or* the religious way of life. To name a few objections: Strauss himself had made that choice early in his life, but that did not solve the problem for him. Moreover, he could never be sure that the decision was justified. And would he still be a seeker for wisdom, a *philosophos*, if he had settled the matter by way of his arbitrary choice? All in all, to stop listening to Jerusalem seems to be the least viable option for Athens to secure its own superiority. The model of Jerusalem and Athens, then, is not that of a mere choice. More than any other Strauss text, "Jerusalem and Athens" shows that the matter cannot be decided—or that any decision may be unjust and therefore in need of revision. The "Western men" in the text resemble the sovereign in Walter Benjamin's *Trauerspiel* book, who in a moment of decision proves unable to decide, caught by *acedia*, dullness of the heart.[82] No matter how confident they were when it came to the task of preserving the roots of Western civilization, the "Western men" were in constant self-doubt over the soundness of their judgment: "By saying that we wish to hear first and then to act to decide, we have already decided in favor of Athens against Jerusalem."[83]

A statement on biblical criticism adds yet another layer of preliminary methodological remarks to the text. This statement, stretching over more than two paragraphs, is a riddle of its own. It starts with the assertion that "[we] must accept" the principle and ends with the confirmation that "we shall not take issue with the findings and even the premises of biblical criticism." But in between these assertions it relegates the impossibility of miracles to "an indemonstrable hypothesis" and repeatedly counters the critical view "from the point of the Bible."[84] The strategy was to grant that the Bible consisted of layers of "myth" and "history" but deny the antitheological implications of this fact. Even if the Bible were a compilation of memories of memories of ancient histories, it has *become* an authoritative text in the process of compilation.

Strauss explained this stance on biblical criticism farther down in the text. Compared with the texts of early Greek thought, it seemed, the Bible is not a book in the proper sense but a compilation of books, of holy speeches. "Confronted with a variety of preexisting holy speeches, which as such had to be treated with utmost respect," Strauss wrote, "[the compilers] excluded only what could not by any stretch of the imagination be rendered compatible with the fundamental and authoritative teaching. . . . Yet by excluding what could not by any stretch of the imagination be rendered compatible with the fundamental and authoritative teaching, they prepared the traditional way of reading the Bible, i.e., the reading of the Bible as if it were a book in the strict sense."[85] This account of how a traditional reading of the Bible was created out of the plurality of possible readings is perhaps the best illustration of what Strauss had in mind when he spoke of a "postcritical Judaism."[86] After biblical criticism, the Bible can be read *as if* it were a holy text without falling back behind the findings of biblical criticism.

The immediate consequence for the question of how to approach the Bible was that even the latest and uppermost textual layer could be as important or authoritative as the earliest ones. "We shall start from the uppermost layer—from what is first for us, even though it may not be the first simply."[87] Strauss believed that this was the point where both the traditional and the historical interpretation of the Bible started, so that he would not need to decide between the two to make a new start. Hence, he would avoid making an advance decision in favor of Athens against Jerusalem.

The ensuing interpretation of the Bible is again immensely concerned with the starting point, the proper way to begin. Strauss started "at the beginning of the beginning," with the account of creation in the book of Genesis. He read this beginning with regard to what is being *said* and *not said* there. The initial question is who speaks the words, "In the beginning God created heaven and earth." Strauss wrote: "We are not told; hence we do not know." Furthermore, it is not clear whether it is actually important—from the viewpoint of the Bible—to know who is speaking. "We have no right to assume that God said it. . . . We shall then assume that the words were spoken by a nameless man. . . . The narrator does not claim to have heard the account from God; perhaps he heard it from some man or men; perhaps he retells a tale."[88]

From the question of voice Strauss turned to the dramatic setting of the beginning of the Bible, translating the account of creation into its spatial arrangement. The initial paragraph on the beginning of the beginning is indeed located at the indifference point of the "traditional" and the "critical" study of the Bible. Strauss sought to articulate the teaching of the Bible "from the point of view of the Bible"[89] to the extent that this point of view could be assumed by the unassisted human mind. He needed to read the Bible more traditionally than the tradition and more critically than biblical criticism. Clearly, the "postcritical" approach was hypercritical from the beginning. It allowed the Bible and Greek philosophy to be read almost as if they had never been read before.

There is another strategic shift at work in the account of the Bible and Greek philosophy: Strauss gave a philosophical interpretation of the Bible and a theological interpretation of Greek philosophy. The interpretation of the Bible is "philosophical" not in the sense of the allegorical method; it did not aim to show that the Bible contains an esoteric philosophical meaning. What made it philosophical is the continuous thinking about the presuppositions of believers and nonbelievers alike. It is "epistemological" inasmuch as it explores the limits of a merely human understanding of a text that claims to be more than human. As Strauss repeatedly emphasized: "Nothing is too wondrous for the lord."[90] In other words, the account of Jerusalem and Athens is guided by Strauss's principal critique of reason. The theological interpretation of Greek philosophy spells out this purpose even more openly. It is designed as a study on God and the gods in Hesiod, Aristotle, Plato, and ultimately Socrates, but clearly there is another dimension here.

The image of Socrates—who was sentenced to death for not believing in the gods worshipped by the citizens of Athens—was a role model for the problem of reason and revelation *before* revelation for Strauss: Socrates denied that he possessed any other than human wisdom, so that he became the guardian of the divine knowledge that remained inaccessible to him. He is wiser than other men because he knows that he knows nothing, that is, nothing regarding the most important things. Strauss's argument is based on Yehuda Halevi's interpretation of the respective passage in Plato's *Apology*. According to Yehuda Halevi, Socrates said he would not deny the divine wisdom, but he could not understand it, for he was wise only in human wisdom. Strauss had subscribed to this interpretation in his earlier discussions of the quote, but now he argued that Yehuda Halevi's interpretation "goes somewhat too far." As he noted, right after denying the possession of any more than human wisdom, Socrates refers to the speech that originated his philosophical mission: the words of the Pythia, who replied on Apollo's behalf at Delphi. It was Socrates's companion Chaerephon who came to Delphi and asked Apollo's oracle whether there was anyone wiser than Socrates. The Pythia replied that no one was wiser, and this reply caused Socrates's mission (*Apology* 21a).[91] As Strauss argued, this mission originated both in human initiative (Chaerephon consulting the oracle) and in divine intervention (for at least Socrates assumed that the Pythia's reply was actually Apollo's reply). Now, while Socrates did not come to doubt the divine origin of the speech, neither did he take for granted that the god's answer was true; he attempted to find men wiser than himself, only to find out that the god's reply was true. "Thus his attempt to refute the oracle turns into a vindication of the oracle. Without intending it, he comes to the assistance of the god; he serves the god; he obeys the god's command."[92]

This image of Socrates, with its alterations and reinterpretations over the course of Strauss's work, contains Strauss's genuine model of the relationship between reason and revelation. The model is not entirely new, for it had been brought up in the introduction to *Philosophy and Law*, and there Strauss had made it clear that Nietzschean atheism would not provide a sufficient basis. But Socratic atheism—understood as the restriction to human wisdom and the abstention from divine wisdom *before* revelation—was another matter. The enigmatic figure of Socrates assisting the god by trying to disprove the god's reply, only to find out that it is true, is the image in which the whole semantic process eventually came to a standstill.

The multilayered, virtually kaleidoscopic narrative of the Bible and Greek philosophy deserves to be explored in a long commentary of its own. The preceding examination can only hope to be helpful in this endeavor. It suggests that both the philosophical project and the methodological strategies of "Jerusalem and Athens" are far more advanced than the initial aura of old-fashionedness suggests. So "returning" in 1967 to the roots of Western civilization, after all, was not just somehow philosophically backward; there is also something entirely new and unheard-of in it.

Conclusion

Leo Strauss and "the Natural Way" of Reading

At the very least, this study will show that reading Leo Strauss is much more complicated than has often been assumed. Strauss himself put great emphasis on proper reading, and he hinted at a close nexus to his writing when he quipped that "one writes as one reads."[1] To understand Leo Strauss as a philosopher, we must understand how he read and wrote.

Strauss-the-careful-reader appeals to students of political philosophy (or philosophy in general) who seek to become careful readers. He offers these students a way to engage with the philosophical thought of the past by way of close and careful reading. They seek to read Strauss as closely and carefully as they read the greatest thinkers of the past. But no matter how slowly and painstakingly carefully they proceed, Strauss's texts pose the greatest difficulties. It would be easy to blame Strauss for this nuisance. Most of his writings are exceedingly complex, if not outright enigmatic. The greater obstacle to reading Strauss, however, is posed by the expectations and preconceptions on the part of his readers. Strauss has long been subjected to a variety of possible "readings," which all too often revolve around certain assumptions about his political position. I occasionally tried to follow how these "readings" have developed a life of their own in Strauss scholarship, up to the point where the respective discourse has lost touch with the writings it pretends to be about. As a rule of thumb, one should engage in such discourses to free the text from the debris of its own afterlife. To understand what the text has to say, one must first remove the obstacles that often result from arbitrary "readings." But for the most part, I have tried to simply follow the argument—or "the argument and the action"—of Strauss's writings. Strauss explained this procedure in his interpretations of classical works. These reflections on how to read Plato, Xenophon, or Aristotle contain numerous indications of how his own writings should be read. Explaining how to interpret the classics, Strauss tells us how to read his interpretations.

But even if Strauss tells us how to read his interpretations, we must not follow his advice in every respect. It is not required to read his writings exclusively in a "Straussian" way, and there is no reason why we should not occasionally understand him better than he understood himself: Strauss was not a perfect author. In a way, the task is more modest, but the claim is also more far-reaching. In the introduction to his study on Xenophon's *Hiero, On Tyranny* (1948), Strauss asserted that there is a "natural way of reading" a classical work.[2] This natural way would retain the openness of reading while limiting the multiplicity of possible (and impossible) readings. Strauss gave a number of hints in his interpretation of the *Hiero*. By instructing us to follow the argument and the action of the text, Strauss guided us to become natural readers.

A basic rule is that every single element of the text must be accounted for. Each detail has a specific "purpose," which reveals itself "in its proper place."[3] No element may be discarded as unintelligible. Insignificant details become intelligible as parts of a larger drama as it unfolds in the action of the dialogue. To understand this "action," one must pay close attention to "what the characters silently do and unintentionally or occasionally reveal."[4] Strauss analyzed the speeches of Simonides and Hiero as a play, in which both overstate their respective cases in order to provoke their opponent into a peculiar position. At one point, Simonides permits Hiero to defeat him, but upon his victory Hiero realizes that he has merely prepared his own downfall.[5] These rhetorical elements are part of a larger drama, namely, the asymmetric confrontation between a wise man and a tyrannical ruler. The tyrant fears the wise man, because he does not understand the meaning and purpose of wisdom, and hence the wise man must fear for his life. Strauss described the awkward moment in the conversation when Simonides seems to reveal his desire for tyrannical power. That moment vanishes when Simonides virtue-signals to Hiero that he does not care about the tyrant's moral flaws. Although he has gained the upper hand in the conversation, he gives Hiero to understand that he would not use his power.[6]

Strauss applied the same principles to philosophical texts, despite their apparent lack of drama. He had a knack for reading philosophical concepts and problems as if they were dramatic characters, whose silent deeds and occasional expressions would reveal the true intention of the philosopher more thoroughly than the philosopher himself had understood it. Contemporaries such as Carl Schmitt and Julius Guttmann sensed this uncanny ability of Leo Strauss to explicate their intentions from early on.

One could summarize the procedure in *On Tyranny* by stating that Strauss read the *Hiero* literally. Even if his own writings need not be read in a "Straussian" way, it seems useful to explore the possibility that they must be read literally as well. I suggest that such a literal reading designates the "natural way" of reading described by Strauss.

The preceding chapters seek to combine a thoroughgoing conceptual concern with a focus on some of the key texts, their larger philosophical contexts, and their particular theoretical problems. As we have seen, the key issue in the triad of culture, religion, and the political is the critique of "culture." This inconspicuous critique migrated from one text to another, and from one phase of Strauss's work to another: it disappeared and all of a sudden reappeared in a different temporal and spatial setting, but it never fully ceased to be a principal concern for Strauss. The same goes for religion and the political. The triad of culture, religion, and the political belongs to the conceptual templates that informed and structured his disparate writings. These templates, which reveal themselves only to long and careful reading, form the clear material basis that turns his writings into a coherent philosophical project. They also determined the choice of texts and the structure of the present study.

A second criterion is that the texts are *significant* in their own right. "Significance" (*Bedeutsamkeit*) is one of the great terms in continental philosophy that cannot be strictly defined, whereas it is indispensable when it comes to describing the production of meaning. As the philosopher Hans Blumenberg wrote on Erich Rothacker's "principle of significance": "Its purpose is that in man's historical world of culture things have 'valences' for attention and for vital distance." The claim is not merely that these things (texts) are *important* for being controversial or some other reason pertaining to their outer history. Blumenberg's main concern was to rebut the notion that significance is merely bestowed upon the object in the act of interpretation. "In significance, the subjective component can indeed be greater than the objective one, but the latter can never return to zero. As a valence that was 'thought up,' significance would have to break down."[7] Ultimately, the openness of the procedure exemplifies the openness of liberal education: each interpretation exemplifies and demonstrates a way of reading. Reading thus understood is not only a "method" but also a way of life: the life with philosophical texts, and the life of writing about these texts, hence creating new texts that—each in a much more modest way—continue the work of the great texts.

Part I describes the conceptual triad of culture, religion, and the political in Strauss's thought in its basis and its genesis. This triad was formed on the model of a prior debate—instigated around 1915 by Hermann Cohen—on the place of religion in the system of philosophy. The systematic problem of religion also provided the template to locate "the political" in its difficult position between a domain of "culture" on the one hand and an intensity that would do away with the cultural differentiation on the other. As I have sought to show, Strauss's masterful review essay on Carl Schmitt's *The Concept of the Political* must be read as a late follow-up to the Cohenian problem. Tracing the history of the problem through a variety of writings from the 1920s and 1930s, we begin to see the precarious double structure of religion *and* the political that bothered Strauss: neither came to rest in a well-structured cultural order, and neither could be located beyond the cultural order.

The larger consideration here concerns the relationship between the historical and the systematic task of philosophy. As opposed to the understanding of philosophical works as a *response* to the immediate historical or social context of their creation, their conceptual and systematic predispositions stem from prior, often remote contexts. The crucial task is to trace these templates and describe how they migrated into the new context. In Strauss's case, they stemmed from phenomenology and neo-Kantianism. To generalize the claim, twentieth-century continental philosophy bids us to pay greater attention to conceptual patterns that migrated from debates of around 1910 to the iconic writings of the 1920s and 1930s, and from here all the way to postwar Jewish thought in America or postwar European philosophy. From here we begin to see some issues of the twenty-first century that are happening in the force field of culture, religion, and the political.

Given Strauss's own discontent with the school, neo-Kantianism is an unlikely starting point to trace this impact, for Strauss did not see himself in this lineage. Nevertheless, we can strictly discern it from his own writings. The point is not a mere "methodological" one. Building his philosophical project upon the Cohenian template, Strauss located the task of philosophy in the force field of culture, religion, and the political. Following his numerous interpretations of his contemporaries, every thinker was caught in this force field. In particular, every thinker had a problem with culturalism.

It is not clear from the outset how this genuinely modern concern matches with the view of Strauss as a "Platonic" philosopher. This question is, of course, far from new. It has been run through Strauss by Hegelians and others to show that he remained trapped in the modern world. But perhaps it can be restated rather noncontroversially. How does he reconcile his Platonism with the utterly un-Platonic concern that expressed itself in the triad of culture, religion, and the political?

Culturalism—as nurtured by German philosophy of culture—was based on the notion that the task of philosophy is to understand the products of man and his civilizational progress. Platonism provided Strauss with an outside perspective on this assumption, which he saw as presumptuous. He sought to restate for twentieth-century thought the view that philosophy is knowledge of one's ignorance. As Plato had Socrates say in the *Apology*: "And surely it is the most blameworthy ignorance to believe than one knows what one does not know. It is perhaps on this point and in this respect, gentlemen, that I differ from the majority of men, and if I were to claim that I am wiser than anyone in anything, it would be in this, that, as I have no adequate knowledge of things in the other world, so I do not think I have" (*Apology* 29b). Strauss morphed this foundational claim of philosophy into a critique of reason. He also understood well that the claim to ignorance had a specific sense here: it was ignorance of the most important things, or *not knowing much about the other world*. More than any other twentieth-century critic of reason, Strauss showed that reason must be understood in its complicated interplay with revelation. A major *critical* concern was to demonstrate that the problem of reason and revelation cannot be understood within the framework of culture.

The major work to address this issue—and the greatest stumbling block in current Strauss scholarship—is *Philosophy and Law*. This early masterwork stretches across multiple epochs and thematic concerns, involving the crisis of contemporary Jewry, a critique of Jewish "culture," the quarrel between ancients and moderns, and the Platonic tradition in medieval Islamic and Jewish thought. And most of all, it provides a bold philosophical interpretation of the medieval Jewish Enlightenment of Maimonides, his Islamic predecessors (Avicenna), and his Jewish successors (Gersonides). Part II of the present study seeks to follow the argument and the action of *Philosophy and Law* and bring its divergent parts and multiple concerns into a unified perspective. The thematic vantage point of the book is a critique of reason: tracing how medieval Islamic and Jewish philosophers sought to defend philosophy vis-à-vis revelation, Strauss described the contours of a "rational critique of reason." This finding is closely related to a methodological point, namely, that the argument and the action of *Philosophy and Law* is anti-exoteric: no matter whether medieval Jewish philosophers subscribed to esotericism (Maimonides) or not (Gersonides), they presupposed the fact of revelation as the necessary basis of philosophizing. *Philosophy and Law* also left a number of unresolved problems that bothered Strauss in his subsequent work and prompted his turn to exoteric writing. As a close examination of the transition from *Philosophy and Law* to the seminal *Persecution and the Art of Writing* (1941/1952) reveals, the turn to exotericism was first and foremost the product of a crisis: a response to a perceived failure.

Just like *Philosophy and Law* itself, the transition from *Philosophy and Law* to *Persecution and the Art of Writing*—and hence also from Strauss's "German-Jewish" writings to his "American" writings—is a crucial moment in the formation of his philosophical project. Most of all, this transition bids us to reexamine the larger case of exotericism (often referred to as esotericism). This topic has largely dominated the debate on Strauss as a reader, and many scholars consider it to be the chief characteristic of his thought. As Irving Kristol summarized Strauss's teaching on the Great Books, these books cannot "simply be 'read,'" they rather "have to be studied, and in a special way." But what is so special about them? For Kristol, the reason is to be found in the fact that the Great Books contain "esoteric doctrines reserved only for the most intelligent and perceptive." Studying rather than merely "reading" the Great Books would therefore reveal those "esoteric doctrines" carefully hidden by the author from superficial readers. Undoubtedly, the same would go for Strauss's own writings—after all, "reading Professor Strauss is not too different an experience from reading Maimonides." Kristol is an early example of a sympathetic Strauss reader acknowledging the difficulty of the task. Reading Strauss, he paid attention to the way Strauss read. He thereby made a few short circuits, which are characteristic of the wider perception of Strauss's work up until today. As if to gloss over the immense difficulties of the doctrine, he ventured: "[I]f they [i.e., the Great Books] are truly great, it is probably their intention to conceal as well as to reveal."[8] In the best case, these words restate a matter of course. Only the worst philosophical writers—those who are not emphatically writers—write as they think. Everyone else has something to hide. This is due to the difference between a philosophical teaching and its presentation in a written form. The possibility of political persecution may add to this *natural* difficulty, which is given with the principal weakness of writing.[9]

Given the wide appeal of Straussian exotericism, we may conclude that exoteric writing is the *exoteric* political dimension of Strauss's political philosophy. But the exoteric reading of his writings is also a sign of hermeneutic weakness. A typical course of action would be as follows: Readers cannot follow the complex argument of the text, because they are not accustomed to close reading and/or unfamiliar with the contexts. They build their interpretation on isolated elements of the text, which necessarily do not add up to a coherent interpretation. To make sense of these elements, they suppose a political meaning—a textual conspiracy in which all random pieces suddenly seem to add up to a whole. This course of overinterpretation is the structure of "politicization" in Strauss scholarship. Another aspect of this fallacy is the widespread expectation that the esoteric meaning is political, whereas the exoteric meaning is philosophical. In the extreme case, this tacit reversal of Strauss's teaching provides the proper basis for a fringe of devoted anti-Straussians, who can make a Strauss text mean whatever they want it to mean. They share a certain obsession with hidden messages placed in the text.

Reading a Strauss text literally, or "as it stands,"[10] helps to get a better sense of its philosophical meaning, including the precise relationship between philosophy and politics. To recall the most important rule: "Reading between the lines is strictly prohibited in all cases where it would be less exact than not doing so. Only such reading between the lines as starts from an exact consideration of the explicit statements of the author is legitimate."[11] For a rule of thumb, reading between the lines would in most—but not in all—cases be less exact than simply following the argument.

Following the argument is not always an easy task. As noted above, Strauss was an extremely careful writer, and most of his writings are exceedingly complex, if not outright enigmatic. He left his readers wondering whether these writings are exoteric—maybe Strauss has been playing them for fools. Perhaps even the much-quoted statement that "one writes as one reads" is exoteric: by confusing the reader, it would safeguard that a controversial claim goes unnoticed. In other words, the exotericism thesis may seem to be the only way out of the uncertainty over where Strauss stood. But it has also fostered a willingness to identify his position too easily. As Strauss indicated, the purpose of the exotericism thesis is to make people read carefully.[12] They would always wonder whether they missed something in the text, and would therefore read it again. Perhaps Kristol was right when he hinted at a similarity between reading Maimonides and reading Strauss. In a 1938 letter that documents the birth of the exotericism thesis, Strauss pointed out to Jacob Klein: "An essential point in Maimonides's technique is *of course* that he says everything completely *in the open*, albeit in places where the idiot wouldn't look for it."[13] Following his early terminology, the "idiot" is the "lazy reader."[14] He would look for a clue just in the middle of the book, for Strauss has taught him to look for important things "somewhere in the middle, i.e., in places least exposed to the curiosity of superficial readers."[15] He would therefore pay too little attention to the two opening paragraphs, in which Strauss dropped a variety of hints and references that are indispensable for understanding the task and the argument of the respective text. Just like Maimonides, Strauss says everything completely in the open. Often he simply explains *how to begin* and *how to proceed* from there. Clues such as these are literally on the surface of things. They are accessible even for readers only modestly familiar with twentieth-century thought, provided that they read carefully. One must merely follow the course of the text from here, and then start over again.

Strauss compared the task of natural reading to "the loathsome business of explaining a joke." As he wrote on the interpretation of Xenophon's *Hiero*, to explain the meaning of a text, "one has to engage in long-winded and sometimes repetitious considerations which can arrest attention only if one sees their purpose, and it is necessary that this purpose should reveal itself in its proper place, which cannot be at the beginning."[16] Interpreting his own writings bids us to repeat this manner to some extent.

The main problem with explaining a joke, of course, is that the joke is not funny. Explaining a joke has been compared to dissecting a frog, which unfortunately dies for the sake of better understanding it. But perhaps it is not the explanation that kills the joke: if somebody does not understand it, was it not already dead? Explaining the joke, then, would be comparable to beating a dead horse. This dreadful business has much in common with the task of explaining the meaning of Leo Strauss's writings. Most of all, they raise the suspicion that there is no secret teaching, or rather, no teaching at all. This suspicion has accompanied Strauss for a long time. Myles Burnyeat famously called Strauss a "sphinx without a secret."[17] For the most part, this insistence that there is *no* hidden message, and hence no teaching, is merely the flip side of the "exoteric" reading. But even Straussians have doubts as to whether Strauss offers a genuine teaching. Perhaps there is nothing behind the act of reading and the beauty it reveals?[18]

It would be unwise to rest satisfied with this explanation. Strauss does offer a philosophical teaching, but it follows to a great extent from the procedure, or the argument and the action, of a text. Moreover, it is difficult to explain this teaching in short without losing what makes it a genuine teaching. First of all, Strauss offers *a change of perspective* on things well known. Second, he provides an epistemic surprise—actually, these things had not been so well known. Third, once a teaching is being understood, it is difficult to grasp how it could have been hitherto overlooked (and how so many previous interpretations could have missed the crucial point). This is the structure of philosophical insight provided by the writings of Leo Strauss. Without much ado, this insight fulfills the Platonic demand to replace opinion by knowledge.

We must take Strauss's preoccupation with the "argument and action" seriously as a philosophical strategy. By reading a philosophical text with regard to its dramatic action, Strauss translated philosophy back into political and social action. There would be much to say about the way in which Strauss's philosophy becomes *political* philosophy, but following the procedure helps to see how he *does* political philosophy. Reading a text with regard to how concepts and problems act out their conflict, Strauss created a spatial setting in which all the references and micro-arguments become part of the unfolding drama of philosophy. This dimension of political thought is difficult to grasp for most present-day schools of philosophy. Strauss adopted much of it from from Platonic and Xenophonic dialogues, but he resolutely turned it into a concern of political philosophizing in the twentieth century.

Part III shows many of these tasks and strategies in action. It provides a fresh commentary on Strauss's 1941 lecture "German Nihilism," a wartime report on a somewhat indeterminate group of "young nihilists" (or conservative revolutionaries) who allegedly paved the way for the rise of National Socialism. To arrive at a comprehensive and homogeneous interpretation of the text, it must be read as a parable on liberal education toward philosophy: The young nihilists are to be led from the nihilistic consequence of their cultural discontent to a qualified embrace of liberal democracy. The political vantage point is that they could become philosophers, and hence insusceptible to the charms of radical politics. The argument on behalf of philosophy—and in particular against the identification of philosophy with its political impact—explains the paradox program of political philosophy as a means to depoliticize philosophy.

The proverbial joke in a Strauss text, then, is the philosophical argument. And for the most part, the philosophical argument is an argument on behalf of philosophy. Strauss often made a relatively simple argument for philosophy—so simple that it can easily be overlooked. It is not clear from the outset what it means to make an argument "for philosophy." Following his interpretations of the Platonic tradition, the point was to secure a space of freedom, of the freedom to philosophize, against political and/

or theological overreach. The spatial setting of this defense is reminiscent of Plato's *Apology*, which Strauss understood as a comedic defense of philosophy before the forum of society.[19] To protect philosophy as a space of intellectual freedom, he needed to defend philosophy against its politicization. The task of the philosopher is to convince the public that it is compatible with society. Accordingly, the political responsibility of the philosopher is to depoliticize philosophy.

This advice is not only clearly paradoxical, it also appears to be in disagreement with the classical notion of the philosopher: once he has left the cave, he cannot be satisfied with his own escape: his love for other people bids him to go back and save as many as possible.[20] Or, to remain true to the Platonic imagery, the natural habitat of the philosopher is the city, especially the marketplace. The question is what he should be doing there. In his response to Alexandre Kojève, who linked the image with a call for political action, Strauss proposed the term *philosophic politics*. As he explained: "The philosopher must go to the market place in order to fish there for potential philosophers. His attempts to convert young men to the philosophic life will necessarily be regarded by the city as an attempt to corrupt the young. The philosopher is therefore forced to defend the cause of philosophy."[21] Philosophic politics is politics on behalf of philosophy, and not politics on behalf of a future society or of any other political idea: it seeks to safeguard philosophy against its unmitigated exposure to the political sphere. According to Strauss, this defense was successfully used by Plato in Greece, Cicero in Rome, Farabi in Islam, and Maimonides in Judaism; and it would also work in a modern democracy, with its peculiar form of persecution (i.e., social ostracism).[22]

Defending the cause of philosophy is clearly more than a matter of exoteric speech here. Otherwise, the defense may not be convincing. The philosopher would also need to *be* a good citizen, and to act responsibly, in order to safeguard philosophy against its exposure to politics. He would need to avoid the pose of political radicalism and convince the public that his work does not pose a threat to the well-being of society.[23]

Needless to say, this claim is far from apolitical. Calls for depoliticization are political, too. There must also be a political reason why the philosopher should, in the last resort, refrain from "mingling in politics."[24] Following the debate with Kojève, mingling in politics would make him complicit with tyranny, ancient or modern, or it would foster the new tyranny of the universal and homogeneous state. However, the philosopher cannot be apolitical because there are too many bad political teachings. Bad political teachings would foster new tyrannies, which would in turn put an end to philosophy. The task of the philosopher is therefore to defend a reasonable course of political action.[25]

The call for depoliticization has little purpose in the world of real politics. Its place is in the universities, namely, in the hyperpolitical world of liberal education. Here, the voice of Leo Strauss is more pertinent than anywhere else. As he understood liberal education, it is education toward philosophy, for "education in the highest sense is philosophy."[26] The "puppies"[27] of the breed—or the "young nihilists" in Strauss's 1941 lecture—are to be led to philosophy. The quest for wisdom would infect their souls with a love for truth and liberate them from the charms of political radicalism. But first of all, Strauss would need to teach them how to read. Depoliticization is an integral part of this teaching: its prime purpose is to evade the projection of political attitudes and predispositions onto philosophical texts—a process in which the great works of the past are being drawn into the culture wars of the present. In this situation, depoliticization serves to clarify the political preconceptions and biases of reading. It restores the possibility of studying the texts and understanding what they have to say. Strauss is a good reference point for this endeavor, not only because he read and taught to read carefully, but also because he located the work of philosophy in the force field of culture, religion, and the political. This inconspicuous change leads to severe consequences. Among other things, it sets a limit to the political pretension of higher education—after all, radical politics as devised in philosophy departments is "only" part of our cultural communication. But it also raises the serious question of how to get from opinion to knowledge under the condition of relativism.

Part IV seeks to reopen the Straussian case against relativism. Strauss has largely been canonized as a staunch opponent of modern relativism, but it is difficult to find a coherent argument against relativism in his writings. A closer look at his critical arguments and strategies shows that he targeted a rather specific form of relativism, whereas he was generally far more concerned with the opposite danger of moral "absolutism." The specific form of relativism goes by the name of cultural relativism, as it was being fostered by the new science of cultural anthropology. Strauss's random remarks on Ruth Benedict's seminal *Patterns of Culture* provide a clear link. A survey of the relevant texts provides that Strauss could ultimately not build a coherent argument against relativism. He settled for a median solution instead, seeking to reap the benefits of relativism for a nonrelativistic purpose—and for better or worse, he was far ahead of his time with this strategy.

The emphasis on Strauss as a reader has a history of its own in Strauss scholarship. As Steven B. Smith stated: "Strauss's most important legacy was teaching his readers how to read."[28] But what exactly did he teach on proper reading? And how does his teaching relate to other teachings in twentieth-century thought? Smith counted Strauss among the "masters of suspicion"[29]—a phrase coined by Paul Ricœur to describe the hermeneutics of Marx, Nietzsche, and Freud. But Strauss must be sharply distinguished from these proto-postmodern heroes of interpretation. There may be debate as to whether the esoteric/exoteric divide belongs to "the relation hidden-shown" (Ricœur)—after all, "the most important truth is the most obvious truth, or the truth of the surface."[30] But Strauss does not fit into the hermeneutic framework of "the three 'destroyers,'" as Ricœur famously described the trinity of Marx, Nietzsche, and Freud. He had no business in deciphering the "false consciousness," and he did not stand in opposition to what Ricœur called the "phenomenology of the sacred." At last, we may wonder whether Strauss's hermeneutic principles are not far closer to the older model of hermeneutics as "a recollection of meaning," which Ricœur—as well as Foucault and others—used as a scapegoat to explain the hermeneutics of suspicion.[31] Strauss utterly modernized the recollection of meaning, but he did not collapse it into the Marx-Nietzsche-Freud nexus.

This reluctance is not surprising, given that his major philosophical impulses stemmed from neo-Kantianism and phenomenology. He combined a phenomenological concern—seeing things for what they are—with a systematic concern: seeing the place of a thing or idea within a larger whole. His philosophical project cannot be integrated into a new hegemonic discourse of the counterculture. It rather marks the beginning of a heteronomous counter-counterculture. As such, it has been a steady source to facilitate a departure from the Marx-Nietzsche-Freud nexus. As Werner Dannhauser recalled his early experience in Strauss's Hobbes seminar at the University of Chicago: "He exposed our opinions as *mere* opinions; he caused us to realize that we were the prisoners of our opinions . . . we all believed in watered-down teachings derived from Marx, Freud and others."[32] Reading texts outside of the canon of "theory" was all about the experience of things beautiful. It combined a micrological view on textual details with a clear appeal to common sense, unmarred by the theoretical desire.

Part V traces the emergence of two different types of reading praxis in the late 1960s. Whereas "theory" emerged as a hyperprogressive political praxis, the Straussian model was based on the notion that it would be better to stand against the world. And whereas "theory" was about the possibility of a future society, the reading praxis fostered by Strauss was meant to facilitate a return. Its purpose was to bring back the *thaumazein* of philosophizing. Often, Strauss left his readers in a state of wonder: he read these texts as if they had never been read, or as if they had hitherto only been skimmed. "Leo Strauss taught us how to read," wrote Dannhauser. "So we would read books carefully, line by line if possible, and we found that a great book is indeed a magic structure. It is wonderful—literally full of wonders, a house of many mansions, secret rooms, labyrinthine passages. Moreover, it is incredibly beautiful. By teaching us to see beauty, he elevated our taste, and we became a bit more pure without exerting any of the self-defeating straining-after-beauty that merely distorts."[33]

The text that exemplifies this type of reading praxis most perspicuously is "Jerusalem and Athens" (1967). Strauss's account of the Bible and Greek philosophy in light of their respective beginnings is replete with paradoxies. To begin with, he provided a philosophical interpretation of the Bible and a theological interpretation of Greek philosophy. Part V traces the emergence of the topic in Strauss's writings, his advanced conceptual strategies, his references to the emerging discourse of postcolonialism, and the double aspect of Jerusalem *and* Athens (the two "roots" of Western civilization) and Jerusalem *or* Athens (revelation or reason). Following how all these aspects intertwine provides a sense of the beauty and the magic described by Dannhauser—after all, "Jerusalem and Athens" is an incredibly beautiful text. Reading how Strauss read and wrote, we gain a better understanding of the contexts, problems, and strategies of his philosophical project.

Notes

Introduction

1. Leo Strauss, *Philosophy and Law: Contributions to the Understanding of Maimonides and His Predecessors*, trans. Eve Adler (Albany: State University of New York Press, 1995), 42.
2. Ibid.
3. Ibid.
4. For a classic reference, see Nicolai Hartmann, "Der philosophische Gedanke und seine Geschichte," in *Kleinere Schriften II: Abhandlungen zur Philosophie-Geschichte* (Berlin: de Gruyter, 1957), 1–48: 3.
5. Strauss, "Das Erkenntnisproblem in der philosophischen Lehre Fr. H. Jacobis," in *Gesammelte Schriften*, vol. 2: *Philosophie und Gesetz. Frühe Schriften*, ed. Heinrich Meier (Stuttgart/Weimar: Metzler, 1997), 247, 283.
6. Ibid., 244.
7. Ibid., 283.
8. Cf. *Leo Strauss on Moses Mendelssohn*, ed. Martin D. Yaffe (Chicago/London: The University of Chicago Press, 2013), esp. 10, 82, 116, 137. In his interpretive essay to the volume, Martin Yaffe contextualized these remarks to highlight how Mendelssohn faced severe difficulties in resolving the tension between philosophy (qua system) and Judaism (qua revealed law). Cf. ibid., esp. 230, 241, 277.
9. Stanley Rosen, *Hermeneutics as Politics* (New Haven/London: Yale University Press, 2003), 120–21.
10. Ibid., 120.
11. Strauss, "German Nihilism," *Interpretation* 26, no. 3 (Spring 1999): 355–78: 363.
12. Strauss, *What Is Political Philosophy? and Other Studies* (Chicago/London: The University of Chicago Press, 1959), 28; cf. *Liberalism Ancient and Modern* (Chicago/London: The University of Chicago Press, 1989), 206–207.
13. Strauss, *Persecution and the Art of Writing* (Chicago/London: The University of Chicago Press, 1988), 24.

14. Strauss, "Notes on Carl Schmitt, *The Concept of the Political*," in Heinrich Meier, *Carl Schmitt & Leo Strauss: The Hidden Dialogue* (Chicago/London: The University of Chicago Press, 1995), 91–119.

15. Strauss, *Liberalism Ancient and Modern*, 13.

16. Strauss, *What Is Political Philosophy?*, 91.

17. Strauss, *The City and Man* (Chicago/London: The University of Chicago Press, 1978), 49.

18. Strauss, *Philosophy and Law*, 124.

19. Ibid., 122–23.

20. Ibid., 55–56.

21. Ibid., 54.

22. Strauss, "Some Remarks on the Political Science of Maimonides and Farabi," in *Leo Strauss on Maimonides: The Complete Writings*, ed. Kenneth Hart Green (Chicago/London: The University of Chicago Press, 2013), 291.

23. Ibid., 282–90.

24. Strauss, *Persecution and the Art of Writing*, 43–46; *Leo Strauss on Maimonides*, 348–51; cf. "How to Begin to Study *The Guide of the Perplexed*," in *Leo Strauss on Maimonides*, 495.

25. Strauss, *Liberalism Ancient and Modern*, 142; *Leo Strauss on Maimonides*, 495.

26. Strauss, *Thoughts on Machiavelli* (Chicago/London: The University of Chicago Press, 1978), 13: "The problem inherent in the surface of things, and only in the surface of things, is the heart of things."

27. Cf. Strauss, *The Argument and the Action of Plato's* Laws (Chicago/London: The University of Chicago Press, 1975).

28. Seth Benardete, "Strauss on Plato," in *The Argument of the Action: Essays on Greek Poetry and Philosophy*, ed. Ronna Burger and Michael Davis (Chicago/London: The University of Chicago Press 2000), 407–17: 409.

29. Strauss, "On a New Interpretation of Plato's Political Philosophy," *Social Research* 13 (1946): 3, 326–67: 352.

30. Benardete, "Strauss on Plato," 409.

31. Strauss, *Persecution and the Art of Writing*, 24.

32. Ibid., 30.

33. Steven B. Smith, review of Robert Howse, "Leo Strauss: Man of Peace," *Notre Dame Philosophical Reviews*, October 18, 2014; http://ndpr.nd.edu/news/53222-leo-strauss-man-of-peace/. See also Michael P. Zuckert and Catherine H. Zuckert, *Leo Strauss and the Problem of Political Philosophy* (Chicago: The University of Chicago Press, 2014), 228: "Rather than standing outside the author and offering an interpretation of his words supported by quotations, Strauss attempts to replicate the thought of the author and present it in the author's own voice. As a result, Strauss's restatement of the thought of the thinker he is interpreting is often taken to be a statement of Strauss's own thought."

34. Strauss, "Introductory Essay for Hermann Cohen, *Religion of Reason out of the Sources of Judaism*," in *Jewish Philosophy and the Crisis of Modernity*, 269.

35. Strauss, *Liberalism Ancient and Modern*, 5.

36. Juvenile gangs, however, are known from Strauss's writings also as an example of the prevalence of certain basic values: Justice "is also required for the preservation of a gang of robbers: the gang could not last a single day if its members did not refrain from hurting one another, if they did not help one another, or if each member did not subordinate his own good to the good of the gang." Strauss, *Natural Right and History*, 105; cf. *Persecution and the Art of Writing*, 132; Plato, *Republic*, book 1, 342b-d.

37. Geoffrey H. Hartman, *The Fateful Question of Culture* (New York: Columbia University Press, 1997), 41.

38. Cf. Strauss, *What Is Political Philosophy?*, 20.

39. Strauss, "German Nihilism," 364.

40. Strauss, *Natural Right and History*, 36.

41. Strauss, *Liberalism Ancient and Modern*, 5.

42. Cf. Philipp von Wussow, "Leo Strauss on Returning: Some Methodological Aspects," *Philosophical Readings* IX (2017): 1, 18–24.

43. Strauss, *Philosophy and Law*, 52.

44. Strauss, *What Is Political Philosophy?*, 50.

45. Marx/Engels, *Collected Works*, vol. 3: 1843–44 (New York: International Publishers, 1975), 175; Nietzsche, *The Anti-Christ, Ecce Homo, Twilight of the Idols, and Other Writings* (Cambridge: Cambridge University Press, 2005), 187; Freud, *The Standard Edition of the Complete Psychological Works*, ed. James Strachey, vol. 21 (1927–1931) (London: The Hogarth Press, 1961), 75.

46. For particulars, cf. Philipp von Wussow, "Marx, Nietzsche, Freud: Towards a History of 'Theory' in Modern Jewish Thought," in *Language as Bridge and Border: Political, Cultural, and Social Constellations in the German-Jewish Context*, ed. Sabine Sander (Berlin: Hentrich & Hentrich, 2015), 225–40.

47. Pierre Manent, "Between Athens and Jerusalem," *First Things*, Feb. 2002; www.firstthings.com/article/2012/02/between-athens-and-jerusalem.

48. Judith N. Shklar, *Legalism* (Cambridge: Harvard University Press, 1964), 20–21.

49. Susan Hegeman, *The Cultural Return* (Berkeley: The University of California Press, 2012), 13.

Chapter 1. Hermann Cohen on the Systematic Place of Religion

1. Strauss, *What Is Political Philosophy?*, 11–14.
2. Ibid., 10–11, 22.

3. Strauss, "Notes on Carl Schmitt, *The Concept of the Political*," 94–95; *Philosophy and Law*, 42.

4. Strauss, *What Is Political Philosophy?*, 93.

5. Strauss, *The City and Man*, 1.

6. Strauss, "Notes on Carl Schmitt," 95.

7. Cf. Strauss, "Preface to Hobbes' *Politische Wissenschaft*," in *Jewish Philosophy and the Crisis of Modernity*, 453; cf. 461–62; "Existentialism," *Interpretation* 22, no. 3 (1995): 303–18: 304–305; "A Giving of Accounts," in *Jewish Philosophy and the Crisis of Modernity*, 460; "Philosophy as Rigorous Science and Political Philosophy," in *Studies in Platonic Political Philosophy*, 31; "The Living Issues of German Postwar Philosophy," Heinrich Meier, *Leo Strauss and the Theologico-Political Problem* (New York: Cambridge University Press, 2006), 115–39: 134–35.

8. Strauss, "Introductory Essay to Hermann Cohen, *Religion of Reason out of the Sources of Judaism*," in *Jewish Philosophy and the Crisis of Modernity*, 268.

9. Cf. Hermann Cohen, *Logik der reinen Erkenntnis*, "Vorrede zur ersten Auflage," *Werke*, vol. 6 (Hildesheim: Olms, 2005), ix.

10. Cf. Karl Löwith, *Aufsätze und Vorträge 1930–1970* (Stuttgart: Kohlhammer, 1971), 125.

11. Cohen, *Der Begriff der Religion im System der Philosophie*, *Werke*, vol. 10 (Hildesheim: Olms, 2002), 8.

12. Ibid., 16, cf. 14.

13. Ibid., 43.

14. Alfred Jospe, *Die Unterscheidung von Mythos und Religion bei Hermann Cohen und Ernst Cassirer in ihrer Bedeutung für die jüdische Religionsphilosophie* (Oppeln: [no publ.], 1932), 59.

15. Heinz Graupe, *Die Stellung der Religion im systematischen Denken der Marburger Schule* (Berlin: [no publ.], 1930), 16.

16. Franz Rosenzweig, "Einleitung," in Hermann Cohen, *Jüdische Schriften*, vol. 1 (Berlin: Schwetschke, 1924), xiii–lxiv.

17. Cohen, *Der Begriff der Religion im System der Philosophie*, 39–41.

18. Ibid., 41.

19. Cohen, *Ethik des reinen Willens*, *Werke*, vol. 7 (Hildesheim: Olms, 2008), 587; cf. *Der Begriff der Religion im System der Philosophie*, 41–42.

20. For a similar three-phase model with a different outcome cf. Helmut Holzhey, "Der systematische Ort der 'Religion der Vernunft' im Gesamtwerk Hermann Cohens," in *"Religion der Vernunft aus den Quellen des Judentums": Tradition und Ursprungsdenken in Hermann Cohens Spätwerk*, ed. Holzhey et al. (Hildesheim: Olms, 1998), 37–59: 43–44.

21. Cohen changed this phrase in a 1914 reissue into "admission [*Aufnahme*] of religion into ethics." Cohen, *Einleitung mit kritischem Nachtrag zur neunten Auflage der Geschichte des Materialismus von Friedrich Albert Lange*, *Werke*, vol. 5, part 2 (Hildesheim: Olms, 1984), 106; cf. Cohen, "Religion und Sittlichkeit" (1907), *Werke*, vol. 15: *Kleinere Schriften 4: 1907–1912* (Hildesheim: Olms, 2009), 1–101.

22. Cohen, *Ethik des reinen Willens*, 586–87.
23. Cf. Holzhey, "Der systematische Ort der 'Religion der Vernunft' im Gesamtwerk Hermann Cohens," 48.
24. Cf. Cohen, "Zur Errichtung von Lehrstühlen für Ethik und Religionsphilosophie an den jüdisch-theologischen Lehranstalten," *Jüdische Schriften*, vol. 2, 108–25.
25. Strauss, "Introductory Essay to Hermann Cohen," 269.
26. Cohen, *Der Begriff der Religion im System der Philosophie*, 42.
27. Ibid., 49.
28. Ibid.
29. Ibid., 49–50.
30. Cohen, *Ästhetik des reinen Gefühls*, vol. 2, *Werke*, vol. 9 (Hildesheim: Olms, 2005), 432.
31. Rosenzweig, "Einleitung," xix.
32. Cohen, *Religion of Reason out of the Sources of Judaism* (New York: Ungar, 1972), 12–13.
33. Cf. Cohen, *Religion der Vernunft aus den Quellen des Judentums* (Frankfurt am Main: J. Kauffmann, 1929), 42. The phrase was omitted in the English translation.
34. Cohen, *Religion of Reason out of the Sources of Judaism*, 13.

Chapter 2. Post-Cohenian Quarrels

1. Franz Rosenzweig, *Briefe und Tagebücher*, vol. 2: 1928–1929 (Dordrecht: Springer, 1979), 918, 958.
2. Franz Rosenzweig, "Einleitung," xlvii. Cf. also Rosenzweig's obituary, "Der Dozent: Eine persönliche Erinnerung," *Neue jüdische Monatshefte*, 17/18 (1918), 376–78.
3. Hans Leisegang, *Die Religionsphilosophie der Gegenwart* (Berlin: Junker und Dünnhaupt, 1930), 62–63.
4. Paul Natorp, *Hermann Cohens philosophische Leistung unter dem Gesichtspunkte des Systems* (Berlin: Reuther und Reichard, 1918), 36.
5. Holzhey, "Der systematische Ort der 'Religion der Vernunft' im Gesamtwerk Hermann Cohens," 46.
6. Cohen, *Der Begriff der Religion im System der Philosophie*, 49.
7. Cf. Alan Udoff, "On Leo Strauss," in *Leo Strauss's Thought: Toward a Critical Engagement*, ed. Alan Udoff (Boulder: Lynne Rienner, 1991), 1–29: 22–23; Kenneth Hart Green, *Jew and Philosopher: The Return to Maimonides in the Jewish Thought of Leo Strauss* (Albany: State University of New York Press, 1993), 185–86n16–17; Michael Zank, "Strauss und Cohen," in *Jüdische Religionsphilosophie als Apologie des Mosaismus* (Tübingen: Mohr Siebeck, 2016), 215–28.
8. Georg Wobbermin, ed., *Religionsphilosophie* (Berlin: Heise, 1924), introduction, part I.: "Begriff, Aufgabe und Methode der Religionsphilosophie," 5–16:

5–6. Michael Zank translated *Vergewaltigung* as "violation" of religion (Strauss, *The Early Writings*, 110).

9. Strauss, *The Early Writings*, 110; *Gesammelte Schriften* 2, 343–44.

10. Strauss, *The Early Writings*, 114; *Gesammelte Schriften* 2, 349.

11. Cf. the editorial remarks by Michael Zank in *The Early Writings*, 115n5. Zank added that he found the criticism against Wobbermin's position "outrageous" (ibid.).

12. Ernst Cassirer, "Paul Natorp," in *Gesammelte Werke*, vol. 23 (Hamburg: Meiner, 2006), 197–226: 222.

13. Strauss, "The 'Jewish Writings' of Hermann Cohen," trans. Michael Zank, *Interpretation* 39, no. 2 (2012): 118–27: 119–20.

14. Walter Kinkel, *Hermann Cohen: Eine Einführung in sein Werk* (Stuttgart: Strecker and Schröder, 1924), 245–46.

15. Strauss, "The 'Jewish Writings' of Hermann Cohen," 123.

16. Strauss, "Introductory Essay to Hermann Cohen, *Religion of Reason out of the Sources of Judaism*," 269.

17. Ibid., 274.

18. Cf. Rosenzweig, *Briefe und Tagebücher*, vol. 2: 1928–29, 957–58.

19. Strauss, "The 'Jewish Writings' of Hermann Cohen," 119–20.

20. Ibid., 126; trans. altered.

21. This opposition is presented most vividly in an anecdote that Rosenzweig reported in his Yehuda Halevi translations: "When Hermann Cohen was still living in Marburg, he explained the idea of God he had developed in his ethics to an old Jew, who listened respectfully. But when Cohen had finished, the old Jew asked: 'But where does that leave the *Bore'olam* [creator of the world]?' Cohen did not answer but broke into tears" (Franz Rosenzweig, *Ninety-Two Poems and Hymns of Yehuda Halevi*, ed. Richard A. Cohen [Albany: State University of New York Press 2000], 19). Strauss, indicating that it was he who had shared the anecdote with Rosenzweig, reported it in *Philosophy and Law*, citing his purported answer "to the objection of an orthodox Jew against his theology: to the objection, 'and what has become of the בורא עולם?,' Cohen had no other answer than—to weep, and thus confess that the gap between his belief and the belief of tradition is unbridgeable" (Strauss, *Philosophy and Law*, 50; cf. 139n6). The anecdote was meant to reflect the disappointment over the gulf between Cohen's functionalized Kantian God and the traditional Jewish faith in the Creator of the World.

22. Cf. Strauss, *Philosophy and Law*, 47. See II.2 below.

Chapter 3. Strauss on Paul Natorp and Ernst Cassirer

1. Strauss, "A Giving of Accounts," in *Jewish Philosophy and the Crisis of Modernity*, 460; cf. "Philosophy as Rigorous Science," in *Studies in Platonic Political Philosophy*, 31.

2. Strauss later referred to his dissertation *Das Erkenntnisproblem in der philosophischen Lehre Fr. H. Jacobis* (1921) as "a disgraceful performance" ("A Giving of Accounts," *Jewish Philosophy and the Crisis of Modernity*, 460), but it is unlikely that he thereby meant to distance himself once again from the neo-Kantian question indicated in the title (which is partly denied by the argument and the presentation of the text). Judging from Cassirer's 1934 letter to Paul Otto Kristeller, Strauss and others regarding the first Cassirer *Festschrift*, the philosophical rift did not translate into a personal one (Ernst Cassirer, *Ausgewählter wissenschaftlicher Briefwechsel*, ed. John Michael Krois [Hamburg: Meiner, 2009], 138–39). The letter refers to a lost typewritten *Festschrift* of his pupils for his sixtieth birthday, and *not* to the collection *Philosophy and History*, ed. Klibansky/Patton (Oxford, 1936). No copy of the former was saved.

3. Strauss, "Kurt Riezler," in *What Is Political Philosophy?*, 246; cf. "Existentialism," 304.

4. Strauss, "Notes on Carl Schmitt," 94–95; cf. "Foreword to a Planned Book on Hobbes," in *Hobbes' Critique of Religion and Related Writings*, ed. G. Bartlett/S. Minkov (Chicago: The University of Chicago Press, 2011), 137–49: 145.

5. Karl Vorländer, "Ethischer Rigorismus und sittliche Schönheit. Mit besonderer Berücksichtigung von Kant und Schiller," *Philosophische Monatshefte* 30 (1894): 225–80, 371–405, 534–77: 375; Theodor Litt, *Möglichkeiten und Grenzen der Pädagogik: Abhandlungen zur gegenwärtigen Lage von Erziehung und Erziehungstheorie* (Leipzig/Berlin: Teubner, 1926), 153.

6. Natorp, *Die Weltalter des Geistes* (Jena: Diederichs, 1918), 119–20; *Philosophische Systematik* (Hamburg: Meiner, 2000), 292.

7. Natorp, *Die Weltalter des Geistes*, 119.

8. Ibid.

9. Cf. Strauss, "Progress or Return," in *Jewish Philosophy and the Crisis of Modernity*, 97.

10. Natorp, *Die Weltalter des Geistes*, 120.

11. In a letter to Löwith from 1960, Strauss noted that Heidegger's *Satz vom Grund* was free from the "provincialisms which reminded me always of Natorp and the oath on the Meissner on the one hand, and 1933 on the other" (Strauss, *Gesammelte Schriften* 3, 684; cf. "A Giving of Accounts," 460). The "oath on the Meissner" refers to the "Erste Freideutsche Jugendtag" on the Hohe Meißner mountain massif (Hessen, Germany), a legendary gathering of the German youth movement that took place on 11-12 October 1913. The Freideutsche Jugendtag was the iconic event that connected many different youth movements under the banner of German nationalism and back-to-naturism. The oath, commonly known as the "Meissner formula," goes as follows: "The Freideutsche Jugend wants to model its life according to its own purpose, for its own responsibility, in inner truthfulness. It collectively defends this inner freedom under all circumstances. For mutual understanding, Freideutsche Jugendtage will be held. All collective activities of the Freideutsche Jugend will be alcohol-free and nicotine-free" (Knud Ahlborn,

"Das Meißnerfest der Freideutschen Jugend 1913," in *Grundschriften der deutschen Jugendbewegung*, ed. Werner Kindt (Düsseldorf/Köln: Diederichs, 1963), 105–15: 109). Natorp was among the participants of the Meissner event (along with other illustrious minds such as Walter Benjamin, Eugen Diederichs, and Adolf Grimme). Similar impressions were reported in the memories of Löwith and Hans-Georg Gadamer. When Löwith came from Freiburg in 1924, he found that Marburg "lacked the free atmosphere" he had encountered there: "everything was mustier and more entangled [*muffiger und verfilzter*]" (Karl Löwith, *My Life in Germany Before and After 1933: A Report*, trans. Elizabeth King [Urbana/Chicago: University of Illinois Press, 1994], 94; *Mein Leben in Deutschland vor und nach 1933: Ein Bericht* [Frankfurt am Main: Fischer, 1989], 65). Gadamer had first encountered academic philosophy through neo-Kantianism in Breslau. He later remembered "the rhetorical pomp" of Eugen Kühnemann, "the polished presentations of Richard Hönigswald and the tortuous chains of argument of Julius Guttmann," adding: "All three were neo-Kantians" (Hans-Georg Gadamer, *Philosophical Apprenticeships*, trans. Robert R. Sullivan [Cambridge, MA/London: MIT Press, 1985], 5). He came to Marburg in 1919 to study in the framework of the Marburg School, only to find that Natorp, Nicolai Hartmann, and Heinz Heimsoeth no longer provided a vivid continuation of this tradition. The provincialism of the "school" is perfectly captured in Gadamer's account of a visit in Frankfurt for a presentation by Kurt Riezler around 1928. The narration creates a sharp contrast between the demise of "Marburg" and the rise of "Frankfurt," a relatively new university where he witnessed a new, progressive blend of philosophy, theology, and social sciences in the making, long before it became the hallmark of the Frankfurt School: "[W]e felt the way a farmer might feel coming for the first time into the big city. Paul Tillich shined, Max Horkheimer provoked, Wiesengrund-Adorno seconded, and Riezler replied in the style of a thoughtful cosmopolitan. The whole style of the debate was such that we felt as if we had just come from a cloister" (ibid., 71–72).

12. Natorp, *Philosophische Systematik*, 292.

13. Ernst Cassirer, *The Philosophy of Symbolic Forms*, vol. 1: Language (New Haven/London: Yale University Press, 1953), 69, 77.

14. Cf. Cassirer, *Language and Myth* (New York: Dover, 1946), esp. 7–8.

15. Cf. *The Philosophy of Symbolic Forms*, vol. 3: *The Phenomenology of Knowledge* (New Haven/London: Yale University Press, 1957), pt. 1.

16. Natorp, *Die Weltalter des Geistes*, 119.

17. Cassirer, "Form und Technik," in *Gesammelte Werke*, vol. 17 (Hamburg: Meiner, 2004), 139–83: 141; English translation in Cassirer, *The Warburg Years (1919–1933): Essays on Language, Art, Myth, and Technology*, ed. S. G. Lofts (New Haven/London: Yale University Press, 2013), 272–316; cf. Aud Sissel Hoel/Ingvild Folkvord, eds., *Ernst Cassirer on Form and Technology* (Basingstoke/New York: Palgrave Macmillan, 2012), 15–53.

18. Cf. Cassirer, *An Essay on Man: An Introduction to a Philosophy of Human Culture* (New Haven: Yale University Press, 1945), 171–206.
19. Cf. Cassirer, *The Philosophy of Symbolic Forms*, vol. 2: *Myth* (New Haven/London: Yale University Press, 1955), xiv.
20. Cassirer, "Die Wandlungs- und Gestaltungsfähigkeit der Idee der Demokratie," in *Zu Philosophie und Politik*, Nachgelassene Manuskripte und Texte, vol. 9, ed. John Michael Krois (Hamburg: Meiner, 2008), 61–79: 61–62.
21. Strauss, "Existentialism," 304.
22. "Davos Disputation between Ernst Cassirer and Martin Heidegger," in Martin Heidegger, *Kant and the Problem of Metaphysics*, trans. Richard Taft (Bloomington/Indianapolis: Indiana University Press, 1990), 179.
23. Ernst Cassirer, *The Philosophy of Symbolic Forms*, vol. 1, 81.
24. Ibid., 82.
25. Ibid.
26. Ibid.
27. Strauss, "On the Argument with European Science," in *The Early Writings*, 113, quoting Cassirer's article "Philosophie der Mythologie" (1924).
28. Cassirer, *The Philosophy of Symbolic Forms*, vol. 2, 261.
29. Letter to Karl Löwith, June 30, 1925, in Heidegger/Löwith, *Briefwechsel 1919–1973*, ed. Alfred Denker (Freiburg/Munich: Karl Alber, 2017), 126. Volume 3 of Cassirer's *Philosophy of Symbolic Forms* (published 1929) was not on art but on scientific knowledge.
30. Strauss, *What Is Political Philosophy?*, 295–96.
31. Strauss, "On the Argument with European Science," in *The Early Writings*, 114; cf. "Zur Auseinandersetzung mit der europäischen Wissenschaft," *Gesammelte Schriften* 2, 349.
32. Strauss, "On the Argument with European Science," 114. As to Strauss's own *philosophical* reservations about Cohen's notion of monotheism, see "Cohen and Maimonides," in *Leo Strauss on Maimonides*, 196.
33. Strauss, "On the Argument with European Science," 114. Cassirer would indeed refer to Jewish monotheism from 1925 onward. But it is doubtful to what extent the reluctant inclusion of Judaism changed his overall position on myth and religion.
34. Ibid.
35. Cassirer, "The Myth of the State," in *Gesammelte Werke*, vol. 24 (Hamburg: Meiner, 2007), 253; *The Myth of the State* (New Haven/London: Yale University Press, 1974), 297.
36. Cf. Toni Cassirer, *Mein Leben mit Ernst Cassirer* (Hildesheim: Gerstenberg, 1981), 179.
37. Cassirer, *The Myth of the State*, 297.
38. Ibid., 298.

39. Cf. Eric Voegelin's review of Cassirer's book in *The Journal of Politics* 9, no. 3 (1947): 445–47.
40. Cassirer, *The Myth of the State*, 297–98.
41. Strauss, *Philosophy and Law*, 42.
42. Strauss, *What Is Political Philosophy?*, 295.

Chapter 4. Returning to Cohen

1. Strauss, "On the Argument with European Science," in *The Early Writings*, 114.
2. Cf. Strauss, *Philosophy and Law*, 47. See II.2 below.
3. Strauss, "A Giving of Accounts," in *Jewish Philosophy and the Crisis of Modernity*, 460; cf. "Cohen and Maimonides," in *Leo Strauss on Maimonides*, 189–90.
4. Strauss, "The 'Jewish Writings' of Hermann Cohen," 118.
5. Strauss, "Cohen and Maimonides," 174.
6. Ibid., 175, cf. 177. "Rambam" (RMbM) is the acronym for Rabbi Moshe ben-Maimon, i.e., Maimonides.
7. Ibid., 177.
8. Ibid., 178.
9. Ibid., 177.
10. Ibid., 175.
11. Cf. the discussion on allegorizing interpretation in "Cohen and Maimonides," 183–86; see also "Cohen's Analysis of Spinoza's Bible Science," in *The Early Writings*, 140; *Spinoza's Critique of Religion* (New York: Schocken, 1965), 25.
12. On the concept cf. also Martin D. Yaffe, "Strauss on Hermann Cohen's 'Idealizing' Appropriation of Maimonides as a Platonist," in *Reorientation: Leo Strauss in the 1930s*, ed. Martin D. Yaffe and Richard S. Ruderman (New York: Palgrave Macmillan, 2014), 69–78.
13. Strauss, "Cohen and Maimonides," 179.
14. Ibid., 191.
15. Cf. the restatement in Strauss, "Jerusalem and Athens," in *Jewish Philosophy and the Crisis of Modernity*, 399.
16. Strauss, "Cohen and Maimonides," 191–92.
17. A first indication of this concern can be found in a 1924 article on the Jewish historican Simon Dubnow, written on occasion of Dubnow's *Neueste Geschichte des jüdischen Volkes* (vol. 3, 1923). Cf. Strauss, "Sociological Historiography?," in *The Early Writings*, 101; "Soziologische Geschichtsschreibung?," *Gesammelte Schriften* 2, 335.
18. Strauss, "Cohen and Maimonides," 192; *Gesammelte Schriften* 2, 406.
19. Strauss, "Cohen and Maimonides," 176; cf. Cohen, *Ethik des reinen Willens*, Werke, vol. 7, part 2 (Hildesheim: Olms, 2008), 1: "*Ethics, as the doctrine of*

man, becomes the center of philosophy. And it is only in this center that philosophy gains independence and uniqueness and soon also unity."

20. Strauss, "Cohen and Maimonides," 176.
21. Cohen, *Ethics of Maimonides*, trans. Almut Sh. Bruckstein (Madison: The University of Wisconsin Press, 2004), 2.
22. Ibid.
23. Cf. Strauss, "Cohen and Maimonides," 188–89.
24. Ibid., 204, 221; cf. Cohen, *Ethics of Maimonides*, 50.
25. Strauss, "Cohen and Maimonides," 193.
26. Ibid., 196.
27. Ibid., 203.
28. Ibid., 200.
29. Ibid., 209–10.
30. Ibid., 210.
31. Ibid., 221; cf. *Philosophy and Law*, 79, 130.
32. Strauss, "Cohen and Maimonides," 221.
33. Ibid., 191.
34. Ibid., 196.
35. Ibid., 222.
36. Ibid.
37. Strauss, "Response to Frankfurt's 'Word of Principle,'" in *The Early Writings*, 67.
38. Strauss, "Notes on Carl Schmitt," 119. The phrase "pure and whole" is rather a creative circumscription of the word *integer,* which would usually be translated as "upright" or "of integrity." While the semantic range of *integer* is perhaps most appropriately covered by the notions of pureness and wholeness, they do not convey the moral surplus of the German term, which resonates with Strauss's notion of *Redlichkeit* ("probity") in *Philosophy and Law* and the Preface to *Spinoza's Critique of Religion*.
39. Strauss, "Notes on Carl Schmitt," 119.

Chapter 5. Strauss and Carl Schmitt

1. Heinrich Meier, *Carl Schmitt and Leo Strauss: The Hidden Dialogue* (Chicago/London: The University of Chicago Press, 2006).
2. Cf. William H. F. Altman, *The German Stranger: Leo Strauss and National Socialism* (Lanham, MD: Lexington, 2011).
3. Robert Howse, *Leo Strauss: Man of Peace* (New York: Cambridge University Press, 2014).
4. Strauss, "Notes on Carl Schmitt," 119.
5. Ibid., 94–95.

6. Carl Schmitt, *The Concept of the Political*, trans. George Schwab, expanded edition (Chicago/London: The University of Chicago Press, 2007), 70–71.

7. Chantal Mouffe, *On the Political* (London/New York: Routledge, 2005), 12.

8. Ibid., 13.

9. Ibid., 5.

10. Ibid., 31.

11. Schmitt, *The Concept of the Political*, 89.

12. The first edition from 1927 appeared as an article in the *Archiv für Sozialgeschichte und Sozialpolitik*. The second edition, often referred to as the 1932 edition, was an extended version published as a book in October 1931. It also contained a revised version of Schmitt's 1929 article "Die europäische Kultur in Zwischenstadien der Neutralisierung," now named "Das Zeitalter der Neutralisierungen und Entpolitisierungen" ("The Age of Neutralizations and Depoliticizations"). When this chapter became accessible to the English-reading audience, it contained the dating "1929," but the translation was based on the 1932 text modified again for the 1963 German reissue. Strauss used the second edition (1932) for his "Notes." The third edition (1933), an abridged and revised version of the second, contained certain "adjustments" to the terminology and the political outlook of National Socialism, but no major revisions concerning the general framework of the book. When Schmitt republished *Der Begriff des Politischen* in 1963, he tacitly resorted to the 1932 edition.

13. Cf. Heinrich Meier, *Carl Schmitt & Leo Strauss*, especially 13–14 on the claim that changes in the third edition of *The Concept of the Political* are a response to Strauss.

14. Schmitt, *The Concept of the Political*, 102n2.

15. To recall the course of events up to that point: Strauss had apparently sent his "Notes" on his own initiative to Schmitt, who helped to secure the publication of the text in the *Archiv für Sozialwissenschaft und Sozialpolitik* (cf. his letter to Ludwig Feuchtwanger, June 10, 1932, quoted in Heinrich Meier, *Carl Schmitt & Leo Strauss*, 8; Strauss's letter to Schmitt, ibid., 123). The second out of three published Strauss letters to Schmitt, written in September 1932, refers to "an oral exchange," suggesting that the two met at least once in 1932. Schmitt did not answer Strauss's letter from July 10, 1933 (English translation in Heinrich Meier, *Carl Schmitt & Leo Strauss*, 127–28). Strauss learned from Jacob Klein about Schmitt's affiliation with the National Socialists in October 1933 (cf. *Gesammelte Schriften* 3, 481). After his nonreply in the summer of 1933, Schmitt communicated with Strauss via references in his written work. For the most part, these references pertain to the interpretation of Thomas Hobbes. Schmitt later told Jacob Taubes that his Hobbes interpretations from 1932 onward were addressed to Strauss (Jacob Taubes/Carl Schmitt, *Briefwechsel mit Materialien* [Paderborn: Fink, 2012], 37, 40, 53, 102). In 1935, Strauss alleged that Schmitt had plagiarized his Hobbes interpretation in the book *Die drei Arten des rechtswissenschaftlichen Denkens* (*On the Three Types of Juristic Thought*). The allegation is documented in Strauss's letter from May 10, 1935, to

Erwin Rosenthal, whom he similarly accused of plagiarism: "Thus far it occurred to me only once that somebody plagiarized me. In this case it was a man who in the meantime had become a National Socialist [handwritten addition: Carl Schmitt!] and thus could not possibly admit his dependence on a Jew. I judge your behavior much more strictly. For if we German Jews do not live up to the highest standards in our work and in our behavior, this can lead to incalculable consequences for the entirety" (Letter to E. Rosenthal, Leo Strauss Papers, The Regenstein Library, University of Chicago, box 4, folder 16. Cf. Strauss to Jacob Klein, 10 October 1934, *Gesammelte Schriften* 3, 524; cf. Erich Langstadt's letter to Strauss on the Rosenthal case [undated, 1935], Leo Strauss Papers, box 2, folder 10). The utterly sarcastic remark on the "mitigating circumstance" that Schmitt "could not possibly admit his dependence from a Jew" after his affiliation with National Socialism serves to denounce Rosenthal's alleged plagiarism in strong moral terms, playing on the moral difference between Nazi and Jew and suggesting that Schmitt as a Nazi was morally irresponsible.

16. As to Buber and Strauss, see Philipp von Wussow, "Martin Buber and Leo Strauss: Notes on a Strained Relationship," in *Martin Buber: His Intellectual and Scholarly Legacy*, ed. Sam Berrin Shonkoff (Leiden/Boston: Brill, 2018), 194–211.

17. Heinrich Meier, *Carl Schmitt & Leo Strauss*, xvii.

18. Schmitt, *The Concept of the Political*, 26.

19. Ibid., 38; translation altered.

20. Schmitt, "Der Begriff des Politischen," *Archiv für Sozialwissenschaft und Sozialpolitik*, 58, no. 1 (1927): 1–33: 3–4.

21. Schmitt, *The Concept of the Political*, 26.

22. As Strauss duly noted, Schmitt used the term *autonomy* only with quotation marks here (Strauss, "Notes on Carl Schmitt," 95). Compare his subsequent statement on "Schmitt's opinion" with his polemical remark on quotation marks in *Natural Right and History*, 53.

23. Compare Schmitt, *Der Begriff des Politischen* (Munich: Duncker und Humblot, 1932), 94, with "Die europäische Kultur in Zwischenstadien der Neutralisierung," *Europäische Revue* 5, no. 8 (1929): 517–30: 529.

24. In one instance, he substituted "kulturelle Sphäre" by "geistige Sphäre," so that the unchanged phrase "der Begriff der Kultur selbst" later in the same sentence has no longer any reference. Compare *Der Begriff des Politischen* (1932), 86, with "Die europäische Kultur in Zwischenstadien der Neutralisierung," 523.

25. Schmitt, "Die europäische Kultur in Zwischenstadien der Neutralisierung," 525.

26. Schmitt, *The Concept of the Political*, 26–27, 38.

27. Harold J. Laski, *Studies in the Problem of Sovereignty* (New Haven: Yale University Press, 1917), 15.

28. Amartya Sen, *Identity and Violence: The Illusion of Destiny* (London/New York: Penguin, 2006), xii–xiii.

29. Carl Schmitt, *The Concept of the Political*, 43, 44, 45.

30. Carl Schmitt, "State Ethics and the Pluralist State," in *Weimar: a Jurisprudence of Crisis*, ed. Arthur J. Jacobsen and Bernhard Schlink (Berkeley: University of California Press, 2000), 300–12: 301–302.

31. Ibid., 303.

32. Strauss, *The City and Man*, 240.

33. Walter Benjamin, *The Arcades Project* (Cambridge, MA/London: Belknap Press, 1999), 389.

34. Helmut Kuhn, Review of Carl Schmitt's "Der Begriff des Politischen" (1933), repr. in Kuhn, *Der Staat: Eine philosophische Darstellung* (Munich: Kösel, 1967), 458.

35. Carl Schmitt, *Political Theology: Four Chapters on the Concept of Sovereignty*, trans. George Schwab (Cambridge, MA/London: MIT Press, 1985), 5.

36. Karl Löwith, "Der okkasionelle Dezisionismus von C. Schmitt," in *Gesammelte Abhandlungen. Zur Kritik der geschichtlichen Existenz* (Stuttgart: Kohlhammer, 1960), 93–126.

37. Letter to Hasso Hofmann, January 27, 1965, Leo Strauss Papers, box 4, folder 9.

38. Strauss, "Notes on Carl Schmitt," 116.

39. Ibid., 93.

40. Ibid., 95–96.

41. Ibid., 97–98.

42. Cf. Benjamin Lazier, *God Interrupted: Heresy and the European Imagination between the World Wars* (Princeton: Princeton University Press, 2008), 111–26.

43. Strauss, "Notes on Carl Schmitt," 101.

44. Ibid., 99.

45. Ibid., 100.

46. Ibid., 101.

47. Ibid., 103, 102.

48. Ibid., 105, cf. 109; *The City and Man*, 5. Schmitt had stated: "One could test all theories of state and political ideas according to their anthropology and thereby classify these as to whether they consciously or unconsciously presuppose man to be by nature evil or by nature good" (Schmitt, *The Concept of the Political*, 58).

49. Strauss, "Notes on Carl Schmitt," 108.

50. Ibid., 113.

51. Ibid., 115.

52. Ibid., 117.

53. Cf. Strauss, "The Origins of Political Science and the Problem of Socrates," *Interpretation* 23, no. 2 (1996): 127–207, especially 163–64, 172–77, 187–88, 193–94.

54. Strauss, "Notes on Carl Schmitt," 91, 118.

55. Ibid., 118.

56. Ibid., 92.

57. Ibid., 119.

Chapter 6. A Hidden Masterpiece of Twentieth-Century Philosophy

1. Cf. Scholem's letter to Strauss, November 7, 1972: "You certainly do not conceal from yourself that your book exerted great influence over the years, as little as this is apparent from its outward circulation" (Strauss, *Gesammelte Schriften* 3, 764). Other readers included Hans-Georg Gadamer, Gerhard Krüger, Jacob Klein, Karl Löwith, Alexandre Kojève, Alexandre Koyré, Ernst Simon, Shlomo Pines, Yitzchak Baer, Paul Kraus, and later Jacob Taubes. Heinrich Meier noted that the book exerted a "subterranean influence from the beginning," concluding: "*Philosophie und Gesetz* had been in print since spring 1935 without ever really having been made public. It remained a book for the few." Heinrich Meier, "How Strauss Became Strauss," in *Reorientation: Leo Strauss in the 1930s*, 14.

2. Lazier, *God Interrupted*, 118.

3. Cf. Walter Benjamin, *The Arcades Project*, 577: "The historical index of the images not only says that they belong to a particular time; it says, above all, that they attain to legibility only at a particular time. And, indeed, this acceding 'to legibility' constitutes a specific critical point in the movement at their interior."

4. Fritz Heinemann, "Philosophie und Gesetz," *Frankfurter Israelitisches Gemeindeblatt* 14, no. 3 (1935): 107–108: 107.

5. Michael Zank, "Leo Strauss' Rediscovery of the Exoteric," in *Religious Apologetics—Philosophical Argumentation*, ed. Yossef Schwartz and Volkhard Krech (Tübingen: Mohr Siebeck, 2004), 185–202: 197.

6. Cf. Jacob Klein's letter to Strauss, January 26, 1934, in *Gesammelte Schriften* 3, 489: "On your Guttmann review I can only say that it is excellent, only that the occasion is too insignificant (this is also Krüger's opinion)."

7. Cf. Strauss's letter to Klein, September 15, 1933, in *Gesammelte Schriften* 3, 470; Meier, "How Strauss Became Strauss," 25n8.

8. According to his status report to Julius Guttmann written on January 22, 1935, it was the last of the three chapters to be sent to the publisher (cf. Meier, "How Strauss Became Strauss," 15). Strauss's slight adjustments to fit the text into the terminology of the book can be traced in *Leo Strauss on Maimonides*, 223–66.

9. Cf. Strauss's letter to Martin Buber, November 27, 1934, JNL, ARV MS.Var. 350 008 786.

10. Cf. Strauss's letters to Scholem (*Gesammelte Schriften* 3, 714) and Guttmann (Leo Strauss Papers, box 1, folder 14), both written on December 14, 1934.

11. Letter to Julius Guttmann, quoted in Meier, "How Strauss Became Strauss," 15.

12. Walter Benjamin, *One-Way Street and Other Writings* (London: NLB, 1979), 49.

13. Cf. Strauss, *Philosophy and Law*, 141n24.

14. Ernst Simon, undated letter to Strauss [1935?], Leo Strauss Papers, box 3, folder 9.
15. Friedrich Schleiermacher, *On Religion: Speeches to Its Cultured Despisers* (Cambridge: Cambridge University Press 1996).
16. Strauss, *Philosophy and Law*, 73, see also 54.
17. Ibid., 135n1.
18. Ibid., 21.
19. Cf. Strauss, "On Abravanel's Philosophical Tendency and Political Teaching," in *Gesammelte Schriften* 2, 207–10; "Ecclesia Militans," in *The Early Writings*, 124–30.
20. Strauss, *Philosophy and Law*, 66.
21. Fred D. Wieck to Leo Strauss, December 10, 1956, Leo Strauss Papers, box 3, folder 18.
22. Fritz Heinemann, "Philosophie und Gesetz," *Frankfurter Israelitisches Gemeindeblatt* 14, no. 3 (1935): 107–108.

Chapter 7. Strauss's Introduction

1. Letter to Kojève, May 9, 1935, Strauss, *On Tyranny*, 230. There is no written reaction of Kojève.
2. Cf. especially Laurence Lampert, *The Enduring Importance of Leo Strauss* (Chicago: The University of Chicago Press, 2013), 189–226.
3. Strauss used the term *Scheinrationalismus* (*Gesammelte Schriften* 2, 9); Adler translates as "a semblance of rationalism" (*Philosophy and Law*, 22).
4. Cf. Strauss, *Spinoza's Critique of Religion*, 31.
5. Ibid.
6. Strauss, *Philosophy and Law*, 39.
7. Ibid., 21–22; trans. altered; *Gesammelte Schriften* 2, 9.
8. The historical *querelle des anciens et des modernes* in the seventeenth and eighteenth centuries started from a relatively minor occasion, Charles Perrault's poem "Le siècle de Louis le Grand" (1687) and the subsequent protest of Nicolas Boileau-Despréaux. But the *querelle* reached far beyond the poetological discourse (imitation versus creation, nature versus art) and continued into the Enlightenment and Romanticism. It was discussed in eighteenth-century Germany by Lessing, Herder, Schiller, and Friedrich Schlegel. Since then the *querelle des anciens et des modernes* also became a metaphor of resistance against the normative claims of modernity (cf. Strauss, "Progress or Return?," in *Jewish Philosophy and the Crisis of Modernity*, 101–102). The task of "renewing" the debate therefore serves as a preparation for a reversal of the commonly accepted opinion.
9. Strauss, *Philosophy and Law*, 22.

10. Ibid., 24.//
11. See Strauss, "Cohen and Maimonides," in *Leo Strauss on Maimonides*, especially 177.
12. Strauss, *Philosophy and Law*, 24.
13. Strauss, *Gesammelte Schriften* 2, 15; Adler translates as "the movement whose goal is to return to the tradition" (*Philosophy and Law*, 26).
14. Strauss, *Philosophy and Law*, 26.
15. Strauss, *Gesammelte Schriften* 3, 414.
16. Strauss, *Philosophy and Law*, 28.
17. Ibid., 26.
18. Ibid., 28–29.
19. Cf. Eve Adler's introduction in Strauss, *Philosophy and Law*, 2; Joel L. Kraemer, "The Medieval Arabic Enlightenment," in *The Cambridge Companion to Leo Strauss*, ed. Steven B. Smith (Cambridge: Cambridge University Press, 2009), 142.
20. Strauss, *Philosophy and Law*, 28.
21. Ibid., 54–55, 66.
22. Ibid., 21.
23. Ibid., 66, cf. 54–55.
24. Ibid., 29.
25. Ibid.
26. Cf. Strauss, *Jewish Philosophy and the Crisis of Modernity*, 94, 344. Strauss traced the concept to Monford Harris, but I have not been able to locate it in *any* of Harris's writings.
27. Michel Foucault, "Nietzsche, Freud, Marx," in *Aesthetics, Method, and Epistemology*, ed. James D. Faubion (New York: The Free Press, 1998), 269–78: 275; trans. altered.
28. Cf. Strauss, *Philosophy and Law*, 31.
29. See Philipp von Wussow, "Marx, Nietzsche, Freud: Towards a History of 'Theory' in Modern Jewish Thought," in *Language as Bridge and Border: Linguistic, Cultural, and Political Constellations in 18th to 20th Century German-Jewish Thought*, ed. Sabine Sander (Berlin: Hentrich und Hentrich, 2015), 225–40.
30. Strauss, *Philosophy and Law*, 29.
31. Ibid., 31.
32. Ibid., 29–30.
33. Ibid., 30.
34. Cf. ibid., 28.
35. Ibid., 30.
36. Ibid., 24, 26, 28.
37. For a similar argument compare Joel L. Kraemer, "The Medieval Arabic Enlightenment," 143–44.
38. Strauss, *Spinoza's Critique of Religion*, 30.

39. Strauss, *Persecution and the Art of Writing*, 20.

40. The fact that Strauss was well familiar with the matter can be seen in the impressive collection of references in *Persecution and the Art of Writing*, 20–21.

41. Strauss, *Philosophy and Law*, 30.

42. Ibid., 33–34; trans. altered; *Gesammelte Schriften* 2, 22.

43. Strauss, *Philosophy and Law*, 31.

44. Ibid., 31–32; cf. *Spinoza's Critique of Religion*, 28–29.

45. Cf. Laurence Lampert, *The Enduring Importance of Leo Strauss*, 204.

46. Cf. Strauss, *Philosophy and Law*, 32.

47. Cf. ibid., 35.

48. Ibid., 33.

49. Laurence Lampert, *The Enduring Importance of Leo Strauss*, 213, cf. 211.

50. Ernst Cassirer, *The Philosophy of the Enlightenment* (Princeton: Princeton University Press, 1951), chs. 7 and 5 respectively. Strauss knew Cassirer's study, as one can follow through his Hobbes book (1936). See Strauss, *The Political Philosophy of Hobbes: Its Basis and Its Genesis* (Chicago/London: The University of Chicago Press/Phoenix Books, 1966), 2n1, 152n1.

51. Cassirer, *The Philosophy of the Enlightenment*, xi.

52. Strauss, *Philosophy and Law*, 35.

53. Ibid., 31.

54. Ibid., 34.

55. Lampert, *The Enduring Importance of Leo Strauss*, 212.

56. Strauss, *Philosophy and Law*, 34.

57. Ibid., 35.

58. Isaac Deutscher, *The Non-Jewish Jew and Other Essays* (London: Oxford University Press, 1968), 26–27.

59. Hannah Arendt, "The Jew as Pariah: A Hidden Tradition," *Jewish Social Studies* 6, no. 2 (1944): 99–122; George Steiner, "Some 'Meta-Rabbis,'" in *Next Year in Jerusalem: Portraits of the Jew in the Twentieth Century*, ed. Douglas Villiers (London: Viking, 1976), 64–76.

60. Judith Butler, *Parting Ways: Jewishness and the Critique of Zionism* (New York: Columbia University Press, 2012), 1.

61. Strauss, letter to Krüger, January 7, 1930, in *Gesammelte Schriften* 3, 378–80.

62. Strauss, *Philosophy and Law*, 35.

63. Ibid., 36.

64. Strauss, *Spinoza's Critique of Religion*, 29.

65. Ibid., 38.

66. Strauss, *Philosophy and Law*, 36; *Spinoza's Critique of Religion*, 30.

67. Strauss, *Gesammelte Schriften* 3, 646.

68. Walter Benjamin and Gershom Scholem, *The Correspondence of Walter Benjamin and Gershom Scholem, 1932–1940*, ed. G. Scholem (Cambridge: Harvard University Press, 1992), 156.

69. Strauss, *Philosophy and Law*, 36; *Gesammelte Schriften* 2, 24.
70. Strauss, *Philosophy and Law*, 38.
71. Ibid., 36–37.
72. Ibid., 37.
73. Nietzsche, *Beyond Good and Evil: Prelude to a Philosophy of the Future*, ed. Rolf-Peter Horstmann and Judith Norman (Cambridge/New York: Cambridge University Press, 2002), 118 (§ 227).
74. Ibid., 123 (§ 230).
75. Strauss, *Philosophy and Law*, 137–38n13. Most notably, Strauss referred to Gerhard Krüger and Karl Löwith to describe probity as the "intellectual conscience" of modern science. Probity then means "the 'inner' sovereignty of science over man, and not just any science, but modern science" (Krüger) and "the impartiality of not being partial to transcendent ideals" (Löwith). Strauss further referred to an unnamed definition of criticism in Alphonse Gratry's *Les Sophistes et la critique* (Paris: Douniol/Lecoffre, 1864) to evoke the antitheological implication of scientific probity: "La critique . . . a pour essence la négation du surnaturel [Criticism is essentially the negation of the supernatural]." At last, Strauss cited Gratry's objection: "L'essence de la critique, c'est l'attention [The essence of criticism is attention]." As he added, it was in this sense that the opposition between probity and love of truth had to be understood: "[T]he open avowal that one is an atheist, and the resolute intention of accepting all the consequences, and in particular of rejecting the semi-theism which was the dogmatic and probity-lacking premise of the post-Enlightenment synthesis, with all its implications, as for example the belief in progress—this has doubtless more probity than any compromises or syntheses; but if one makes atheism, which is admittedly not demonstrable, into a positive, dogmatic premise, then the probity expressed by it is something very different from the love of truth." Strauss maintained the sharp distinction between probity and love of truth only with regard to two types of critique (and not to the larger issue of critique versus philosophy, as has sometimes been argued): a type of critique that remains open to what it criticizes, and a type of critique that degenerates into dogma. The structuring difference is between rejecting and accepting a dogmatic premise. Hence, the footnote explicates the difference between a critical and a dogmatic version of atheism, and it takes a side for the former against the latter.
76. Strauss, *Philosophy and Law*, 37.
77. Ibid.
78. Ibid.
79. Cf. John P. McCormick, "Post-Enlightenment Sources of Political Authority: Biblical Atheism, Political Theology, and the Schmitt-Strauss Exchange," *History of European Ideas* 37, no. 2 (2011): 175–80.
80. Strauss, "Note on the Plan of Nietzsche's *Beyond Good and Evil*," in *Studies in Platonic Political Philosophy*, 178–79.
81. Ibid., 180.
82. Strauss, *Philosophy and Law*, 38.

83. Ibid.

84. David Janssens, *Between Athens and Jerusalem: Philosophy, Prophecy, and Politics in Leo Strauss's Early Thought* (Albany: State University of New York Press, 2008), 94.

85. Strauss, *Spinoza's Critique of Religion*, 30.

86. Robert C. Miner, "Leo Strauss's Adherence to Nietzsche's 'Atheism From Intellectual Probity,'" *Perspectives on Political Science* 41 (2012): 155–64: 155.

87. Cf. Robert C. Miner, "Nietzsche, Schmitt, and Heidegger in the Anti-Liberalism of Leo Strauss," *Telos* 60 (2012): 9–27.

88. Stanley Rosen, *Hermeneutic as Politics*, 121; cf. Strauss, *Spinoza's Critique of Religion*, 12, on the close connection between probity, philosophy as an act of will, and the overman.

89. Strauss, "Note on the Plan of Nietzsche's *Beyond Good and Evil*," in *Studies in Platonic Political Philosophy*, 188.

90. Nietzsche, *Beyond Good and Evil*, 123 (§ 230).

91. Strauss, *Philosophy and Law*, 38.

92. Ibid.

93. Ibid.

94. Strauss did not touch upon the history of Jewish Nietzscheanism, from the debate between Micha Berdyczewski and Achad Ha'am to the fierce declamations of Martin Buber and the young Gershom Scholem and Oscar Levy's open letter to Adolf Hitler. But he was certainly familiar with those interpretations that described the task of Jewry in terms of the Nietzschean "overman," and they found no resonance in his project. For an overview of Jewish Nietzscheanism, see Philipp von Wussow, "Übervolk," in *Enzyklopädie jüdischer Geschichte und Kultur*, ed. Dan Diner, vol. 6 (Stuttgart: Metzler, 2015), 201–207.

95. Strauss, *Philosophy and Law*, 38.

96. Ibid., 39. I do not follow Eve Adler's occasional capitalization of the term "law" here and elsewhere.

Chapter 8. Leo Strauss and Julius Guttmann on the History of Jewish Philosophy

1. Julius Guttmann, *Die Philosophie des Judentums* (Munich: Reinhardt, 1933); *Philosophies of Judaism: The History of Jewish Philosophy from Biblical Times to Franz Rosenzweig*, trans. David W. Silverman (Garden City: Anchor Books 1966).

2. Cf. Eve Adler's introduction, *Philosophy and Law*, 6.

3. Strauss, *What Is Political Philosophy?*, 10.

4. Strauss, *Philosophy and Law*, 122–23; see especially 55–56 on the difference between modern and premodern divisions of philosophy.

5. Ibid., 41; cf. Guttmann, *Philosophies of Judaism*, 4.

6. See the defense of this approach vis-à-vis Strauss in Julius Guttmann, "Philosophie der Religion oder Philosophie des Gesetzes?," *Proceedings of the Israel Academy of Sciences and Humanities* 5, no. 6 (1974): 148–73: 150.

7. Guttmann, *Philosophies of Judaism*, 4.

8. Guttmann, *Die Philosophie des Judentums*, 10.

9. Guttmann, *Philosophies of Judaism*, 4. The suggestion that Guttmann had modified his position due to Strauss's criticism was made by Eliezer Schweid, referring to Guttmann's Jerusalem lectures *On the Philosophy of Religion*. Cf. Eliezer Schweid, "Religion and Philosophy: The Scholarly-Theological Debate Between Julius Guttmann and Leo Strauss," in *Maimonidean Studies*, ed. Arthur Hyman, vol. 1 (New York: Yeshiva University Press, 1990), 163–95; Yitzhak Julius Guttmann, *On the Philosophy of Religion*, ed. Nathan Rotenstreich (Jerusalem: Magnes Press, 1976).

10. Guttmann, *Philosophies of Judaism*, 4.

11. Ibid.

12. Cf. Kenneth Seeskin, *Jewish Philosophy in a Secular Age* (Albany: State University of New York Press, 1990), 3–4.

13. Cf. Thomas Meyer, *Zwischen Philosophie und Gesetz. Jüdische Philosophie und Theologie von 1933 bis 1938* (Leiden/Boston: Brill, 2009), 76; see also 100.

14. Strauss, *Philosophy and Law*, 42.

15. Ibid. The first page reference is to *Die Philosophie des Judentums* (1933), the second to *Religion und Wissenschaft im mittelalterlichen und im modernen Denken* (Berlin: Philo, 1922). References within Strauss's quotes starting with an "R" are to the latter text.

16. Ibid., 138n2.

17. For example, Jewish religion in the Greek (Guttmann, *Philosophies of Judaism*, 18, 22, 45), Islamic (ibid., 4, 54–55, 207), or modern European (ibid., 327–28) culture. More specifically, the German text refers to these "cultures" as *Kulturkreise*, a notion which had been popularized by Oswald Spengler. Guttmann's proposition that the "culture of the Italian and Dutch Jews" until the eighteenth century "was only peripherally affected by modern culture" (ibid., 327) employs two different notions of culture in the same sentence, but this is due to the inaccuracy of the English translation. The German original uses the terms *Bildung* and *Kulturelemente* here (Guttmann, *Die Philosophie des Judentums*, 301). Inaccuracies are often to be found in the translation of German philosophic terminology, for which the path via Hebrew was apparently not very helpful.

18. Guttmann, *Philosophies of Judaism*, 4; cf. Guttmann, *Religion und Wissenschaft im mittelalterlichen und im modernen Denken*, 3.

19. Guttmann, *Philosophies of Judaism*, 101, cf. 68.

20. Ibid., 53.

21. Ibid., 289–91.

22. Strauss, *Philosophy and Law*, 51.

23. Ibid., 43.

24. Ibid., 44.
25. Ibid., 45.
26. Ibid., 44; Guttmann, *Philosophies of Judaism*, 332; *Die Philosophie des Judentums*, 305.
27. Strauss, *Philosophy and Law*, 44; Guttmann, *Philosophies of Judaism*, 344; *Die Philosophie des Judentums*, 317.
28. Strauss, *Philosophy and Law*, 44.
29. Joel Abraham List, "A Society for the Preservation of the Jewish People" (1819), quoted in Paul R. Mendes-Flohr and Jehuda Reinharz, eds., *The Jew in the Modern World: A Documentary History*, 2nd edition (New York/Oxford: Oxford University Press, 1995), 211–12.
30. Alexander Altmann, "Theology in Twentieth-Century German Jewry," *Leo Baeck Institute Year Book*, 1956, 193–216: 193.
31. Cf. Gershom Scholem, *Judaica* 1 (Frankfurt am Main: Suhrkamp, 1963), 152–53.
32. Gershom Scholem, *Judaica 6: Die Wissenschaft vom Judentum* (Frankfurt am Main: Suhrkamp, 1997), 23.
33. Strauss, *Philosophy and Law*, 45; cf. Guttmann, *Philosophies of Judaism*, 396.
34. Strauss, *Philosophy and Law*, 45.
35. Ibid., 46; trans. altered.
36. Ibid., 45.
37. Ibid., 47; trans. altered. Strauss quickly added that this inability to "conceive of God as a reality" was by no means characteristic for Cohen alone but for modern philosophy of religion as a whole.
38. This was the strategy of Julius Guttmann to cast doubt on Strauss's interpretation: "The philosophical convictions underlying this judgment are those of modern existential philosophy. . . . The superiority of the category of law over the [category] of religious consciousness is the superiority of the existential over the validity-philosophical [*geltungsphilosophischen*] interpretation of revelation" (Guttmann, "Philosophie der Religion," 151). *Geltungsphilosophie* (philosophy of validity) is another name for neo-Kantianism, with its emphasis on the multiple "spheres of validity." As to existentialism, see also Guttmann's "Existence and Idea: Critical Observations on the Existential Philosophy," in *Scripta Hierosolymitana*, vol. 6: Studies in Philosophy, ed. S. H. Bergman (Jerusalem: Magnes, 1960), 9–40.
39. Strauss, *Gesammelte Schriften* 3, 489.
40. Franz Rosenzweig, "Einleitung," Hermann Cohen, *Jüdische Schriften*, vol. 1 (Berlin: Schwetschke, 1924), xlvii.
41. Strauss, *Philosophy and Law*, 47.
42. Ibid., 52.
43. Cf. *Franz Rosenzweig's "The New Thinking,"* ed. Alan Udoff and Barbara E. Galli (Syracuse: Syracuse University Press, 1999).
44. Strauss, *Philosophy and Law*, 47.
45. Ibid., 45, 52.

46. Ibid., 51, cf. 52.
47. Cf. ibid., 51.
48. Ibid., 53.
49. Ibid.
50. Ibid., 58.
51. Ibid., 81.
52. Ibid., 59.
53. Strauss, *Gesammelte Schriften* 3, 704–705.
54. Ibid., 706.
55. Strauss saw this difference very sharply. Cf. ibid., 707.
56. Guttmann, "Philosophie der Religion," 153; the reference is to Strauss, *Philosophy and Law*, 81.
57. Ibid., 152.
58. Guttmann, *Philosophies of Judaism*, 201–202.
59. Ibid., 227–28.
60. Cf. ibid., 3–5.
61. Strauss, *Philosophy and Law*, 54.
62. Although Guttmann spoke out primarily as a critic of exotericism, he reproduced the exotericism thesis even in his criticism, and he needed it for his own project. Cf. Strauss's comments on the doctrine of the twofold truth, ibid., 65–66.
63. Ibid., 58, 57.
64. Ibid., 57–58.
65. Ibid., 58.
66. Ibid., 139n10.
67. Ibid., 83.
68. Ibid., 84.
69. Ibid., 87.
70. Ibid., 88.
71. Guttmann, "Philosophie der Religion oder Philosophie des Gesetzes?," 153.
72. Strauss, *Philosophy and Law*, 91.
73. Ibid., 99.
74. Strauss, letter to Cyrus Adler, September 30, 1933, Leo Strauss Papers, box 4, folder 1.
75. Cf. Strauss's letter to Krüger, June 26, 1930, in *Gesammelte Schriften* 3, 382.
76. Leo Strauss, "Die Lehre des R. Lewi ben Gershom," typewritten manuscript, Leo Strauss Papers, box 16, folder 32.
77. Strauss, *Philosophy and Law*, 77.
78. Ibid., 92, cf. 88.
79. Ibid., 100.
80. Ibid., 26.
81. Guttmann, "Philosophie der Religion oder Philosophie des Gesetzes?," 172; cf. Heinrich Meier, *Leo Strauss and the Theologico-Political Problem* (Cambridge/New York: Cambridge University Press, 2006), 20.

82. Strauss, *Philosophy and Law*, 58.
83. Ibid., 58–59.
84. Ibid., 59.
85. Guttmann, "Philosophie der Religion oder Philosophie des Gesetzes?," 155.
86. Strauss, *Philosophy and Law*, 60.
87. Ibid., 59.
88. Ibid., 83–84.
89. Ibid., 59.
90. Cf. Benjamin Aldes Wurgaft, "Culture and Law in Weimar Jewish Medievalism: Leo Strauss's Critique of Julius Guttmann," *Modern Intellectual History* 11, no. 1 (2014): 119–46: 132.
91. Strauss, "Cohen and Maimonides," in *Leo Strauss on Maimonides*, 219.
92. Strauss, *Philosophy and Law*, 60.
93. Ibid.
94. Ibid.; cf. 88, 92.
95. Ibid., 60; *Gesammelte Schriften* 2, 47–48.
96. Ibid., 61.
97. Strauss, "How to Study Medieval Philosophy," in *Leo Strauss on Maimonides*, 105.
98. Cf. ibid.
99. Strauss, *Philosophy and Law*, 61–65.
100. Ibid., 61–63.
101. Ibid., 60.
102. Ibid., 63.
103. Ibid., 64.
104. Ibid., 140n16.
105. Ibid., 65; trans. altered; cf. 108; *Gesammelte Schriften* 2, 52.
106. See Daniel Tanguay, *Leo Strauss: An Intellectual Biography*, especially 52; Heinrich Meier, "How Strauss Became Strauss," in *Reorientation*, 19–20.
107. Strauss, *Philosophy and Law*, 108.
108. Ibid., 66.
109. Ibid., 38.
110. Ibid., 66; *Gesammelte Schriften* 2, 52.
111. Strauss, *Philosophy and Law*, 67.
112. Ibid.
113. Ibid.
114. Ibid., 67.
115. Ibid., 68.
116. Ibid., 70.
117. Ibid., 71.
118. Guttmann, "Philosophie der Religion oder Philosophie des Gesetzes?," 172.

119. Strauss, *Natural Right and History*, 6.
120. Strauss, *Philosophy and Law*, 73.
121. Ibid.; cf. *Persecution and the Art of Writing*, 9–10.
122. Strauss, *Philosophy and Law*, 102–103.
123. Ibid., 103.
124. Ibid., 103–104.
125. Ibid., 105, cf. 91.
126. Ibid., 105.
127. Ibid., 106–107.
128. Ibid., 106–11.
129. Ibid., 113–19.
130. Ibid., 119.
131. Ibid., 120.
132. Ibid.
133. Ibid., 122, 123.
134. Cf. Heinrich Meier, "How Strauss became Strauss," in *Reorientation*, 17.
135. Strauss, "A Giving of Accounts," in *Jewish Philosophy and the Crisis of Modernity*, 463.
136. Cf. Strauss, *Gesammelte Schriften* 2, 126, 198, 425.
137. Strauss, *The Argument and the Action of Plato's Laws* (Chicago/London: The University of Chicago Press, 1975), 1.
138. Strauss, *Philosophy and Law*, 122–23. As to the construction of the quote, the edition referred to by Strauss mentions two books on the *Laws* without naming their authors, but Strauss attributes the books expressly to Plato and Aristotle. To do so, he referred to a Gotha manuscript. Only with the help of this manuscript could he create a link between Avicenna and Plato's *Laws*. The assertion that the *Politics* treats the religious laws and the difference between divine and false prophecy is missing in both versions of the text. Georges Tamer therefore refers to the quote as a "construction," contending that Strauss "creates a link between Avicenna and Plato which in fact does not exist." Georges Tamer, *Islamische Philosophie und die Krise der Moderne. Das Verhältnis von Leo Strauss zu Alfarabi, Avicenna, und Averroes* (Leiden: Brill, 2001), 64, 86. Cf. numerous references in Joel L. Kraemer, "The Medieval Arabic Enlightenment," in *The Cambridge Companion to Leo Strauss*, 153n58.
139. Cf. Strauss, *Philosophy and Law*, 123.
140. Ibid., 122.
141. Ibid., 124–25.
142. Cf. ibid., 76. For two somewhat different explanations of the change of orientation provided by the quote, see Georges Tamer, *Islamische Philosophie und die Krise der Moderne*, 61.
143. Strauss, *Philosophy and Law*, 125.
144. Cf. Strauss, "On Abravanel's Philosophical Tendency and Political Teaching," in *Gesammelte Schriften* 2, 196–98; *Persecution and the Art of Writing*, 8–9.

145. Cf. Strauss, *The Argument and the Action of Plato's Laws*, 1.
146. Strauss, *Philosophy and Law*, 127–28.
147. Ibid., 128; trans. altered; *Gesammelte Schriften* 2, 118.
148. Strauss, *Philosophy and Law*, 128.
149. Ibid., 132–33.
150. Ibid., 79, 130.
151. Strauss, "Cohen and Maimonides," in *Leo Strauss on Maimonides*, 179.
152. Strauss, *Philosophy and Law*, 129.
153. Ibid., 130–31.
154. Ibid., 130; cf. Cohen, *Ethics of Maimonides*, trans. Almut Sh. Bruckstein (Madison: The University of Wisconsin Press, 2004), 50.
155. Strauss, *Philosophy and Law*, 131; trans. altered; *Gesammelte Schriften* 2, 121.
156. Cf. Strauss, *Philosophy and Law*, 132–33.
157. Ibid., 61, 76, 81.
158. Strauss, *Gesammelte Schriften* 3, 538.
159. Strauss, *Philosophy and Law*, 132.
160. Ibid.
161. Ibid., 72; trans. altered; *Gesammelte Schriften* 2, 60.
162. Strauss, *Philosophy and Law*, 72.
163. Ibid., 73; see also the ensuing footnote 25.
164. Ibid., 75.
165. Ibid.; trans. altered; *Gesammelte Schriften* 2, 63.
166. Ibid., 76–79. Strauss added a footnote here pointing out Mendelssohn's indebtedness to Hobbes. From here one can put together the meaning of his ironic remark that he planned to "publish an introduction to the *Moreh* [*Guide*] with the title: 'Hobbes' Political Science in its Development,' which should come out next year with Oxford University Press" (Strauss, *Gesammelte Schriften* 3, 716).
167. Strauss, *Philosophy and Law*, 79.

Chapter 9. A Complex Afterlife

1. Heinrich Meier, *Carl Schmitt and Leo Strauss: The Hidden Dialogue*, xvii.
2. Guttmann had sought to publish this article in the *Jewish Quarterly Review*, but the plan never materialized. See Fritz Bamberger's letter to Strauss from January 9, 1960 (quoting from Guttmann's letters to Ismar Elbogen), Leo Strauss Papers, box 1, folder 2.
3. Cf. Strauss, *Gesammelte Schriften* 3, 722.
4. Cf. Strauss's letter from December 14, 1934: "To my very great regret I do not have the inner and outer calm at the moment to reply to your objections to my remarks." He nevertheless asked Guttmann to recommend his text to Schocken.

On January 22, 1935, he thanked Guttmann for his detailed study of his review and added: "To my very great regret I do not have the opportunity at the moment to reply to you in this regard. Instead I merely wish to ask you today if you would possibly be willing to review my little writing and to develop your anti-critical concerns more precisely on that occasion. I believe this would be welcomed not only by myself." Strauss repeated his plea for a review of his book on March 27, 1935. (For all letters, cf. Leo Strauss Papers, box 8, folder 4.) We can safely say that Strauss's main concerns at this stage were the publication of his book and the subsequent public debate, not the argument with Guttmann.

5. Letter to Guttmann, May 20, 1949, Leo Strauss Papers, box 4, folder 8.

6. Strauss, *Gesammelte Schriften* 3, 728, trans. cited in Heinrich Meier, "How Strauss Became Strauss," in *Reorientation*, 29n29. I shall discuss this letter at greater length below.

7. Letter to Julius Guttmann, May 22, 1929, quoted in Heinrich Meier, "Vorwort zur zweiten Auflage," Strauss, *Gesammelte Schriften* 1: *Die Religionskritik Spinozas und zugehörige Schriften*, ed. Heinrich Meier, 3rd ed. (Stuttgart/Weimar: Metzler, 2008), xix n 10.

8. Letter to Strauss, December 28, 1933, in *Gesammelte Schriften* 3, 483.

9. Eliezer Schweid, "Religion and Philosophy: The Scholarly-Theological Debate Between Julius Guttmann and Leo Strauss," 163.

10. For some exceptions see Mari Rethelyi, "Guttmann's Critique of Strauss's Modernist Approach to Medieval Philosophy: Some Arguments Toward a Counter-Critique," *The Journal of Textual Reasoning* 3, no. 1 (2004): http://jtr.lib.virginia.edu/volume-3-number-1/; Chiara Adorisio, "Philosophy of Religion or Political Philosophy?: The Debate Between Leo Strauss and Julius Guttmann," *European Journal of Jewish Studies* 1 (2007): 135–55; Paul Mendes-Flohr, "The Philosophy of Religion or the Philosophy of Law?," *Archivio di filosofia* 1, no. 2 (2007): 145–56.

11. See letter to Jacob Klein, October 10, 1939, in *Gesammelte Schriften* 3, 583, cf. 525.

12. Cf. Benjamin Wurgaft, "Culture and Law in Weimar Jewish Medievalism," 120; Leora Batnitzky, "Leo Strauss and the 'Theologico-Political Predicament," in *The Cambridge Companion to Leo Strauss*, 50; Joel L. Kraemer, "The Medieval Arabic Enlightenment," ibid., 138; Stephan Steiner, *Weimar in Amerika*, 92.

13. Cf. Thomas Meyer, *Zwischen Philosophie und Gesetz*, 103; Stephan Steiner, *Weimar in Amerika*, 92–95.

14. Guttmann, "Philosophie der Religion oder Philosophie des Gesetzes?," 149.

15. Ibid., 163.

16. Ibid., 151.

17. Ibid., 172.

18. Ibid., 164.

19. Guttmann, *Philosophies of Judaism*, 204, cf. 501n125.

20. Strauss, *Philosophy and Law*, 78–79.

21. Ibid., 124.
22. Guttmann, "Philosophie der Religion oder Philosophie des Gesetzes?," 172.
23. Strauss, *Philosophy and Law*, 71.
24. Ibid., 121, cf. 123.
25. Ibid., 120.
26. Guttmann, "Philosophie der Religion oder Philosophie des Gesetzes?," 172.
27. Strauss, *Gesammelte Schriften* 3, 765.
28. Guttmann, *Philosophies of Judaism*, 203–204.
29. Ibid., 502n125.
30. Strauss, *Philosophy and Law*, 42.
31. Strauss, *Gesammelte Schriften* 3, 726.
32. Ibid., 727–28; English translation cited in Heinrich Meier, "How Strauss Became Strauss," in *Reorientation*, 29n29. Strauss eventually received the Guttmann manuscript shortly before his death, from Scholem; cf. *Gesammelte Schriften* 3, 765.
33. Following Michael Zank, readers have understood the phrase with regard to Strauss's overall turn to medieval thought: "In order to dig his way back from Marburg (or Davos) to Athens he proceeded backward in history to the world against which the modern critique of tradition arose. What has been dubbed a 'return to Maimonides' (Green) in the work of Strauss is, however, strictly speaking only a half-way station, a 'Jewish-Thomistic detour,' as Strauss judged in hindsight, on the way to the original difficulties of pursuing philosophy addressed in Plato's parable of the cave" (Michael Zank, "Leo Strauss' Rediscovery of the Exoteric," 195–96). But "Jewish Thomism" was by no means meant to designate Strauss's overall medievalism as a "detour" on the way to Plato. The more specific meaning and purpose was pointed out by Leora Batnitzky, who showed that Strauss's statement "means that he had viewed revelation as a matter of knowledge" before realizing that the understanding of revelation as knowledge rather than legislation was a domain of Christian scholasticism (Batnitzky, *Leo Strauss and Emmanuel Levinas*, 242n22, cf. 123; cf. also Randi L. Rashkover, "Justifying Philosophy and Restoring Revelation: Assessing Strauss's Medieval Return," in *Encountering the Medieval in Modern Jewish Thought* [Leiden/Boston: Brill, 2012], 229–57: 243). The problem with this interpretation is its uneasy relationship to Batnitzky's presuppostion that this understanding of Jewish and Islamic versus Christian theology runs through Strauss's thought from early on. If it is a continuous strand in Strauss's thought, there is no reason why he should have made a "path via a Jewish Thomism" in *Philosophy and Law* and why he should have henceforth moved away from it. The bottom line is that one must pay greater attention to the specific context of Strauss's phrase and the changes in his interpretation of the medievals. "Jewish Thomism" marks an unresolved problem in the theoretical design of *Philosophy and Law*, but Strauss's later refutations and clarifications—most of all in *Persecution and the Art of Writing*—only aggravated the problem.
34. Josef Sermoneta, "Pour une histoire du thomisme juif," in *Aquinas and Problems of his Time*, ed. G. Verbeke and D. Verhelst (Leuven/The Hague: Leuven

University Press/Martinus Nijhoff, 1976), 130–35. As Seymour Feldman explained: "At a time when in southern France Maimonidean philosophy took a 'radical' turn towards Averroes, resulting in the 'esoteric' Maimonides, the Italian Maimonideans tended to be more moderate and 'conservative.' In this regard, they were fortified and influenced by Christian medieval thinkers, such as Thomas Aquinas, who also recoiled from several of the more radical ideas of Averroes. This receptivity to Christian philosophical thought became characteristic of Italian Jewish philosophical literature and persisted throughout the Renaissance." Seymour Feldman, *Philosophy in a Time of Crisis. Don Isaac Abravael: Defender of the Faith* (New York/London: Routledge Curzon, 2003), 165.

35. Cf. Strauss, *Gesammelte Schriften* 2, 616.
36. Strauss, *Philosophy and Law*, 67–68.
37. Cf. Strauss, *Persecution and the Art of Writing*, 19.
38. Strauss, *Philosophy and Law*, 21.
39. Strauss, Introduction to Alexander Altmann, "The Encounter of Faith and Reason in the Western Tradition and its Significance Today," October 1961, unpublished tape recording, Leo Strauss Papers, box 67.
40. Cf. Heinrich Meier, "How Strauss Became Strauss," in *Reorientation*, 29n29.
41. Cf. also Strauss, "An Epilogue," in *The Scientific Study of Politics*, ed. Herbert J. Storing (New York: Holt, Rinehart, and Winston, 1963), 307–27: 308.
42. Letter to Paul Kraus, May 17, 1936, in *Gesammelte Schriften* 3, xxxii n 41.
43. Letter to Jacob Klein, February 16, 1938, in *Gesammelte Schriften* 3, 549, cf. 545, 550, 553–54, 558–59, 562, 567, 586. As to previous, hitherto unpublished letters to Norbert Nahum Glatzer with the same edge, see Susanne Klingenstein, "Of Greeks and Jews: Old Letters Throw New Light on Leo Strauss," *The Weekly Standard*, October 25, 2010; www.weeklystandard.com/of-greeks-and-jews/article/508813.
44. Daniel Tanguay, *Leo Strauss: An Intellectual Biography*, 50–53.
45. Strauss, *Natural Right and History*, 20–21.
46. "His method, in general, of quieting the doubts of the 'perplexed' is the old one—as old as Philo and beyond—of regarding Biblical phrases as metaphors and allegories, containing an esoteric meaning beside or opposed to the literal." Isaac Husik, *A History of Mediaeval Jewish Philosophy* (New York: Macmillan, 1916), 240, cf. xvi, 79, 242, 303.
47. Strauss, *Philosophy and Law*, 95.
48. Ibid., 95–96.
49. Ibid., 82.
50. Ibid., 102.
51. Cf. Heinrich Meier, "How Strauss Became Strauss," *Reorientation*, 14.
52. The conventional viewpoint is not limited to the German-Jewish context. Beside Guttmann, some of the principal scholars to be addressed by Strauss were Harry A. Wolfson and Isaac Husik, as well as E. I. J. Rosenthal, Richard Walzer, and Franz Rosenthal. Cf. Joshua Parens, "Escaping the Scholastic Paradigm: The Dispute Between Strauss and his Contemporaries about How to Approach Islamic

and Jewish Medieval Philosophy," in *Encountering the Medieval in Modern Jewish Thought*, ed. James A. Diamond and Aaron W. Hughes (Leiden/Boston: Brill, 2012), 203–27; repr. in Parens, *Leo Strauss and the Recovery of Medieval Political Philosophy* (Rochester: University of Rochester Press, 2016), 39–54; see also Kenneth Hart Green, *Leo Strauss and the Rediscovery of Maimonides* (Chicago/London: The University of Chicago Press, 2013), 17–41.

53. Strauss, *Persecution and the Art of Writing*, 11; cf. also Kenneth Hart Green, *Jew and Philosopher: The Return to Maimonides in the Jewish Thought of Leo Strauss*, 113–14.

54. Strauss, "Some Remarks on the Political Science of Maimonides and Farabi," in *Leo Strauss on Maimonides*, 284; cf. "Quelques remarques sur la science politique de Maïmonide et de Fârâbî," in *Gesammelte Schriften* 2, 125–58: 132–33.

55. Ibid., 284–85.

56. Strauss, "On Abravanel's Philosophical Tendency and Political Teaching," in *Gesammelte Schriften* 2, 199.

57. Ibid., 200.

58. Cf. ibid., 203.

59. Ibid., 207.

60. Ibid., 208–209.

61. Ibid., 225.

62. Guttmann, *Philosophies of Judaism*, 289–91.

63. Cf. Strauss, *Persecution and the Art of Writing*, 81, 124–26.

64. See, however, ibid., 34–35.

65. William H. F. Altman, *The German Stranger: Leo Strauss and National Socialism* (Lanham, MD: Lexington, 2011), 30. The belief that Strauss *was* an exoteric writer is shared by Eugene Sheppard, *Leo Strauss and the Politics of Exile: The Making of a Political Philosopher* (Waltham, MA: Brandeis University Press, 2006), 100; Joel L. Kraemer, "The Medieval Arabic Enlightenment," in *The Cambridge Companion to Leo Strauss*, 138. Steven B. Smith's exposition on Strauss as a reader is more ambiguous in this respect (*Reading Leo Strauss: Politics, Philosophy, Judaism* [Chicago/London: The University of Chicago Press, 2006], 7–9). For the argument against this understanding, see Catherine Zuckert and Michael Zuckert, *The Truth about Leo Strauss. Political Philosophy and American Democracy*, 127–28; Lars Fischer, "After the Strauss Wars," *East European Jewish Affairs* 40, no. 1 (2010): 61–79: 67–68.

66. Strauss, *What Is Political Philosophy?*, 230.

67. Cf. his letter to Scholem from June 1952, in *Gesammelte Schriften*, 726, as cited at length above.

68. As to the "between the lines" metaphor, cf. Strauss, *Persecution and the Art of Writing*, 25, 36.

69. Ibid., 35n17.

70. Cf. Steven B. Smith, *Reading Leo Strauss: Politics, Philosophy, Judaism*, 7.

71. Strauss, "Religious Situation of the Present," in *Reorientation*, 230.

72. Strauss, "On a Forgotten Kind of Writing," in *What is Political Philosophy?*, 232; cf. "Exoteric Teaching," in *The Rebirth of Classical Political Rationalism*, 68.
73. Strauss, *Persecution and the Art of Writing*, 24–25.
74. Ibid., 185.
75. Ibid., 30.

Chapter 10. Genealogies of National Socialism

1. Leo Strauss, "German Nihilism," *Interpretation* 26, no. 3 (Spring 1999): 355–78. The text was edited from the manuscript of a lecture delivered in February 1941 at the New School for Social Research in New York to the General Seminar of the Graduate Faculty of Political and Social Science. The overall seminar topic, according to the manuscript, was "Experiences of the Second World War." Although the thematic semblance and temporal proximity may suggest otherwise, "German Nihilism" was not yet a contribution to the legendary Study Group on Germany, which had its first meeting on November 18, 1942, and lasted for nine months, before it was absorbed into the Institute of World Affairs. The Study Group, which had Strauss among its members, alongside Erich Hula, Adolph Lowe, Eduard Heimann, Horace Kallen, Felix Kaufmann, Kurt Riezler, Carl Mayer, and Albert Salomon, is nevertheless an important reference point for understanding the text. Later guests were Fernando de los Ríos and Felix Gilbert. Ernst Karl Winter, whom Strauss mentioned in his "Historicism" lecture, was to give a paper on Plato and Aristotle. For some of the discussions of that group cf. Thomas Meyer, "Die Macht der Ideen. Albert Salomon im Kontext zweier ideengeschichtlicher Debatten: Weimar und Exil," in *Verlassene Stufen der Reflexion. Albert Salomon und die Aufklärung der Soziologie*, ed. Peter Gostmann and Claudius Härpfer (Wiesbaden: VS Verlag für Sozialwissenschaften, 2011), 157–77; Almut Stoletzki, "The Study Group on Germany: Exploring the Transatlantic Dynamics in an Exile Debate of the 1940s," *Traversea* 2 (2012): 80–100. Stoletzki names Strauss as one of the two "most vital discussants of the group," the other being Carl Mayer (ibid., 86). These recent studies build upon the foundation laid by older works such as John G. Gunnell, *The Descent of Political Theory* (Chicago/London: The University of Chicago Press, 1993), ch. "Coming to America"; Peter M. Rutkoff/William B. Scott, *New School. A History of The New School for Social Research* (New York: The Free Press, 1986); Claus-Dieter Krohn, *Wissenschaft im Exil. Deutsche Sozial- und Wirtschaftswissenschaftler in den USA und die New School for Social Research* (Frankfurt am Main/New York: Campus, 1987).
2. Susan Shell, "'To Spare the Vanquished and Crush the Arrogant': Leo Strauss's Lecture on 'German Nihilism,'" in *The Cambridge Companion to Leo Strauss*, 171–91: 172.
3. William H. F. Altman, "Leo Strauss on 'German Nihilism': Learning the Art of Writing," *Journal of the History of Ideas* 68, no. 4 (2007): 587–612.

4. Stephan Steiner, *Weimar in America: Leo Strauss' Politische Philosophie* (Tübingen: Mohr Siebeck, 2013), 124.

5. Strauss, "German Nihilism," 362.

6. Cf. ibid., 365.

7. Strauss, *Persecution and the Art of Writing*, 37.

8. Strauss, *Natural Right and History*, 42–43.

9. Karl Popper, *Die offene Gesellschaft und ihre Feinde*, Preface to the seventh German ed. (Tübingen: Mohr Siebeck, 2002), ix. The preface is not included in the English edition.

10. Wolf Lepenies, *The Seduction of Culture in German History* (Princeton: Princeton University Press, 2006), 15. As a matter of fact, many of the small states each had a national theatre before 1871.

11. For a classical description of this double character of German thought, cf. Theodor W. Adorno, "On the Question: 'What is German?,'" in *Critical Models: Interventions and Catchwords*, trans. Henry W. Pickford (New York: Columbia University Press, 1998), 205–14.

12. Wolf Lepenies, *The Seduction of Culture in German History*, 12.

13. Cf. Hannah Arendt, "Approaches to the 'German Problem,'" in *Essays in Understanding, 1930–1954: Formation, Exile, and Totalitarianism* (New York: Schocken, 1994), 106–20: 108: "Nazism owes nothing to any part of the Western tradition, be it German or not, Catholic or Protestant, Christian, Greek, or Roman. Whether we like Thomas Aquinas or Machiavelli or Luther or Kant or Hegel or Nietzsche . . . they have not the least responsibility for what is happening in the extermination camps."

14. Friedrich Meinecke, *Die deutsche Katastrophe* (Wiesbaden: Brockhaus, 1946); translated as *The German Catastrophe* (Cambridge: Harvard University Press, 1950).

15. Cf. Walter Benjamin, "On the Concept of History," in *Selected Writings*, vol. 4: 1938–1940, ed. Howard Eiland and Michael W. Jennings (Cambridge, MA/London: Belknap Press, 2003), 389–400: 391.

16. Ernst Cassirer, *The Myth of the State*, 4. (See also chapter 3 above.)

17. Albert Salomon, "The Spirit of the Soldier and Nazi Militarism," *Social Research* 9 (1942): 82–103: 82.

18. Erich Hula, "Review of Ernst Fraenkel's *The Dual State*," *Social Research* 9 (1942): 271–73: 273.

19. Strauss, *Spinoza's Critique of Religion*, 1.

20. Cf. Ernst Troeltsch's wartime article "Der Geist der deutschen Kultur," in *Deutschland und der Weltkrieg*, ed. Otto Hintze and Friedrich Meinecke (Leipzig: Teubner, 1915), 52–90: 52.

21. Cf. Edmond Vermeil, *The German Scene (Social, Political, Cultural) 1890 to the Present Day* (London: Harrap, 1956).

22. Crane Brinton, *Nietzsche* (New York: Harper and Row, 1965) (first publ. 1941), 200–201. "As the war went on, Nietzsche, Treitschke, and von Bernhardi

tended to fade out of the picture a bit, to be replaced by more immediate matters. They were revived again in their full horror in the middle of the war, when it became necessary to key the Americans up to the fight" (ibid., 204).

23. Benjamin, "On the Concept of History," 391.

24. Vansittart himself had a surprisingly favorable view of Nietzsche, especially for his psychological account of the German soul. Vansittartism—the position that an aggressive foreign policy is part of the German national character—was sidelined by Neville Chamberlain, the champion of appeasement politics. The discussion in England successively shifted away from Nietzsche in favor of longer genealogical lines. Cf. Jörg Später, *Vansittart: Britische Debatten über Deutsche und Nazis 1902–1945* (Göttingen: Wallstein, 2003), 273–76.

25. Rutkoff and Scott, *New School*, 137.

26. Alvin Johnson, "War and the Scholar," *Social Research* 9 (1942): 1–3: 3.

27. Rutkoff and Scott, *New School*, 137.

28. William Montgomery McGovern, *From Luther to Hitler: The History of Fascist-Nazi Political Philosophy* (New York: Houghton Mifflin, 1973), 17.

29. Reinhold Niebuhr, *Christianity and Power Politics* (New York: Charles Scribner's Sons, 1940), 49.

30. Carl Mayer, "On the Intellectual Origin of National Socialism," *Social Research* 9, no. 2 (1942): 225–47: 228.

31. Cf. Niebuhr, *Christianity and Power Politics*, 57.

32. Peter F. Wiener, *Martin Luther: Hitler's Spiritual Ancestor* (London/New York: Hutchinson, 1945), 9, passim.

33. Ibid., 72. See also Wiener's slurs against Martin Niemöller, 75–78.

34. United Nations Educational, Scientific and Cultural Organization, "The Roots of National Socialism and Causes of the Transformation of the National-Socialist Movement into an Overwhelming Political Force," UNESCO/SS/W/1, Paris, July 31, 1949; http://unesdoc.unesco.org/images/0017/001781/178108eb.pdf, 3: "The Lutheran tradition, which divides wordly life into 'Ordnungen' (governed by laws of their own and not directly subject to the principle of the Gospel) led to an uncritical acceptance of every command of the competent authorities, and even to the acceptance of the authority of every man actually holding any power. This explained why in practice the machinery of the State and the 'Wehrmacht' placed itself unconditionally at the disposal of the National-Socialist movement from 30 January 1933 onwards."

35. Helmuth Plessner, *Die verspätete Nation: Über die politische Verführbarkeit bürgerlichen Geistes* (Frankfurt am Main: Suhrkamp, 1974), 79, 75.

36. Eric Voegelin, "Nietzsche, the Crisis, and the War," *Published Essays 1940–1952*, Collected Works, vol. 10 (Columbia/London: University of Missouri Press, 2000), 126–56: 131.

37. Rohan Butler, *The Roots of National Socialism* (London: Faber and Faber, 1941), 276. Strauss wrote on the notions of "folk minds," i.e., on the assumption that nations or ethnic groups are organic units, in *Natural Right and History*, 16.

38. Paul Viereck, *Metapolitics: From Wagner and the German Romantics to Hitler* (New Brunswick/London: Transaction Publishers, 2007).
39. Ibid., 5.
40. Ibid., 7, following Ernst Troeltsch, *Deutscher Geist und Westeuropa* (Tübingen: Mohr, 1925).
41. Ibid., 8.
42. Ibid., 91.
43. This transformation in Thomas Mann's understanding of culture and politics is the guiding theme in Wolf Lepenies, *The Seduction of Culture in German History*, passim.
44. Viereck, *Metapolitics*, li, lv, lvii.
45. Cf. Theodor W. Adorno and Thomas Mann, *Correspondence 1943–1955*, ed. Christoph Gödde and Thomas Sprecher (Cambridge/Malden: Polity, 2006).
46. Viereck, *Metapolitics*, lviii–lix.
47. George Santayana, *Egotism in German Philosophy* (London/Toronto: J. M. Dent and Sons, 1916), 5–6.
48. Cf. ibid., 21, on the negligence of "technical" discussions.
49. Ibid., 5.
50. Ibid., 12.
51. Ibid., 15.
52. George Santayana, "German Philosophy and Politics" [review], *The Journal of Philosophy, Psychology and Scientific Methods* 12, no. 24 (1915): 645–49: 649.
53. Ibid.
54. Cf. Dewey's 1916 review of Santayana's book: "The Tragedy of the German Soul: Egotism in German Philosophy," in Dewey, *The Middle Works, 1899–1924*, vol. 10: *Journal Articles, Essays, and Miscellany Published in the 1916–1917 Period*, ed. Jo Ann Boydston (Carbondale/Edwardsville: Southern Illinois University Press, 2008), 305–309: 308–309.
55. Dewey, *German Philosophy and Politics*, The Middle Works, 1899–1924, Vol. 8: *Essays on Education and Politics, 1915*, ed. Jo Ann Boydston (Carbondale/Edwardsville: Southern Illinois University Press, 1985), 198.
56. Cf. Werner Stegmaier and Daniel Krochmalnik, eds., *Jüdischer Nietzscheanismus* (Berlin/New York: de Gruyter, 1997), 196. Levy, however, would not have agreed with Dewey's actual point that Nietzsche was *epigonal* to Kant—a mere "superficial and transitory wave of opinion" that had no effect upon the course of German philosophy and politics (Dewey, *German Philosophy and Politics*, 151).
57. Dewey, *German Philosophy and Politics*, 151.
58. Ibid.
59. Dewey, The Middle Works, vol. 8, 421–23.
60. Cf. Stephan Steiner, *Weimar in Amerika*, passim.
61. Robert Horwitz, "John Dewey," in *History of Political Philosophy*, ed. Leo Strauss and Joseph Cropsey, 3d ed. (Chicago/London: The University of Chicago Press, 1987), 851–69: 851.

62. Dewey, *German Philosophy and Politics*, 144.
63. Ibid., 152.
64. Ibid., 182.
65. William Ernest Hocking, "Political Philosophy in Germany," repr. in John Dewey, The Middle Works, 1899–1924, Vol. 8: *Essays on Education and Politics, 1915*, ed. Jo Ann Boydston (Carbondale/Edwardsville: Southern Illinois University Press, 1985), 473–77: 474–75.
66. Dewey, The Middle Works, vol. 8, 419.
67. Dewey, *German Philosophy and Politics*, 144.
68. Ibid., 141.
69. John Dewey, "Philosophy and Civilization," The Later Works, 1925–1953, vol. 3: *1927–1928*, ed. Jo Ann Boydston (Carbondale/Edwardsville: Southern Illinois University Press, 1984), 3–10: 3.
70. Cf. ibid., 4.
71. Strauss, *What Is Political Philosophy?*, 279–80.
72. Ibid., 281; cf. Dewey, *German Philosophy and Politics*, 151.
73. Cf. Strauss, *Natural Right and History*, 1–2.
74. Eric Voegelin, "Nietzsche, the Crisis, and the War," 126.
75. Crane Brinton, *Nietzsche*, 216.
76. Ibid., 213–15.
77. Ibid., 216.
78. Ibid., 231.
79. Ibid., 216, 222.
80. Rohan Butler, *The Roots of National Socialism*, 295.
81. Karl Löwith, *My Life in Germany Before and After 1933*, 5–6.
82. Karl Löwith, *Nietzsche*, in *Sämtliche Schriften*, vol. 6 (Stuttgart: Metzler, 1987), 399.
83. Ibid., 398.
84. Ibid., 402.
85. *The Nietzsche Reader*, ed. Keith A. Pearson and Duncan Large (Malden/Oxford/Carlton: Blackwell, 2006), 388; cf. Nietzsche, *Kritische Studienausgabe*, vol. 12: Nachgelassene Fragmente 1885–1887, ed. Giorgio Colli/Mazziono Montinari (Munich: dtv, 1988), 216.
86. Strauss, *Gesammelte Schriften*, vol. 3: *Hobbes' politische Wissenschaft und zugehörige Schriften—Briefe*, ed. Heinrich/Wiebke Meier, 2nd ed. (Stuttgart/Weimar: Metzler, 2008), 648. Strauss's late testimony must be treated with the same care and reservation as other autobiographical statements he made in the 1960s. But the statement also points to a decisive shift: the end of his Nietzschean phase was the beginning of Strauss's Platonism. This turn from Nietzsche to Plato is well documented in his correspondence of that time. As he wrote to Krüger in December 1932, the "fundamental obscurity" of Nietzsche "could only be overcome by advancing to Platonic philosophy" (Strauss, *Gesammelte Schriften* 3, 415). In May 1933, he wrote to Löwith: "When I encountered Plato's Laws I realized that, by recalling certain

Platonic doctrines, the questions of Nietzsche—i.e., *our* questions—pose themselves much more simply, clearly, and originally" (ibid., 620–21).

87. Strauss, "German Nihilism," 364.
88. Ibid.
89. Ibid., 372; cf. "The Three Waves of Modernity," in *An Introduction to Political Philosophy*, ed. Hilail Gildin (Detroit: Wayne State University Press, 1989), 98: "In a sense, all political use of Nietzsche is a perversion of his teaching. Nevertheless, what he said was read by political men and inspired them. He is as little responsible for fascism as Rousseau is responsible for Jacobinism. This means, however, that he is as much responsible for fascism as Rousseau was responsible for Jacobinism."
90. Cf. Strauss, *What Is Political Philosophy?*, 54–55.
91. Carl Mayer, "On the Intellectual Origins of National Socialism," 228–33.
92. Ibid., 228, 230; emphasis added.
93. Ibid., 234–38.
94. Ibid., 240–42.
95. Ibid., 246.
96. Ibid., 242.
97. Ibid., 247.
98. Carl Landauer, "Comment on Mayer's Analysis of National Socialism," *Social Research* 9, no. 3 (1942): 402–404: 403.
99. Ibid., 402.
100. Ibid., 404.
101. Cf. Hannah Arendt, "Approaches to the 'German Problem,'" in *Essays in Understanding*, 110.
102. Strauss, *Spinoza's Critique of Religion*, 1. This social stability and resistance to fascism, particularly in England, had been the guiding theme in Adolph Lowe's *The Price of Liberty* (1937).

Chapter 11. Strauss's Argument

1. Strauss, "German Nihilism," 357.
2. Ibid.
3. Ibid., 359.
4. Ibid., 358–59.
5. Ibid., 358. As to the distinction between the open society and the closed society, see also Strauss's letter to Löwith, August 15, 1946, in *Gesammelte Schriften* 3, 662–63.
6. Cf. Altman, "Leo Strauss on 'German Nihilism,'" 596, 598; Steiner, *Weimar in Amerika*, 118–19.
7. Strauss, "German Nihilism," 358.

8. Strauss, *The City and Man*, 101; cf. "On the *Euthydemus*," *Studies in Platonic Political Philosophy*, 79; *Liberalism Ancient and Modern*, 11, 14. Kurt Riezler's essay "Play and Seriousness" was published in the same year, 1941, in the *Journal of Philosophy*.

9. The "serious life" as imagined by the German nihilists is obviously different from the virtue of seriousness in Straussian political philosophy, or it is fundamentally transformed by philosophy. The seriousness of the German proto-nihilists is also a counterpoint to the probity of the biblical atheist in *Philosophy and Law*, who lives in a constant tension between the two highest aims of man: philosophical and religious wisdom. See in this context Strauss's emphasis on "the fact that the young nihilists were atheists," and more specifically, post-Nietzschean atheists of the Right (Strauss, "German Nihilism," 361–62).

10. Ibid., 359.
11. Strauss, *The City and Man*, 97; Plato, *Republic*, 471b-c.
12. Strauss, *The City and Man*, 95.
13. Ibid., 97.
14. Strauss, "German Nihilism," 359.
15. Ibid., 359–60.
16. Ibid., 355; cf. 356.
17. Emil Lederer, *State of the Masses: The Threat of the Classless Society* (New York: Norton, 1940). At the New School, the economist and sociologist Emil Lederer had been a co-founder of the University in Exile, and the dean of the Graduate Faculty (the successor of the University in Exile) until his death in 1939.
18. Ibid., 138.
19. Ibid., 149–50. Criticism was largely directed at Lederer's equation of classes and social groups.
20. Ibid., 151.
21. Ibid., 19.
22. Ibid., 159, 169.
23. Strauss, "German Nihilism," 360.
24. Nietzsche, *Thus Spoke Zarathustra*, Prologue, 5, in *The Nietzsche Reader*, 258.
25. Winston Churchill, speech to the House of Commons, May 13, 1940: "I would say to the House, as I said to those who have joined this Government: I have nothing to offer but blood, toil, tears and sweat."
26. Strauss, "German Nihilism," 372.
27. Ibid., 360.
28. Rosa Luxemburg, *The Crisis in the German Social Democracy* (*The "Junius" Pamphlet*) (New York: The Socialist Publication Society, 1919), 18.
29. Strauss, "German Nihilism," 360.
30. Strauss, "Historicism," *Toward* Natural Right and History*: Lectures and Essay by Leo Strauss*, 1937–1946, ed. J. A. Colen and Svetozar Minkov (Chicago/London: The University of Chicago Press, 2018), 68–93.

31. Strauss, "The Living Issues of German Postwar Philosophy," 118–25, 131–33; cf. *What Is Political Philosophy?*, 27.

32. Strauss, "Notes on Carl Schmitt," 117.

33. Strauss, "German Nihilism," 363–64.

34. Altman, "Leo Strauss on 'German Nihilism,'" 603; cf. 606 on the same quote: "Strauss compares the Nazis to clouds." Cf. also Steiner, *Weimar in Amerika*, 120.

35. Strauss, "German Nihilism," 364.

36. Ernst Jünger, "Über den Schmerz," in *Blätter und Steine* (Hamburg: Hanseatische Verlagsanstalt, 1934), 154–213: 212.

37. As to the personnel, Strauss's notion of the German nihilists is somewhat synthetic. He first mentioned Oswald Spengler, Arthur Moeller van den Bruck, Carl Schmitt, Alfred Baeumler, Ernst Jünger, and Martin Heidegger as the *teachers* of the young nihilists ("German Nihilism," 362) and referred to Spengler as "one of their greatest teachers" (363). With the exception of Heidegger (who does not fully fit into the picture for several reasons), these people belonged to what has retrospectively been named the "conservative revolution." Special emphasis is on Jünger, who was also named by Strauss as a "German nihilist" proper (369) and as one of the "spokesmen" of German nihilism (360). Jünger, as it were, combines most seamlessly the traits of a historicist, an aestheticist, and a lover of war. On Jünger, see also Strauss, "The Living Issues of German Postwar Philosophy," 128.

38. Strauss, *On Tyranny*, 208. The connection between Kojève's end state and the Nietzschean "last man" was first made in Strauss's letter to Kojève from August 22, 1948 (ibid., 239).

39. Ibid., 209–10. On the "conversion to philosophy" cf. *Persecution and the Art of Writing*, 109.

40. Strauss, "German Nihilism," 364.

41. Ibid., 370.

42. Ibid., 365.

43. Cf. ibid., 365–66.

44. Ibid., 365.

45. Ibid.

46. Ibid.

47. Ibid.

48. Ibid., 364.

49. Ibid., 363.

50. For the opposite case, compare Sheppard, *Leo Strauss and the Politics of Exile*, 96.

51. Strauss, "German Nihilism," 360.

52. Strauss, *Persecution and the Art of Writing*, 36. The emphasis on the nihilists' adolescence, then, partially confirms the suspicion that "German Nihilism"

is in some way related to the article "Persecution and the Art of Writing" that was written in the same year. But the link is not some "secret teaching": it is the fact that the young nihilists, just like those "puppies" of liberal education, are "potential philosophers" (ibid.).

53. Cf. Strauss, "German Nihilism," 370.

54. Ibid., 362.

55. "Cassirer represented the established academic position. He was a distinguished professor of philosophy but he was no philosopher. He was erudite but he had no passion" (Strauss, "Kurt Riezler," in *What is Political Philosophy?*, 246).

56. Walter Benjamin, "On the Concept of History," in *Selected Writings* 4, 392; trans. altered.

57. Michael André Bernstein, *Five Portraits. Modernity and the Imagination in Twentieth-Century German Writing* (Evanston: Northwestern University Press, 2000), 82–83.

58. Strauss, "The Living Issues of German Postwar Philosophy," 115.

59. Strauss, "German Nihilism," 370.

60. Cf. Strauss, *What is Political Philosophy?*, 41; *On Tyranny*, 192.

61. Strauss, "German Nihilism," 370–71.

62. Ibid., 371–72.

63. Strauss, "The Living Issues of German Postwar Philosophy," 115.

64. Ibid.

65. Ibid.

66. Strauss, "Existentialism," 306.

67. Strauss, "Philosophy as Rigorous Science and Political Philosophy," in *Studies in Platonic Political Philosophy*, 30.

68. Strauss, *Nietzsche's* Beyond Good and Evil*: A Course Offered in 1971/72*, ed. Mark Blitz, The Leo Strauss Center, University of Chicago; http://leostrauss-center.uchicago.edu/sites/default/files/Nietzsche's %20Beyond%20Good%20and%20 Evil.pdf, 1.

69. Strauss, "Existentialism," 305. See also his statement in a letter to Scholem written in January 1973: "Luther, Hamann and Heidegger seem to be the most conspicuous examples of high class intelligence and low class character which are probably more characteristic of Germany than any other country" (Strauss, *Gesammelte Schriften*, vol. 3, 766).

70. Strauss referred to the "other Germany" thesis in his Dewey review, arguing that the question "why Germany is different" is "evaded by those who refer to the 'Other Germany,' to the Germany which is not 'different,' which takes its bearings not by blood and iron nor by blood and soil but by philosophy." He dismissed this view by arguing that "the question concerns precisely not the mere existence but the political existence, the political efficiency, of the 'Other Germany'" (Strauss, *What Is Political Philosophy?*, 279).

71. Rutkoff and Scott, *New School*, 140.

72. Strauss, "The Re-Education of Axis Countries Concerning the Jews," *The Review of Politics* 69 (2007): 530–38.
73. Karl Popper, *Die offene Gesellschaft und ihre Feinde*, ix.
74. Cf. Adorno and Horkheimer, *Dialectic of Enlightenment*. Adorno had a knack for a certain type of historical short-circuit when it came to the intellectual origins of National Socialism. In *Minima Moralia*, he held that "there is a straight line of development" between the gospel of happiness and the construction of extermination camps (Adorno, *Minima Moralia: Reflections From Damaged Life* [London/New York: Verso, 2005], 63; cf. 79).
75. Adorno, Theodor W. et al., *The Positivist Dispute in German Sociology*, trans. Glyn Adeyand David Frisby (New York: Harper and Row, 1976).
76. Georg Lukács, *The Destruction of Reason* (Atlantic Highlands, NJ: Humanities, 1981); Jürgen Habermas, *The Philosophical Discourse of Modernity* (Cambridge, MA: Polity Press, 1990).

Chapter 12. From "Culture" to "Cultures"

1. For a proper sociohistorical explanation, see Fritz Ringer, *The Decline of the German Mandarins: The German Academic Community, 1890–1933* (Cambridge: Harvard University Press, 1969); for an adaptation of Ringer's general analysis to Strauss's specific situation, cf. Jürgen Gebhardt, "Leo Strauss: The Quest for Truth in Times of Perplexity," in *Hannah Arendt and Leo Strauss. German Émigrés and American Political Thought after World War II*, ed. Peter Graf Kielmannsegg, Horst Mewes, and Elisabeth Glaser-Schmidt (Cambridge/New York: Cambridge University Press, 1995), 81–104.
2. Some examples: David Biale, "Leo Strauss: The Philosopher as Weimar Jew," in *Leo Strauss's Thought: Toward a Critical Engagement*, ed. Alan Udoff (Boulder: Lynne Rienner, 1991), 31–40; Eugene Sheppard, *Leo Strauss and the Politics of Exile*; Adi Armon, "Just before the 'Straussians.' The Development of Leo Strauss's Political Thought from the Weimar Republic to America," *New German Critique* 37 (Autumn 2010): 173–98; Stephan Steiner, *Weimar in Amerika. Leo Strauss' politische Philosophie* (Tübingen: Mohr Siebeck, 2013).
3. Steven Aschheim, *Beyond the Border: The German-Jewish Legacy Abroad* (Princeton/Oxford: Princeton University Press, 2007), 87.
4. Quoted in Susan Hegeman, *Patterns for America: Modernism and the Concept of Culture* (Princeton: Princeton University Press, 1999), 3.
5. Warren I. Susman, "The Culture of the Thirties," in *Culture as History: The Transformation of American Society in the Twentieth Century* (New York: Pantheon, 1985), 153.
6. Matthew Arnold, *Culture and Anarchy*, ed. Jane Garnett (Oxford: Oxford University Press, 2006), 34.

7. Ibid., 6.
8. Ibid., 9 and passim. The phrase "sweetness and light" referred to "the two noblest of things" in Swift's *The Battle of the Books* (1697/1704); cf. Arnold, *Culture and Anarchy*, 40.
9. Susman, "The Culture of the Thirties," 153–54.
10. Grace de Laguna, "Cultural Relativism and Science," *The Philosophical Review* 51, no. 2 (1942): 141–66: 144.
11. Hegeman, *Patterns for America*, 4.
12. Claus-Dieter Krohn et al., eds., *Handbuch der deutschsprachigen Emigration 1933–1945*, 2nd ed. (Darmstadt: WBG, 2008).
13. This view is summed up in Krohn, *Handbuch der deutschsprachigen Emigration 1933–1945*, 446–66.
14. Cf. Joel Isaac, "The Curious Cultural Logic of Intellectual Migration: Rudolf Carnap and Leo Strauss," in *The Legacy of Leo Strauss*, ed. Tony Burns and James Connelly (Exeter: Imprint Academic, 2010), 161–80.
15. Cf. Steven Aschheim, *Beyond the Border*; see especially ch. 3, "Icons beyond the Border: Why Do We Love (Hate) Theodor Adorno, Hannah Arendt, Walter Benjamin, Franz Rosenzweig, Gershom Scholem, and Leo Strauss?," 81–118.
16. Allan Bloom, *The Closing of the American Mind* (New York: Simon and Schuster, 1987), 141–42.
17. Ibid., 146–47.
18. Cf. Till Kinzel, *Platonische Kulturkritik in Amerika: Studien zu Allan Blooms* The Closing of the American Mind (Berlin: Duncker und Humblot, 2002).
19. Strauss, *Natural Right and History*, 2.
20. Ibid., 1–2; cf. Ernst Troeltsch, "The Ideas of Natural Law and Humanity in World Politics," in Otto Gierke, *Natural Law and the Theory of Society* (Boston: Beacon Press, 1960), 201–22, esp. 217.
21. Strauss, "The Living Issues of German Postwar Philosophy," 115.

Chapter 13. Cannibalism

1. Strauss, *Natural Right and History*, 9.
2. Edward Westermarck, *The Origin and Development of the Moral Ideas* (New York: Johnson Reprint, 1971), 762.
3. Edward Westermarck, *Ethical Relativity* (London: Routledge, 2000), 184–85.
4. Ibid., 185; *The Origin and Development of the Moral Ideas*, 422–23, 553.
5. Jomo Kenyatta, *Facing Mount Kenya: The Tribal Life of the Gikuyu* (London: Mercury Books, 1965), 309, 134–35; cf. Steven Lukes, *Moral Relativism* (New York: Picador, 2008), 105–106.

6. Steven Lukes, *Liberals and Cannibals: The Implications of Diversity* (London/New York: Verso, 2003), 28.

7. Strauss, *Natural Right and History*, 3; see "Progress or Return?," in *Jewish Philosophy and the Crisis of Modernity*, 101; "Introduction to Maimonides' *The Guide of the Perplexed*," in *Leo Strauss on Maimonides*, 427.

8. Strauss, *What Is Political Philosophy?*, 51.

9. Strauss, "Social Science and Humanism," in *The Rebirth of Classical Political Rationalism*, 9.

10. Strauss, "Relativism," in *Relativism and the Study of Man*, ed. Helmut Schoeck and James W. Wiggins (Princeton: Van Nostrand, 1961), 142.

11. This section, stretching over more than four pages in the original publication ("Relativism," in *Relativism and the Study of Man*, 135–57: 141–45), was omitted in *The Rebirth of Classical Political Rationalism* (13–26). The editor explained that he had "omitted some portions of the original essay that were redundant" in the light of other chapters of the volume (ibid., 272n13), but the portion on cultural anthropology does not qualify as redundant. The missing section was restored in the reprint in Harry V. Jaffa, *Crisis of the Strauss Divided: Essays on Leo Strauss and Straussianism, East and West* (Lanham, MD: Rowman and Littlefield, 2012), 167–83.

12. Cf. Arnold Brecht, "The Rise of Relativism in Legal and Political Philosophy," *Social Research* 6 (1939): 392–414; cf. Brecht, "The Search for Absolutes in Political and Legal Philosophy," *Social Research* 7 (1940): 201–28.

13. Arnold Brecht, *Political Theory* (Princeton: Princeton University Press, 1959), 550, cf. 263–65.

14. Ibid.

15. Strauss, "Relativism," in *Relativism and the Study of Man*, 141–44.

16. Ruth Benedict, "The Uses of Cannibalism," in *An Anthroplogist at Work: Writings of Ruth Benedict*, ed. Margaret Mead (London: Secker and Warburg, 1959), 44–45.

17. Ibid., 47.

18. Ibid., 46, 48.

19. Ibid., 47.

20. Ibid., 47–48.

21. Ruth Benedict, *Patterns of Culture* (Boston/New York: Houghton Mifflin, 2005), 45.

22. Leo Strauss, *Plato's Gorgias*, ed. Devin Stauffer, The Leo Strauss Center, University of Chicago; https://leostrausscenter.uchicago.edu/sites/default/files/Plato's%20Gorgias%201963.pdf, 173.

23. Leo Strauss, *Seminar on Montesquieu, 1966*, ed. Thomas L. Pangle, The Leo Strauss Center, University of Chicago; http://leostrausscenter.uchicago.edu/sites/default/files/Montesquieu%2C%20spring%201966.pdf, 147.

24. Cf. Strauss, *Historicism and Modern Relativism*, Leo Strauss Papers, box 11, folder 10–11, 2. Strauss's slip of the tongue may be also understood as a witty criticism of Ruth Benedict. After all, the name of Benedict Arnold commonly stands for treason or betrayal in the United States.

25. See Strauss, "On a Forgotten Kind of Writing," in *What Is Political Philosophy?*, 227, with reference to Carl Becker and George Sabine.

26. Strauss, *Natural Right and History*, 125, see also 26; on the term *comprehensive view*, ibid., 25–27.

27. Strauss, *Historicism and Modern Relativism*, 30–31.

28. Cf. Franz Boas, "Aryans and Non-Aryans" (New York: Information and Service Associates, 1934); Ruth Benedict and Gene Weltfish, *The Races of Mankind* (New York: Public Affairs Committee, 1943).

29. See the selected correspondence in *An Anthroplogist at Work: Writings of Ruth Benedict*, 399–418, and Benedict's obituary for Boas, ibid., 419–22.

30. Cf. ibid., 210–11.

31. Ibid.

32. Ruth Benedict, *Patterns of Culture*, xxi–xxiii.

33. Ibid., 45.

34. Ibid.

35. Ibid., 3.

36. Ibid.

37. Ibid., 7.

38. Ibid., 11.

39. Melville J. Herskovits, *Man and his Works: the Science of Cultural Anthropology*, 7th print (New York: Knopf, 1960), 68.

40. Strauss, "Social Science and Humanism," in *The Rebirth of Classical Political Rationalism*, 12.

41. Cf. Steven Lukes, *Moral Relativism*.

42. Strauss, *Historicism and Modern Relativism*, 29.

43. Strauss, "Jerusalem and Athens," in *Jewish Philosophy and the Crisis of Modernity*, 379.

Chapter 14. Irrationalism and the Remnants of the Social Question

1. Cf. Strauss, *Natural Right and History*, introduction; "Restatement," in *On Tyranny*, 177–212.

2. Strauss, *Natural Right and History*, 4.

3. Ibid.

4. Cf. Strauss, *Philosophy and Law*, 135n1.

5. Strauss, "Relativism," 144.
6. Wilhelm Windelband, *A History of Philosophy: With Special Reference to the Formation and Development of Its Problems and Conceptions* (New York: Macmillan, 1901), 615–16.
7. Cf. Strauss, *Natural Right and History*, 7–8 and ch. II.
8. Max Weber, *Gesammelte Aufsätze zur Wissenschaftslehre* (Tübingen: Mohr, 1922), 35.
9. Ibid., 64, 133 ("unberechenbar"), 67–68 ("Undeutbarkeit").
10. Strauss, *Natural Right and History*, 43, cf. 60–61n22, 77.
11. Ibid., 47–48, cf. 44.
12. Ibid., 42, 49.
13. Alfred Baeumler, *Das Irrationalitätsproblem in der Ästhetik und Logik des 18. Jahrhunderts bis zur Kritik der Urteilskraft* (Darmstadt: WBG, 1967) (first publ. 1923).
14. Emil Lask, "Die Logik der Philosophie und die Seinskategorien," in *Gesammelte Schriften*, ed. Eugen Herrigel, vol. 2 (Tübingen: Mohr, 1923), 76; cf. 80 on "the rationality of form and the irrationality of the material."
15. Cf. Tom Rockmore, *Irrationalism: Lukács and the Marxist View of Reason* (Philadelphia: Temple University Press, 1992).
16. Georg Lukács, *History and Class Consciousness: Studies in Marxist Dialectics* (Cambridge: MIT Press, 1971), 116–19.
17. Cf. Lukács, *The Destruction of Reason* (Atlantic Highlands, NJ: Humanities, 1981), especially ch. III: "Nietzsche as Founder of Irrationalism in the Imperialist Period."
18. As to the difference between irrationality and irrationalism, see Lask's early comparison of the terms. Emil Lask, "Die Logik der philosophischen Kategorien," in *Gesammelte Schriften*, vol. 2, 212–22.
19. Strauss, *Natural Right and History*, 42.
20. This distinction between "crisis" and "catastrophe" was *not* drawn by Strauss, who used the two terms in different contexts without providing a link. As a rule of thumb, he referred to an ongoing "crisis" of the West that was rather confirmed and aggravated by the "catastrophes and horrors of a magnitude hitherto unknown" (Strauss, "Jerusalem and Athens," 399). His rare references to National Socialism leave open whether the catastrophes of National Socialism and Stalinism marked a decisive break or a mere continuation of the crisis of modernity.
21. Strauss, *Natural Right and History*, 44.
22. Ibid., 4.
23. Cf. Adorno/Horkheimer, *Dialectic of Enlightenment: Philosophical Fragments*, trans. E. Jephcott (Stanford: Stanford University Press, 2002), passim.
24. Karl Marx, *A Contribution to the Critique of Political Economy* (Chicago: Kerr, 1904), 13; cf. Adorno and Horkheimer, *Dialectic of Enlightenment*, 165; Horkheimer, "Die Juden und Europa," in *Gesammelte Schriften*, vol. 4: Schriften 1936–1941 (Frankfurt am Main: Fischer, 1988), 328; Adorno, "Über Statik und

Dynamik als sozialwissenschaftliche Kategorien," in *Gesammelte Schriften*, vol. 8: Soziologische Schriften I (Frankfurt am Main: Suhrkamp, 2003), 232–34.

25. Strauss, *Natural Right and History*, 20–21.
26. Ibid., 21.
27. Strauss, "Progress or Return?," in *Jewish Philosophy and the Crisis of Modernity*, 98, 101.
28. Ibid.; cf. *The City and Man*, 5.
29. Strauss, "Progress or Return?," 94.
30. Friedrich Engels, "Ludwig Feuerbach und der Ausgang der klassischen deutschen Philosophie," in Marx/Engels, *Werke*, vol. 21 (Berlin: Dietz, 1962), 263–307: 267–69.
31. Strauss, "Progress or Return," 97; cf. *Natural Right and History*, 176n10; *What Is Political Philosophy?*, 130.
32. Strauss, "Progress or Return," 97.
33. Strauss, *Spinoza's Critique of Religion*, 1.
34. Strauss, *Natural Right and History*, 143.
35. Strauss, "Relativism," 145–48.
36. Lukács, *The Destruction of Reason*, 576.
37. Strauss, "Relativism," 146.
38. Lukács, *The Destruction of Reason*, 228; *History and Class Consciousness*, 234–35.
39. Strauss, "Relativism," 147.
40. Strauss attributed this expression to the Austrian writer Robert Musil, apparently quoting from memory. The actual expression in Musil's novel *Der Mann ohne Eigenschaften* (1930) is *fortwursteln*. Cf. Strauss, "The Living Issues of Postwar German Philosophy," 124; Robert Musil, *Der Mann ohne Eigenschaften* (Reinbek: Rowohlt, 1980), 115, 195.
41. Strauss, "Relativism," 148.
42. Strauss, "Historicism," 76.
43. Strauss, *Natural Right and History*, 26n9.
44. Strauss, *What Is Political Philosophy?*, 27.
45. Strauss, "Historicism," 76; cf. "The Living Issues of German Postwar Philosophy," 125–31, on the turn from reason to authority; "German Nihilism" on liberal democrats, Nazis, and communists as covert historicists. Wherever Strauss described the flight of German philosophy and politics as a turn from reason to authority, that flight was facilitated by "history."
46. Strauss, *What Is Political Philosophy?*, 57; cf. "Historicism," 72, 75.
47. Strauss, *Natural Right and History*, 12.

Chapter 15. Two Types of Relativism

1. Cf. Strauss, *Natural Right and History*, 146–64.

2. Strauss, "Relativism," 137–38.
3. Strauss, "Social Science and Humanism," in *The Rebirth of Classical Political Philosophy*, 9. If not otherwise noted, all subsequent quotes ibid., 8–12.
4. Allan Bloom, *The Closing of the American Mind*, 25.
5. Ibid., 26.
6. Ibid., 29.
7. Strauss, "Social Science and Humanism," 10.
8. Ibid., 11.
9. Ibid., 12.
10. Ibid., 11.
11. Strauss, *Philosophy and Law*, 21.

Chapter 16. Jerusalem and Athens or Jerusalem versus Athens?

1. Pierre Manent, "Between Athens and Jerusalem," *First Things*, February 2002; www.firstthings.com/article/2012/02/between-athens-and-jerusalem.
2. Stanley Rosen, *Hermeneutics as Politics*, 112.
3. Strauss, "Jerusalem and Athens, 1950," The Leo Strauss Center, University of Chicago; https://leostrausscenter.uchicago.edu/jerusalem-and-athens; cf. "Progress or Return?," in *Jewish Philosophy and the Crisis of Modernity*, 104–105.
4. Strauss, "Jerusalem and Athens," in *Jewish Philosophy and the Crisis of Modernity*, 377, 380.
5. Ibid., 377.
6. Ibid.
7. Strauss, "Progress or Return?," 87.
8. Ibid., 89, 90. See also the "Preface" to *Spinoza's Critique of Religion*.
9. Jacob Taubes, *To Carl Schmitt: Letters and Reflections* (New York: Columbia University Press, 2013), 14.
10. Theodor W. Adorno, *Negative Dialectics* (London: Routledge, 1973), 3.
11. See the documentation in *Frankfurter Adorno Blätter*, vol. 6, ed. Rolf Tiedemann (Munich: Edition text + kritik, 2000); Wolfgang Kraushaar, *Frankfurter Schule und Studentenbewegung: Von der Flaschenpost zum Molotowcocktail* (Frankfurt am Main: Rogner und Bernhard, 1998).
12. From a leaflet of the Kommune, quoted in Rolf Tiedemann, "Iphigenie bei den Berliner Studenten," *Frankfurter Adorno Blätter* 6: 122–27: 122. Anti-American (as well as anti-Jewish) sentiments were an integral part of the radical students' ideology.
13. Cf. Philipp Felsch, *Der lange Sommer der Theorie: Geschichte einer Revolte, 1960–1990* (Munich: Beck, 2015).
14. Irving Kristol, *Neoconservatism: The Autobiography of an Idea* (New York: Free Press, 1995), 7.
15. Gary Dorrien, *The Neoconservative Mind: Politics, Culture, and the War of Ideology* (Philadelphia: Temple University Press, 1993), 73, 111. Ken Green cites

Gertrude Himmelfarb, Kristol's wife, who conveyed that it was *Persecution and the Art of Writing* that hooked Kristol up with Strauss's works (Green, *Leo Strauss on Maimonides*, 7–8). Kristol published a review of *Persecution and the Art of Writing* in *Commentary* 14 (1952): 392–97.

16. Hadley Arkes, "Athens and Jerusalem: The Legacy of Leo Strauss," in *Leo Strauss and Judaism. Jerusalem and Athens Critically Revisited*, ed. David Novak (Lanham, MD: Rowman and Littlefield, 1996), 1–23: 4.

17. Anne Norton, *Leo Strauss and the Politics of the American Empire* (New Haven/London: Yale University Press, 2004), 23.

18. Strauss, *Liberalism Ancient and Modern*, 3.

19. Ibid., 6.

20. Strauss, "German Nihilism," 362.

21. Jacob Taubes, *To Carl Schmitt: Letters and Reflections*, 9.

22. Cf. Karl I. Solibakke, "The Pride and Prejudice of the Western World: The Iconicity of the Great Books," *Postscripts* 6, nos. 1–3 (2010): 261–75.

23. Strauss, *Liberalism Ancient and Modern*, 5.

24. Friedrich Nietzsche, *Nachgelassene Fragmente 1882–1884*, *Werke*, vol. 10, ed. Giorgio Colli and Mazzino Montinari (Munich: dtv, 1980), 244.

25. Susan Orr, *Jerusalem and Athens: Reason and Revelation in the Works of Leo Strauss* (Lanham, MD: Rowman and Littlefield, 1995), 24.

26. Strauss, "Jerusalem and Athens," 377.

27. Ibid., 377–78.

28. Ibid., 378–79.

29. Hermann Cohen, "Das soziale Ideal bei Platon und den Propheten," in *Jüdische Schriften*, ed. Bruno Strauß (Berlin: Schwetschke, 1924), vol. 1, 306–30: 306. Eva Jospe translated: "Plato and the prophets constitute the most important well-springs of modern culture" (Cohen, "The Social Ideal as Seen by Plato and by the Prophets," in *Reason and Hope: Selections from the Jewish Writings of Hermann Cohen*, ed. Eva Jospe [Cincinnati: Hebrew Union College, 1993], 66–77: 66).

30. Strauss, "Jerusalem and Athens," 399.

31. Ibid.

32. Ibid.

33. Ibid.

34. Gilles Deleuze, *Proust and Signs* (Minneapolis: University of Minnesota Press, 2000), 105.

35. Ibid.

36. Raoul Mortley, *French Philosophers in Conversation* (London: Routledge, 1991), 18.

37. Howard Caygill, *Levinas and the Political* (London/New York: Routledge, 2003), 211n11; Robert Eaglestone, "Postcolonial Thought and Levinas's Double Vision," in *Radicalizing Levinas*, ed. Peter Atterton and Matthew Calarco (Albany: State University of New York Press, 2010), 57–68: 58. For Simon Critchley, too, the statement was "frankly racist" (Critchley, "Five Problems in Levinas's View of

Politics and a Sketch of a Solution to Them," in *Levinas, Law, Politics*, ed. Marinos Diamantides [Abingdon/New York: Routledge-Cavendish, 2007], 93–105: 96).

38. Sonia Sikka, "The Delightful Other: Portraits of the Feminine in Kierkegaard, Nietzsche, and Levinas," in *Feminist Interpretations of Emmanuel Levinas*, ed. Tina Chanter (University Park: The State University of Pennsylvania Press, 2001), 98–118: 113–14.

39. Mortley, *French Philosophers in Conversation*, 18.

40. Levinas, *Humanismus des anderen Menschen* (Hamburg: Meiner 1989), 140.

41. The question of Strauss's encounter with "otherness" can be understood in different ways. Grant Havers suggested viewing Jerusalem and Athens as each other's "other." In particular, Jerusalem is the "other" of reason. Cf. Grant Havers, "Between Athens and Jerusalem: Western Otherness in the Thought of Leo Strauss and Hannah Arendt," *The European Legacy* 9, no. 1 (2004): 19–29. This understanding is based on the inside view of the irreconcilable opposition between Jerusalem and Athens. We come to an entirely different understanding of "otherness" if we start from Jerusalem *and* Athens as the two pillars of the West, and hence view the dichotomy in its opposition to, or its encounter with, the non-West.

42. Strauss, *Liberalism Ancient and Modern*, 7.

43. Strauss, "Why We Remain Jews: Can Jewish Faith and History Still Speak to Us?," in *Jewish Philosophy and the Crisis of Modernity*, 336–37.

44. Ibid., 320; as to "folk dances" see also 345.

45. Strauss, *Liberalism Ancient and Modern*, 4.

46. Strauss, "1001 Nights," Leo Strauss Papers, box 20, folder 2.

47. Strauss, "Jerusalem and Athens," 378.

48. Strauss, *The City and Man*, 3, cf. 5 on the lesson of communism for the West.

49. Cf. Strauss, "Progress or Return?," in *Jewish Philosophy and the Crisis of Modernity*, passim; "The Three Waves of Modernity," in *An Introduction to Political Philosophy*; *The City and Man*, introduction.

50. Samuel P. Huntington, *The Clash of Civilizations and the Remaking of World Order* (New York: Simon and Schuster, 1996), 93.

51. Strauss, "Progress or Return?," 116, 117.

52. Samuel Huntington, *The Clash of Civilizations*, 51.

53. Niall Ferguson, *Civilization: The Six Killer Apps of Western Power* (London: Penguin, 2012).

54. Daniel Tanguay, *Leo Strauss: An Intellectual Biography*, 144–45.

55. Cf. Jeffrey A. Bernstein, *Leo Strauss on the Borders of Judaism, Philosophy, and History* (Albany: State University of New York Press, 2015), 5–11; Daniel Tanguay, *Leo Strauss: An Intellectual Biography*, 145–46.

56. Strauss, "Progress or Return?," 104.

57. Cf. David Janssens, *Between Athens and Jerusalem: Philosophy, Prophecy, and Politics in Leo Strauss's Early Thought* (Albany: State University of New York

Press, 2008); Jeffrey A. Bernstein, *Leo Strauss on the Borders of Judaism, Philosophy, and History* (Albany: State University of New York Press, 2015).

58. Strauss, "The Future of an Illusion," in *The Early Writings*, 204; J. W. Goethe, "Noten und Abhandlungen zum besseren Verständnis des West-östlichen Divans," *Werke*, Hamburger Ausgabe, vol. 2 (Munich: dtv, 1998), 208.

59. "But the question is precisely whether there is no alternative to Biblical faith on the one hand, and *modern* unbelief on the other. . . . The alternative which I have in mind, is exactly philosophy in its original or pre-modern meaning" (Strauss, "Reason or Revelation," 143).

60. Cassirer, *The Myth of the State*, 219.

61. Strauss, "The Future of an Illusion," in *The Early Writings*, 204; cf. *Persecution and the Art of Writing*, 107n35.

62. Cited in Heinrich Meier, *Leo Strauss and the Theologico-Political Problem*, 29n1.

63. Strauss, *Gesammelte Schriften* 3, 660, cf. 663, 666.

64. Strauss, "Reason and Revelation," 148–49.

65. Cf. Strauss, "Relativism," in *Relativism and the Study of Man*, 151; "Existentialism," 312–13.

66. Heinrich Meier, *Leo Strauss and the Theologico-Political Problem*, xvi n 17. The manuscript has been preserved but thus far neither been published nor made available.

67. Leo Strauss, "Jerualem and Athens, 1950," https://leostrausscenter.uchicago.edu/jerusalem-and-athens.

68. Strauss, "Plan of a Book Tentatively Entitled: *Philosophy and the Law: Historical Essays*," in *Jewish Philosophy and the Crisis of Modernity*, 468.

69. Strauss, "Reason and Revelation," 149–50.

70. Ibid., 161–64.

71. Ibid., 150.

72. Ibid., 29n1.

73. Strauss, *Philosophy and Law*, 31–32.

74. Strauss, "Progress or Return?," in *Jewish Philosophy and the Crisis of Modernity*, 117–32.

75. Strauss, *Natural Right and History*, 62–63.

76. Ibid., 75.

77. Ibid., 76.

78. Ibid., 76–78, cf. 65.

79. Strauss, "Jerusalem and Athens," 379.

80. In the second chapter Strauss changed this reference point to the "mission" of the prophets and Socrates; cf. ibid., 400–404.

81. Ibid., 379–80.

82. Cf. Walter Benjamin, *The Origin of German Tragic Drama* (London/New York: Verso, 1998), 155–57.

83. Strauss, "Jerusalem and Athens," 380.
84. Ibid., 380–81.
85. Ibid., 394. For this reason biblical criticism is not per se on the side of Athens. I beg to disagree in this respect with Kim A. Sorensen, *Discourses on Strauss: Reason and Revelation in Leo Strauss and His Critical Study of Machiavelli* (Notre Dame: University of Notre Dame Press, 2006), 32.
86. Strauss, "Progress or Return?," in *Jewish Philosophy and the Crisis of Modernity*, 94; "Why We Remain Jews," ibid., 344.
87. Strauss, "Jerusalem and Athens," 382.
88. Ibid.
89. Ibid., 381.
90. Ibid., 391, 392.
91. Ibid., 402.
92. Ibid.

Conclusion

1. Strauss, *What Is Political Philosophy?*, 230.
2. Strauss, *On Tyranny*, 25.
3. Ibid., 28; cf. 34–35.
4. Ibid., 78.
5. Ibid., 86.
6. Ibid., 55–56, 58–59.
7. Hans Blumenberg, *Work on Myth*, trans. Robert M. Wallace (Cambridge/London: MIT Press, 1985), 67–68.
8. Irving Kristol, "The Philosophers' Hidden Truth: *Persecution and the Art of Writing* by Leo Strauss," *Commentary*, October 1, 1952; www.commentarymagazine.com/articles/persecution-and-the-art-of-writing-by-leo-strauss/.
9. Cf. Plato, Seventh Letter, 341c-e.
10. Strauss, *Persecution and the Art of Writing*, 30; Plato, *Politeia*, 519b-d.
11. Ibid.
12. Strauss, "On a Forgotten Kind of Writing," in *What Is Political Philosophy?*, 232.
13. Strauss, *Gesammelte Schriften* 3, 550.
14. Strauss, "Religious Situation of the Present," in *Reorientation*, 230.
15. Strauss, *Persecution and the Art of Writing*, 185.
16. Strauss, *On Tyranny*, 28.
17. M. F. Burnyeat, *Explorations in Ancient and Modern Philosophy*, vol. 2 (Cambridge/New York: Cambridge University Press, 2012), 289–304.
18. Cf. Werner J. Dannhauser, "Leo Strauss: Becoming Naive Again," *The American Scholar* 44 (1974–75): 641, cf. 640.

19. Cf. Strauss, *Gesammelte Schriften* 3, 562.
20. Cf. Strauss, *What Is Political Philosophy?*, 32.
21. Strauss, *On Tyranny*, 205.
22. Cf. Strauss, *Persecution and the Art of Writing*, 205–206.
23. Cf. ibid.
24. Strauss, *On Tyranny*, 206.
25. Strauss, "What Can We Learn from Political Theory?," in *Toward Natural Right and History: Lectures and Essay by Leo Strauss*, 1937–1946, ed. J. A. Colen and Svetozar Minkov (Chicago/London: The University of Chicago Press, 2018), 33–51.
26. Strauss, *Liberalism Ancient and Modern*, 6.
27. Strauss, *Persecution and the Art of Writing*, 36.
28. Steven B. Smith, *Reading Leo Strauss: Politics, Philosophy, Judaism* (Chicago/London: The University of Chicago Press, 2006), 7.
29. Ibid.
30. Strauss, "The Problem of Socrates," in *The Rebirth of Classical Political Rationalism*, 142; cf. *Thoughts on Machiavelli*, 13.
31. All quotes from Paul Ricœur, *Freud and Philosophy: An Essay on Interpretation* (New Haven/London: Yale University Press, 1970), 33–36.
32. Werner J. Dannhauser, "Leo Strauss: Becoming Naive Again," 638.
33. Ibid., 640.

Bibliography

Adorisio, Chiara. "Philosophy of Religion or Political Philosophy?: The Debate between Leo Strauss and Julius Guttmann." *European Journal of Jewish Studies* 1 (2007): 135–55.

Adorno, Theodor W. *Critical Models: Interventions and Catchwords*. Translated by Henry W. Pickford (New York: Columbia University Press, 1998).

———. *Gesammelte Schriften* (Frankfurt am Main: Suhrkamp, 2003).

———. *Minima Moralia: Reflections From Damaged Life* (London/New York: Verso, 2005).

———. *Negative Dialectics*. Translated by E. B. Ashton (London: Routledge, 1973).

———. et al. *The Positivist Dispute in German Sociology*. Translated by Glyn Adey and David Frisby (New York: Harper and Row, 1976).

Adorno, Theodor W., and Max Horkheimer. *Dialectic of Enlightenment: Philosophical Fragments*. Translated by E. Jephcott (Stanford: Stanford University Press, 2002).

Adorno, Theodor W., and Thomas Mann. *Correspondence 1943–1955*. Edited by Christoph Gödde and Thomas Sprecher (Cambridge/Malden: Polity, 2006).

Ahlborn, Knud. "Das Meißnerfest der Freideutschen Jugend 1913." In *Grundschriften der deutschen Jugendbewegung*, edited by Werner Kindt (Düsseldorf/Köln: Diederichs, 1963), 105–15.

Altman, William H. F. "Leo Strauss on 'German Nihilism': Learning the Art of Writing." *Journal of the History of Ideas* 68, no. 4 (2007): 587–612.

———. *The German Stranger: Leo Strauss and National Socialism* (Lanham, MD: Lexington, 2011).

Altmann, Alexander. "Review of Julius Guttmann, *Philosophies of Judaism*." *Conservative Judaism* 19, no. 1 (1964): 73–77.

———. "The Encounter of Faith and Reason in the Western Tradition and its Significance Today." October 1961, unpublished tape recording, Leo Strauss Papers, box 67.

———. "Theology in Twentieth-Century German Jewry." *Leo Baeck Institute Year Book*, 1956, 193–216.

Arendt, Hannah. "Approaches to the 'German Problem.'" In *Essays in Understanding, 1930–1954: Formation, Exile, and Totalitarianism* (New York: Schocken, 1994), 106–20.

———. "The Jew as Pariah: A Hidden Tradition." *Jewish Social Studies* 6, no. 2 (1944): 99–122.

Arkes, Hadley. "Athens and Jerusalem: The Legacy of Leo Strauss." In *Leo Strauss and Judaism. Jerusalem and Athens Critically Revisited*, edited by David Novak (Lanham, MD: Rowman and Littlefield, 1996), 1–23.

Armon, Adi. "Just before the 'Straussians.' The Development of Leo Strauss's Political Thought from the Weimar Republic to America." *New German Critique* 37 (Autumn 2010): 173–98.

Arnold, Matthew. *Culture and Anarchy*. Edited by Jane Garnett (Oxford: Oxford University Press, 2006).

Aschheim, Steven. *Beyond the Border: The German-Jewish Legacy Abroad* (Princeton/Oxford: Princeton University Press, 2007).

Baeumler, Alfred. *Das Irrationalitätsproblem in der Ästhetik und Logik des 18. Jahrhunderts bis zur Kritik der Urteilskraft* (Darmstadt: WBG, 1967).

Batnitzky, Leora. *Leo Strauss and Emmanuel Levinas: Philosophy and the Politics of Revelation* (Cambridge: Cambridge University Press, 2006).

Benardete, Seth. "Strauss on Plato." In *The Argument of the Action: Essays on Greek Poetry and Philosophy*, edited by Ronna Burger and Michael Davis (Chicago/London: The University of Chicago Press, 2000), 407–17.

Benedict, Ruth. *An Anthroplogist at Work: Writings of Ruth Benedict*. Edited by Margaret Mead (London: Secker and Warburg, 1959).

———. *Patterns of Culture* (Boston/New York: Houghton Mifflin, 2005).

Benedict, Ruth, and Gene Weltfish. *The Races of Mankind* (New York: Public Affairs Committee, 1943).

Benjamin, Walter. *The Arcades Project* (Cambridge, MA/London: Belknap Press of Harvard University Press, 1999).

———. *Gesammelte Schriften*. Edited by Rolf Tiedemann (Frankfurt am Main: Suhrkamp, 1997).

———. "On the Concept of History." In *Selected Writings*, vol. 4: 1938–1940, edited by Howard Eiland and Michael W. Jennings (Cambridge, MA/London: Belknap Press, 2003), 389–400.

———. *One-Way Street and Other Writings* (London: NLB, 1979).

———. *The Origin of German Tragic Drama* (London/New York: Verso, 1998).

———, and Gershom Scholem. *The Correspondence of Walter Benjamin and Gershom Scholem, 1932–1940*. Edited by G. Scholem (Cambridge: Harvard University Press, 1992).

Bernstein, Jeffrey A. *Leo Strauss on the Borders of Judaism, Philosophy, and History* (Albany: State University of New York Press, 2015).

Bernstein, Michael André. *Five Portraits: Modernity and the Imagination in Twentieth-Century German Writing* (Evanston: Northwestern University Press, 2000).
Biale, David. "Leo Strauss: The Philosopher as Weimar Jew." In *Leo Strauss's Thought: Toward a Critical Engagement*, edited by Alan Udoff (Boulder: Lynne Rienner, 1991), 31–40.
Bloom, Allan. *The Closing of the American Mind* (New York: Simon and Schuster, 1987).
Blumenberg, Hans. *Work on Myth*. Translated by Robert M. Wallace (Cambridge/London: MIT Press, 1985).
Boas, Franz. *Aryans and Non-Aryans* (New York: Information and Service Associates, 1934).
Brecht, Arnold. *Political Theory* (Princeton: Princeton University Press, 1959).
———. "The Rise of Relativism in Legal and Political Philosophy." *Social Research* 6 (1939): 392–414.
———. "The Search for Absolutes in Political and Legal Philosophy." *Social Research* 7 (1940): 201–28.
Brinton, Crane. *Nietzsche* (New York: Harper and Row, 1965).
Burnyeat, M. F. *Explorations in Ancient and Modern Philosophy*, vol. 2 (Cambridge/New York: Cambridge University Press, 2012).
Butler, Judith. *Parting Ways: Jewishness and the Critique of Zionism* (New York: Columbia University Press, 2012).
Butler, Rohan. *The Roots of National Socialism* (London: Faber and Faber, 1941).
Cassirer, Ernst. *An Essay on Man: An Introduction to a Philosophy of Human Culture* (New Haven: Yale University Press, 1945).
———. *Ausgewählter wissenschaftlicher Briefwechsel*. Edited by John Michael Krois (Hamburg: Meiner, 2009).
———. *Ernst Cassirer on Form and Technology*. Edited by Aud Sissel Hoel and Ingvild Folkvord (Basingstoke/New York: Palgrave Macmillan, 2012).
———. *Language and Myth* (New York: Dover, 1946).
———. "Form und Technik." In *Gesammelte Werke*, vol. 17 (Hamburg: Meiner, 2004).
———. "Paul Natorp." In *Gesammelte Werke*, vol. 23 (Hamburg: Meiner, 2006), 197–226.
———. "The Myth of the State." In *Gesammelte Werke*, vol. 24 (Hamburg: Meiner, 2007), 251–66.
———. *The Myth of the State* (New Haven/London: Yale University Press, 1974).
———. *The Philosophy of Symbolic Forms*, vol. 1: Language (New Haven/London: Yale University Press, 1953).
———. *The Philosophy of Symbolic Forms*, vol. 2: Myth (New Haven/London: Yale University Press, 1955).
———. *The Philosophy of Symbolic Forms*, vol. 3: The Phenomenology of Knowledge (New Haven/London: Yale University Press, 1957).

———. *The Philosophy of the Enlightenment* (Princeton: Princeton University Press, 195).

———. *The Warburg Years (1919–1933): Essays on Language, Art, Myth, and Technology*. Edited by S. G. Lofts (New Haven/London: Yale University Press, 2013).

———. *Zu Philosophie und Politik*, Nachgelassene Manuskripte und Texte, vol. 9. Edited by John Michael Krois (Hamburg: Meiner, 2008).

Cassirer, Toni. *Mein Leben mit Ernst Cassirer* (Hildesheim: Gerstenberg, 1981).

Caygill, Howard. *Levinas and the Political* (London/New York: Routledge, 2003).

Cohen, Hermann. *Ästhetik des reinen Gefühls*, vol. 2, Werke, vol. 9 (Hildesheim: Olms, 2005).

———. *Der Begriff der Religion im System der Philosophie*, Werke, vol. 10 (Hildesheim: Olms, 2002).

———. *Einleitung mit kritischem Nachtrag zur neunten Auflage der Geschichte des Materialismus von Friedrich Albert Lange*, Werke, vol. 5 [part 2]. Edited by H. Holzhey (Hildesheim: Olms, 1984).

———. *Ethics of Maimonides*. Translated by Almut Sh. Bruckstein (Madison: The University of Wisconsin Press, 2004).

———. *Ethik des reinen Willens*, Werke, vol. 7, part 2 (Hildesheim: Olms, 2008).

———. *Jüdische Schriften*. 3 vols. (Berlin: Schwetschke, 1924).

———. *Logik der reinen Erkenntnis*, Werke, vol. 6 (Hildesheim: Olms, 2005).

———. *Religion der Vernunft aus den Quellen des Judentums* (Frankfurt am Main: J. Kauffmann, 1929).

———. *Religion of Reason out of the Sources of Judaism*. Translated by Simon Kaplan (New York: Ungar, 1972).

———. "Religion und Sittlichkeit." In Werke, vol. 15: *Kleinere Schriften 4: 1907–1912*. Edited by H. Wiedebach (Hildesheim: Olms, 2009), 1–101.

———. "The Social Ideal as Seen by Plato and by the Prophets." In *Reason and Hope: Selections from the Jewish Writings of Hermann Cohen*, edited by Eva Jospe (Cincinnati: Hebrew Union College, 1993), 66–77.

Critchley, Simon. "Five Problems in Levinas's View of Politics and a Sketch of a Solution to Them." In *Levinas, Law, Politics*, edited by Marinos Diamantides (Abingdon/New York: Routledge-Cavendish 2007), 93–105.

Dannhauser, Werner J. "Leo Strauss: Becoming Naive Again." *The American Scholar* 44 (1974–75): 636–42.

de Laguna, Grace. "Cultural Relativism and Science." *The Philosophical Review* 51, no. 2 (1942): 141–66.

Deleuze, Gilles. *Proust and Signs* (Minneapolis: University of Minnesota Press, 2000).

Deutscher, Isaac. *The Non-Jewish Jew and Other Essays* (London: Oxford University Press, 196).

Dewey, John. *German Philosophy and Politics*, The Middle Works, 1899–1924, Vol. 8: *Essays on Education and Politics, 1915*. Edited by Jo Ann Boydston (Carbondale/Edwardsville: Southern Illinois University Press, 1985).

———. "Philosophy and Civilization." In *The Later Works, 1925–1953*, vol. 3: *1927–1928*. Edited by Jo Ann Boydston (Carbondale/Edwardsville: Southern Illinois University Press, 1984), 3–10.

———. "The Tragedy of the German Soul: Egotism in German Philosophy." In The Middle Works, 1899–1924, vol. 10: *Journal Articles, Essays, and Miscellany Published in the 1916–1917 Period*. Edited by Jo Ann Boydston (Carbondale/Edwardsville: Southern Illinois University Press, 2008), 305–309.

Dorrien, Gary. *The Neoconservative Mind: Politics, Culture, and the War of Ideology* (Philadelphia: Temple University Press, 1993).

Eaglestone, Robert. "Postcolonial Thought and Levinas's Double Vision." In *Radicalizing Levinas*, edited by Peter Atterton and Matthew Calarco (Albany: State University of New York Press, 2010), 57–68.

Engels, Friedrich. "Ludwig Feuerbach und der Ausgang der klassischen deutschen Philosophie." In Marx/Engels, *Werke*, vol. 21 (Berlin: Dietz, 1962), 263–307.

Feldman, Seymour. *Philosophy in a Time of Crisis. Don Isaac Abravael: Defender of the Faith* (New York/London: Routledge Curzon, 2003).

Felsch, Philipp. *Der lange Sommer der Theorie: Geschichte einer Revolte, 1960–1990* (Munich: Beck, 2015).

Ferguson, Niall. *Civilization: The Six Killer Apps of Western Power* (London: Penguin, 2012).

Fischer, Lars. "After the Strauss Wars." *East European Jewish Affairs* 40, no. 1 (2010): 61–79.

Foucault, Michel. "Nietzsche, Freud, Marx." In *Aesthetics, Method, and Epistemology*, edited by James D. Faubion (New York: The Free Press, 1998), 269–78.

Freud, Sigmund. *The Standard Edition of the Complete Psychological Works*, vol. 21 (1927–1931). Edited by James Strachey (London: The Hogarth Press, 1961).

Gadamer, Hans-Georg. *Philosophical Apprenticeships*. Translated by Robert R. Sullivan (Cambridge, MA/London: MIT Press, 1985).

Gebhardt, Jürgen. "Leo Strauss: The Quest for Truth in Times of Perplexity." In *Hannah Arendt and Leo Strauss. German Émigrés and American Political Thought after World War II*, edited by Peter Graf Kielmannsegg, Horst Mewes, and Elisabeth Glaser-Schmidt (Cambridge/New York: Cambridge University Press, 1995), 81–104.

Goethe, Johann Wolfgang. *Werke*, Hamburger Ausgabe, vol. 2 (Munich: dtv, 1998).

Gratry, Alphonse. *Les Sophistes et la critique* (Paris: Douniol/Lecoffre, 1864).

Graupe, Heinz. *Die Stellung der Religion im systematischen Denken der Marburger Schule* (Berlin: [no publ.], 1930).

Green, Kenneth Hart. *Jew and Philosopher: The Return to Maimonides in the Jewish Thought of Leo Strauss* (Albany: State University of New York Press, 1993).

———. *Leo Strauss and the Rediscovery of Maimonides* (Chicago/London: The University of Chicago Press, 2013).

Gunnell, John G. *The Descent of Political Theory* (Chicago/London: The University of Chicago Press, 1993).
Guttmann, Julius. *Die Philosophie des Judentums* (Munich: Reinhardt, 1933).
———. "Existence and Idea: Critical Observations on the Existential Philosophy." In *Scripta Hierosolymitana*, vol. 6: Studies in Philosophy. Edited by S. H. Bergman (Jerusalem: Magnes, 196), 9–40.
———. "Philosophie der Religion oder Philosophie des Gesetzes?," *Proceedings of the Israel Academy of Sciences and Humanities* 5, no. 6 (1974): 148–73.
———. *Philosophies of Judaism: The History of Jewish Philosophy from Biblical Times to Franz Rosenzweig*. Translated by David W. Silverman (Garden City: Anchor Books, 1966).
———. *Religion und Wissenschaft im mittelalterlichen und im modernen Denken* (Berlin: Philo, 1922).
Guttmann, Yitzhak Julius. *On the Philosophy of Religion*. Edited by Nathan Rotenstreich (Jerusalem: Magnes Press, 1976).
Habermas, Jürgen. *The Philosophical Discourse of Modernity* (Cambridge, MA: Polity Press, 1990).
Hartman, Geoffrey H. *The Fateful Question of Culture* (New York: Columbia University Press, 1997).
Hartmann, Nicolai. "Der philosophische Gedanke und seine Geschichte." In *Kleinere Schriften II: Abhandlungen zur Philosophie-Geschichte* (Berlin: de Gruyter, 1957), 1–48.
Havers, Grant. "Between Athens and Jerusalem: Western Otherness in the Thought of Leo Strauss and Hannah Arendt." *The European Legacy* 9, no. 1 (2004): 19–29.
Hegeman, Susan. *Patterns for America: Modernism and the Concept of Culture* (Princeton: Princeton University Press, 1999).
———. *The Cultural Return* (Berkeley: The University of California Press, 2012).
Heidegger, Martin. *Kant and the Problem of Metaphysics*. Translated by Richard Taft (Bloomington/Indianapolis: Indiana University Press, 1990).
Heidegger, Martin/Karl Löwith. *Briefwechsel 1919–1973*. Edited by Alfred Denker (Freiburg/Munich: Karl Alber, 2017).
Heinemann, Fritz. "Philosophie und Gesetz." *Frankfurter Israelitisches Gemeindeblatt* 14, no. 3 (1935): 107–108.
Herskovits, Melville J. *Man and His Works: The Science of Cultural Anthropology*, 7th print (New York: Knopf, 1960).
Hocking, William Ernest. "Political Philosophy in Germany." In John Dewey, *The Middle Works, 1899–1924*, Vol. 8: *Essays on Education and Politics, 1915*. Edited by Jo Ann Boydston (Carbondale/Edwardsville: Southern Illinois University Press, 1985), 473–77.
Holzhey, Helmut. "Der systematische Ort der 'Religion der Vernunft' im Gesamtwerk Hermann Cohens." In *"Religion der Vernunft aus den Quellen des Judentums": Tradition und Ursprungsdenken in Hermann Cohens Spätwerk*, edited by Holzhey et al. (Hildesheim: Olms, 1998), 37–58.

Horkheimer, Max. *Gesammelte Schriften*, vol. 4: *Schriften 1936–1941* (Frankfurt am Main: Fischer, 198).

Horwitz, Robert. "John Dewey." In *History of Political Philosophy*, edited by Leo Strauss and Joseph Cropsey, 3rd ed. (Chicago/London: The University of Chicago Press, 1987), 851–69.

Howse, Robert. *Leo Strauss: Man of Peace* (New York: Cambridge University Press, 2014).

Hula, Erich. "Review of Ernst Fraenkel's *The Dual State*." *Social Research* 9 (1942): 271–73.

Huntington, Samuel P. *The Clash of Civilizations and the Remaking of World Order* (New York: Simon and Schuster, 1996).

Husik, Isaac. *A History of Mediaeval Jewish Philosophy* (New York: Macmillan, 1916).

Isaac, Joel. "The Curious Cultural Logic of Intellectual Migration: Rudolf Carnap and Leo Strauss." In *The Legacy of Leo Strauss*, edited by Tony Burns and James Connelly (Exeter: Imprint Academic, 2010), 161–80.

Jaffa, Harry V. *Crisis of the Strauss Divided: Essays on Leo Strauss and Straussianism*, East and West (Lanham, MD: Rowman and Littlefield, 2012).

Janssens, David. *Between Athens and Jerusalem: Philosophy, Prophecy, and Politics in Leo Strauss's Early Thought* (Albany: State University of New York Press 2008).

Johnson, Alvin. "War and the Scholar." *Social Research* 9 (1942): 1–3.

Jospe, Alfred. *Die Unterscheidung von Mythos und Religion bei Hermann Cohen und Ernst Cassirer in ihrer Bedeutung für die jüdische Religionsphilosophie* (Oppeln: [no publ.], 1932).

Jünger, Ernst. "Über den Schmerz." In *Blätter und Steine* (Hamburg: Hanseatische Verlagsanstalt, 1934), 154–213.

Kenyatta, Jomo. *Facing Mount Kenya: The Tribal Life of the Gikuyu* (London: Mercury Books, 1965).

Kinkel, Walter. *Hermann Cohen: Eine Einführung in sein Werk* (Stuttgart: Strecker und Schröder, 1924).

Kinzel, Till. *Platonische Kulturkritik in Amerika: Studien zu Allan Blooms* The Closing of the American Mind (Berlin: Duncker und Humblot, 2002).

Klingenstein, Susanne. "Of Greeks and Jews: Old Letters Throw New Light on Leo Strauss." *The Weekly Standard*, October 25, 2010; www.weeklystandard.com/of-greeks-and-jews/article/508813.

Kraushaar, Wolfgang. *Frankfurter Schule und Studentenbewegung: Von der Flaschenpost zum Molotowcocktail* (Frankfurt am Main: Rogner und Bernhard, 1998).

Kristol, Irving. *Neoconservatism: The Autobiography of an Idea* (New York: Free Press, 1995).

———. "The Philosophers' Hidden Truth: *Persecution and the Art of Writing* by Leo Strauss," *Commentary*, October 1, 1952; www.commentarymagazine.com/articles/persecution-and-the-art-of-writing-by-leo-strauss/.

Krohn, Claus-Dieter. *Handbuch der deutschsprachigen Emigration 1933–1945*, 2nd ed. (Darmstadt: WBG, 2008).

———. *Wissenschaft im Exil. Deutsche Sozial- und Wirtschaftswissenschaftler in den USA und die New School for Social Research* (Frankfurt am Main/New York: Campus, 1987).

Kuhn, Helmut. *Der Staat: Eine philosophische Darstellung* (Munich: Kösel, 1967).

Lampert, Laurence. *The Enduring Importance of Leo Strauss* (Chicago: University of Chicago Press, 2013).

Landauer, Carl. "Comment on Mayer's Analysis of National Socialism." *Social Research* 9, no. 3 (1942): 402–404.

Lask, Emil. *Gesammelte Schriften*. Edited by Eugen Herrigel, vol. 2 (Tübingen: Mohr, 1923).

Laski, Harold J. *Studies in the Problem of Sovereignty* (New Haven: Yale University Press, 1917).

Lazier, Benjamin. *God Interrupted: Heresy and the European Imagination between the World Wars* (Princeton: Princeton University Press, 2008).

Lederer, Emil. *State of the Masses: The Threat of the Classless Society* (New York: Norton, 1940).

Leisegang, Hans. *Die Religionsphilosophie der Gegenwart* (Berlin: Junker und Dünnhaupt, 1930).

Lepenies, Wolf. *The Seduction of Culture in German History* (Princeton: Princeton University Press, 2006).

Levinas, Emmanuel. *Humanismus des anderen Menschen* (Hamburg: Meiner, 1989).

Litt, Theodor. *Möglichkeiten und Grenzen der Pädagogik: Abhandlungen zur gegenwärtigen Lage von Erziehung und Erziehungstheorie* (Leipzig/Berlin: Teubner, 1926).

Löwith, Karl. *Aufsätze und Vorträge 1930–1970* (Stuttgart: Kohlhammer, 1971).

———. *Gesammelte Abhandlungen: Zur Kritik der geschichtlichen Existenz* (Stuttgart: Kohlhammer, 1960).

———. *Mein Leben in Deutschland vor und nach 1933: Ein Bericht* (Frankfurt am Main: Fischer, 1989).

———. *My Life in Germany Before and After 1933: A Report*. Translated by Elizabeth King (Urbana/Chicago: University of Illinois Press, 1994).

———. *Sämtliche Schriften*, vol. 6: *Nietzsche* (Stuttgart: Metzler, 1987).

Lukács, Georg. *History and Class Consciousness: Studies in Marxist Dialectics* (Cambridge: MIT Press, 1971).

———. *The Destruction of Reason* (Atlantic Highlands, NJ: Humanities Press, 1981).

Lukes, Steven. *Liberals and Cannibals: The Implications of Diversity* (London/New York: Verso, 2003).

———. *Moral Relativism* (New York: Picador, 2008).

Luxemburg, Rosa. *The Crisis in the German Social Democracy (The "Junius" Pamphlet)* (New York: The Socialist Publication Society, 1919).

Manent, Pierre. "Between Athens and Jerusalem," First Things, February 2002; www.firstthings.com/article/2012/02/between-athens-and-jerusalem.

Marx, Karl. *A Contribution to the Critique of Political Economy* (Chicago: Kerr, 1904).

Marx, Karl, and Friedrich Engels. *Collected Works*, vol. 3: 1843–44 (New York: International Publishers, 1975).
Mayer, Carl. "On the Intellectual Origin of National Socialism." *Social Research* 9, no. 2 (1942): 225–47.
McCormick, John P. "Post-Enlightenment Sources of Political Authority: Biblical Atheism, Political Theology, and the Schmitt-Strauss Exchange." *History of European Ideas* 37, no. 2 (2011): 175–80.
McGovern, William Montgomery. *From Luther to Hitler: The History of Fascist-Nazi Political Philosophy* (New York: Houghton Mifflin, 1973).
Meier, Heinrich. *Carl Schmitt and Leo Strauss: The Hidden Dialogue* (Chicago/London: The University of Chicago Press, 1995).
———. *Leo Strauss and the Theologico-Political Problem* (New York: Cambridge University Press, 200).
Meinecke, Friedrich. *Die deutsche Katastrophe* (Wiesbaden: Brockhaus, 1946).
———. *The German Catastrophe* (Cambridge: Harvard University Press, 1950).
Mendes-Flohr, Paul. "The Philosophy of Religion or the Philosophy of Law?" *Archivio di filosofia* 1, no. 2 (2007): 145–56.
———, and Jehuda Reinharz, eds. *The Jew in the Modern World: A Documentary History*, 2nd ed. (New York/Oxford: Oxford University Press, 1995).
Meyer, Thomas. "Die Macht der Ideen. Albert Salomon im Kontext zweier ideengeschichtlicher Debatten: Weimar und Exil." In *Verlassene Stufen der Reflexion. Albert Salomon und die Aufklärung der Soziologie*, edited by Peter Gostmann and Claudius Härpfer (Wiesbaden: VS Verlag für Sozialwissenschaften, 2011), 157–77.
———. *Zwischen Philosophie und Gesetz. Jüdische Philosophie und Theologie von 1933 bis 1938* (Leiden/Boston: Brill, 2009).
Miner, Robert C. "Leo Strauss's Adherence to Nietzsche's 'Atheism From Intellectual Probity.'" *Perspectives on Political Science* 41 (2012): 155–64.
———. "Nietzsche, Schmitt, and Heidegger in the Anti-Liberalism of Leo Strauss." *Telos* 60 (2012): 9–27.
Mortley, Raoul. *French Philosophers in Conversation* (London: Routledge, 1991).
Mouffe, Chantal. *On the Political* (London/New York: Routledge, 2005).
Musil, Robert. *Der Mann ohne Eigenschaften* (Reinbek: Rowohlt, 1980).
Natorp, Paul. *Die Weltalter des Geistes* (Jena: Diederichs, 1918).
———. *Hermann Cohens philosophische Leistung unter dem Gesichtspunkte des Systems* (Berlin: Reuther und Reichard, 1918).
———. *Philosophische Systematik* (Hamburg: Meiner, 2000).
Niebuhr, Reinhold. *Christianity and Power Politics* (New York: Charles Scribner's Sons, 1940).
Nietzsche, Friedrich. *Beyond Good and Evil: Prelude to a Philosophy of the Future* (Cambridge/New York: Cambridge University Press, 200).
———. *Kritische Studienausgabe*, vol. 10: *Nachgelassene Fragmente 1882–1884*. Edited by Giorgio Colli and Mazzino Montinari (Munich: dtv, 1980).

———. *Kritische Studienausgabe*, vol. 12: *Nachgelassene Fragmente 1885–1887*. Edited by Giorgio Colli and Mazziono Montinari (Munich: dtv, 1988).

———. *The Anti-Christ, Ecce Homo, Twilight of the Idols, and Other Writings* (Cambridge: Cambridge University Press, 2005).

———. *The Nietzsche Reader*. Edited by Keith A. Pearson and Duncan Large (Malden/Oxford/Carlton: Blackwell, 2006).

Norton, Anne. *Leo Strauss and the Politics of American Empire* (New Haven/London: Yale University Press, 2004).

Orr, Susan. *Jerusalem and Athens: Reason and Revelation in the Works of Leo Strauss* (Lanham, MD: Rowman and Littlefield, 1995).

Parens, Joshua. "Escaping the Scholastic Paradigm: The Dispute between Strauss and his Contemporaries about How to Approach Islamic and Jewish Medieval Philosophy." In *Encountering the Medieval in Modern Jewish Thought*, edited by James A. Diamond and Aaron W. Hughes (Leiden/Boston: Brill, 2012), 203–27.

———. *Leo Strauss and the Recovery of Medieval Political Philosophy* (Rochester: University of Rochester Press, 2016).

Plessner, Helmuth. *Die verspätete Nation: Über die politische Verführbarkeit bürgerlichen Geistes* (Frankfurt am Main: Suhrkamp, 1974).

Popper, Karl. *Die offene Gesellschaft und ihre Feinde*, 8th ed. (Tübingen: Mohr Siebeck, 2002).

Rashkover, Randi L. "Justifying Philosophy and Restoring Revelation: Assessing Strauss's Medieval Return." In *Encountering the Medieval in Modern Jewish Thought*, edited by James A. Diamond and Aaron W. Hughes (Leiden/Boston: Brill, 2012), 229–57.

Rethelyi, Mari. "Guttmann's Critique of Strauss's Modernist Approach to Medieval Philosophy: Some Arguments Toward a Counter-Critique." *The Journal of Textual Reasoning* 3, no. 1 (2004); http://jtr.lib.virginia.edu/volume-3-number-1/.

Ricœur, Paul. *Freud and Philosophy: An Essay on Interpretation* (New Haven/London: Yale University Press, 1970).

Ringer, Fritz. *The Decline of the German Mandarins: The German Academic Community, 1890–1933* (Cambridge: Harvard University Press, 1969).

Rockmore, Tom. *Irrationalism: Lukács and the Marxist View of Reason* (Philadelphia: Temple University Press, 1992).

Rosen, Stanley. *Hermeneutics as Politics* (New Haven/London: Yale University Press, 2003).

Rosenzweig, Franz. *Briefe und Tagebücher*, vol. 2: 1928–1929 (Dordrecht: Springer, 1979).

———. "Der Dozent: Eine persönliche Erinnerung." *Neue jüdische Monatshefte* 17/18 (1918): 376–78.

———. "Einleitung." In Hermann Cohen, *Jüdische Schriften*, vol. 1 (Berlin: Schwetschke, 1924), xii–lxiv.

———. *Ninety-Two Poems and Hymns of Yehuda Halevi*. Edited by Richard A. Cohen (Albany: State University of New York Press, 2000).

Rutkoff, Peter M., and William B. Scott. *New School. A History of The New School for Social Research* (New York: The Free Press, 1986).
Salomon, Albert. "The Spirit of the Soldier and Nazi Militarism." *Social Research* 9 (1942): 82–103.
Santayana, George. *Egotism in German Philosophy* (London/Toronto: J. M. Dent and Sons, 1916).
———. "German Philosophy and Politics [review]." *The Journal of Philosophy, Psychology and Scientific Methods* 12, no. 24 (1915): 645–49.
Schleiermacher, Friedrich. *On Religion: Speeches to Its Cultured Despisers* (Cambridge: Cambridge University Press, 1996).
Schmitt, Carl. "Der Begriff des Politischen." *Archiv für Sozialwissenschaft und Sozialpolitik* 58, no 1 (1927): 1–33.
———. *Der Begriff des Politischen* (Munich: Duncker und Humblot, 1932).
———. *Der Begriff des Politischen* (Hamburg: Hanseatische Verlagsanstalt, 1933).
———. *Der Begriff des Politischen: Text von 1932 mit einem Vorwort und drei Corollarien* (Berlin: Duncker und Humblot, 1963).
———. "Die europäische Kultur in Zwischenstadien der Neutralisierung." *Europäische Revue* 5, no. 8 (1929): 517–30.
———. *Political Theology: Four Chapters on the Concept of Sovereignty*. Translated by George Schwab (Cambridge, MA/London: MIT Press, 1985).
———. "State Ethics and the Pluralist State." In *Weimar: A Jurisprudence of Crisis*, edited by Arthur J. Jacobsen and Bernhard Schlink (Berkeley: University of California Press, 2000), 300–12.
———. *The Concept of the Political*. Translated by George Schwab, expanded edition (Chicago/London: The University of Chicago Press, 2007).
Scholem, Gershom. *Judaica*, vol. 1 (Frankfurt am Main: Suhrkamp, 1963).
———. *Judaica*, vol. 6: *Die Wissenschaft vom Judentum* (Frankfurt am Main: Suhrkamp, 1997).
Schweid, Eliezer. "Religion and Philosophy: The Scholarly-Theological Debate between Julius Guttmann and Leo Strauss." In *Maimonidean Studies*, edited by Arthur Hyman, vol. 1 (New York: Yeshiva University Press, 1990), 163–95.
Seeskin, Kenneth. *Jewish Philosophy in a Secular Age* (Albany: State University of New York Press 1990).
Sen, Amartya. *Identity and Violence: The Illusion of Destiny* (London/New York: Penguin, 2006).
Sermoneta, Josef. "Pour une histoire du thomisme juif." In *Aquinas and Problems of His Time*, edited by G. Verbeke and D. Verhelst (Leuven/The Hague: Leuven University Press/Martinus Nijhoff, 1976), 130–35.
Sheppard, Eugene. *Leo Strauss and the Politics of Exile: The Making of a Political Philosopher* (Waltham, MA: Brandeis University Press, 2006).
Shklar, Judith N. *Legalism* (Cambridge Harvard University Press, 1964).
Sikka, Sonia. "The Delightful Other: Portraits of the Feminine in Kierkegaard, Nietzsche, and Levinas." In *Feminist Interpretations of Emmanuel Levinas*,

edited by Tina Chanter (University Park: The State University of Pennsylvania Press, 2001), 98–118.
Smith, Steven B. *Reading Leo Strauss: Politics, Philosophy, Judaism* (Chicago/London: The University of Chicago Press, 2006).
———. Review of Robert Howse, "Leo Strauss: Man of Peace." *Notre Dame Philosophical Reviews*, October 18, 2014; http://ndpr.nd.edu/news/53222-leo-strauss-man-of-peace/.
———, ed. *The Cambridge Companion to Leo Strauss* (Cambridge: Cambridge University Press, 2009).
Solibakke, Karl I. "The Pride and Prejudice of the Western World: The Iconicity of the Great Books." *Postscripts* 6, nos. 1–3 (2010): 261–75.
Sorensen, Kim A. *Discourses on Strauss: Reason and Revelation in Leo Strauss and His Critical Study of Machiavelli* (Notre Dame: University of Notre Dame Press, 2006).
Später, Jörg. *Vansittart: Britische Debatten über Deutsche und Nazis 1902–1945* (Göttingen: Wallstein, 2003).
Stegmaier, Werner, and Daniel Krochmalnik, eds. *Jüdischer Nietzscheanismus* (Berlin/New York: de Gruyter, 1997).
Steiner, George. "Some 'Meta-Rabbis,'" In *Next Year in Jerusalem: Portraits of the Jew in the Twentieth Century*, edited by Douglas Villiers (London: Viking, 1976), 64–76.
Steiner, Stephan. *Weimar in America: Leo Strauss' Politische Philosophie* (Tübingen: Mohr Siebeck, 2013).
Stoletzki, Almut. "The Study Group on Germany: Exploring the Transatlantic Dynamics in an Exile Debate of the 1940s." *Traversea* 2 (2012): 80–100.
Strauss, Leo. "1001 Nights." Leo Strauss Papers, box 20, folder 2.
———. "An Epilogue." In *The Scientific Study of Politics*, edited by Herbert J. Storing (New York: Holt, Rinehart, and Winston, 1963), 307–27.
———. *An Introduction to Political Philosophy*. Edited by Hilail Gildin (Detroit: Wayne State University Press, 1989).
———. "Existentialism." *Interpretation* 22, no. 3 (1995): 303–18.
———. "Foreword to a Planned Book on Hobbes." In *Hobbes' Critique of Religion and Related Writings*, edited by G. Bartlett and S. Minkov (Chicago: The University of Chicago Press, 2011), 137–49.
———. "German Nihilism." *Interpretation* 26, no. 3 (Spring 1999): 355–78.
———. *Gesammelte Schriften*, vol. 1: *Die Religionskritik Spinozas und zugehörige Schriften*. Edited by Heinrich Meier, 3rd ed. (Stuttgart/Weimar: Metzler, 2008).
———. *Gesammelte Schriften*, vol. 2: *Philosophie und Gesetz. Frühe Schriften*. Edited by Heinrich Meier (Stuttgart/Weimar: Metzler, 1997).
———. *Gesammelte Schriften*, vol. 3: *Hobbes' politische Wissenschaft und zugehörige Schriften—Briefe*. Edited by Heinrich/Wiebke Meier, 2nd ed. (Stuttgart/Weimar: Metzler, 2008).

———. "Historicism." In *Toward* Natural Right and History: *Lectures and Essay by Leo Strauss*, 1937–1946, edited by J. A. Colen and Svetozar Minkov (Chicago/London: The University of Chicago Press, 2018), 68–93.

———. *Historicism and Modern Relativism*. Unpublished seminar transcript, Leo Strauss Papers, box 11, folder 10–11.

———. Introduction to Alexander Altmann, "The Encounter of Faith and Reason in the Western Tradition and its Significance Today." October 1961. Unpublished tape recording, Leo Strauss Papers, box 67.

———. "Jerusalem and Athens, 1950," The Leo Strauss Center, University of Chicago; https://leostrausscenter.uchicago.edu/jerusalem-and-athens.

———. *Jewish Philosophy and the Crisis of Modernity: Essays and Lectures in Modern Jewish Thought*. Edited by Kenneth Hart Green (Albany: State University of New York Press, 1997).

———. *Leo Strauss on Maimonides: The Complete Writings*. Edited by Kenneth Hart Green (Chicago/London: The University of Chicago Press, 2013).

———. *Liberalism Ancient and Modern* (Chicago/London: The University of Chicago Press, 1995).

———. *Natural Right and History* (Chicago/London: The University of Chicago Press, 1965).

———. *Nietzsche's* Beyond Good and Evil: *A Course Offered in 1971/72*. Edited by Mark Blitz. The Leo Strauss Center, University of Chicago; http://leostrausscenter.uchicago.edu/sites/default/files/Nietzsche's%20Beyond%20Good%20and%20Evil.pdf.

———. "Notes on Carl Schmitt, The Concept of the Political." In Heinrich Meier, *Carl Schmitt & Leo Strauss: The Hidden Dialogue* (Chicago/London: The University of Chicago Press, 1995), 91–119.

———. "On a New Interpretation of Plato's Political Philosophy." *Social Research* 13, no. 3 (1946): 326–67.

———. "On Classical Political Philosophy." *Social Research* 12, no. 1 (1945): 98–117.

———. *On Tyranny. Including the Strauss-Kojève Correspondence*. Edited by Victor Gourevitch and Michael Roth (Chicago/London: The University of Chicago Press, 2000).

———. *Persecution and the Art of Writing* (Chicago/London: The University of Chicago Press, 1988).

———. *Philosophy and Law: Contributions to the Understanding of Maimonides and his Predecessors*. Translated by Eve Adler (Albany: State University of New York Press, 1995).

———. *Plato's Gorgias*. Edited by Devin Stauffer. The Leo Strauss Center, University of Chicago; https://leostrausscenter.uchicago.edu/sites/default/files/Plato's%20Gorgias%201963.pdf.

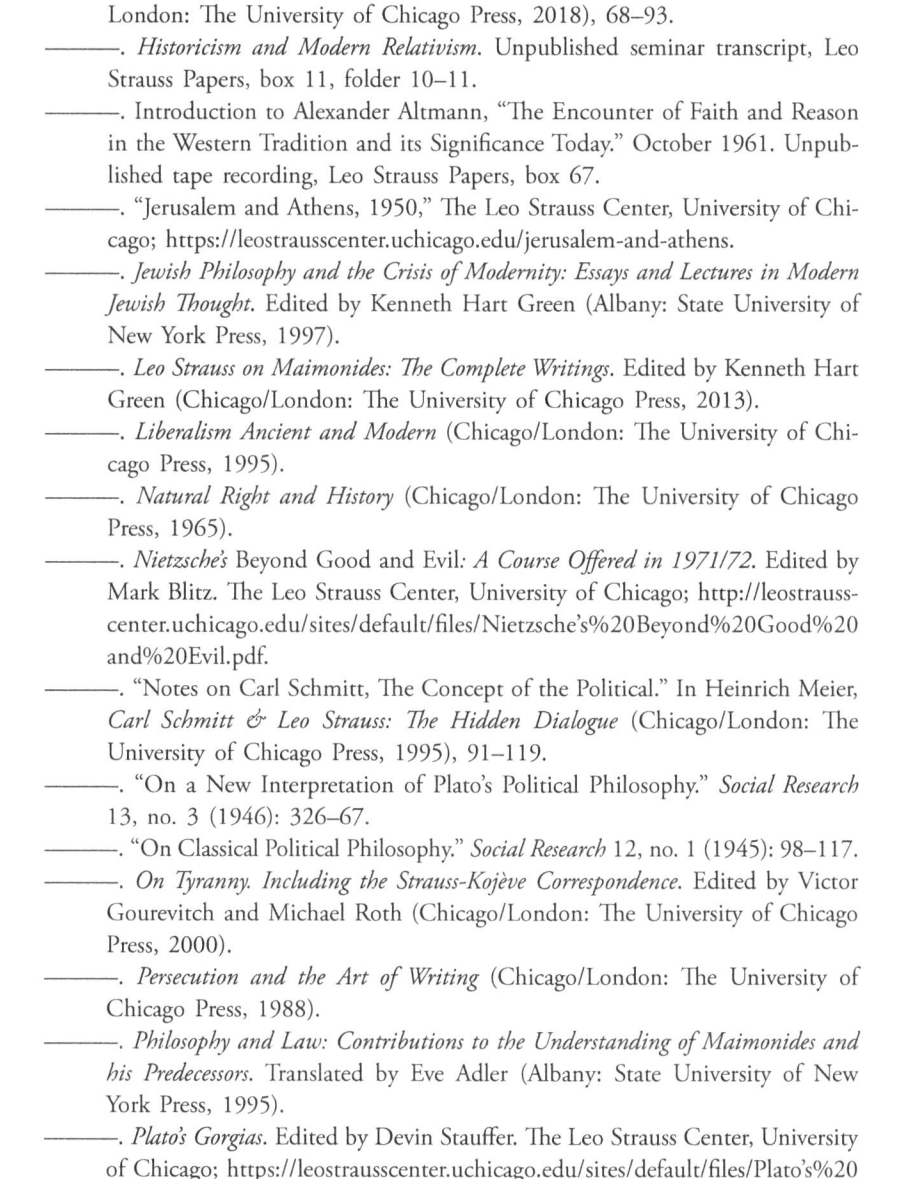

———. "Reason and Revelation." In Heinrich Meier, *Leo Strauss and the Theologico-Political Problem* (New York: Cambridge University Press, 2006), 141–80.

———. "Relativism." In *Relativism and the Study of Man*, edited by Helmut Schoeck and James W. Wiggins (Princeton: Van Nostrand, 1961), 135–57.

———. *Rousseau, 1962*. Edited by Jonathan Marks. The Leo Strauss Center, University of Chicago; https://leostrausscenter.uchicago.edu/sites/default/files/Rousseau%201962.pdf.

———. *Seminar on Montesquieu, 1966*. Edited by Thomas L. Pangle. The Leo Strauss Center, University of Chicago; http://leostrausscenter.uchicago.edu/sites/default/files/Montesquieu%2C%20spring%201966.pdf.

———. *Spinoza's Critique of Religion* (New York: Schocken, 1965).

———. *Studies in Platonic Political Philosophy* (Chicago/London: The University of Chicago Press, 1986).

———. *The Argument and the Action of Plato's Laws* (Chicago/London: The University of Chicago Press, 1975).

———. *The City and Man* (Chicago/London: The University of Chicago Press, 1978).

———. *The Early Writings*. Edited by Michael Zank (Albany: State University of New York Press, 2002).

———. "The 'Jewish Writings' of Hermann Cohen." Translated by Michael Zank. *Interpretation* 39, no. 2 (2012): 118–27.

———. "The Living Issues of German Postwar Philosophy." In Heinrich Meier, *Leo Strauss and the Theologico-Political Problem* (New York: Cambridge University Press, 2006), 115–39.

———. "The Origins of Political Science and the Problem of Socrates." *Interpretation* 23, no. 2 (1996): 127–207.

———. *The Political Philosophy of Hobbes: Its Basis and Its Genesis* (Chicago/London: The University of Chicago Press/Phoenix Books, 1966).

———. *The Rebirth of Classical Political Rationalism: An Introduction to the Thought of Leo Strauss*. Edited by Thomas L. Pangle (Chicago/London: The University of Chicago Press, 1989).

———. "The Re-Education of Axis Countries Concerning the Jews." *The Review of Politics* 69 (2007): 530–38.

———. *Thoughts on Machiavelli* (Chicago/London: The University of Chicago Press, 1978).

———. "What Can We Learn from Political Theory?" In *Toward* Natural Right and History: *Lectures and Essay by Leo Strauss*, 1937–1946, edited by J. A. Colen and Svetozar Minkov (Chicago/London: The University of Chicago Press, 2018), 33–51.

———. *What Is Political Philosophy? and Other Studies* (Chicago/London: The University of Chicago Press, 1988).

———, and Joseph Cropsey, eds. *History of Political Philosophy*, 3rd ed. (Chicago/London: The University of Chicago Press, 1987).

Susman, Warren I. "The Culture of the Thirties." In *Culture as History: The Transformation of American Society in the Twentieth Century* (New York: Pantheon, 1985), 150–83.

Tamer, Georges. *Islamische Philosophie und die Krise der Moderne. Das Verhältnis von Leo Strauss zu Alfarabi, Avicenna und Averroes* (Leiden: Brill, 2001).
Tanguay, Daniel. *Leo Strauss. An Intellectual Biography* (New Haven/London: Yale University Press, 2007).
Taubes, Jacob. *To Carl Schmitt: Letters and Reflections* (New York: Columbia University Press, 2013).
Taubes, Jacob/Carl Schmitt. *Briefwechsel mit Materialien* (Paderborn: Fink, 2012).
Tiedemann, Rolf, ed. *Frankfurter Adorno Blätter*, vol. 6 (Munich: Edition text + kritik, 200).
Troeltsch, Ernst. "Der Geist der deutschen Kultur." In *Deutschland und der Weltkrieg*, edited by Otto Hintze/Friedrich Meinecke (Leipzig: Teubner, 1915), 52–90.
———. *Deutscher Geist und Westeuropa* (Tübingen: Mohr, 1925).
———. "The Ideas of Natural Law and Humanity in World Politics." In Otto Gierke, *Natural Law and the Theory of Society* (Boston: Beacon Press, 1960), 201–22.
Udoff, Alan, ed. *Leo Strauss's Thought: Toward a Critical Engagement* (Boulder: Lynne Rienner, 1991).
———, and Barbara E. Galli, eds. *Franz Rosenzweig's "The New Thinking"* (Syracuse: Syracuse University Press, 1999).
United Nations Educational, Scientific and Cultural Organization. "The Roots of National Socialism and Causes of the Transformation of the National-Socialist Movement into an Overwhelming Political Force." UNESCO/SS/W/1, Paris, July 31, 1949; http://unesdoc.unesco.org/images/0017/001781/178108eb.pdf.
Vermeil, Edmond. *The German Scene (Social, Political, Cultural) 1890 to the Present Day* (London: Harrap, 1956).
Viereck, Paul. *Metapolitics: From Wagner and the German Romantics to Hitler* (New Brunswick/London: Transaction Publishers, 2007).
Voegelin, Eric. "Nietzsche, the Crisis, and the War." In *Collected Works*, vol. 10: *Published Essays 1940–1952* (Columbia/London: University of Missouri Press, 2000), 126–56.
———. Review of Cassirer's *The Myth of the State*. *The Journal of Politics* 9, no. 3 (1947): 445–47.
von Wussow, Philipp. "Anerkennung." In *Enzyklopädie jüdischer Geschichte und Kultur*, edited by Dan Diner, vol. 1 (Stuttgart: Metzler, 2011), 88–94.
———. "Leo Strauss on Returning: Some Methodological Aspects." *Philosophical Readings* IX, no. 1 (2017): 18–24.
———. "Martin Buber and Leo Strauss: Notes on a Strained Relationship." In *Martin Buber: His Intellectual and Scholarly Legacy*, edited by Sam Berrin Shonkoff (Leiden/Boston: Brill, 2018), 194–211.
———. "Marx, Nietzsche, Freud: Towards a History of 'Theory' in Modern Jewish Thought." In *Language as Bridge and Border: Political, Cultural, and Social Constellations in the German-Jewish Context*, edited by Sabine Sander (Berlin: Hentrich und Hentrich, 2015), 225–40.

———. "Übervolk." In *Enzyklopädie jüdischer Geschichte und Kultur*, edited by Dan Diner, vol. 6 (Stuttgart: Metzler, 2015), 201–207.

Vorländer, Karl. "Ethischer Rigorismus und sittliche Schönheit. Mit besonderer Berücksichtigung von Kant und Schiller." *Philosophische Monatshefte* 30 (1894): 225–80, 371–405, 534–77.

Weber, Max. *Gesammelte Aufsätze zur Wissenschaftslehre* (Tübingen: Mohr, 1922).

Westermarck, Edward. *Ethical Relativity* (London: Routledge, 2000).

———. *The Origin and Development of the Moral Ideas* (New York: Johnson Reprint, 1971).

Wiener, Peter F. *Martin Luther: Hitler's Spiritual Ancestor* (London/New York: Hutchinson, 1945).

Windelband, Wilhelm. *A History of Philosophy: With Special Reference to the Formation and Development of Its Problems and Conceptions* (New York: Macmillan, 1901).

Wobbermin, Georg, ed. *Religionsphilosophie* (Berlin: Heise, 1924).

Wurgaft, Benjamin Aldes. "Culture and Law in Weimar Jewish Medievalism: Leo Strauss's Critique of Julius Guttmann." *Modern Intellectual History* 11, no. 1 (2014): 119–46.

Yaffe, Martin D., and Richard S. Ruderman, eds. *Reorientation: Leo Strauss in the 1930s* (New York: Palgrave Macmillan, 2014).

Zank, Michael. "Apikoros." In *Enzyklopädie jüdischer Geschichte und Kultur*, edited by Dan Diner, vol. 1 (Stuttgart: Metzler, 2011), 124–27.

———. "Leo Strauss' Rediscovery of the Exoteric." In *Religious Apologetics—Philosophical Argumentation*, edited by Yossef Schwartz and Volkhard Krech (Tübingen: Mohr Siebeck, 2004), 185–202.

———. "Strauss und Cohen." In *Jüdische Religionsphilosophie als Apologie des Mosaismus* (Tübingen: Mohr Siebeck, 2016), 215–28.

Zuckert, Catherine H. *Postmodern Platos: Nietzsche, Heidegger, Gadamer, Strauss, Derrida* (Chicago/London: The University of Chicago Press, 1996).

Zuckert, Catherine, and Michael Zuckert. *The Truth about Leo Strauss: Political Philosophy and American Democracy* (Chicago/London: The University of Chicago Press, 2006).

Zuckert, Michael P., and Catherine H. Zuckert. *Leo Strauss and the Problem of Political Philosophy* (Chicago/London: The University of Chicago Press, 2014).

Index

absolutism, xxi, 173, 181, 184, 225, 227, 237, 247, 249–252, 295
Abravanel, Isaac, 98, 154–155
Achad Ha'am, 318
Adler, Cyrus, 111, 321
Adler, Eve, 314–315, 318
Adler, Mortimer, 261
Adorisio, Chiara, 325
Adorno, Theodor W., 58, 169, 177, 214, 243, 257–259, 306, 330, 332, 338, 342, 344
Ahlborn, Knut, 305
Albalag, Isaac, 108
Alexander of Aphrodisias, 109
Alfarabi, *see* Farabi
Allen, Woody, 224
Altman, W. H. F., 156, 202, 309, 328–329, 334, 336
Altmann, Alexander, 101, 144–145, 320, 327
apikoros, 79–81
Arendt, Hannah, 80, 167, 191, 223, 316, 330, 334
Aristotle, xiii, 33–38, 111, 124, 128–131, 260, 282, 286, 323, 329
Arkes, Hadley, 260, 345
Armon, Adi, 338
Arnold, Benedict, 232, 341
Arnold, Matthew, 220, 271, 338–339
Aschheim, Steven, 219, 338–339

atheism, 61–62, 82, 84–89, 92, 120, 133–134, 146, 198, 248, 282, 317, 335
Auerbach, Erich, 272
Augustine, 271
Averroes (Ibn Rushd, Ibn Rošd), 107, 110–112, 115–116, 148, 151, 327
Avicenna, 92, 126–129, 289, 323

Baer, Yitzchak, 313
Baeumler, Alfred, 215, 241, 336, 342
Bamberger, Fritz, 324
barbarism, 26, 28, 176, 200, 228, 230, 235, 243
Barth, Karl, 273
Batnitzky, Leora, 325–326
Becker, Carl, 341
Benardete, Seth, xvii–xviii, 300
Benedict, Ruth, xx, 220, 222, 225, 230–237, 295, 340–341
Benjamin, Walter, 49, 59–60, 168, 170, 208, 280, 306, 312–313, 316, 330–331, 337, 347
Berdyczewski, Micha, 318
Berlin, Isaiah, 247
Bergson, Henri, 194
Bernhardi, Friedrich von, 169, 330
Bernstein, Jeffrey A., 346–347
Bernstein, Michael, 208, 337

Biale, David, 338
biblical criticism, 280–281, 348
Bildung, 171, 259, 319
Bloom, Allan, 224–225, 248–249, 339, 344
Blumenberg, Hans, 287, 348
Boas, Franz, 234, 341
Bodin, Jean, 173
Boileu-Despréaux, Nicolas, 314
Borkenau, Franz, 223
Brecht, Arnold, 230, 340
Brinton, Crane, 185–186, 330, 333
Buber, Martin, 45, 67–68, 70, 135, 311, 313, 318
Burke, Edmund, 173
Burnyeat, Miles, 292, 348
Butler, Judith, 80, 316
Butler, Rohan, 176, 186, 331, 333

cannibalism, xxi, 228–231, 239, 248, 250
Carlyle, Thomas, 191
Cassirer, Ernst, 10, 14, 19, 21–28, 31, 51, 76–77, 168, 208, 273, 304–308, 316, 330, 337, 347
Cassirer, Toni, 307
cave, 109, 119, 246, 294, 326
Caygill, Howard, 266, 345
Chamberlain, Houston Stewart, 176
Chamberlain, Neville, 331
chosenness, 108–109
Churchill, Winston, 199, 335
Cicero, 294
civilization, xix, xxiv–xxv, 52, 75, 78–79, 81, 83, 155–156, 176, 179, 184, 186, 193–194, 197–200, 206–212, 225, 239, 246, 257–258, 261, 265–266, 270–271, 280, 283, 297
  and cannibalism, 229–231, 248, 250–251
  critique of, 155, 225
  nihilistic desire to destroy, 193–194, 199
  "Western civilization," xxiv–xxv, 186, 199, 207, 251, 257–258, 260, 265–266, 270–271, 280, 283, 297
Cohen, Hermann, vii, xiii, xix, xxiv, 3–17, 19, 21–23, 25–26, 28–29, 31–38, 42, 46, 50, 67–68, 70, 91, 93–96, 99–100, 102–103, 130–131, 134, 145, 182, 263–266, 272, 288, 302–304, 307–309, 324, 345
creation, 22, 25, 27–28, 51, 62, 67, 71, 74, 77–78, 103–104, 111, 155, 281, 314
Critchley, Simon, 345
Cropsey, Joseph, 260
cultural anthropology, xx–xxi, xxiv, 176, 220–222, 225, 227–232, 234–238, 263, 269, 278, 295, 340
culture, xxv–xxvi, 5–7, 32–33, 36, 42–46, 74–75, 78, 92, 96–99, 155, 175–177, 205–207, 220–221, 225, 228–229, 234, 246, 249, 252, 259–265, 268, 278, 345
  American culture, 183, 222, 248
  and barbarism, 26, 28, 243
  and civilization, xix, 75, 78, 164, 199, 204–207, 209
  and cultures, xx–xxi, xxiv, 183, 185, 220–222, 230, 232–235, 237–238, 262–263, 265–269, 319
  and Judaism, 15–16, 93–94, 101, 108–109, 142, 268, 289
  as creation, 51, 77–78
  conflict between culture and religion, x, 3, 11–13, 99–100, 115
  critique of, ix–xi, 43, 51–52, 75, 78, 98, 155, 220, 262, 287

cultural provinces (Natorp), 2, 19–21, 42–43, 51
  domains of, x, 38, 42, 44–45, 50–51, 96–97, 115, 206, 288
  education toward, 261
  German culture, 7, 163, 167–168, 170, 175, 177, 205, 210, 220, 273
  Jerusalem and Athens as two cultures, 262–263, 265–266, 278
  systematic question of, 5–29, 42, 45–47, 50–53, 94, 96
culture war, culture wars, 169, 181, 215, 259–260, 295

Dannhauser, Werner, 296–297, 348–349
d'Annunzio, Gabriele, 187
Deleuze, Gilles, 265, 272, 345
de los Ríos, Fernando, 329
Derrida, Jacques, 257, 265
Descartes, René, 66, 76, 184
Deutscher, Isaac, 80, 316
Dewey, John, 170–172, 177, 179–185, 232, 234, 332–333, 337
Diederichs, Eugen, 306
Dilthey, Wilhelm, 234
Dorrien, Gary, 344
double truth, 108–109
Dubnow, Simon, 308
Dutschke, Rudi, 258

Eaglestone, Robert, 345
education, xix, 124, 157, 165, 196, 206–209, 215, 261, 268, 287, 293, 295, 337
Elbogen, Ismar, 324
Elisha ben Abuya, 79–80
Engels, Friedrich, 20, 85, 200, 244, 301, 343
Epicureanism, 79–82, 85, 134
Epicurus, 79, 81

existentialism, 17, 103–104, 138, 250, 320
exotericism, xiii, xvi–xix, 58, 87, 92, 106–109, 114–116, 119, 124, 129, 132, 136–137, 143, 146–160, 164–165, 202, 273–274, 290–292, 294, 296, 321, 328

Farabi (al-Farabi, Alfarabi), xvi, 126, 147–149, 153–154, 294
Feldman, Seymour, 327
Felsch, Philipp, 344
Ferguson, Niall, 346
Fichte, Johann Gottlob, 173, 176
Fischer, Lars, 328
Formstecher, Salomon, 67
Foucault, Michel, 71–72, 290, 315
Fraenkel, Ernst, 169, 223
Freud, Sigmund, xxiii, 70–72, 80, 86, 273, 296, 301
Fromm, Erich, 224

Gadamer, Hans-Georg, 306, 313
Gebhardt, Jürgen, 338
Gersonides (Levi ben Gerson), 59, 110–112, 134, 150–151, 289–290
Gide, André, 187
Gilbert, Felix, 329
Glatzer, Norbert Nahum, 148, 327
Glaucon, 195–197
Goethe, Johann Wolfgang, 168, 178, 258, 273, 347
Gogarten, Friedrich, 104
Gratry, Alphonse, 317
Graupe, Heinz, 6, 302
Green, Kenneth Hart, 303, 326, 328, 344–345
Grimme, Adolf, 306
Gunnell, John G., 329
Guttmann, Julius, x, xv, 45, 59–61, 66, 91–110, 112–114, 117–119, 121–123, 132, 134–147, 150,

Guttmann, Julius *(continued)*
  155, 287, 306, 313, 318–322,
  324–328

Habermas, Jürgen, 44, 215, 338
Halevi, Yehuda, 282, 304
Hamann, Johann Georg, 337
Harris, Monford, 315
Hartman, Geoffrey, xx, 301
Hartmann, Nicolai, 299, 306
Havers, Grant, 346
Hegel, Georg Wilhelm Friedrich,
  33–34, 37, 68, 82, 166, 173–174,
  176–177, 189, 245–246, 258,
  330
Hegeman, Susan, xxv, 222, 301,
  338–339
Hesiod, 282
Heidegger, Martin, xix, 23, 25, 58, 76,
  166, 212–213, 215, 224, 246,
  305, 307, 336–337
Heimann, Eduard, 170, 172, 329
Heimsoeth, Heinz, 306
Heine, Heinrich, 171
Heinemann, Fritz, 59, 63, 313–314
Herder, Johann Gottfried, 175–176,
  314
Herskovits, Melville, 236, 341
Hillel ben Samuel, 144
Himmelfarb, Gertrude, 345
Hirsch, Samuel, 67
historicism, 66, 77, 155, 201–202,
  204, 209, 220, 225, 227, 229,
  232, 245–246, 278, 343
Hitler, Adolf, 26, 166–168, 171–173,
  175–176, 185–186, 201–203,
  205, 208, 211–214, 243, 264,
  318
Hobbes, Thomas, 52, 66, 173, 296,
  310, 316, 324
Hocking, William Ernest, 181–182,
  333

Hönigswald, Richard, 306
Hofmann, Hasso, 50, 312
Holocaust, 100, 164–165, 169, 213,
  243
Holzhey, Helmut, 13, 302–303
Homer, 175, 214
Horkheimer, Max, 58, 169, 243, 306,
  338, 342
Horwitz, Robert, 180, 332
Howse, Robert, 300, 309
Hula, Erich, 169–170, 329–330
Humboldt, Wilhelm von, 221
Huntington, Samuel, 269–270, 346
Husik, Isaac, 144, 150, 327
Hutchins, Robert Maynard, 261

Ibsen, Henrik, 178
Idealism, xix, 5–6, 10, 75–77, 103–
  104, 167, 172, 174, 177–184,
  241
interpretation, xxiii, 31–34, 61, 71–72,
  77–79, 110, 137, 142, 159, 181,
  285–286, 296
irrationalism, 172, 174, 189, 240,
  242–243, 342
irrationality, 61, 240–242, 342
Isaac, Joel, 339

Jabotinsky, Ze'ev (Vladimir), xv
Jacobi, Friedrich Heinrich, xii
Jaffa, Harry V., 340
Jahn, Friedrich Ludwig (Father Jahn),
  176
James, William, 185
Janssens, David, 86–87, 318, 346
Jewish philosophy, x, xiii, 4, 95–96,
  98, 102, 107–108, 113, 117,
  131–132, 152, 273
  and philosophy, 113, 152
  German-Jewish, 68, 152
  medieval, ix, 57–58, 65–66, 92–94,
    98, 100, 104, 106–107, 109–110,

112, 116, 119, 121–123, 129,
   133, 137–139, 144, 146, 151,
   155, 289–290
Johnson, Alvin, 171, 331
Jospe, Alfred, 6, 302
Jospe, Eva, 345
Judaism, xxiii, 26, 31–32, 36, 68,
   79–80, 88, 94–95, 100–103, 105,
   108, 123, 130–131, 142, 145, 148,
   154, 258, 268, 273, 299, 307
   and German culture, 7–8
   and the system of philosophy
      (Cohen), 7, 14–17
   internalization of, 73
   medieval understanding of, 93
   modern reinterpretations of, xxiii
   orthodoxy and the Enlightenment,
      66–68, 71, 73
   philosophy of (Guttmann), 94–96,
      99, 117
   "post-critical Judaism," 71, 280
   return to, 88–89
Jünger, Ernst, 203, 336

Kallen, Horace, 171–172, 329
Kant, Immanuel, 5–7, 33–34, 37,
   68, 76, 96, 108, 166–167, 173,
   177–181, 184–185, 206, 241,
   330, 332
Kaufmann, Felix, 170, 172, 329
Kelsen, Hans, 170
Kenyatta, Jomo, 228, 339
Kierkegaard, Søren, 274–275
Kinkel, Walter, 15, 304
Kinzel, Till, 339
Klein, Jacob, 103, 131, 136, 148, 291,
   310–311, 313, 325, 327
Klingenstein, Susanne, 327
Kluckhohn, Clyde, 220
Kohn, Hans, 272
Kojève, Alexandre, 65, 136, 203–204,
   258, 294, 313–314, 336

Koyré, Alexandre, 313
Kraemer, Joel L., 315, 323, 325, 328
Kraus, Paul, 137, 147, 313, 327
Kraushaar, Wolfgang, 344
Kristeller, Paul Otto, 305
Kristol, Irving, 259–260, 290–291,
   344–345, 348
Kroeber, A. L., 220
Krochmalnik, Daniel, 332
Krohn, Claus-Dieter, 329, 339
Krüger, Gerhard, 80, 136, 313,
   316–317, 321, 333
Kühnemann, Eugen, 306
Kuhn, Helmut, 49, 312
Kultur (see also *culture*), xix, 46,
   176–177, 259
Kulturkritik, 163–164, 199, 224
Kulturprovinzen (Paul Natorp), *see*
   culture

Laguna, Grace de, 221–222, 339
Lampert, Laurence, 76, 78, 314, 316
Lamprecht, Karl, 181
Landauer, Carl, 188, 190–191, 193,
   334
Langstadt, Erich, 311
Lask, Emil, 241–242, 342
Laski, Harold, 47–48, 311
last man, 157, 199, 203, 244–245,
   262, 336
law, 17, 22, 37, 58, 61–62, 67–68,
   79, 81, 90, 110–119, 122–123,
   125, 127–134, 137–141, 150–
   151, 154, 241, 299, 318, 320,
   323
Lazarus, Moritz, 221
Lazier, Benjamin, 312–313
Lederer, Emil, 198, 335
Leisegang, Hans, 12, 303
Lepenies, Wolf, 167, 330, 332
Lerner, Ralph, 260
Lessing, Gotthold Ephraim, 314

Levinas, Emmanuel, 266–269, 271, 345–346
Levy, Oscar, 179, 318, 332
Lewin, Kurt, 223
List, Joel Abraham, 100, 320
Litt, Theodor, 19, 305
Lowe, Adolph, 170, 172, 214, 329, 334
Löwith, Karl, 50, 82, 186–187, 213, 274, 302, 305–307, 312–313, 317, 333–334
Lukács, Georg, 215, 240, 242–246, 338, 342–343
Lukes, Steven, 339–341
Luther, Martin, 166–167, 172–175, 179, 185–189, 330–331, 337
Luxemburg, Rosa, 80, 200, 335

Machiavelli, Niccolò, 330
Maimonides, Moses, xvi, 32–33, 35–38, 61–62, 65–66, 68–69, 88–90, 96, 108–113, 119–120, 124–127, 130–131, 134, 136, 139, 141, 144–151, 153–155, 164, 204, 289–292, 294, 308, 326–327
Maistre, Joseph de, 173
Malinowski, Bronislaw, 228
Manent, Pierre, xxiv, 255, 301, 344
Mann, Thomas, 177, 332
Marburg School, 5, 31, 306
Marcuse, Herbert, 259
Marx, Karl, xxiii, 70–72, 80, 85–86, 166, 181, 243, 245, 296, 301, 342
Marxism, 169, 242–246
Mayer, Carl, 170, 173, 188–191, 329, 331, 334
McCormick, John P., 317
McGovern, William, 173, 191, 331
Meier, Heinrich, 309–311, 313, 321–327, 347

Meinecke, Friedrich, 168, 330
Mendelssohn, Moses, xii, 8, 99–100, 103, 133–134, 299, 324
Mendes-Flohr, Paul, 325
Meyer, Thomas, 319, 325, 329
Miner, Robert, 86–87, 318
miracles, 62, 67, 70–71, 73–74, 126–127, 155, 276, 280
Moeller van den Bruck, Arthur, 336
Mortley, Raoul, 345–346
Moses, 125
Mouffe, Chantal, 43–44, 310
Mozart, Wolfgang Amadeus, 168
Musil, Robert, 343
Mussolini, Benito, xv, 185
myth, 21–22, 24–28, 58, 122, 168, 259, 280, 307

National Socialism, 108, 234
  Cassirer on, 28
  origins of, xix, 163–169, 172–177, 180, 182, 185–191, 202, 205, 207–209, 211–215, 293, 331, 338
  period in German-Jewish thought, 57–58
  Schmitt's affiliation with, xv, 2, 41, 310–311
  socio-economic explanation of, 169
  Strauss's stance on, xiv, xix, 163–164, 166, 198, 202, 209, 212–213, 342
Natorp, Paul, 12–14, 19–22, 28, 31, 42–43, 51, 303, 305–306
nature, 51–52, 212, 314
neo-Kantianism, vii, xiii, xv, 3–4, 6, 12, 15, 19, 21, 31, 42–43, 46, 92–94, 96–99, 206, 240–242, 288, 296, 305–306, 320
Neumann, Franz, 169, 214, 223
Newton, Isaac, 76

Niebuhr, Reinhold, 173–174, 331
Niemöller, Martin, 331
Nietzsche, Friedrich, xix, xxiii, 65,
 70–72, 78, 82–89, 133–134,
 156–157, 166–167, 169, 174,
 178–179, 185–190, 194–195,
 199, 203, 212, 215, 224, 234,
 242, 244, 246, 262, 263, 268,
 275, 282, 296, 301, 317–318,
 330–336, 345
nihilism, 163–164, 187–190, 193–209,
 335–337
Norton, Anne, 260, 345

Orr, Susan, 262, 345
orthodoxy, 61–62, 67–75, 77–79,
 81–84, 86–89, 92
otherness, 236, 267, 270, 346

Parens, Joshua, 327–328
Perrault, Charles, 314
phenomenology, 4, 98, 170, 246, 288,
 296
Philo, 327
philosophy of culture, x, xiii, xxiv, 3,
 9–10, 21, 24, 28, 38, 79, 94,
 96–98, 142, 206, 262–263, 273,
 289
philosophy of religion, xv, 3, 11–12,
 14–15, 61, 82, 92–93, 95–96,
 100, 103–104, 118, 122, 132,
 320
Pines, Shlomo, 313
Plato, xviii, xxii, 33–38, 65, 111, 119,
 123, 127–134, 139, 141, 154,
 156–157, 166, 175, 180, 196,
 204, 246, 251–252, 263–264,
 282, 286, 289, 293–294, 301,
 323, 326, 329, 333–335, 345,
 348
Plessner, Helmut, 170, 175, 331
pluralism, 24, 47–49, 171, 238

political, the, ix–xi, xiii–xiv, xxi, 2–3,
 22, 28–29, 34–36, 39, 42–53,
 58–59, 70, 78, 97, 287–288
political philosophy, ix–x, xiii–xiv,
 xxii, 1–4, 29, 33, 35–36, 38, 41,
 63, 123, 129, 131, 133, 138,
 140, 153, 155–157, 163, 184,
 195, 204, 206, 269, 285, 290,
 293
Popper, Karl, 166, 214, 330, 338
positivism, 180, 211, 220, 225, 227,
 229–230, 232, 234, 246, 278
postcolonialism, xxiv, 266–267, 269,
 297
pragmatism, 169, 172, 178, 180–185,
 246
probity, 84–89, 309, 317–318
progress, progressivism, 20, 38, 85, 89,
 149, 195, 197, 201, 203–204,
 207–208, 243–246, 257, 264–265
prophecy, 111, 125–129, 140–141, 323
prophetology, 59, 62, 92, 112,
 122–123, 125–129, 134, 142,
 149, 151
Proust, Marcel, 265

Rashkover, Randi, 326
rationalism, 61, 62, 65–66, 68–69, 73,
 79, 87, 92, 112, 118–119, 121,
 131, 138, 140, 143, 145–148,
 151, 156, 242, 314
Rauschning, Hermann, 172, 187
reality, 5–6, 8, 17, 21, 24–25, 31,
 48–49, 52, 61, 67, 98, 103,
 105–106, 113–114, 241, 259,
 278, 320
reason, xii, 9–10, 17, 24, 49, 61–62,
 65, 69, 72, 79, 110, 118, 120,
 176, 182–183, 189, 204, 206,
 238–243, 266, 289, 343
 and revelation, xxiii, 58, 61, 65,
 69–70, 73–74, 87, 92, 99,

reason, and revelation *(continued)*
    113, 118–121, 123, 132, 134,
    142–148, 150, 255, 262–263,
    272–274, 277–278, 282, 289,
    297, 346
  critique of, 62, 69, 120–121, 238,
    281, 289
  insufficiency of, 112, 119–121, 146,
    150
reeducation, 214
relativism, xii, xx–xxii, 71, 78, 139,
    205, 220, 224–225, 227–231,
    234, 236–240, 244–252, 260,
    269, 278, 295–296
religion, x–xi, xxiii–xxiv, 3, 31, 42–43,
    50, 61, 68, 70, 78, 89, 94–100,
    109, 115, 175, 228, 255, 273,
    276, 304, 307, 319
  critique of, xxiii, 61–62, 70–72,
    78–81, 83, 85–86, 134
  in the system of philosophy, xiii,
    3–17, 19–22, 24–29, 46, 92–96,
    103, 177, 288, 302
Rethelyi, Mari, 325
return, ix, xiv, xxii, 15–17, 28, 31–33,
    37–38, 65, 68, 88–90, 104,
    257–258, 264–266, 278, 283,
    297, 315, 326
revelation, 17, 26, 61–62, 67, 69–70,
    83, 86, 89, 93, 98–100, 102,
    108–109, 111–125, 127–134,
    138–139, 141–147, 150–151,
    256, 268, 274, 276–278, 290,
    320, 326
  and reason, *see* reason
  excess over reason, 121, 144–146
  formal recognition of, 105–107,
    112–114, 117
  reality of, 61, 98, 100, 109,
    113–114, 123, 131
Rickert, Heinrich, 241–242
Ricœur, Paul, 296, 349

Riesman, David, 224
Riezler, Kurt, 170, 172, 306, 329, 335
Ringer, Fritz, 338
Rockmore, Tom, 342
Romano, Judah, 144
Romanticism, xix, 172, 175–176, 178,
    189, 314
Rosen, Stanley, xiii, 87, 255, 299, 318,
    344
Rosenberg, Alfred, 176, 215
Rosenthal, Erwin, 311, 327
Rosenthal, Franz, 327
Rosenzweig, Franz, 3, 9–12, 14–17,
    31, 67–68, 70, 102–104,
    302–304, 320
Rothacker, Erich, 287
Rousseau, Jean-Jacques, 188, 195, 229,
    334
Rutkoff, Peter M., 171–172, 329, 331,
    337

Sabine, George, 341
Salomon, Albert, 168, 170, 329–330
Santayana, George, 170–172, 177–180,
    332
Schelling, Friedrich Wilhelm Joseph,
    166–167, 189, 241
Schiller, Friedrich, 314
Schlegel, Friedrich, 314
Schleiermacher, Friedrich, 12–13, 61,
    68, 96, 108, 132, 314
Schmitt, Carl, vii, xi, xiii–xv, 19, 34,
    38–39, 41–53, 135, 137, 195,
    201, 287–288, 310–312, 336
Schmoller, Gustav von, 181
Scholem, Gershom, 82, 101, 106–107,
    136, 140, 143, 313, 316, 318,
    320, 326, 328, 337
Schweid, Eliezer, 319, 325
Scott, William B., 171–172, 329, 331,
    337
Seeskin, Kenneth, 319

Sen, Amartya, 47, 311
Seneca, 155
Sermoneta, Josef (Giuseppe), 144, 326
Shell, Susan, 163, 329
Sheppard, Eugene, 328, 336, 338
Shestov, Leo, 271
Shklar, Judith, xxiv–xxv, 301
Sikka, Sonia, 346
Simmel, Georg, 24
Simon, Ernst, 61, 313–314
Smith, Steven B., xviii, 296, 300, 328, 349
social science, ix, xx–xxi, 164, 169, 171, 219–221, 223, 227–228, 232, 238–241, 244–245, 248, 276, 278, 306
Socrates, xviii, 35–36, 133–134, 196, 282, 289, 347
Solibakke, Karl I., 345
Sorensen, Kim A., 348
Später, Jörg, 331
Spengler, Oswald, 78, 203, 221, 225, 232–234, 319, 336
Spinoza, Baruch (Benedict), 33, 80, 157, 184
Stalin, Joseph, 166
Stalinism, 342
Stegmaier, Werner, 332
Steiner, George, 80, 316
Steiner, Stephan, 325, 330, 332, 334, 336, 338
Steinheim, Salomon Ludwig, 67
Steinschneider, Moritz, 101
Steinthal, Heymann, 221
Stoletzki, Almut, 329
Susman, Warren, 220, 338–339
Swift, Jonathan, 339
system, xi–xiv, 3–17, 19, 21–25, 29, 31, 35, 43, 50–51, 53, 60, 74–76, 92, 103, 242, 299

Tamer, Georges, 323

Tanguay, Daniel, 149, 271, 322, 327, 346
Taubes, Jacob, 258, 261, 310, 313, 344–345
Tertullian, 271
theory, 32, 102, 124–125, 130–131, 151, 259–260, 274, 296–297
Thomas Aquinas, 144–145, 148, 327, 330
Tiedemann, Rolf, 344
Tillich, Paul, 170, 306
Treitschke, Heinrich von, 169, 330
Troeltsch, Ernst, 176, 225, 330, 332, 339
Trotsky, Leon, 80

Udoff, Alan, 303

Vansittart, Robert, 170, 331
Verkade, 174
Vermeil, Edmond, 169, 330
Viereck, Paul, 176–177, 332
Voegelin, Eric, 175, 185, 308, 331, 333
Vorländer, Karl, 19, 305

Wagner, Richard, 176–177
Walzer, Richard, 327
Weber, Max, 225, 227, 241, 244, 248, 276, 278, 342
Weil, Gotthold, 101
Weltanschauung, 232–234, 246
Weltfish, Gene, 341
Wertheimer, Max, 223
Westermarck, Edward, 228, 339
Wieck, Fred, 62–63, 314
Wiener, Peter, 174, 331
Windelband, Wilhelm, 241, 342
Winter, Ernst Karl, 329
Wissenschaft des Judentums, 99–102, 108, 118, 142–143
Wittgenstein, Ludwig, 58

Wobbermin, Georg, 14, 303–304
Wolfson, Harry A., 327
Wolzogen, Christoph von, 267
Wurgaft, Benjamin Aldes, 322, 325

Xenophon, 136, 203, 286, 292–293

Yaffe, Martin, 299, 308

Zank, Michael, 59, 303–304, 313, 326
Zionism, xv, 88
Zuckert, Catherine, 300, 328
Zuckert, Michael, 300, 328
Zunz, Leopold, 101

CPSIA information can be obtained
at www.ICGtesting.com
Printed in the USA
BVHW042308140223
658548BV00005B/65